THE ARMCHAIR ANGLER

THE ARMCHAIR LIBRARY

THE ARMCHAIR
ANGLER

Edited by Terry Brykczynski
and David Reuther
with John Thorn

Illustrations by Bill Elliott

COLLIER BOOKS
Macmillan Publishing Company
New York

Maxwell Macmillan Canada
Toronto

Maxwell Macmillan International
New York   Oxford   Singapore   Sydney

Collier Books
Macmillan Publishing Company
866 Third Avenue
New York, NY 10022

Maxwell Macmillan Canada, Inc.
1200 Eglinton Avenue East
Suite 200
Don Mills, Ontario M3C 3N1

Macmillan Publishing Company is part of the Maxwell Communication Group of Companies.

Library of Congress Cataloging-in-Publication Data
The armchair angler / edited by Terry Brykczynski and David Reuther,
    with John Thorn; illustrations by Bill Elliott.
        p.   cm.
    Originally published: New York: Scribner, 1986.
    ISBN 0-02-017801-8
    1. Fishing.   I. Brykczynski, Terry.   II. Reuther, David.
III. Thorn, John, 1947–   .
[SH441.A68   1993]   92-2403   CIP
799.1—dc20

Macmillan books are available at special discounts for bulk purchases for sales promotions, premiums, fund-raising, or educational use. For details, contact:

Special Sales Director
Macmillan Publishing Company
866 Third Avenue
New York, NY 10022

First Collier Books Edition 1993

10 9 8 7 6 5 4 3 2 1

Printed in the United States of America

CONTENTS

Introduction

Angling is not the sport of kings, even though the best opportunity for royal-spotting is Scotland's River Dee. Nor is fishing the racket of knaves, if one overlooks the occasional bit of poaching. It is instead, as Philip Wylie pointed out, the one true international national sport.

Take a kid fishing and you've got him hooked for life. Give that kid a pen along with some tackle and in all probability he'll want to record his experiences on paper. What is it about angling that makes writing about it so compulsory, so urgent? Certainly it isn't the necessity to document complicated technique—the basic skills of fishing haven't changed in a hundred, a thousand years. The Walton of 1653 would find only his duds out of fashion on the banks of today's rivers. And while falconry may have a slight chronological headstart in literature, that's only a glitch of history—it's tough to fish Arabian deserts. Perhaps a better question would be, "What attracts the best writers to fishing?" The fact is plain, the fiction an overwhelming corroboration, that no other sport can match angling for sheer quantity of first-rate writing.

Getting a grip on this body of literature is an almost insuperable task. Any number of collections have attempted an overview, some with historical perspectives, others with surveys of techniques or compendia of lore—legitimate approaches, but ones that can lose sight even as they focus in, and run the risk of leaving the reader ultimately unsatisfied. The problems are these—the finest writing often lies dormant in sources long out of print, overshadowed by reams of subsequent dross, or—worse yet—is overlooked because the author hasn't been "classified" an expert in the field. The criterion for inclusion in the present anthology is just good writing. Sometimes plain, but never simple. Prose of the highest order.

These pieces have been written three hundred years ago—or three. They have been printed originally by handset type on parchment bound in vellum or slugged out by linotype and slapped on newsprint pulp. They have first appeared in glossy mass circulation periodicals or limited runs of discerning poetry journals. It doesn't matter when or where—only that they were excellently written then and remain excellent reading now.

Any field has its groundbreaking prototypes, its innovative set pieces that define the form. Angling abounds with the "Me 'n' Joe" story, the screaming reeler, and the one-that-got-away—examples that are included here not as a concession to popularity but rather as a demonstration of the heights to which these genres can attain. But special effort has been made to prospect in areas not normally considered typical angling territory, the search yielding rich pay dirt from sources as unexpected as Charles Dodgson (Lewis Carroll), T. H. White, Roy Blount, Jr., and William Jay Smith. The last two decades in particular have seen a phalanx of writers emerge whose influence transcends traditional boundaries. Thomas McGuane, Russell Chatham, and Bill Barich, among others, can be welcomed to the ranks of contemporary masters.

Sophisticated readers will recognize some classic pieces that have appeared in previous anthologies; it is hoped that they will recall the enjoyment of reading them for the first time and allow a new generation that opportunity.

Among those who have aided the editors in assembling this collection and whose help is gratefully acknowledged are: Margery Peters, Library of the General Society of Mechanics and Tradesmen; Elizabeth Davis, Pierpont Morgan Library; Gerard Belliveau, Jr., Racquet & Tennis Club Library; Carol Brener, Murder Ink; Paula Deitz, Frederick Morgan, and Julia Stephen, "Hudson Review"; and, especially, Andrea Miller.

THE ARMCHAIR
ANGLER

Out of necessity anglers become observers. Painters in particular seem attracted to the sport. If we must label Atherton's style, call it Magic Realism. The Museum of Modern Art does. Look for the telling detail and the carefully limned tableaux.

JOHN ATHERTON

Youth

It seemed to me that my good fortune was almost overwhelming when I caught my first fish. As it happened, the fish was a good one, a great-headed pike that weighed four pounds and was almost as long as I. Such a sizable trophy was not only thrilling, but its bestial aspect—the big jaws filled with sharp teeth, and its long powerful body—was doubly exciting. It seemed to live for hours. I tried to dispatch it by various means but only succeeded after dragging it home and chopping its head completely off with the camp ax. Since that early day the expectancy and thrill of capture, whether of a trout, a lordly salmon, or a six-inch bluegill, has lessened none in its intensity, and I hardly expect that it ever will.

Since then, the paths to the fishing waters have led to many interesting and wonderful places to cast a fly: the Washington rivers like the Spokane and the Little Spokane, the Satsop, Wynoochie, and Humptulips (even the names are wonderful), the Cle-Elum, the Cedar, Deep Creek; and, in Oregon, the Deschutes, Crooked, and Crescent Creek; in California the Pit, the Feather, the Merced, and the Klamath; the charming streams of New England, the Catskills and Adirondacks—the Beaverkill, the Neversink, the Willowemoc, the Schoharie; the Ausable and the Battenkill. The mountain lakes in Idaho in the

Coeur d'Alenes, the lakes in the Cascades of Washington and Oregon; the clear waters of the Sierras have all brought their own unique contributions. And the salmon rivers of New Brunswick and Cape Breton with their long gravel bars and dark spruces, the bright silvery fish up from the sea and the campfires on the river banks; the canoe on the brown waters of Maine, with the deer standing at the edge when we rounded a bend—these are all memorable and their remembrance brings lasting pleasures.

Angling has been responsible, to a great extent, for a life and a philosophy well suited to the temperament of the artist. It has taught me about art, as art has led to interesting theories and experiments in angling. Thinking and fishing go well together somehow. And the thinking is usually of the creative sort rather than the summing up of those difficulties with which we are all beset at times.

One of the great qualities of the sport is that it is noncompetitive. Americans, in particular, seem to me well enough supplied with competition not to include fishing as well. The least flavor of the competitive destroys its most charming qualities, lending it an atmosphere of sly haste, pervading its associations with petty jealousies, envy, and resentments. The angler who is determined to catch the biggest fish or the most of them, by his own determination becomes a competitor and is self-poisoned.

How wonderful to the fisherman is the anticipation of an angling excursion. The reality of experience often finds itself obliged to take second place to the pictures the mind can summon. In imagination, the angler is provided with unique sensations. In the fleeting moment he visualizes them, he enjoys emotions impossible to have been experienced in reality in such a short space of time. A whole day's happenings can be brought to the imagination in the twinkling of an eye. The mind can visualize the scenes frequented by the angler, with great beauty rarely found in actuality. The trees, filled with singing birds, are never in the way of his cast and are only placed there to afford him shade or shelter. The trout never come with difficulty, and he can make them in his mind's eye of a size in proportion to his enthusiasm.

I know a man who, due to ill health, is unable to go out on the river. He finds, instead, a great peace of mind and a great deal of enjoyment in taking what he calls a trip to a good trout stream. He will fish an entire river in imagination, working up from pool to pool, casting his flies to imaginary trout, raising some, leaving others unmolested and occasionally finding a good one, which he confidently works over and takes with a masterly approach.

When one knows a trout stream after many years of having fished it, the experience of going back again, even by so remote a method as through spirit alone, can afford some delightful occasions. It is all gold and no dross.

In youth, of course, the angler does not need to rely on memory, imagination, or those quiet hours of contemplation so pleasant after long experience. His is the active pursuit. He loves to explore new waters. He stalks his quarry with an enthusiasm and determination that rely more on strength and endurance than on guile. He may be prone to do a little poaching of the innocent sort, and his methods savor more of the hunter than the purist.

I remember well that my own youth brought few exceptions to these rules. Even though angling was beginning to be regarded more philosophically, and the beauties of the contemplative point of view finding roots in an active nature, I was apt to revert to impulsive and often unpredictable tactics. "Dapping" was one.

Did you ever "dap" for trout? If not, you have undoubtedly been deprived of one of the definitely exciting experiences of angling with the fly. Part of its fascination lies, no doubt, in the faint flavor of the poacher's art, the lack of which in any angler, particularly a young and intrepid one, is to be deplored rather than commended. It requires a certain stealth. It is flavored with an atmosphere typical of the small boy who creeps up to hook his quarry and fling it over his head with a shout of joy.

One year during my early angling wanderings, I spent a summer in Yosemite Valley, in California. The Merced River there, a lovely crystal-clear stream that hurls itself over great cliffs and rushes down between the boulders, flows out more calmly when it reaches the valley floor. There its banks become heavily overgrown in places, and there are sections where either it is impossible to enter the stream or one has no room to cast. There were places where the bushy cover extended out, over, and even into the water for several feet.

Naturally these difficult spots had trout in them. By curious maneuvering one could peer down and see the heavy fish, secure in their environment.

The method I adopted to suit that occasion was hardly to be called the most pure, but it did produce some excellent results. I will only offer the apology that my tender years were responsible. I remember distinctly how delicious those trout tasted, due to their unusual method of capture I am sure!

Dapping, an ancient practice, is still used in Great Britain for catching trout during hatches of the large mayflies. It usually consists of fastening the actual insect to the hook and allowing it just to touch the water where trout can be expected, not by casting, but by a mere lowering of the rod point, the angler being concealed, of course.

My own method was much simpler. I used a rather bushy dry fly, on heavy gut, and fished it on a short line, at most no longer than the rod. Only the fly touched the water.

At the time I visited that dramatically beautiful valley, the roads were scarcely more than sheep trails and we spent the entire day driving up from San Francisco. There was a great deal less travel then than now, and consequently only a fraction of the number of tourists and anglers.

My quarters were in the old inn called Cedar Cottage, named from the enormous tree that grew right up through the building. It was only a stone's throw to the river and early each morning it was my habit to take a rod and try to catch a trout for breakfast. Along the bank there was a row of large trees, their roots making fine hides. One particular spot nearly always held a fish. If I caught him, another would appear a day or so later, and this favorite place furnished me with many a fine meal.

When I learned how to fish it properly, by the stealthy approach and the dapped fly, I could walk up carefully behind a big tree trunk, slowly push my rod around the tree and drop my fly without even seeing the water. Frequently I was only aware of the subsequent rise by hearing it, or by feeling the strong pull of the fish. It became almost automatic, this early morning execution, and you may be sure I was careful not to advertise my method. The trout in that particular spot varied little in size. They were exactly right to furnish a solid and substantial breakfast, so I needed only one.

There were other good spots along the banks that also produced their trout at times. And there was considerable smashed gear, as often a heavy fish would be too much to handle in the tangle of branches and roots. Whenever possible I would haul the larger trout quickly up the bank, violently flopping. The small and medium-sized ones could be levered out through the air as my rod was husky and my gear stout. With only the fly touching the water, heavier leaders could be used and they, of course, held many a fish that might otherwise have been lost. The fly patterns seemed to matter very little to the fish. It was the dapping that did the trick.

These daily expeditions brought me a certain reputation, and the cooks planned on the trout as an everyday article for my breakfast menu. But if I failed to deliver I was badgered unmercifully, and it was with a certain loss of face that I was compelled to order a substitute.

One day I took a fish of about a pound in weight that seemed overcorpulent, and to find the cause, I opened him at once. The autopsy showed an animal entirely new to me. About the size of a mouse, but longer and more slender, with soft, molelike fur and a flattened rudderlike tail, it was still in perfect preservation.

There was a natural history museum in Yosemite then, maintained by the Park Service, and I took my strange trophy over to see if they could identify it. The young man in charge was greatly surprised and remarked that only one other such specimen had ever been found there. It turned out to be a navigator shrew, and he begged it for his collection. The occasion led to a pleasant and long friendship.

There have been a lot of years and many casts since that memorable summer. My appetite for breakfast trout has diminished somewhat and an inherent laziness has increased considerably. With the conservatism of middle age, my angling has become more leisurely and, looking backward, it seems long ago that I last crawled up to a bank and hung my fly over an unsuspecting trout, ready to lever him out and hurry him home to the waiting skillet.

But there are still occasions when, standing out in the current and correctly casting my fly to the edge of the bushes, I have a recurrence of that early urge to more Indian-like tactics. Who knows, tomorrow it may get the best of me.

Many people choose to fish on party boats, public piers, and crowded riverbanks on opening day. R. Palmer Baker, Jr., however, prefers a more solitary aspect to his sport. It is his perfect antidote for modern life.

R. PALMER BAKER, JR.

The Solitary and Friendly Sport

In this story three fishermen stop their car at a crossroad and ask a back-woodsman the way to Beaver Creek.

"What you fellers lookin' for?"

They say they are going fishing. Trout fishing.

In due course the backwoodsman tells them the way.

"You fellers got any whiskey with you?"

They say no.

"How about a little 'baccy?"

They say they don't smoke.

"Well, now," says the backwoodsman, "I thought you fellers said you was goin' fishin'."

There is something to this story. Trout fishing is the most solitary yet the most companionable of sports. It can be very elegant and very disreputable.

One of my companions was equally devoted to dry-fly fishing and bridge. His idea of a successful trip was to play cards most of the night, fish in the morning, sleep away the afternoon, and then fish the evening rise. When he died, at a sadly early age, his friends knew that this was his idea of heaven. He used to admire and not just laugh at Webster's wonderful cartoon of the four salmon fishermen playing bridge in a hut near the river. Outside, another member of the party staggers under the weight of an enormous fish and calls for attention. "George, you're dummy," says one of the players, "you go look at the damn fish."

On a Thursday before Decoration Day, the bridge master and I left the city with two other friends to fish the New York waters of the Battenkill. One member of our party did not have a license, so we looked for the office of the town clerk at the county seat. Misdirected, we entered a lawyer's office. After learning of our mistake and apologizing to his secretary, we said—three of the party being lawyers—that we should like to meet him. This was not possible, she told us. This was the month of May, and every Thursday afternoon he went fishing.

The afternoon was a fine one, and we got out on the stream as quickly as we could, knowing that a long evening of bridge lay ahead of us. Cahills were coming off the water in numbers, and the trout were taking them with regularity. Our bridge master was in his element. He caught and released one fish after another. Downstream, a worm fisherman could contain himself no longer. He came up along the bank, just as another trout was landed.

"Hey, mister! What bait you usin'?"

The bridge master drew himself up.

"My dear fellow," he said, "this is a dry fly." Then retribution followed. Turning toward shore, he stepped into a hole. Quietly the bridge master went under, holding his Leonard aloft like Excalibur. His fishing hat gently floated downstream, and a moment later, walruslike, he emerged.

This companionable kind of fishing is one of the happiest aspects of the sport. Yet it is also rewarding now and then to fish by yourself. Solitude, particularly for the city man, is at the heart of fishing for trout.

The best times for this are days stolen from work, the beginnings of vacations, the end of some sustained endeavor. I remember one day at the close of college, when I was released—how temporarily!—from intellectual bondage. It was on the Vermont-New York line, and I did not have a care in the world.

Early in the morning a big trout kept rising at the center of the biggest pool in the river. I almost drowned trying to reach him with the fly, but he was much too far out for me. At that time I scorned the wearing of waders, and when I came out of the water I was numb with cold; but neither this nor the failure to catch the trout diminished the pleasure of the morning.

In the afternoon I fished a meadow tributary. The best pools were open and without cover, so it was necessary to cast while lying almost prone. If the fly landed properly, the trout jumped when they took it.

After the war I returned to the river again, staying with my wife's sister, who was opening her country house for the summer. At six o'clock the June morning was glorious. Since I did not have my license, I had to wait until after breakfast before fishing, so I dressed and walked through the village and across the fields to look at the stream before the household was awake.

The nearest pool was bordered on one side by hayfields and on the other by the slope of a wooded hill. Seated on a tree root at the head of the pool, comfortably smoking his pipe, was a local fisherman of great repute. He had been fishing with minnows and was through for the day. Together, the two trout in his basket weighed at least five pounds. I admired them with envy and delight.

The rest of the day was like standing at the gates of paradise. In the morning we bought the license, did the shopping, and got the house ready for the summer. At noon neighbors insisted on having us for lunch. In the afternoon we had to follow a golf tournament. But then my hostess took pity.

After the tournament, we ate an early supper and drove quickly back to the house. While we were passing a graveyard I was told to hold my breath and make a wish. "Now," she said, as I drew my breath, "you will catch your trout."

There were two good hours of daylight ahead of me. Off I went, through the village and across the fields, with my rod.

At dusk the swallows began to dive and circle, feeding on the mayflies that were coming off the water. The little trout started splashing at the flies on the surface.

Then two bigger fish began to rise steadily in a little bay at the head of the pool. The current swirled there against a high grassy bank where two Guernsey cows were feeding, now and then lifting their heads to look with curiosity at the fisherman below them. Each time a mayfly drifted along this bank there was a dimple on the surface and the insect disappeared.

Kneeling on a gravel bar, I was able to get very close to this location and, for once, to float my fly, a Cahill, without drag to one of the rising trout. He took it with a dimple, followed the pressure of the line, and allowed himself to be landed in the pool below the gravel bar. He was a brook trout, not too common in this part of the river, June-fat and a foot long.

The second trout along the bank took the fly in the same way. It was a brown trout, almost identical in size, and so I had a good brace. Having been defeated by this river more than once, I placed the fish in my bag and walked back to the house with satisfaction.

My hostess and her husband were standing in the kitchen. When I held the two fish out to her, one in each hand, she said, "My goodness, they're still alive; they're quivering."

"No," I said. "That's me." And I thanked her for the graveyard wish and what had turned out to be a perfect day.

When you are fishing alone, you had better bring your fish home if you want your friends and family to believe you. On the other hand, the return of a large trout to the stream without a witness can result in a fine sense of moral superiority.

The fact is that the fly-fisherman is likely to raise his biggest and most difficult trout when he is on the stream alone, concentrating and undisturbed. One spring morning, when I looked from the office window, the sun was sparkling on the waters of the North River, the city plane trees were green, and the pigeons were wheeling on a fresh west wind. The thought of that day wasted in the city was intolerable. I closed my desk and left.

Two hours later I was on one of the streams in the Croton watershed. Although heavily fished at the beginning of the season, some of these are good brown trout waters. They have a cool and constant flow from the reservoir outlets and their banks are shaded and protected from siltation. Most of the fish are stocked, but now and then the fly-fisherman takes a wild trout, and once in a while a big one comes up from the reservoir below.

This was one of those occasions—an escape from the city—when solitude is a joy. I walked upstream for fifteen minutes before making the first cast. Violets were blooming along the edge of the woods. The red-winged blackbirds called to each other as they nested at the edges of the swamp. Presently I was walking in a grove of hemlocks, approaching the first pool.

The first attempt was made with a dun variant, a smoky-gray fly with a long hackle. Immediately two little trout splashed and jumped over it. At about the same time, a hatch of small red-gray flies was seen coming off the water. When the fly was changed to a Red Quill, one of the little trout took it at once. He was returned to his family and I proceeded upstream.

None of the rising fish was of any size, but one came up in virtually every pool. When I came to one of the larger pools I fished the lower end carefully, but there was no response. This was odd. There should have been several small trout at the tail of the pool. Then I looked upstream, to the very head of the pool, where the current flowed between two big rocks. There was a tiny splash in the current.

On another occasion I had seen a splash like this and later had been able to identify it. The splash was caused not by a little fish but by the flick of a big trout's tail as it turned in the current. Suddenly I was convinced that this was a similar occasion, particularly since the absence of small fish at the tail indicated that a big one might have driven them off.

The Red Quill was dried, oiled, and dipped in the stream to wash off the excess dressing. I got it into the air and began lengthening the cast. Back and forth went the line, along the side of the pool so as not to throw its shadow over the trout. In a moment all was in readiness for the final delivery when the back cast hung solidly up in a hemlock branch.

Good-bye, Red Quill; good-bye, leader. At this point I was not going to move from my position and disturb the pool. After drawing the line tight and cursing a little, I broke off the fly and the first tippet of the leader. With shaking hands I finally succeeded in tying on a new tippet and another Red Quill.

This time more care was used with the back cast. The fly landed in the current between the rocks, floated two inches, and simply disappeared.

If I had not already been sure, I would have known this was a big fish when I tightened on the line. For a moment he did not move. Then he jumped. He jumped six times. He was certainly fifteen inches long—a monster for the stream. He began to run up and down the pool, powerfully, frantically. Because I was now standing at the tail, he turned each time he saw me. He wanted badly to go downstream toward the reservoir from which he no doubt had recently come.

Now he raced upstream, into the current between the rocks where he had taken the fly, and in an instant he was fighting in the pool above me. Then I made the mistake of stepping out on the bank to follow. I am convinced that he saw me. He came back downstream with a leap, raced through the pool, and was into the fast water below me. When I stripped in line and snubbed him he jumped one more time and was gone.

There is a catharsis in this kind of experience. The next day I was again prepared for work. My angling friends who know the stream nod their heads and say they believe me when I tell the story. I think some do. And some may not.

Barich packs us along on his travels. We poke our head out of his knapsack and peer over his shoulder. The view is quite extraordinary.

BILL BARICH

Hat Creek and the McCloud

Every autumn, I try to make a trip into the mountains of northern California to do some trout fishing, and this past year was no exception. I was more eager than ever, in fact, because I hadn't done any fishing for a while, and I felt an acute biological need for open spaces. On our return from Europe, we'd settled in San Francisco, and the honk and nonsense of the city was already getting to me. I suppose the noise wasn't really any worse than the noise of London or Florence, but it had an echo of permanence about it. Gone were the days of carefree wandering. Anyway, I got out of bed one morning and stared through my apartment window at the tree on my block and noticed that six or seven of its pauperish leaves had turned red. That was my signal—a mere urban reflection of what would be going on in the Trinity Alps or the Cascade Range.

In my closet, I had a shoebox file of fishing maps, and I pulled it out to help me decide which river to fish. I chose Hat Creek, a famous California stream in Siskiyou County I'd never hit before. Hat Creek flows south through the granite and lava of the Cascades until it dead-ends in Lassen Volcanic National Park. In its lower reaches, it is among the richest trout streams in the United States, on a par with the Firehole River, in Wyoming, and the Letort Spring

Run, in Pennsylvania. It is capable of producing enough food to support as many as 3,200 trout over five miles of water. All the trout in lower Hat Creek are wild, not hatchery reared, and they can grow to considerable size. This section of the stream is elegant and challenging. It attracts anglers from all over the world. Fishing pressure is often intense, especially during the legendary insect hatches that explode in clockwork fashion in the summer months— little yellow stone flies in June, pale morning duns in July, tricorythodes spinners in August. In order to preserve the quality of lower Hat Creek, the California Department of Fish and Game has instituted a stringent set of regulations. Only artificial flies and lures with single barbless hooks may be used, so that fish can be released with as little damage to them as possible. (A study done at Hat Creek in 1973 revealed that anglers let go 63 percent of the fish they'd hooked.) The daily creel limit is two trout. The trout must be at least eighteen inches long—big fish, that is, the kind that set your heart to pumping.

Hat Creek is so productive because it's a spring creek, pure and translucent, fed primarily by underground springs rather than rain or snowmelt. Like most spring creeks, it has a high concentration of bound carbon dioxide—sixty to eighty parts per million, as compared to ten or twenty for an average stream. As the creek percolates up through the volcanic subsoil of the region, the carbon dioxide in it dissolves deposits of marl and lime that have formed around the fossilized skeletons of crustaceans, snails, shellfish, and plants. This makes the creek very alkaline. It has large quantities of calcium and magnesium carbonates. Alkalinity encourages an abundance of insect life—particularly of those species most favored by trout. It also promotes weed growth (weeds provide cover for fish and oxygenate a stream through photosynthesis) and, in general, helps to create excellent habitat for German browns and rainbows. The trout of Hat Creek are stocky, brilliantly colored, and difficult to catch even in autumn, after the tourists have all gone home.

I spent the evening before I left sorting through my tackle. I wanted to get rid of the worthless stuff, but I couldn't bring myself to throw out anything. Nostalgia seems to infuse every aspect of fishing, including the gear. When I came across a handful of streamer flies tied for steelhead, I started thinking about my friend Paul Deeds, who taught me almost everything I know about those ungovernable fish. I hadn't seen Deeds for more than a year. I'd sent him some postcards, but I knew even as I mailed them that they were destined to wind up in the flyblown cellar of his house. Deeds never answers his mail. He doesn't have much affection for the telephone, either—he regards it as an instrument of torture. I'd called him a couple of times since I'd been back, just to say hello, but I'd felt as though I were talking to a doorjamb. What we'd shared could not in any way be counted as conversations. I thought I'd give him one more try, though, because I missed him and I was in the mood for company on Hat Creek.

I dialed Deeds's number. The phone rang and rang. I could see him sitting in his ratty kitchen with a cup of coffee at his elbow, looking out into the prune orchard that surrounds his place and hoping that the ringing would stop.

"Who is it?" he asked when he picked up the receiver. He must have been holding it yards from his mouth; I could barely hear him.

I told him who it was, and what I had in mind.

"You're crazy," Deeds said. "Hat Creek is too crowded. There'll be all kinds of people around."

"It's almost October, Paul. It won't be too bad."

"Maybe not for a city person," he said.

Deeds can be very stubborn when it comes to matters of principle or opinion. From his reluctance to discuss Hat Creek, I figured that he'd probably been there once when four or five other anglers were on the river, and that this horrible *crowd* had so disconcerted him that he swore never to return.

"If you were making a trip, where would you go?" I asked.

"McCloud River," he said. "Down in the canyon, near the Nature Conservancy preserve. I'd camp at Ah-Di-Na Meadow. I'd fish downstream from there to Ladybug Creek. Hang on for a second, my dog wants to get out."

The only part of the McCloud that I was familiar with was a tame stretch than runs parallel to Interstate 5 near Dunsmuir. It's a decent but unspectacular stream in that region, similar to many other streams that border highways and are subject to the passing fancies of motorist-anglers. The McCloud that runs through the canyon is completely different—far less accessible and so less popular. It flows through rugged terrain that still has a few bears and mountain lions. In the canyon, the trout are wild.

"It's getting cold out there," Deeds said, when he came back on the line.

"You don't think it'll be crowded on the McCloud?"

"I sincerely doubt it. The road in is about eight miles of bad dirt."

I checked a map of Siskiyou County. The town of McCloud was just fifty miles or so from where I'd be. "Suppose I fish Hat Creek first, then meet you in McCloud?"

"I can't just drop everything and take off."

This made me laugh. Deeds is divorced. He has no job. He lives off his faltering prune crop and the small portfolio of stocks and bonds that he inherited.

"What can be so pressing?" I asked. "The harvest is over."

"There's still the dog to be fed."

After further negotiations, he agreed to call me in the morning. I told him not to be too late, since I wanted to get an early start, but I didn't have to worry. Deeds woke me just after six o'clock, while the sky was still black. "Friday at the McCloud Hotel," he said. "I'll meet you there about noon."

Almost nothing makes me happier than to leave on a fishing trip. I feel like I'm doing something active for a change instead of hanging around on a street corner waiting for a bus to jump the curb and run me over. One of the secret terrors of the age is that we are all dying slowly of complacency. I carried my tackle to the car and put it in the trunk. The sky was red now, streaked with pink clouds. I could tell from the haze and stillness that it was going to be hot. By the time I'd reached Redding, around midmorning, the temperature had risen to eighty-four degrees. Redding is at the northern tip of the Sacramento Valley. It's a wonderful spot to experience heat, since it's hemmed in by two mountain ranges—the Salmons and the Cascades—and the air in town moves not at all.

I stopped at a tackle shop that specializes in materials and gear for those who fish with flies. The clerk told me that the fishing on Hat Creek had only been fair for the last week or so. He said that I shouldn't look for much in the way of insect hatches, except for orange caddis flies and maybe a few blue-wing olives. The trout would most likely be feeding below the surface. They'd go for nymphs and streamers. (Nymphs imitate insect larvae; streamers imitate baitfish.) He suggested that I use a fly line with a sinking tip. I bought one and also some stone-fly nymphs and some leeches. When I asked the clerk about places to stay, he recommended Lava Creek Lodge, in Glenburn.

That afternoon, I got my first glimpse of Hat Creek. It snuck up on me without any fanfare. I went over a highway bridge just past Burney and saw a stream on both sides of me and then a sign that said HAT CREEK. I turned the car around and pulled down an access road that led to a picnic area by the water. After Deeds's warning, I expected the picnic tables to be occupied by hundreds of chubby guys in T-shirts and funny hats, but nobody was there. Nobody was fishing, either. I walked to the creek and knelt on the bank. The water was very clear. I could see almost to the stream bed—about five feet down, I guessed. There were weeds—red, brown, purple, many shades of green—shifting around in the current. The motion had a witchery to it. In spite of what the clerk had told me, there was a good hatch of mayflies going on. The bugs floated toward heaven on lacy wings.

The setting was so serene, and so perfect for trout, that it was hard to remember that Hat Creek was once a decimated stream. Its transformation began in 1968, around the time that the Department of Fish and Game came under pressure from conservation-minded angling organizations for having let the quality of trout fishing in California deteriorate. The department had been slow to protect prime habitat against environmental degradation, and there were fewer and fewer productive wild trout streams around. To make up for its losses, the department relied on what's known as a "put-and-take" program. In essence, the state kept dumping millions of small, hatchery-reared trout into rivers as fast as anglers reeled in the old ones. That's pretty fast—hatchery fish are easy to catch. At the hatchery, they've been trained to answer the dinner bell. They'll chase after almost any type of bait—worms, salmon eggs, even mini-marshmallows. They've never learned any survival skills, so when they're planted in a stream, they panic and school together in fear. Most of them are hooked right away. Predators pitch in to make short work of others. Only a few hatchery fish in any river manage to last from one season to the next.

The put-and-take program was (and is) popular with weekend anglers who were only interested in filling their creel, but it didn't satisfy the purists. The project to reclaim lower Hat Creek was an attempt to please them. When the project started, trash fish made up about 95 percent of the creek's population. They'd eaten or otherwise interfered with most of the native trout in the project area—a three-and-a-half-mile stretch between Lake Britton and Baum Lake. Biologists went to the stream and captured wild strains of rainbow and German brown for later restocking. The stream was then treated with chemicals. About seven tons of trash fish eventually turned belly-up—Sacramento suckers, hardmouths, buffalo fish. Next, a barrier was constructed at the northern end of the creek to prevent the trash fish in Lake Britton from moving upstream. The wild trout were planted again, and they flourished. They had more food, less danger and competition. The project was such a success that, in 1971, the department established a more elaborate wild trout program to restore and perpetuate quality angling throughout the state. Currently, seventeen streams and a lake are designated for wild trout management.

For a while, I sat on the riverbank, watching the insects hatch. The sunshine felt good, a tonic to the bones. Every now and then, I saw a dimple on the water when a trout rose to swallow a fallen bug. I had to stifle my desire to run to the car and grab my rod. The sitting still was an act of discipline. The notion was to be calm instead of frenzied, as I usually am on the first day. I concentrated on the creek, its flow, the channels where fish were feeding, trying to commit the details to memory. It takes a long time before you begin to see things with any degree of actuality. After thirty minutes of meditation, I got to my feet, stretched my legs, and drove to the lodge.

Glenburn is not so much a real town as a name on a map. It's located in the Fall River Valley at an elevation of about 3,500 feet. The valley has a cowboy feel to it. Beef cattle are the major agricultural industry, so pastureland is conspicuous. I passed fields of grass and alfalfa, of grain hay. There were sprinklers in the fields—the sort with long pipes and spoked wheels. Blackbirds were riding them. I saw hundreds of mallards overhead, beginning their annual migration, winging south along the course of the Fall River. Like Hat Creek, the Fall is spring fed and extremely productive. It supports an estimated 2,000 trout to the mile. The property that borders the river is all privately owned. The only way to fish the Fall (unless you've got a rancher friend) is by boat. A boat opens up twelve miles of countryside. You drift by farms and ranches, weathered barns, aspens, grazing cattle. Sometimes you catch a glimpse of Mount Shasta with its eternally snowcapped peak.

Lava Creek is a relatively new place. It consists of a lodge with a bar and a restaurant. The lodge sits right on the edge of a pretty little lake called Eastman. There are a few cabins, too, set among scrubby pines, and I rented one. It came equipped with a dented pot-and-pan combo and several back issues of *Family Circle* and *Cosmopolitan*. I don't think I've ever rented a cabin anywhere that didn't have at least two or three women's magazines on the kitchen table. Some Gideon-like organization must be responsible for distributing them to resorts throughout the Pacific Northwest.

After I unloaded the car, I took a stroll to see if I could ferret out any hot angling tips from the locals. Near my cabin, I ran into a young guy in a down vest who was chopping wood. By the look of the pile he'd stacked against a shed, he was preparing for a cold winter. His name was Kyle. He and his wife managed the place. He told me that Hat Creek was going to be a tough mother to fish. I'd have to cast perfectly if I hoped to score, because the water was clear and slow moving and wouldn't disguise my mistakes. Most of the big trout had already been caught, then released, and they were especially wary. Kyle knew guides who refused to let their clients even *try* to cast. Instead, the clients had to *deposit* their flies on the water, then strip line from their reels by hand until the flies floated in front of feeding trout. For novices, Kyle said, the best spot on the creek was fifty yards of broken, riffly water that flowed out from a Pacific Gas and Electric Company powerhouse. The riffles helped to hide a faulty presentation. Your fly didn't have to land as smoothly there, since the water was in a state of perturbation and even real insects bobbed around like mad. "You try there first," Kyle said.

I got to the powerhouse at six o'clock. It was just off the main highway, down a well-maintained utility company road. Four men were already fishing in the riffles. They'd left enough space for me to sneak in among them, but I hated it when somebody did that to me, so I put on my waders, climbed over a stile, and walked upstream toward slacker water that rolled idly through a meadow. Some black Angus cattle were plodding around on the opposite hillside, their heads lowered to the ground. The trees at the edge of the meadow were incense cedars. Their bark was red-brown, ridged and covered with scales.

The calm attitude I'd cultivated during my meditation vanished completely once I had my rod assembled. Trout were rising everywhere, making circles with their lips on the smooth, slick creek. Occasionally, I heard an explosion—some really monstrous lunker leaping into the air to nab a bug. I couldn't decide what the fish were taking, so I tried a leech that I'd bought in Redding. Properly speaking, leeches are ugly, segmented, bloodsucking worms of the type that attached themselves to Humphrey Bogart in *The African Queen*. The imitation is not so repulsive. It's a feathery black fly that's best fished just under the surface.

Once I had the leech tied to my leader, I moved closer to the stream. I wanted to wade it, like the men below me in the riffles, but it was too deep where I was, and I had to do my casting from shore. Whenever you're casting, the idea is to fall into a hypnotic rhythm, so that you and the rod become one—so that *thinking* becomes impossible—but I failed to accomplish that. The rod and I were bitter enemies. It wouldn't do a thing I asked it to. I kept hooking the leech on the tall star nettles and giant mulleins behind me. It seemed to me that if I went farther upstream, where the banks were not so overgrown, I might do better, but the soil there proved to be marshy and I slid into it up to my knees.

The whole scenario would have been tragic if it hadn't happened to me so many times before. One of the few advantages of maturity is that petty failures no longer make you break rods, get drunk, and curse at strangers. I brushed the muck from my waders, then wiped my hands on my shirt. (In a pinch, fishing clothes are a tolerable substitute for towels or handkerchiefs.) I snipped off the leech and tied on an orange caddis. It was a dry fly, so it floated. With its wings propped up, it looked like a princely specimen, but it found no takers. Neither did the mosquito I tried next.

As I was trading the mosquito for a black ant, I glanced up and saw a mangy cocker spaniel running toward me. For some reason, fishermen's dogs are always friendly. They love to dance around and do tricks and stick out their tongues in a totally joyous way. Some of their masters' joy at being outside in the good world God made must get transmitted to them. I patted the spaniel on the head, and he licked my hand. His master came along in a minute or two—a stocky guy who was grunting from the effort of walking. He'd chewed his cigar to an interesting mass. I asked him how he'd done, and he said he'd taken two minor league trout the night before, but that he'd been skunked this evening. "The moon, it's almost full," he said. "Those fish have been stuffing themselves on caddis all month long."

At dusk, I packed it in. About seven or eight men were in the riffles now, pressed in much too tightly. I watched them for a bit—they were all using nymphs and streamers—but none of them got any action. I opened a can of beer and drove to the lodge. The country night was sweet. I pushed the accelerator to the floor, enjoying a rush of speed, and the liberating sensation of being unpoliced. Traffic cops are scarce in the Fall River Valley. The dark, twisty roads impose the laws. I pushed the radio button and on came Charley Pride singing "You're So Good When You're Bad." A little later, the white clapboard face of Glenburn church jumped out at me. It was built in 1886. Services are still held in it once a month, even in winter, when the deacons have to fire up a potbellied stove to ward off the chill.

There was frost on my windshield when I left the lodge the next morning. I was tempted to go back inside, crawl under the covers, and read *Family Circle* until the sun was higher in the sky, but I pushed myself forward, into the wintry air and then out into the valley. A man and his son were launching a skiff in the Fall, and they both waved and smiled, blowing clouds of breath. The leaves of the aspens along the river had died some more during the night, and they were a brighter yellow than ever. A powder of new snow was on the mountains. The light was intense, a shock to the eyes.

I hoped that I'd be rewarded for bucking the cold, but the powerhouse riffles were again occupied by several anglers. One guy was wearing earmuffs and gloves. The sight of this coward so unnerved me that I had a very Deedsian reaction and took off in a huff for the picnic area I'd stopped at the first afternoon. It was still deserted. I followed a trail that went under the highway bridge into another meadow, thinking it might lead me to a secret, uninhabited, fruitful run of water.

The trail took me around a bend in the creek. Ahead, I saw a short stretch of fast water. It wasn't as fast as the riffle water, but it was fast enough to sink a wet fly. I chose a stone fly nymph from my fly box. Western stone flies emerge in spring and summer, but, as nymphs, they're present in streams at other times, and they're an important food for trout. The fly must be fished deep to be effective, so I wrapped a little piece of lead around my line. This made casting more awkward. I kept wishing for an insect hatch; the trout would start feeding, and I'd know which imitation to use. But the bugs stayed quiet all morning, and I had to fish blind. Around one o'clock, hunger got the best of me, and I walked to the car to eat. I had a sandwich of Safeway cheese, and then an apple, and then I had a nap. I must have been tired, because I didn't wake until midafternoon. I went to the creek and washed my face, then drove to the powerhouse again. All the back-and-forth driving was beginning to take the shine off my fishing experience.

On the utility company road, I had to brake to a halt when a porcupine raced in front of me. Actually, "raced" is too strong a word to apply to any porcupine, even if the animal is moving at top speed. The porcupine waddled. It seemed as surprised to see me as I was to see it. In the mountains, you get used to the chipmunk and squirrel kamikazes who are always darting in front of your tires, risking their existence for a thrill, but porcupines are pretty rare. They appear to have stumbled into the wrong century, and they're not happy about it. Once this porcupine made it across the road, he waddled into a gully and started climbing a hummock, toward the shelter of some toyon bushes. The hummock was wet from the morning's frost, and the porcupine had difficulty with his footing. He'd almost make it to the toyons and then the earth would give beneath his feet and down he'd roll, quills first, into the gully. The show was so good that I switched off the motor and sat there watching him. The curious thing was that he never bothered to look back. I knew that if I were doing the climbing, and I sensed the presence of an intruder, I'd be peeking over my shoulder whenever I could. Maybe that's a good definition of neurosis—to be constantly peeking over your shoulder to check what might be wrong. The porcupine was incredibly determined. He must have fallen fifteen times before he finally reached his goal. I wanted to applaud him. In fact, I would have applauded him if I thought he'd care, but he didn't even stop at the top of the hummock to celebrate. He wasn't anywhere close to being human.

For once, nobody was in the powerhouse riffles—I had the spot to myself. I tied on a new leader with a very fine taper and, to that, I tied a caddis nymph. I waded into the creek rather cautiously—the current was strong—and began to cast. It went well for a change. I was able to concentrate on what I was doing, but after thirty fishless minutes, a thought unrelated to angling came into my head, and then another thought came—inconsequential, both these thoughts—and I drifted off in pursuit of them. Of course, I had an immediate strike. A trout with a sense of humor grabbed the nymph while I was playing around with the little fist in my skull. The bite was like a reminder from nature. It brought me back to attention, but then I drifted off again, into a fantasy about how I'd tell Kyle of Lava Creek that I'd hooked and lost a terrific fish. The fantasy gave way to speculation about why anglers are pathological liars, and before I knew it I'd worked myself to the end of the riffles.

I took a rest on the bank. Late afternoon sunshine was coming through the cedar branches. Suddenly, insects began to hatch. It was very exciting, because I could see them so clearly—orange caddis flies. I snapped a spool with a floating line into my reel and tied on an imitation caddis, size 18. There was some water that was already in shade, and I worked it first. I made short, delicate casts to cut down on mistakes. I knew that I was doing a good job of presenting the fly, but I was still surprised when a rainbow trout took it. I had so little line on the water that I landed the trout with no trouble. It was about thirteen inches long, stout and boxy, bearing the bright pinks and reds and silvers of a wild trout. Hatchery fish have the same colors, but they always seem muted, like bad reproductions of great art. When I gripped the trout to remove my hook, I could feel its flailing muscles, a tremendous focusing of power. Because the hook was barbless, it slipped out easily, leaving just a tiny tear in the trout's lip. I released it into the creek and watched it dart into the depths. Nothing disappears as quickly as a trout redeemed.

That evening, after dinner, I went to the lodge for a drink. No doubt I was looking for a chance to mention my trout, but I couldn't get a word in edgewise with the four other angler-guests at the bar. They were fly-fishing bullies—the kind of guys who dress in unsoiled flannel, down, and khaki garments and spend thousands of dollars on tackle and far-flung vacations. These bullies are always yakking about their last trip to New Zealand or Patagonia, and it's very depressing to listen to them, since by their insistence on the value of all the things in life that *don't* matter, they violate the essence of the sport—which combines, as Izaak Walton noted, humility and a calmness of spirit. I only lasted through a single bourbon. Instead of going to my cabin, I walked to Eastman Lake and sat on the shore for a few minutes, just staring at the moonlight on the water. Moonlight never gets old.

Robert Bell takes a somewhat sobering stance on the live vs. artificial bait controversy.

ROBERT BELL

The Fisherman

Beside the turbid stream of life
Sits the grim fisherman, who plies
His rod above the troubled strife,
Patient and watchful, nor denies
Any by reason of its size.

And I, too, on some careless day,
Shall feel the hook I had not guessed;
And I shall try to break away,
And go, after a brief protest,
Into the basket, with the rest.

As the longtime angling editor of *Outdoor Life,* Ray Bergman comes as close as anyone to perpetuating the standards set by Theodore Gordon. A generation cut its teeth on Bergman's book, *Trout.*

RAY BERGMAN

Steelhead of the Umpqua

Having been born and raised on the East Coast and not being wealthy, it took me a great many years to satisfy my desire to fish in waters west of the Mississippi. The first trip, with a five-year-old Model A Ford, took us to that river, from Canada to New Orleans, and out into the Atlantic as well: that is, to the island of Ocracoke, North Carolina. The next year, with a new car, we made a trip that brought us plenty of fishing in Michigan, Colorado, Wyoming, Missouri, Arkansas, and Mississippi.

During these years Clarence Gordon, of Oregon, had been corresponding with me. His letters about the steelhead fishing on the North Umpqua, in the vicinity of Steamboat where he had a delightful camp, painted such fascinating pictures that my wife and I couldn't resist them. We put aside other projects we had considered and surrendered to the lure of Oregon, California, and West Texas for that year. We have always been glad that we did. We feel that we owe Clarence a debt of gratitude for having hastened our first trip to the Pacific Coast.

A friend, Fred Gerken, of Tombstone, Arizona, also had a great desire to fish for steelhead, so the result was a meeting at the Wilcox Ranch on Encampment Creek, Wyoming. I'd become attached to this stream from a previous trip, and after ten days of splendid fishing there, we started for Oregon.

22

We went by way of the Columbia River Highway. My first glimpse of Mount Hood was enthralling. It fulfilled all my dreams of what a high mountain should look like. There were many forest fires raging at the time, and by some freak of the air currents the smoke obscured the lower part of the mountain, but not the valley, leaving the peak suspended in mid-air—pointed, majestic, and fascinating. We'd seen higher mountains before but none more spectacular, for Hood rises from comparatively low country while the others rise from very high altitudes to begin with, thus losing much impressiveness. Next to Mount Hood, the Tetons hold my memory most. They are so rugged and jagged, and rise so high above the surrounding country, that they get your nervous system responding with inward heart quivers.

We had another thrill when we left Roseburg for the trip up the North Umpqua to Steamboat. The first few miles were not so much, but once above Glide it was as picturesque and tortuous a route as one could imagine. You felt sure you were going places, and you really were.

The river is wild and beautiful, and at first sight a bit terrifying. You wonder how you are going to be able to wade it without getting into difficulties. Despite this it isn't so bad once you learn to read the bottom. On the bottom are narrow strips of gravel that wander here and there and crisscross like old-time city streets. By walking in these and stepping only on reasonably flat, clean rocks or on other rocks where you can see the mark of previous footsteps, you wade with fair comfort and safety. The rocks of the routes between most of the good pools are plainly marked by the tread of many feet, and as long as you know what to look for you have no trouble. But do not hurry—watch each step closely unless you have the activity and surefootedness of a mountain goat or a Clarence Gordon. When he gets to a hard spot he makes a hop, skip, and jump and lands just where he wants, while you gingerly and sometimes painfully make your way after him, arriving a few minutes later. He waits apparently patiently, but probably in his heart wishing you would move quicker. He finds it so easy it must seem ridiculous to him for anyone to be so slow and faltering. I once thought I was agile (I was, from what others tell me), but Clarence—well, just ask those who have fished with him.

Never having fished for steelhead, I decided to watch Gordon a while before trying my luck. From experience I know that you can learn plenty by watching someone who knows the water from concentrated fishing. The time of the year may make a difference in the places where the best fishing is found. At the season we have fished the North Umpqua, steelhead were found only in certain sections of the main channel. In addition, not all waters containing large steelhead were suitable for fly fishing. If of greater depth than six to eight feet, the trout were not much interested in a fly, although now and then one would take.

I fished first at the Fighting Hole, so named because it was all fast water and short, with white and fast water below, so that there was always a good chance of the fish getting out of the hole and into the rapids and thus taking you for a ride that often led to disaster in some degree. Usually this meant only the loss of the fish, but sometimes it meant the loss of a bit of tackle as well.

The first thing I noted was the way Clarence handled the fly. He cast quartering across and slightly downstream. When the fly touched water his rod tip began to dip and rise rhythmically about every three seconds. At the same time he retrieved a little line with his other hand—about a foot or two all told during the entire drift of the fly. On the first cast the fly did not submerge. Before making the next cast he soaked it thoroughly, and from then on it sank readily. He explained that in low, clear water a fly dragging over the surface was likely to spoil your chances. This was good trout-fishing lore. Many times I have soaked flies in mud to make them sink quickly for the same reasons when fishing for wary browns.

The Fighting Hole did not produce, so we moved down to the Mott Pool. This was a long fast run that terminated in a fairly wide basin. Almost at once Clarence hooked a fish. As it struck he let go the slack line he had been holding. The reel screeched as the fish dashed downstream. He broke water some hundred and fifty feet below and then started a dogged resistance. At this time Clarence gave me a little more information: "Most trout fishermen after steelhead for the first time make the mistake of stripping line when playing them. They do it with other fish and think they can do it with these, but you have got to play them on the reel: otherwise there is sure to be trouble." As I watched I knew this was true. As with Atlantic salmon, it would be certain suicide to your chances to attempt to play them by stripping. Those strong rushes—some as long as a hundred and fifty feet—those vicious tugs when like a bulldog they figuratively shook their heads savagely, would make it well nigh impossible to handle them in any other way except on the reel. The slightest kink, the slightest undue pressure, and something would break.

Watching Clarence fight this fish was too much for my resolve not to fish until I learned something about the game. Besides, I had learned how to manipulate the fly; the rest would be the same as grilse or landlocked salmon—or at least so I thought.

The lower end of the Mott failed me. Clarence said it was probably because his fish had run into it several times and so disturbed the rest located there. I hooked a steelhead in the next hole—I think it is called the Bologna for the reason that when a fish goes over there it is gone; and as they usually do go over, it is just bologna to fish the hole; but I did not know it at this time. There was an irresistible vibrant pull at the strike, the reel screeched a few seconds, and then the line was slack. I had lost my first fish.

"You'd have lost the fish when he went over anyway," soothed Clarence. "It is usually over quickly in this hole," and then he told me why. "Going over" on the Umpqua means that a fish leaves the pool it has been hooked in and runs into the white water below. If this stretch of bad water is of any great length, a fish that "goes over" is usually lost. When it gets away the fish is said to have "cleaned" the angler.

It seemed as if the Umpqua steelhead had it in for me—at least I made a poor showing the first three days. I hooked five fish and lost them all. Three pulled out after a short fight, and two cleaned me out good and proper. I was in the doldrums. The only thing that cheered me at all was the fact that Clarence Gordon insisted my hard luck was due to bad breaks and not to poor fishing. "Besides," he said, "I have really been giving you the works—bringing you to places that always mean trouble when you hook a fish. Take that hole right here—I've never landed a fish here yet, and I have hooked plenty."

On the other hand Fred Gerken seemed to take the game with the greatest nonchalance and was making a record for himself. On the first day he used his four-and-a-half-ounce trout rod, thirty yards of line, and a 3x leader, went out on the Kitchen Pool, and took a five-pounder as if he were catching a one-pound rainbow. But he did not tempt fate by continuing the use of the trout outfit. The next day he assembled his nine-and-a-half-footer and really went after business. Well did he uphold his grand start—a fish the second day, and no others were brought into camp. He did the same thing the third day, although he wasn't the only one. Phil Edson, of Pasadena, brought one in about four pounds bigger than Fred's. But still I had nothing to show. It was always excuses—this happened, that happened—well, you know how it is. To make it look worse my wife took a five-and-a-quarter-pounder at noon on the fourth day, and while she is a good bait caster she had never done a lot of trout fishing. We started her out with the bait-casting rod, and she did not like it a bit. But to be a good sport she kept using it for three days. Then she rebelled—she wanted to fish with a fly like the rest of us. So I took her out on the Kitchen Pool to give her a little coaching. About a half hour of this and she decided she could go it alone. I had seen a steelhead jump at the lower part of the pool, so was only too glad to rush ashore for my rod. I had just reached the tackle tent when I heard my wife give a call. I rushed back and found her fast to a fish—I believe the very one I went in to get my rod for. As I say, she had not had much experience fly fishing, but she had turned the trick and handled the hooked fish like a veteran. She was proud of her five-and-a-quarter-pounder, but not as happy about it as I thought she had a right to be. I soon learned why. She said: "It was all luck. The cast that took him was the worst I made." I knew exactly how she felt. Dr. Phil Edson, a guest at the camp who had been an observer of the operations, remarked, "A sloppy cast—in the Kitchen Pool

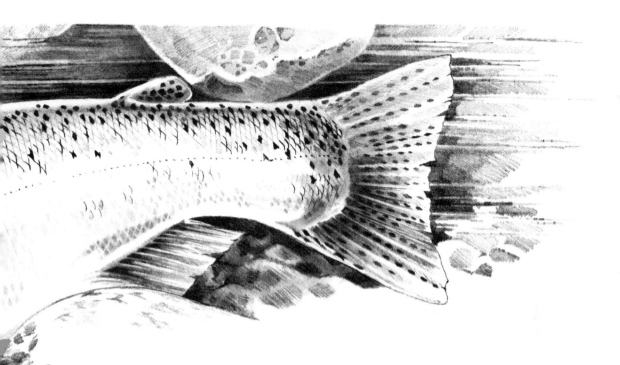

and at midday in a bright sun. That's something to make us think. Morning and evening, say the experts, and be sure to drop your fly lightly. I wonder what they will say about this?" (To my knowledge no one ever questioned this. They couldn't, as a matter of fact, because it actually happened.)

To make Phil's remarks even more pointed, immediately after lunch I slipped down to the Mott Pool and about halfway through hooked a fish. The singing of the reel was music to my ears. Nothing went wrong this time, and I had the satisfaction of looking up toward the end of the fight to see Fred, Grace, and Phil watching me. Phil was so anxious that I save the fish that he took off his shoes and stockings and with bare feet waded that treacherous water between us, just so that he could be on hand to help me land it in a most difficult spot. That is sportsmanship to commend. I shall never forget this spontaneous act of his as long as I live. It showed the real soul of the man, his unselfish desire to see that I got my fish. It was all very satisfying.

Now Clarence showed his angling acumen. For several days he had been planning his next move so that it would be most advantageous to me. He explained it, now that it was time to carry it through. It seems that when steelhead are not moving much, they become indifferent to flies fished repeatedly from one side of a pool. Mott Pool had been fished hard from the camp side for some time and was going a bit sour. But it hadn't been fished from the opposite side for at least a week—first because not many would tackle it from that side alone, because of the difficulty of wading, and second because Clarence always made an excuse when anyone mentioned going there. He wanted it to get *hot* before taking me there. Even after being taken to the other side by canoe there was plenty of rough wading before reaching the place from which you started fishing. If it hadn't been for Clarence showing me the bad spots and how to avoid them, I'd probably have floundered many times. As it was I never lost my footing.

When we reached the upper end of the hole that I was to fish, Clarence gave me some sage advice. "There are big fish here," he warned. "When one strikes, just keep a taut line and let him go. Don't strike back." Nothing happened until my fly drifted and cut across the tail on the pool. Here I felt a tug but did not connect. But on the next cast I hooked a heavy fish. For the moment he simply held steady, then moved to the center of the pool. Once there he sulked for five minutes or more, and I could not move him. Suddenly he started doing things, and I have but a vague idea of what happened. The reel screeched, its handle knocked my knuckles, my fingers burned as the line sped beneath them as I was reeling in frantically to get the best of a forward run. At the end of this exhibition, in which were included several jumps, he started a steady and rather slow but irresistible run that made the backing on my reel melt away. Clarence was by my side looking at my reel drum. "He's gone over," he said. My heart sank. Then for some unaccountable reason, perhaps an unknown ledge below, he stopped running. I started to pump him—work him— and he came right along. I reeled as fast as I could, and still he kept coming. My spirits revived with this chance of success. By this time he was only thirty feet away. But the fish suddenly decided he had come far enough and started edging off sideways. I could not stop him. He made a short fast run into shallow water at the right, and then all I felt was a vibrant weight. "I'm hung up," I groaned. I walked from one side of the ledge to the other, I knocked the rod, gave slack line, did everything I possibly could, but he did not come loose. I could feel the fish, so I knew we were still connected.

It was partly dark by this time, and the water between me and the fish was treacherous. I had never waded it in daylight and could not attempt it in the dark. But Gordon took the chance even though he had never waded the place before. "The leader is caught on a board," he called. "There—he is all yours." I felt a tug, saw and heard a splash, and the fish was gone. "About a twelve-pounder," said Gordon. "It's a wonder the leader didn't break the instant you snagged." For this is what happened: the leader had finally frayed on the board and broken. The board had floated down from some bridge-construction work upstream.

And that night Fred brought in another fish. But fortune treated me better from then on. The very next evening I brought in two fish, one weighing seven and a half pounds and the other ten and three-quarters. The latter was the largest fish of the season, although a week after we left, Phil Edson took one of ten and a half pounds. From then on my luck ran better than average, but Fred's held true to form to the last day. At that time his score was seven hooked and seven landed—some record when 50 percent is an excellent score. Clarence and the rest of us decided something must be done about it. The result of this conference was a trip down to the opposite side of Mott Pool. That night Fred hooked one he couldn't do much with, but even so he might have upheld the honor of his standing except for an unlucky break. The fish had been hooked lightly and pulled out. Anyway, he came in without his fish—the only day out of eight that this happened.

It is strange the way things sometimes happen. Dr. Dewey, of Pasadena, arrived at camp a few days before we did, took his limit of three fish two days in succession and never lost one. But after that it was different. He hooked a number of fish, but something always went wrong. Some "pulled out," and one "went over." He tried to follow the latter, stumbled, and fell in. He came in wet, bedraggled, and muddy. He hooked a number of other fish on flies from which the points of the hooks had been broken on rocks, and of course he held these only a second or two. Twice his leader frayed on sharp rocks and broke at a critical moment. But this was good medicine. It taught him that it pays to inspect tackle frequently to avoid such needless losses. The complaints, "If I had only changed my leader," or "If I had only looked at my fly to see if the hook was all right," should never have to be made.

I experimented considerably with flies. I tried streamers, standard salmon patterns, and all sorts of flies that had brought me success in various sections of North America, but none of them produced. The best fly of all was the Umpqua. It had been designed especially for this stream. The Cummings was a close rival and often effective when the Umpqua would not produce.

From my own experience and from many talks with the fellows who fish the North Umpqua every season I gathered that only two sizes were needed—numbers 4 and 6. I used 4's most, but when a fish was missed I would change to a 6. Sometimes the smaller fly worked.

The day before we left Steamboat I concentrated on two pools, the Sawtooth and the Surveyor's. The Sawtooth got its name from the sharp-topped rocks that divide it. If a fish ever ran your leader over the center or sawtooth rock, it was good-bye to fish and whatever part of your terminal tackle below where it was cut by the rock.

The first time I had fished this pool both Clarence and Phil Edson were watching me. There was a suspicious smirk on their faces, but at the moment I didn't tumble to the reason. When I hooked a fish I could fairly feel their expectant joy in my downfall. I almost played directly into their hands too. I led the fish upstream, and only their uncontrolled chuckles put me wise that this might spell disaster because of the sharp rocks. In time I changed my tactics and landed the fish, and so spoiled their chance for a horse laugh on me.

But on this last day I took my first trout from this hole with incredible ease. It was a fair fish, a bit over six pounds, and took the fly on my side of the sharp rock. By giving it the butt of the rod and showing no quarter I kept it from crossing the dangerous spot, and for some reason it gave up not long after. But the next fish gave me a taste of what a Sawtooth trout could really do. This one took in the center of the hole, on the other side of the sharp-edged rock. When he struck the shock was so great that it almost took the rod from my hands, and after getting hooked he quickly wrapped the leader around the rock and it cut through as if it had been a piece of cheese. It happened so fast that it temporarily dazed me. That was all the action I got from the Sawtooth that day.

At the Surveyor's Pool it was not necessary to make a long cast. The first one I made wasn't more than twenty feet, and a six-pounder took it at the very moment it touched the water. Landing this fish made me feel quite satisfied with myself. Two six-pounders in an hour was mighty good fishing no matter how you looked at it.

I rested the pool a half hour and then tried again. This time I had four rises that I missed, and then I connected with a fish that took slowly but surely. He was the heaviest one I had yet come in contact with. For twenty minutes I just held on. The fish didn't either run or tug; he simply bored to bottom and stayed there. Nothing I could do would budge him, even the taking of the line in my hand and pulling with that. But finally he must have become tired of the continual strain, because he suddenly started to kick up a general rumpus. First, he came direct from the bottom with express train speed and continued into the air until the force of his rush had been expended. When he hit the water he did so broadside, making a splash that might have been heard a quarter of a mile. He then lashed the pool to a froth, made a few more less spectacular jumps, and finally came to rest out in midstream and near the surface.

It looked to me as if he had used up his energy, so I put on all the pressure the rod would bear, thinking he'd come in docilely. Vain hope. I couldn't move him any more than I could when he had been hugging the bottom. He just lay there with a wicked look in his eye and sapped the strength from my arm. Finally I had to release the pressure a bit. I couldn't take it. As I did this he started fanning his tail and his fins. I knew something was going to happen, but I didn't know what. I soon found out. Turning quickly he started downstream, and this time I could tell he was going places. There was no stopping him. I braked as much as I dared, burned my fingers as well as knocked my knuckles, but the line melted away. When I looked at my reel the end was near. He was in the fast water below the pool and gaining speed each instant, so I pointed the rod tip at him and prayed that only the leader would break. Then something snapped, and the strain was gone. The leader had broken at the fly, and the fish had "cleaned" me. The landing of the ten-and-three-quarter-pounder in the Mott Pool had been thrilling, but it did not affect me like this complete rout. Now that time has lent perspective to the experience, I know that this particular incident was my most memorable angling adventure. And it is that way all along the line. In every species of fish I've angled for, it is the ones that have got away that thrill me most, the ones that keep fresh in my memory. So I say it is good to lose fish. If we didn't, much of the thrill of angling would be gone.

The author of *Lorna Doone*, Blackmore has been credited by no less an angling authority than Henry van Dyke with writing the greatest English fishing story. Crocker's Hole is a pool fed by a river flowing for eternity.

R. D. BLACKMORE

Crocker's Hole

The Culm, which rises in Somersetshire, and hastening into a fairer land (as the border waters wisely do) falls into the Exe near Killerton, formerly was a lovely trout stream, such as perverts the Devonshire angler from due respect toward Father Thames and the other canals round London. In the Devonshire valleys it is sweet to see how soon a spring becomes a rill, and a rill runs on into a rivulet, and a rivulet swells into a brook; and before one has time to say, "What are you at?"—before the first tree it ever spoke to is a dummy, or the first hill it ever ran down has turned blue, here we have all the airs and graces, demands and assertions of a full-grown river.

But what is the test of a river? Who shall say? "The power to drown a man," replies the river darkly. But rudeness is not argument. Rather shall we say that the power to work a good undershot wheel, without being dammed up all night in a pond, and leaving a tidy back-stream to spare at the bottom of the orchard, is a fair certificate of riverhood. If so, many Devonshire streams attain that rank within five miles of their spring; aye, and rapidly add to it. At every turn they gather aid, from ash-clad dingle and aldered meadow, mossy rock and ferny wall, hedge-trough roofed with bramble netting, where the baby water lurks, and lanes that coming down to ford bring suicidal tribute. Arrogant, all-engrossing river, now it has claimed a great valley of its own; and whatever falls within the hill scoop, sooner or later belongs to itself. Even the crystal "shutt" that crosses the farmyard by the woodrick, and glides down an aqueduct of last year's bark for Mary to fill the kettle from; and even the tricklets that have no organs for telling or knowing their business, but only get into unwary oozings in and among the water-grass, and there make moss and forget themselves among it—one and all, they come to the same thing at last, and that is the river.

The Culm used to be a good river at Culmstock, tormented already by a factory, but not strangled as yet by a railroad. How it is now the present writer does not know, and is afraid to ask, having heard of a vile "Culm Valley Line." But Culmstock bridge was a very pretty place to stand and contemplate the ways of trout; which is easier work than to catch them. When I was just big enough to peep above the rim, or to lie upon it with one leg inside for fear of tumbling over, what a mighty river it used to seem, for it takes a treat there and spreads itself. Above the bridge the factory stream falls in again, having done its business, and washing its hands in the innocent half that has strayed down the meadows. Then under the arches they both rejoice and come to a slide of about two feet, and make a short, wide pool below, and indulge themselves in perhaps two islands, through which a little river always magnifies itself, and maintains a mysterious middle. But after that, all of it used to come together, and make off in one body for the meadows, intent upon nurturing trout with rapid stickles, and buttercuppy corners where fat flies may tumble in. And here you may find in the very first meadow, or at any rate you might have found, forty years ago, the celebrated "Crocker's Hole."

The story of Crocker is unknown to me, and interesting as it doubtless was, I do not deal with him, but with his Hole. Tradition said that he was a baker's boy who, during his basket-rounds, fell in love with a maiden who received the cottage-loaf, or perhaps good "Households," for her master's use. No doubt she was charming, as a girl should be, but whether she encouraged the youthful baker and then betrayed him with false *rôle*, or whether she "consisted" throughout,—as our cousins across the water express it,—is known to their *manes* only. Enough that she would not have the floury lad; and that he, after giving in his books and money, sought an untimely grave among the trout. And this was the first pool below the bread-walk deep enough to drown a five-foot baker boy. Sad it was; but such things must be, and bread must still be delivered daily.

A truce to such reflections,—as our foremost writers always say, when they do not see how to go on with them,—but it is a serious thing to know what Crocker's Hole was like; because at a time when (if he had only persevered, and married the maid, and succeeded to the oven, and reared a large family of short-weight bakers) he might have been leaning on his crutch beside the pool, and teaching his grandson to swim by precept (that beautiful proxy for practice)—at such a time, I say, there lived a remarkably fine trout in that hole. Anglers are notoriously truthful, especially as to what they catch, or even more frequently have not caught. Though I may have written fiction, among many other sins,—as a nice old lady told me once,—now I have to deal with facts; and foul scorn would I count it ever to make believe that I caught that fish. My length at that time was not more than the butt of a four-jointed rod, and all I could catch was a minnow with a pine, which our cook Lydia would not cook, but used to say, "Oh, what a shame, Master Richard! they would have been trout in the summer, please God! if you would only a' let 'em grow on." She is living now, and will bear me out in this.

But upon every great occasion there arises a great man; or to put it more accurately, in the present instance, a mighty and distinguished boy. My father, being the parson of the parish, and getting, need it be said, small pay, took sundry pupils, very pleasant fellows, about to adorn the universities. Among them was the original "Bude Light," as he was satirically called at Cambridge, for he came from Bude, and there was no light in him. Among them also was John Pike, a born Zebedee, if ever there was one.

John Pike was a thick-set younker, with a large and bushy head, keen blue eyes that could see through water, and the proper slouch of shoulder into which great anglers ripen; but greater still are born with it; and of these was Master John. It mattered little what the weather was, and scarcely more as to the time of year, John Pike must have his fishing every day, and on Sundays he read about it, and made flies. All the rest of the time he was thinking about it.

My father was coaching him in the fourth book of the Æneid and all those wonderful speeches of Dido, where passion disdains construction; but the only line Pike cared for was of horsehair. "I fear, Mr. Pike, that you are not giving me your entire attention," my father used to say in his mild dry way; and once when Pike was more than usually abroad, his tutor begged to share his meditations. "Well, sir," said Pike, who was very truthful, "I can see a green drake by the strawberry tree, the first of the season, and your derivation of 'barbarous' put me in mind of my barberry dye." In those days it was a very nice point to get the right tint for the mallard's feather.

No sooner was lesson done than Pike, whose rod was ready upon the lawn, dashed away always for the river, rushing headlong down the hill, and away to the left through a private yard, where "no thoroughfare" was put up, and a big dog stationed to enforce it. But Cerberus himself could not have stopped John Pike; his conscience backed him up in trespass the most sinful when his heart was inditing of a trout upon the rise.

All this, however, is preliminary, as the boy said when he put his father's coat upon his grandfather's tenterhooks, with felonious intent upon his grand-mother's apples; the main point to be understood is this, that nothing—neither brazen tower, hundred-eyed Argus, nor Cretan Minotaur—could stop John Pike from getting at a good stickle. But, even as the world knows nothing of its greatest men, its greatest men know nothing of the world beneath their very nose, till fortune sneezes dexter. For two years John Pike must have been whipping the water as hard as Xerxes, without having ever once dreamed of the glorious trout that lived in Crocker's Hole. But why, when he ought to have been at least on bowing terms with every fish as long as his middle finger, why had he failed to know this champion? The answer is simple—because of his short cuts. Flying as he did like an arrow from a bow, Pike used to hit his beloved river at an elbow, some furlong below Crocker's Hole, where a sweet little stickle sailed away down stream, whereas for the length of a meadow upward the water lay smooth, clear, and shallow; therefore the youth, with so little time to spare, rushed into the downward joy.

And here it may be noted that the leading maxim of the present period, that man can discharge his duty only by going counter to the stream, was scarcely mooted in those days. My grandfather (who was a wonderful man, if he was accustomed to fill a cart in two days of fly-fishing on the Barle) regularly fished down stream; and what more than a cartload need anyone put into his basket?

And surely it is more genial and pleasant to behold our friend the river growing and thriving as we go on, strengthening its voice and enlargening its bosom, and sparkling through each successive meadow with richer plenitude of silver, than to trace it against its own grain and good-will toward weakness, and littleness, and immature conceptions.

However, you will say that if John Pike had fished up stream, he would have found this trout much sooner. And that is true; but still, as it was, the trout had more time to grow into such a prize. And the way in which John found him out was this. For some days he had been tormented with a very painful tooth, which even poisoned all the joys of fishing. Therefore he resolved to have it out, and sturdily entered the shop of John Sweetland, the village black-smith, and there paid his sixpence. Sweetland extracted the teeth of the village, whenever they required it, in the simplest and most effectual way. A piece of fine wire was fastened round the tooth, and the other end round the anvil's nose, then the sturdy blacksmith shut the lower half of his shop door, which was about breast-high, with the patient outside and the anvil within; a strong push of the foot upset the anvil, and the tooth flew out like a well-thrown fly.

When John Pike had suffered this very bravely, "Ah, Master Pike," said the blacksmith, with a grin, "I reckon you won't pull out thic there big vish,"—the smithy commanded a view of the river,—"clever as you be, quite so peart as thiccy."

"What big fish?" asked the boy, with deepest interest, though his mouth was bleeding fearfully.

"Why that girt mortial of a vish as hath his hover in Crocker's Hole. Zum on 'em saith as a' must be a zammon."

Off went Pike with his handkerchief to his mouth, and after him ran Alec Bolt, one of his fellow-pupils, who had come to the shop to enjoy the extraction.

"Oh, my!" was all that Pike could utter, when by craftily posting himself he had obtained a good view of this grand fish.

"I'll lay you a crown you don't catch him!" cried Bolt, an impatient youth, who scorned angling.

"How long will you give me?" asked the wary Pike, who never made rash wagers.

"Oh! till the holidays if you like; or, if that won't do, till Michaelmas."

Now the midsummer holidays were six weeks off—boys used not to talk of "vacations" then, still less of "recesses."

"I think I'll bet you," said Pike, in his slow way, bending forward carefully, with his keen eyes on this monster; "but it would not be fair to take till Michaelmas. I'll bet you a crown that I catch him before the holidays—at least, unless some other fellow does."

The day of that most momentous interview must have been the 14th of May. Of the year I will not be so sure; for children take more note of days than of years, for which the latter have their full revenge thereafter. It must have been the 14th, because the morrow was our holiday, given upon the 15th of May, in honour of a birthday.

Now, John Pike was beyond his years wary as well as enterprising, calm as well as ardent, quite as rich in patience as in promptitude and vigour. But Alec Bolt was a headlong youth, volatile, hot, and hasty, fit only to fish the Maëlstrom, or a torrent of new lava. And the moment he had laid that wager he expected his crown piece; though time, as the lawyers phrase it, was "expressly of the essence of the contract." And now he demanded that Pike should spend the holiday in trying to catch that trout.

"I shall not go near him" that lad replied, "until I have got a new collar." No piece of personal adornment was it, without which he would not act, but rather that which now is called the fly-cast, or the gut-cast, or the trace, or what it may be. "And another thing," continued Pike; "the bet is off if you go near him, either now or at any other time, without asking my leave first, and then only going as I tell you."

"What do I want with the great slimy beggar?" the arrogant Bolt made answer. "A good rat is worth fifty of him. No fear of my going near him, Pike. You shan't get out of it that way."

Pike showed his remarkable qualities that day, by fishing exactly as he would have fished without having heard of the great Crockerite. He was up and away upon the mill-stream before breakfast; and the forenoon he devoted to his favourite course—first down the Craddock stream, a very pretty confluent of the Culm, and from its junction, down the pleasant hams, where the river winds toward Uffculme. It was my privilege to accompany this hero, as his humble Sancho; while Bolt and the faster race went up the river ratting. We were back in time to have Pike's trout (which ranged between two ounces and one-half pound) fried for the early dinner; and here it may be lawful to remark that the trout of the Culm are of the very purest excellence, by reason of the flinty bottom, at any rate in these the upper regions. For the valley is the western outlet of the Black-down range, with the Beacon hill upon the north, and Hackpen long ridge to the south; and beyond that again the Whetstone hill, upon whose western end dark port-holes scarped with white grit mark the pits. But flint is the staple of the broad Culm Valley, under good, well-pastured loam; and here are chalcedonies and agate stones.

At dinner everybody had a brace of trout—large for the larger folk, little for the little ones, with coughing and some patting on the back for bones. What of equal purport could the fierce rat-hunter show? Pike explained many points in the history of each fish, seeming to know them none the worse, and love them all the better, for being fried. We banqueted, neither a whit did soul get stinted of banquet impartial. Then the wielder of the magic rod very modestly sought leave of absence at the tea time.

"Fishing again, Mr. Pike, I suppose," my father answered pleasantly; "I used to be fond of it at your age; but never so entirely wrapped up in it as you are."

"No, sir; I am not going fishing again. I want to walk to Wellington, to get some things at Cherry's."

"Books, Mr. Pike? Ah! I am very glad of that. But I fear it can only be fly-books."

"I want a little Horace for eighteen-pence—the Cambridge one just published, to carry in my pocket—and a new hank of gut."

"Which of the two is more important? Put that into Latin, and answer it."

"Utrum pluris facio? Flaccum flocci. Viscera magni." With this vast effort Pike turned as red as any trout spot.

"After that who could refuse you?" said my father. "You always tell the truth, my boy, in Latin or in English."

Although it was a long walk, some fourteen miles to Wellington and back, I got permission to go with Pike; and as we crossed the bridge and saw the tree that overhung Crocker's Hole, I begged him to show me that mighty fish.

"Not a bit of it," he replied. "It would bring the blackguards. If the blackguards once find him out, it is all over with him."

"The blackguards are all in factory now, and I am sure they cannot see us from the windows. They won't be out till five o'clock."

With the true liberality of young England, which abides even now as large and glorious as ever, we always called the free and enlightened operatives of the period by the courteous name above set down, and it must be acknowledged that some of them deserved it, although perhaps they poached with less of science than their sons. But the cowardly murder of fish by liming the water was already prevalent.

Yielding to my request and perhaps his own desire—manfully kept in check that morning—Pike very carefully approached that pool, commanding me to sit down while he reconnoitred from the meadow upon the right bank of the stream. And the place which had so sadly quenched the fire of the poor baker's love filled my childish heart with dread and deep wonder at the cruelty of women. But as for John Pike, all he thought of was the fish and the best way to get at him.

Very likely that hole is "holed out" now, as the Yankees well express it, or at any rate changed out of knowledge. Even in my time a very heavy flood entirely altered its character; but to the eager eye of Pike it seemed pretty much as follows, and possibly it may have come to such a form again:

The river, after passing through a hurdle fence at the head of the meadow, takes a little turn or two of bright and shallow indifference, then gathers itself into a good strong slide, as if going down a slope instead of steps. The right bank is high and beetles over with yellow loam and grassy fringe; but the other side is of flinty shingle, low and bare and washed by floods. At the end of this rapid, the stream turns sharply under an ancient alder tree into a larger, deep, calm repose, cool, unruffled, and sheltered from the sun by branch and leaf— and that is the hole of poor Crocker.

At the head of the pool (where the hasty current rushes in so eagerly, with noisy excitement and much ado) the quieter waters from below, having rested and enlarged themselves, come lapping up round either curve, with some recollection of their past career, the hoary experience of foam. And sidling toward the new arrival of the impulsive column, where they meet it, things go on, which no man can describe without his mouth being full of water. A "V" is formed, a fancy letter V, beyond any designer's tracery, and even beyond his imagination, a perpetually fluctuating limpid wedge, perpetually crenelled and rippled into by little ups and downs that try to make an impress, but can only glide away upon either side or sink in dimples under it. And here a gray bough of the ancient alder stretches across, like a thirsty giant's arm, and makes it a very ticklish place to throw a fly. Yet this was the very spot our John Pike must put his fly into, or lose his crown.

Because of the great tenant of Crocker's Hole, who allowed no other fish to wag a fin there, and from strict monopoly had grown so fat, kept his victualing yard—if so low an expression can be used concerning him—within about a square yard of this spot. He had a sweet hover, both for rest and recreation, under the bank, in a placid antre, where the water made no noise, but tickled his belly in digestive ease. The loftier the character is of any being, the slower and more dignified his movements are. No true psychologist could have behaved—as Sweetland the blacksmith did, and Mr. Pook the tinman—that this trout could ever be the embodiment of Crocker. For this was the last trout in the universal world to drown himself for love; if truly any trout has done so.

"You may come now, and try to look along my back," John Pike, with a reverential whisper, said to me. "Now don't be in a hurry, young stupid; kneel down. He is not to be disturbed at his dinner, mind. You keep behind me, and look along my back; I never clapped eyes on such a whopper."

I had to kneel down in a tender reminiscence of pasture land, and gaze carefully; and not having eyes like those of our Zebedee (who offered his spine for a camera, as he crawled on all fours in front of me), it took me a long time to descry an object most distinct to all who have that special gift of piercing with their eyes the water. See what is said upon this subject in that delicious book, "The Gamekeeper at Home."

"You are no better than a muff," said Pike, and it was not in my power to deny it.

"If the sun would only leave off," I said. But the sun, who was having a very pleasant play with the sparkle of the water and the twinkle of the leaves, had no inclination to leave off yet, but kept the rippling crystal in a dance of flashing facets, and the quivering verdure in a steady flush of gold.

But suddenly a May-fly, a luscious gray-drake, richer and more delicate than canvas-back or woodcock, with a dart and a leap and a merry zigzag, began to enjoy a little game above the stream. Rising and falling like a gnat, thrilling her gauzy wings, and arching her elegant pellucid frame, every now and then she almost dipped her three long tapering whisks into the dimples of the water.

"He sees her! He'll have her as sure as a gun!" cried Pike, with a gulp, as if he himself were "rising." "Now, can you see him, stupid?"

"Crikey, crokums!" I exclaimed, with classic elegance; "I have seen that long thing for five minutes; but I took it for a tree."

"You little"—animal quite early in the alphabet—"now don't you stir a peg, or I'll dig my elbow into you."

The great trout was stationary almost as a stone, in the middle of the "V" above described. He was gently fanning with his large clear fins, but holding his own against the current mainly by the wagging of his broad-fluked tail. As soon as my slow eyes had once defined him, he grew upon them mightily, moulding himself in the matrix of the water, as a thing put into jelly does.

And I doubt whether even John Pike saw him more accurately than I did. His size was such, or seemed to be such, that I fear to say a word about it; not because language does not contain the word, but from dread of exaggeration. But his shape and colour may be reasonably told without wounding the feeling of an age whose incredulity springs from self-knowledge.

His head was truly small, his shoulders vast; the spring of his back was like a rainbow when the sun is southing; the generous sweep of his deep elastic belly, nobly pulped out with rich nurture, showed what the power of his brain must be, and seemed to undulate, time for time, with the vibrant vigilance of his large wise eyes. His latter end was consistent also. An elegant taper run of counter, coming almost to a cylinder, as a mackerel does, boldly developed with a hugeous spread to a glorious amplitude of swallow-tail. His colour was all that can well be desired, but ill-described by any poor word-palette. Enough that he seemed to tone away from olive and umber, with carmine stars, to glowing gold and soft pure silver, mantled with a subtle flush of rose and fawn and opal.

Swoop came a swallow, as we gazed, and was gone with a flick, having missed the May-fly. But the wind of his passage, or the skir of wing, struck the merry dancer down, so that he fluttered for one instant on the wave, and that instant was enough. Swift as the swallow, and more true of aim, the great trout made one dart, and a sound, deeper than a tinkle, but as silvery as a bell, rang the poor ephemerid's knell. The rapid water scarcely showed a break; but a bubble sailed down the pool, and the dark hollow echoed with the music of a rise.

"He knows how to take a fly," said Pike; "he has had too many to be tricked with mine. Have him I must; but how ever shall I do it?"

All the way to Wellington he uttered not a word, but shambled along with a mind full of care. When I ventured to look up now and then, to surmise what was going on beneath his hat, deeply set eyes and a wrinkled forehead, relieved at long intervals by a solid shake, proved that there are meditations deeper than those of philosopher or statesman.

Surely no trout could have been misled by the artificial May-fly of that time, unless he were either a very young fish, quite new to entomology, or else one afflicted with a combination of myopy and bulimy. Even now there is room for plenty of improvement in our counterfeit presentment; but in those days the body was made with yellow mohair, ribbed with red silk and gold twist, and as thick as a fertile bumble-bee. John Pike perceived that to offer such a thing to Crocker's trout would probably consign him—even if his great stamina should overget the horror—to an uneatable death, through just and natural indignation. On the other hand, while the May-fly lasted, a trout so cultured, so highly refined, so full of light and sweetness, would never demean himself to low bait, or any coarse son of a maggot.

Meanwhile Alec Bolt allowed poor Pike no peaceful thought, no calm absorption of high mind into the world of flies, no placid period of cobblers' wax, floss-silk, turned hackles, and dubbing. For in making of flies John Pike had his special moments of inspiration, times of clearer insight into the everlasting verities, times of brighter conception and more subtle execution, tails of more elastic grace and heads of a neater and nattier expression. As a poet labours at one immortal line, compressing worlds of wisdom into the music of ten syllables, so toiled the patient Pike about the fabric of a fly comprising all the excellence that ever sprang from maggot. Yet Bolt rejoiced to jerk his elbow at the moment of sublimest art. And a swarm of flies was blighted thus.

Peaceful, therefore, and long-suffering, and full of resignation as he was, John Pike came slowly to the sad perception that arts avail not without arms. The elbow, so often jerked, at last took a voluntary jerk from the shoulder, and Alec Bolt lay prostrate, with his right eye full of cobbler's wax. This put a desirable check upon his energies for a week or more, and by that time Pike had flown his fly.

When the honeymoon of spring and summer (which they are now too fashionable to celebrate in this country), the hey-day of the whole year marked by the budding of the wild rose, the start of the wheat-ear from its sheath, the feathering of the lesser plantain, and flowering of the meadowsweet, and, foremost for the angler's joy, the caracole of May-flies—when these things are to be seen and felt (which has not happened at all this year), then rivers should be mild and bright, skies blue and white with fleecy cloud, the west wind blowing softly, and the trout in charming appetite.

On such a day came Pike to the bank of Culm, with a loudly beating heart. A fly there is, not ignominious, or of cowdab origin, neither gross and heavy-bodied, from cradlehood of slimy stones, nor yet of menacing aspect and suggesting deeds of poison, but elegant, bland, and of sunny nature, and obviously good to eat. Him or her—why quest we which?—the shepherd of the dale, contemptuous of gender, except in his own species, has called, and as long as they two coexist will call, the "Yellow Sally." A fly that does not waste the day in giddy dances and the fervid waltz, but undergoes family incidents with decorum and discretion. He or she, as the case may be,—for the natural history of the river bank is a book to come hereafter, and of fifty men who make flies not one knows the name of the fly he is making,—in the early morning of June, or else in the second quarter of the afternoon, this Yellow Sally fares abroad, with a nice well-ordered flutter.

Despairing of the May-fly, as it still may be despaired of, Pike came down to the river with his master-piece of portraiture. The artificial Yellow Sally is generally always—as they say in Cheshire—a mile or more too yellow. On the other hand, the "Yellow Dun" conveys no idea of any Sally. But Pike had made a very decent Sally, not perfect (for he was young as well as wise), but far above any counterfeit to be had in fishing-tackle shops. How he made it, he told nobody. But if he lives now, as I hope he does, any of my readers may ask him through the G.P.O., and hope to get an answer.

It fluttered beautifully on the breeze, and in such living form, that a brother or sister Sally came up to see it, and went away sadder and wiser. Then Pike said: "Get away, you young wretch," to your humble servant who tells this tale; yet being better than his words, allowed that pious follower to lie down upon his digestive organs and with deep attention watch. There must have been great things to see, but to see them so was difficult. And if I huddle up what happened, excitement also shares the blame.

Pike has fashioned well the time and manner of this overture. He knew that the giant Crockerite was satiate now with May-flies, or began to find their flavour failing, as happens to us with asparagus, marrow-fat peas, or straw-berries, when we have had a month of them. And he thought that the first Yellow Sally of the season, inferior though it were, might have the special charm of novelty. With the skill of a Zulu, he stole up through the branches over the lower pool till he came to a spot where a yard-wide opening gave just space for spring of rod. Then he saw his desirable friend at dinner, wagging his tail, as a hungry gentleman dining with the Lord Mayor agitates his coat. With one dexterous whirl, untaught by any of the many books upon the subject, John Pike laid his Yellow Sally (for he cast with one fly only) as lightly as gossamer upon the rapid, about a yard in front of the big trout's head. A moment's pause, and then, too quick for words, was the thing that happened.

A heavy plunge was followed by a fearful rush. Forgetful of current the river was ridged, as if with a plough driven under it; the strong line, though given out as fast as might be, twanged like a harp-string as it cut the wave, and then Pike stood up, like a ship dismasted, with the butt of his rod snapped below the ferrule. He had one of those foolish things, just invented, a hollow butt of hickory; and the finial ring of his spare top looked out, to ask what had happened to the rest of it. "Bad luck!" cried the fisherman; "but never mind, I shall have him next time, to a certainty."

When this great issue came to be considered, the cause of it was sadly obvious. The fish, being hooked, had made off with the rush of a shark for the bottom of the pool. A thicket of saplings below the alder tree had stopped the judicious hooker from all possibility of following; and when he strove to turn him by elastic pliance, his rod broke at the breach of pliability. "I have learned a sad lesson," said John Pike, looking sadly.

How many fellows would have given up this matter, and glorified themselves for having hooked so grand a fish, while explaining that they must have caught him, if they could have done it! But Pike only told me not to say a word about it, and began to make ready for another tug of war. He made himself a splice-rod, short and handy, of well-seasoned ash, with a stout top of bamboo, tapered so discreetly, and so balanced in its spring, that verily it formed an arc, with any pressure on it, as perfect as a leafy poplar in a stormy summer. "Now break it if you can," he said, "by any amount of rushes; I'll hook you by your jacket collar; you cut away now, and I'll land you."

This was highly skilful, and he did it many times; and whenever I was landed well, I got a lollypop, so that I was careful not to break his tackle. Moreover he made him a landing net, with a kidney-bean stick, a ring of wire, and his own best nightcap of strong cotton net. Then he got the farmer's leave, and lopped obnoxious bushes; and now the chiefest question was: what bait, and when to offer it? In spite of his sad rebuff, the spirit of John Pike had been equable. The genuine angling mind is steadfast, large, and self-supported, and to the vapid, ignominious chaff, tossed by swine upon the idle wind, it pays as much heed as a big trout does to a dance of midges. People put their fingers to their noses and said: "Master Pike, have you caught him yet?" and Pike only answered: "Wait a bit." If ever this fortitude and perseverence is to be recovered as the English Brand (the one thing that has made us what we are, and may yet redeem us from niddering shame), a degenerate age should encourage the habit of fishing and never despairing. And the brightest sign yet for our future is the increasing demand for hooks and gut.

Pike fished in a manlier age, when nobody would dream of cowering from a savage because he was clever at skulking; and when, if a big fish broke the rod, a stronger rod was made for him, according to the usage of Great Britain. And though the young angler had been defeated, he did not sit down and have a good cry over it.

About the second week in June, when the May-fly had danced its day, and died,—for the season was an early one,—and Crocker's trout had recovered from the wound to his feelings and philanthropy, there came a night of gentle rain, of pleasant tinkling upon window ledges, and a soothing patter among young leaves, and the Culm was yellow in the morning. "I mean to do it this afternoon," Pike whispered to me, as he came back panting. "When the water clears there will be a splendid time."

The lover of the rose knows well a gay voluptuous beetle, whose pleasure is to lie embedded in a fount of beauty. Deep among the incurving petals of the blushing fragrance, he loses himself in his joys sometimes, till a breezy waft reveals him. And when the sunlight breaks upon his luscious dissipation, few would have the heart to oust him, such a gem from such a setting. All his back is emerald sparkles; all his front red Indian gold, and here and there he grows white spots to save the eye from aching. Pike put his finger in and fetched him out, and offered him a little change of joys, by putting a Limerick hook through his thorax, and bringing it out between his elytra. *Cetonia aurata* liked it not, but pawed the air very naturally, and fluttered with his wings attractively.

"I meant to have tried with a fern-web," said the angler; "until I saw one of these beggars this morning. If he works like that upon the water, he will do. It was hopeless to try artificials again. What a lovely colour the water is! Only three days now to the holidays. I have run it very close. You be ready, younker."

With these words he stepped upon a branch of the alder, for the tone of the waters allowed approach, being soft and sublustrous, without any mud. Also Master Pike's own tone was such as becomes the fisherman, calm, deliberate, free from nerve, but full of eye and muscle. He stepped upon the alder bough to get as near as might be to the fish, for he could not cast this beetle like a fly; it must be dropped gently and allowed to play. "You may come and look," he said to me; "when the water is so, they have no eyes in their tails."

The rose-beetle trod upon the water prettily, under a lively vibration, and he looked quite as happy, and considerably more active, than when he had been cradled in the anthers of the rose. To the eyes of a fish he was a strong individual, fighting courageously with the current, but sure to be beaten through lack of fins; and mercy suggested, as well as appetite, that the proper solution was to gulp him.

"Hooked him in the gullet. He can't get off!" cried John Pike, labouring to keep his nerves under; "every inch of tackle is as strong as a bell-pull. Now, if I don't land him, I will never fish again!"

Providence, which had constructed Pike, foremost of all things, for lofty angling—disdainful of worm and even minnow—Providence, I say, at this adjuration, pronounced that Pike must catch that trout. Not many anglers are heaven-born; and for one to drop off the hook halfway through his teens would be infinitely worse than to slay the champion trout. Pike felt the force of this, and rushing through the rushes, shouted: "I am sure to have him, Dick! Be ready with my night-cap."

Rod in a bow, like a springle-riser; line on the hum, like the string of Paganini; winch on the gallop, like a harpoon wheel, Pike, the head-centre of everything, dashing through thick and thin, and once taken overhead—for he jumped into the hole, when he must have lost him else, but the fish too impetuously towed him out, and made off in passion for another pool, when, if he had only retired to his hover, the angler might have shared the baker's fate—all these things (I tell you, for they all come up again, as if the day were yesterday) so scared me of my never very steadfast wits, that I could only holloa! But one thing I did, I kept the night-cap ready.

"He is pretty nearly spent, I do believe," said Pike; and his voice was like balm of Gilead, as we came to Farmer Anning's meadow, a quarter of a mile below Crocker's Hole. "Take it coolly, my dear boy, and we shall be safe to have him."

Never have I felt, through forty years, such tremendous responsibility. I had not the faintest notion how to use a landing net; but a mighty general directed me. "Don't let him see it; don't let him see it! Don't clap it over him; go under him, you stupid! If he makes another rush, he will get off, after all. Bring it up his tail. Well done! You have him!"

The mighty trout lay in the night-cap of Pike, which was half a fathom long, with a tassel at the end, for his mother had made it in the winter evenings. "Come and hold the rod, if you can't lift him," my master shouted, and so I did. Then, with both arms straining, and his mouth wide open, John Pike made a mighty sweep, and we both fell upon the grass and rolled, with the giant of the deep flapping heavily between us, and no power left to us, except to cry, "Hurrah!"

It's been said that there are two types of people in the world—those who divide people into types and those who don't. Anglers fish for fun, right? Oh, they might sputter some noble-sounding excuse, some ethical rationalization. Roy Blount, Jr., met a group with quite a different motivation. Although this dispatch was filed several years ago, before the infamous "bait and twitch" maneuvers scandalized the pro circuit, his analysis remains a model of reportage.

ROY BLOUNT, JR.

5,760 Casts a Day: Now That's Plugging

A man goes bass fishing in order to get away, breathe free, eat sardines and suck on his teeth in peace, right? So why is that Cajun crop-duster pilot posing for pictures in front of a big tank full of lemon-lime-colored liquid, saying, "Thank you very much, fish" to a bass in the tank and holding up a check for $15,000?

Because he, Jack Hains of Rayne, Louisiana, has just won the fifth annual BASS Masters ("Mystery") Classic at Currituck Sound near Kitty Hawk, North Carolina. He has whipped eighteen of that fish's peers and twenty-nine of his own, including Jimmy Houston of Tehlequah, Oklahoma, who fishes in white pants with red and blue stars embroidered down the seams and a red shirt with his name and BILL NORMAN LURES stitched on it. The outfit comes with a little white jacket, too, that he . . .

He fishes in *what*? Wait a minute! Who ever heard of a bass fisherman dressed like that? This is not some kind of Yippie making a mockery of bass fishing, is it? We will attend to Hains and his flashy check and peculiar ceremony later. First, let us go back three days' time, to practice day of the Classic, and take a closer look at Houston.

He is standing vividly in the bow of a boat, casting toward one of Currituck's grassy banks. He *sounds* like a bass fisherman. "I'm gonna fish this water right here. There's a terrible amount of good water right here. They're up in under them roots."

He holds up a lure known as a Pico Pop. It looks suitable enough, like a chunky, scared-to-death baitfish or legless, streamlined frog. It is designed to be twitched on top of the water. "I've caught a laaaht of big fish on these," says Houston. He casts and twitches. "Look at that rascal! Looks *good*. I just can't imagine something not coming up and getting ahold of that."

He casts, twitches. "I know they're up in under there. Up under them old grass roots. Them old stump roots. I don't know why a man couldn't catch a *lot* of fish in this water."

Casts, twitches. "This is *pretty* water."

It is not even out of character for Houston to have blond hair way down below his collar. You don't have to be a hippie these days, even up under the old grass roots of Tahlequah, to have a lot of hair. Houston is thirty, and when he has time he sells insurance. "I hate to give up that insurance agency," he says. "It's like selling an old shotgun." Insurance, you figure, is a reasonable thing for a bass fisherman to be in.

But he is also in that garish costume! Who ever heard of a bass fisherman looking like Evel Knievel?

Then again, many people think of a fishing *boat* as . . . comfortable. Maybe grubby. You could spill a couple of beers, some ketchup, a can of oil, or some of that soggy fuzz that worms come in and it wouldn't be noticed.

But the boat Houston is fishing in—standard issue for the tournament— looks like you ought to drive it to the country club dance. With its 115-horsepower motor, it lists for $7,884. It is made of white and green fiber glass inlaid with bits of glitter. It has a Poly-Turfed deck and cushioned swivel chairs on pedestals. Pedestals!

But Houston doesn't lounge around in that comfort. He never sits in his seat, except to drive distances. When he fishes he always stands, operating his electric trolling motor with his knee and raising and lowering his electric anchor with his foot. If he wants to fish different water, he can consult his sonar depth-finder or his water-temperature gauge or the meter that measures the amount of oxygen in the water. From a boat nearby, a local news crew is *televising* him.

Maybe you think of fishing as a leisure activity. Watch Houston work his four different casting and spinning rigs. When one lure gets hung on the bottom he will put that rod down and use another one until the boat moves to where the snag is. He isn't relaxing.

"A lot of guys aren't here to win and don't work as diligently as they should," he says. "You hear guys saying, 'I hope I don't blank out today.' Never enters my mind to blank out. The same guys always win. They fish hard."

Fish *hard!* Houston may not be as fierce a competitor as Ricky Green of Arkadelphia, Arkansas, who says, "I don't like to go fishing by myself. I want to go out with someone to strap it on his backside." But Houston does say, "You've got to have total mental and physical concentration." Houston may not be as high-gear a caster as Tommy Martin of Hemphill, Texas, who once was clocked at twelve casts per minute over a full eight-hour day. But Houston does try to launch a lure about every eight seconds—underhand to save time, like a second baseman feeding a shortstop.

One other thing Jimmy Houston has on his boat, besides a tackle box containing, oh, maybe 192 crankbaits, eighty spinner-baits, twenty top-waters and a couple hundred plastic worms. He has a clean white towel. "My wife made me bring it for these white pants. I have a tendency to wipe my hands on 'em when I catch a fish." He catches a bass that would go about two pounds, unhooks it, and tosses it back. He wipes his hands carefully on the towel. "I want you to tell my wife," he says.

Well, most people would just as soon eat barbeque without licking their lips as catch fish without wiping their hands on their pants. It takes the fun out of it. But this isn't fishing for fun. After this practice day, Jimmy Houston will be popping everything he catches, that's as long as twelve inches, into his live well. The fisherman who brings in the most pounds and ounces of keeper black or Kentucky bass within the daily limit during a three-day period wins $15,000 and greatly improves the value of his face in ads selling lures, lines, boats, and motors.

The strange truth is that amiable Jimmy Houston is a *professional* bass fisherman. So is amiable Jack Hains, which is why we saw him holding that check and thanking that fish. The lurid green tint of the water in the tank was caused by an antiseptic. Fussy as bass pros are, the fish have to be protected from catching things from them.

"Pro fishing has its critics," concedes Bob Cobb, vice-president of the Montgomery, Alabama-based Bass Anglers Sportsman Society, or BASS, which is the pioneering and still most prominent sponsor of big-time bass tournaments. "Some folks claim to fish for pay is as bad as bad women."

And the way they go about it, it sometimes seems as fancy as fancy women. Few pro bassers (as they are sometimes called) dress as colorfully as Houston, but some have been known to spray deodorant on their plastic worms and wash their hands with detergent every time they mess with their motors. Haven't they ever read that best-selling postcard that goes, "Old Fishermen Never Die . . . They Just Smell That Way"?

If they have, they don't care. Bass fishing, which used to be not all that much more uptown than coon hunting, or anyway dove shooting, has in recent years become nearly as tied up in money, tips from the tops (pros hold "bass seminars" at men's clubs), official memberships, and shiny equipment as has golf. *Gentleman's Quarterly* isn't previewing the season's new bassing togs yet, but as the president and founder of BASS, Ray Scott, puts it, "Old boys who can't buy their wife a coat are buying $5,000 boats."

And a new profession, if not exactly a new breed of men, is arising. The elite of bass fisherman now make $30,000 a year or more from tournaments, endorsements, appearances, and tie-ins—even if they don't have their own TV shows or scented-worm gold mines. Men can now give up their trusty old insurance agencies, shop classes, sales routes or Dairy Queen franchises, and live like doctors and lawyers on fishing. Hard.

These pros would like to get network TV exposure, and expect to when prize money increases. Big money and recognition are already available in other areas. Ten years ago Tom Mann of Eufaula, Alabama, worked for the state Game and Fish Commission, angled for pleasure, fooled around with a spinner-bait he called Little George (after his boss at the time, Governor Wallace), and poured liquid plastic into worm molds in his wife's kitchen. Now, thanks to his BASS exposure, he is a prominent sports figure in thousands of barbershops and homes. He is the owner of a bait company that makes and sells not only Little George (which *Popular Mechanics* named one of the Twenty Alltime Great Bass Fishing Lures) but also extremely popular strawberry-, blackberry-, blueberry-, and watermelon-flavored plastic worms. You might think that worm-flavored strawberries would taste better to bass, but things don't seem to work that way. Mann also is a millionaire.

Bass fishing has arrived. There are steely cool bass pros, bass pros who pace the floor all night before a tournament, straight-arrow pros, pros who stay up all night before a tournament on purpose and even, here and there, bass-fishing groupies. So far the sport is biggest in the South and Southwest, where artificial lakes or impoundments created by Corps of Engineers dams and filled with bass, are most plentiful.

But BASS is no isolated phenomenon. It has 260,000 members, the vast majority of them nonpros who pay $12 annual dues for access to information, merchandise, sew-on patches, and small local tournaments. There is a BASS chapter in the Bronx—and as far away as Rhodesia. As might be expected, other groups have arisen to claim chunks of the bass-boom pie: American Bass Fishermen, headquartered in Cocoa Beach, Florida; Bass Casters Association, Mattoon, Illinois; the now defunct but formerly big-spending Project Sports, Inc., Dallas; the Po' Boys, Tulsa; and, for women, the Tulsa Bass Belles. By often giving away more money at their tournaments, these competing organizations have made BASS sweeten its own pots considerably.

Trout fishing still is more prestigious, but trout are sacred and their pursuit a more and more rarefied proposition. "The trout you catch Friday morning were brought in in a truck and put there Tuesday night," grumbles one of the original BASS pros, John Powell. "It's like staking out pheasant to hunt. You have to kick them to make them fly. Or else shoot them standing there on the ground." Bass, on the other hand, are hardy and plentiful nationwide. And in catching them you can be emulating the superstars you see on non-network TV and in the bait ads.

Bud Leavitt, the outdoor editor of the Bangor (Maine) *Daily News*, who trout fishes with Ted Williams and Red Smith—or, rather, they trout fish with him— expects that bass fishing will soon catch on in places where it has been scorned, like New England. Eastern Establishment paranoids on the alert for evidence of a power shift toward the so-called "Southern Rim" can find it in bass fishing.

When Leavitt first attended the BASS Mystery Classic, the annual grand championship tournament—the top twenty-four to thirty bass pros, their wives, and some forty outdoor writers are flown to a fishing site undisturbed until the plane takes off—he was skeptical of what is sometimes called "cast-for-cash" angling. He says, "Fishing you think of as a contemplative thing, with your son, with your brother, with your dad." But Leavitt stayed to praise, especially after he saw a pro named Bobby Meador point to a Marlboro pack "and cast eighty feet and hit it. Then it drifted so he had to cast under a limb, and he hit it again. These guys know what they're doing. And these tournaments give fishing a peg—something to attract attention to it as a big-time sport."

Not every outdoorsman is ready to agree with Leavitt. Some sports editors refuse to cover bass tournaments because they may threaten stocks of fish— a few years ago you could see pickup truck loads being hauled off at the end of the day—and because they are too commercial. But Scott and Cobb are major league PR men, and BASS is as resourceful as the NFL at getting the word out about itself. The working press that attends the Mystery Classic can get free transportation and accommodations and also, from manufacturers, free lines, lures, and a big tackle box. And a chance to fish with a pro every day of the tournament. And cash prizes for the biggest press fish. And contacts with people who can get other things for them wholesale. And Cobb, an ex-newsman, was seen writing one outdoor writer's story for him. If none of that works, BASS puts out two slick magazines of its own.

Sensitive to charges that tournaments destroy too many fish, BASS speaks often of its "Don't Kill Your Catch" program. An extra ounce is awarded for each live fish weighed in, special measures are taken to protect the fish from infection (such as that stuff in the holding tank), and the great bulk of the "harvest" is released alive every day. Sometimes a little boy will sit at the release point, catching a few fish as they hang, disoriented, in the shallow water. Others die from handling. But research tends to show that most of the freed fish resume active lives. BASS has also attracted favorable notice by lobbying against water pollution; and is now working on computerizing the sentiments of its members so as to bring to bear a quarter of a million votes' influence on conservation issues.

As for the question of commercialization, well, nobody will ever accuse pro bass fishing of neglecting the economic factor. As many business cards are swapped at tournaments as fish stories. Company reps are on hand saying, "Super sport, super people. Anything we can do for you?" Sew-on patches— RABBLE ROUSER, SWEET OKIE BUG, MISTER TWISTER, BASS PRO SHOPS— are big. Nonpros send off for them, pros get considerations in return for wearing them. Pros get free gear and expense backing for using and boosting a given company's products. "Gotten so I'm afraid to use somebody else's lures," one pro lamented during the 1975 Mystery Classic, "for fear I'll win on them."

"Did you ever hear the word 'lie'?" asked another pro.

"Yeah, but they got cameras on you out there."

Ricky Green, thirty-one, was a chemist till the fishing money got good. His father was an Arkansas revenuer who, when Ricky hooked his first bass at the age of six, made him land it himself. Green is not so outgoing a self-promoter as Bill Dance of Memphis and Roland Martin of Broken Arrow, Oklahoma, the only two pros who rank ahead of him in all-time BASS earnings, and he doesn't have syndicated TV shows as they do. And even though he was second only to Haines in prize money last year, his BASS purses totaled just $10,385 and those from other groups' tournaments $7,500. Still, he says he should be able to clear $50,000 in 1976, because this year the prize money is way up, and he also has deals with a bait company, a boat company, an electronics company, a rod company, a trolling-motor company, and a company that makes "a liquid that you put in your trailer tires. There are eight or ten things it does for your tires."

All these benefits flow from the quantitative achievement of horsing a lot of bass pounds into a boat. Considerable skill, study, and effort are required, but not so much of what a man who catches thirty-pound salmon on a fly rod and ten-pound tippet would call artistry. Stout rod and twelve-to-twenty-pound-test lines are standard, and the kept bass range from about a pound to a rare ten-pounder; most of the fish fall in the one-to-three-pound range.

Striking and landing bass require delicacy and timing, of course, but the main thing is to "get on fish"—to find out where they are congregating—and to figure out what to "throw at them." Much of a bass fisherman's science might be compared to market research.

Still, it is a homey science. Around the weigh-in point at the end of the day, as competitors come in and their scores are posted on a big board, people chew the fat and compare notes:

"Put a willow-leaf blade on it and they just started eating it up. Switched to the lime green, buzzing it real close to the top, slowed it down, ran it down underneath. . . ."

"He's got some *nice* fish. Woo-*ee*"

"Dropped it over the logs, fluttered it, jerked it, and they just cooperated real well."

"Purple blowtail."

"Somebody's putting out an artificial butterfly. See there on that man's hat that says ARDMORE FEED AND SEED."

"Naw, that's a real butterfly. It just flew off."

"Bunch of little old bitty ones. Don't matter how hard you work 'em if you ain't on 'em good."

"Well, but I don't care how good you are on 'em, you still got to catch 'em."

"I'm so tired of looking at willers I could die."

"Them root wads . . ."

There are those who don't hold by too much calculation. "People say they have theories, know where to find fish," says Tommy Martin, who works as a guide and won the 1974 Classic. "I just go out there and throw as many different things as I can. And fish hard. I never know when I'm going to catch a fish."

But most of the leading pros worry about "patterns." They're not patterned in a pattern hard," complained Houston one day. "I like it when they're patterned hard." In search of patterns they fill their minds with data about water temperature, clarity, topographic map coordinates, amount of light, color of worm, and the lay of the "structure." Structure is submerged stuff—logs, docks, buildings, roadways—around which bass cluster, the way people do around water. Artificial impoundment bottoms are rich in structure; in some cases, whole towns were flooded over when dams were constructed. Bill Dance has several books out on how to find structure—it shows up on maps and sonar— and how to drag the right plastic worms provocatively, sensitively, over and around it. When you have learned to tell the difference between the feel of a plastic worm dropping off the side of a submerged log and that of a plastic worm being hit by a bass—quickly enough to react to the latter by snatching hard enough to "cross his eyes" or "break his neck"—you are well on your way to becoming a modern bass master.

There are also those, like Green and Houston, who prefer casting spinnerbaits (so called for the attached metal disks that flutter and sparkle in the water as the lure is reeled in) or crankbaits (lures that rise or descend depending on the speed with which they are reeled in) or top-water lures in shallow water toward roots and pilings and other surface structure features.

Tom Shockley, who recently started fishing in big tournaments, was amazed at all there was to learn. "Spinnerbaits. I had fished 'em two ways: buzz 'em or let 'em sink. I found out you can swim 'em, spin 'em, float 'em. . . ." BASS people point to the explosion of knowledge brought about by tournaments' drawing experts out of the bushes—bass fishermen used to be loners—to exchange tips with others from other bushes. Occasionally a revolutionary technique arises. Dee Thomas of Newark, California, caught a lot of fish at a tournament last year when nobody else did. It turned out he was taking a seven-and-a-half-foot rod with a small jig on the end, knocking a hole in the muck along the banks and swinging, rather than casting, the jig into the hole. Thomas called this technique "flippin.' " Now a company has a rod called the Flippin' Stik, and will send you a pamphlet entitled *The Whole Flippin' Story*.

Traditionalists will be pleased to learn that lying is still one of the tricks of the fishing trade. Or, more precisely, being less than wholly straightforward about answering other competitors' questions when they are trying to expand their knowledge in time to beat you the next morning. "Where'd you catch that big fish, Billy?" someone may ask.

"Like to had another'n too," says Billy. "Had him right up to the boat. Woulda been bigger than that one."

"Where'd you catch him?"

"Throwed a purple and yellow worm out there."

"Where, though?"

"One 'em little pockets."

"Which pockets?"

"Yep, one 'em little pockets in there."

"Where? Which end of the lake?"

"You got any frog chunks?"

This brings us to delicate social considerations. What is to keep everybody from following the Dances and Martins around and taking advantage of their expertise? For one thing, that would be bad form. The pros on the circuit might be broken down loosely into several different crowds, but the regulars form a fairly close-knit fraternity. Even so, there is tension between established figures and aspiring youngsters, especially when the latter are from near the site of the tournament and local fisherman are suspected of spying for the home boy. "I had a terrific problem today," said Roland Martin one evening during a tournament at Lake Texoma, on the Texas-Oklahoma border. "A guy followed me the entire day. Some local bass club guy. I couldn't really see what he looked like. Then when I started catching 'em the guy started talking to me on the CB. 'Hey, that's a good one, Roland.' I hung a gigantic fish. 'What was that, Roland?' Then I see him writing things down. 'Roland,' he says, 'I got what I come for. To see you fish structure.'

" 'I don't appreciate that,' I said. He got all huffy. I don't mind somebody watching me, but he's stealing my effort."

All of which carries bass fishing a long way from the days Jimmy Harris

remembers. The other pros call Harris "Skinny D." One afternoon when he was wearing a pair of voluminous waterproof pants somebody told him, "You look like a straw in a paper sack." He owns a lot of Mississippi cotton land now, and still competes in tournaments for the enjoyment. But back in the 1930s, when he and his friends would fish along the Mississippi River levees, they had no organization behind them, or in their way, and they made do with simple materials. "We'd take the string off the packages for line, and we'd have one plug to cast so we had to go in after it when it was lost. We caught a lot of bass. And then we'd take an iron skillet, some lard, some meal, build a fire, and throw those fish on it. Make some hush puppies, too. That was *good.'*

John Powell, who looks like a well-seasoned Howdy Doody, has been fishing for bass for forty years and has been associated with BASS since its earliest days. He makes a good living speaking to groups, representing a few products, fishing enough tournaments to stay up among the top thirty pros. At a cocktail party during the 1975 Classic, he got to talking to a couple of reporters. "I don't have the killer instinct anymore," he said. "Why should I? I did. I can make 3,500 casts in one day if I'm willing to submit myself to fourteen hours of hard concentration. I used to catch 12,000 fish a year. Now, about 2,000. Maybe keep half a dozen a month.

"I can enjoy fishing without meat in the boat. Work up and down that bank over there. Compete against Mr. Bass. He's the only one that's a pro. He don't read your cotton-picking Solunar Tables—he got his own computer. If I get a big strike and lose him, I'm not going to throw back in that same spot. I'm gonna move on. We played that one, he won. But in a tournament . . . gotta get that meat in the boat."

Powell has his hand open, gesturing. Ray Scott comes by and closes Powell's fingers into a fist. He is kidding, but also implying that Powell may be waxing

heretical. Scott, big, energetic, engaging, moves on. "The people in this room," says Powell after grunting slightly, "are responsible for all the bass boats, all the monofilament line, the hooks, the techniques. You go into a store and buy a rod and reel today, there was some influence on it from this room. This guy Ray Scott, the guy that just come over here and made fun of me and folded my fingers down, he's the greatest thing ever happened to bass fishing. He's six people in one."

Powell looks off into the distance, as if scanning the days ahead for structure. "I hope it's always fun and not commercial. I caught my first bass when I was six years old, took the day off from working in the fields and caught an eight-pound bass with a cane pole and a spotted minnow. Fished thirty-five years without a depth finder. Now I've got in the habit. Soon as I get a strike, I'm looking right at that depth finder."

A couple of corporate monofilament types are edgily summoning Powell away. "Don't ever get obligated to anybody," he advises, and he joins them for dinner.

A good deal of the evening entertainment at the Classic is provided by the fishing stars and choreographed by Scott. After the whole crowd ate a big buffet dinner, Scott blithely got them up front to do outrageous things. Such as those men with the biggest stomachs dancing the hula shirtless. After winning the most applause for his hula and therefore the prize of a Johnson spoon, Bo Dowden of Natchitoches, Louisiana, grinning boyishly, asked Scott to give him the microphone. "Let me talk over that thing."

"You can't talk over this thing!" cried Scott in mock dismay. "What you mean? You a *fisherman*."

"We're a demagogic system," Scott later told the group, blandly. "What's that word? Dictatorial. It's very nice when a hundred people are doing what's set up for them to do."

For instance, the fishermen and accompanying press went out on the last day of the 1975 Classic in cold forty-mph winds and flat-bottom bass boats not designed to cope with the ragged swells. The night before, pro Billy Westmorland of Celina, Tennessee, was asked whether he thought the boats would go out as expected. "Scott would send us out if it was raining pitchforks and Chinese babies," Westmorland said.

Conditions have been hazardous at previous BASS tournaments. One year at Lake Eufaula, Oklahoma, a norther blew up and started sinking boats. Wes Woosley of Tulsa had to be saved twice from drowning.

No one was hurt on the final day of last year's Classic, but waves knocked several boats out of commission, and a number of the competitors went all day—7 A.M. to 8 P.M.—without catching a fish. That evening when he checked in, Al Lindner of Brainerd, Minnesota, the only prominent northern bass pro, was asked, "What'd you get?"

"In," said Lindner.

"This is what makes bass fishing," said Scott expansively. "We've had those bluebird days—bluebirds singing, wives sitting out making goo-goo eyes at the weather. And then we've had it turn bad. I've seen it so cold . . . I saw a flag sticking out frozen."

Nothing seems to put Scott out of the mood for bass-fishing administration, and nobody denies that he and his operations man, Harold Sharp, are good at it. Scott was selling insurance very successfully in 1967 when he got the idea of putting on up-and-up bass tournaments. From that idea has come a very pretty dollar for Scott and the profession of bass catching. Before BASS, tournaments had tended to be chaotic local affairs won by locals—that aspect wasn't chaotic. BASS tournaments are aboveboard and policed. When one fisherman was found to have brought in fish he had previously planted in a basket on the water, BASS suspended him for life and suspended another fisherman, who failed to report him, for one year, then sent out a press release about the whole thing.

Fishermen do criticize Scott for not giving them much of a voice in rules and for not paying enough prize money. This year the Classic will pay a total of $50,000 with $25,000 to the winner. The other BASS tournaments also are worth $50,000 each, as compared to $23,000 last year, and first-prize money is up from $4,140 to $14,000, but pros complain that a portion of the overall "money" is not cash but boats, and they don't need any more boats. What kind of deals BASS might have with boat companies, even chambers of commerce interested in attracting tournaments to their localities, is a subject of speculation.

If deals do exist, they only sweeten the pot. BASS gets some $4.6 million in annual dues; it costs $250 to enter a tournament, and BASS operates a three-city franchise outdoor specialty store called Outhouse, a boat-and-tackle store in Montgomery, a motel on a fishing river, and a mail-order merchandising service.

This is a pool of money well worth casting into, even in a storm. The men who do it range, as John Powell says, "from millionaires to guys who had to hock their shotgun to pay the entry fee." As it happens, many of the best-known fishermen—Dance, Roland Martin, Tom and Don Mann, Westmorland—are big, beefy men with county-sheriff bellies. "Fat is where it's at," says Martin. "This stomach keeps me warm. When I get thin I get cold, sick, nervous." Then, too, there are the lean wrangler types—you wouldn't ask for a better Marlboro man than Tommy Martin. Many of them, fat or thin, are distinctively marked by suntan from the cheekbones down; cap brims and dark glasses keep them pale on the forehead and around the eyes. Their hands are horny as farmers'. Scott speaks proudly of "two-fisted hairy-legged knotheads."

The only two men who have won the Angler of the Year award since it was first given in 1971 are Roland Martin, four times; and Dance, once. Though Martin is blond, Dance seems to be the fair-haired boy. Scott introduces him as "bass fishing's first superstar" and is pleased that he represents the sport so personably. "He could've been one of these old harelip country boys with snuff running down both corners of his mouth," says Scott.

An intensely accommodating and cordial fraternity-president type who gave up the furniture business for professional fishing, Dance, age thirty-five, speaks a lot of desire, dedication, and the exchange of ideas. "I've never been in a boat with a man in my life," he says, "that I didn't learn something. I may have learned not to ever get in the boat with him again, but at least I've learned something. I love to try to figure fish out. It's seeking the unknown.

"But competitive fishing—the pressure really wears on me. I can't sleep. I remember when I was six years old and my granddaddy was going to take me fishing the next morning. I'd wake up every two hours. It's the same now. And there's a lot of traveling, with the TV show and appearances. I slept in my own bed only five nights in the first four months of last year.

"But if I don't promote Bill Dance, nobody will. My fishing has improved 500 percent since I started fishing tournaments, and my income is ten times what it was. It's all a result of BASS. I look back and thank the good Lord for it."

Roland Martin has shaggier hair than Dance and a more complicated face. He didn't dance in the hula contest, but he and his wife Mary Ann did name their first son, Scott, after Ray. Martin is thirty-six years old, brawny, blond, clever looking, prepossessing, intense. "I'm trying to be more amiable lately," he says, discussing his in-boat presence. "I've been accused of being a real ass. Won't talk to my partner, won't communicate.

"The guy you're paired with is supposed to control the boat 50 percent of the time. But I just tell him, 'Let's go catch a bunch of fish. If you have something to contribute, fine. But mainly I want to catch some fish.' A guy is going to go for my deal.

"When I was nineteen I caught a big fish, by accident, and entered it in a local contest and won a little trophy. It sat on the mantelpiece, people started saying, 'That Roland catches big fish.' I kept entering and winning contests. I'd send in to *Field and Stream* and get a button to wear on my hat. A button with a little picture of a fish on it.

"My parents discouraged me. My father was a professional man, never fished a lick, and my mother was a drama major. They thought I was wasting my time. One time I missed dinner fishing, came in late, and Dad got so mad at me that when I walked in with my solid fiber glass rod he yelled, 'I'm going to bend that thing!'

"He bends it. It springs back. He hits it into the wall. It lays grooves in the wall. He throws it down and jumps on it. It still keeps its shape. Then he runs out of the room.

"I picked up the rod. It was bent a little bit but it would still work. I loved my Dad, but I never fished with him."

Somewhere in that story there are a couple of proverbs about sparing the rod and bending the twig. At any rate, Martin never looked forward to taking up the profession of outfishing other people, because there was no such thing. But after college he was traveling in Europe with his parents when they were killed in an auto accident in which he was badly injured. To recuperate, and to get away from expressions of sympathy, he went off to Santee-Cooper Reservoir in South Carolina. He stayed down there for five years, fishing, doing a little writing and guiding, building his bass-catching reputation and being "a bachelor bum."

In 1970 he started fishing tournaments. "Competition's done this for me," he says. "I always had this pride that I was a good fisherman, but I never had a ruler to measure by. Now I can very legitimately say I have proved my merit."

It was at a BASS tournament that he met his wife. "She had on a big stocking cap and a snowmobile suit and was carrying a big stringer of fish," he says.

"He thought I was a little fat man walking up the hill," says Mary Ann.

Roland recalls, "I said to Dance, 'Hey, that's a funny-looking guy.' Dance said, 'That's Mary Ann Colbert, twenty-five-year-old whiz-kid fisherman.'"

"Roland and I courted so much during that tournament, Bill Dance beat him by one ounce," says Mary Ann.

"*Seven* ounces," says Roland.

The Martins travel together, working on his TV show. She fishes in tournaments herself, but not BASS ones. No women are allowed. Competitors are paired by lot and, well, what if a man and a woman, unmarried, were sharing a boat and one of them experienced a call of nature?" "He can just turn his head," says Mary Ann, but BASS doesn't agree. She has done some figurative boat-rocking on this count, but the gender bar remains unlifted.

Racially, too, BASS competition is homogeneous. The whole operation, and much of the bass boom, has a white southern flavor. University of North Carolina English Professor Louis Rubin, a noncompetitive bass fisherman and longtime student of Southern literature and ways, goes so far as to say, "The artificial impoundment has done more for race relations in the South than anything else. It has gotten the good old boys away from the general store stirring things up and out onto the water chasing the black bass."

And true, between contract negotiations, there still is front-porch talk to be heard at any BASS gathering. "When I was a boy," said Scott one evening as conversation at dinner turned to wart remedies, "people said the only way to lose warts was to take something like a button and hide it and then forget where you put it. As soon as you forget, the wart falls off. I *still* remember where I put that button. I can see it right now on that top shelf in my uncle's house. I can't forget it to save my life."

Bass fishing has not forgotten its roots, either. It may be advancing to higher levels of finance and technical sophistication, but on the whole it retains a small-town church-social flavor. Superstars Dance and Martin pitch in to help unload baggage. Dance, Martin, and Green sneak a brick into Jimmy Houston's tackle box before it is weighed in (only ten pounds of tackle is allowed each man). High school clog dancers and Lonzo and Oscar from the Grand Ole' Opry fill out the evening entertainment.

It is all part of fishing hard. Which makes you wonder, if a man fishes hard, what is he going to do easy? The main reason a good many people go into the professions of law and medicine is to make enough money to be able to take off afternoons and fish. What's going to be the point of becoming a doctor or lawyer now? So you can go home and watch people fish on the *American Sportsman*? Then, too, pretty soon people are going to be watching television hard. Sleeping in hammocks hard. Whittling hard, humming hard, chewing tobacco and 'lowing as how hard it is.

It's hard to knock such developments, though, as long as they stay down to earth. Jack Hains is being interviewed after winning the Classic, with eighteen live bass weighing a total of forty-five pounds four ounces. He says, "I eat bass nearly every night. I just love it. Filet 'em out and save some for breakfast."

"What color worm you use today, Jack?" (Nicklaus never gets questions like this.)

"Purple with a yellow tail."

"What length worm, Jack?"

"Six-inch. That's about as long a worm as I throw."

"Where'd you go to school?"

"Rayne High School. And University of Southwestern Louisiana. Didn't graduate there. Quit and went to flying. My father owns a crop-dusting service and farms beans some. I work rice and soybeans, dusting."

He says, yes, crop dusting is daredevil seat-of-the-pants precision work that a man can take pride in, and he likes it, "but not enough." Not enough to stay in it much longer, that is, now that he has a fishing career.

"Why don't you take off your waterproof suit for the pictures?"

"Ain't got no britches on. Had to get out and wade and got 'em wet."

"Look at that bass behind you in the tank. He's talking to you."

"I told you I wouldn't hurt you," says Hains to the bass.

The bass swims away. Scott comes forward to speak to the bass. "He says, 'Naw, I don't want to start any more foolishness with you.'" Then Scott asks the other fish in the tank, "Anybody else in there want to be interviewed?"

"Pooly," Scott says to the black man he brings from Montgomery to help out at such moments as this, "swirl a stick around in here, get us a fish who wants to talk."

A lady with three different colors of semiprecious stones on her eyeglasses is watching. So is a man wearing a patch advertising a jumpsuit concern. Nearby, a fat man is challenging a skinny man to go quail hunting with him sometime. "I'll show you how a fat man can walk," he says. "I've done walked two bird dogs to death."

Another fish looks out toward the camera. This is when Hains, holding up his first-prize check, says, "Thank you very much, fish." The fish looks noncommittal.

"Just look at Jack," says somebody. "Grinning like a cat eating yellow jackets."

"And talking to a fish. Only in America," says another man. *He* is wearing a hat that says FIELD TESTER, YUM YUM WORMS.

The best primers on any subject are deceptively brief, eloquently compact. This piece, penned in 1900, qualifies as an archetype.

CHARLES BRADFORD

Trout Truths

What is the best season of the year to go a-fishing?

I think the best time is when you feel like it and can leave home and business. The desire for fishing is like some diseases, in attacking a man with great severity without notice. It can be no more resisted than falling in love can be resisted, and, like love, the best treatment is its gratification.

What is the best time o'day for fishing?

Any time after breakfast. Never go before, for trout are not early risers. I have known men to get out of bed at daylight, making much noise, to the disgust of those who wished to sleep, and rush off with an empty stomach save perhaps for a drink of whiskey, and return several hours later to a cold breakfast, having captured nothing but a headache. Trout will bite just when they feel like it, and the best way to ascertain their biting time is to give them a frequent opportunity.

How about the wind and the weather?

Trout will bite when the wind blows and when it does not. A cloudy day is best except when they rise better on a bright, sunny one. They also often bite well when it rains.

What fly is best?

The fly the trout seem to fancy most on the day you are out. I never go without at least fifty varieties. You may as well ask a woman what style of bonnet she prefers. The taste of trout and women is governed by a similar law, and they change it quite as often. I once made a fly that was so ugly that it frightened my cat out of the room, and yet it proved a great killer. The surest way is to have every known specimen, and to try them all.

What kind of hook is best?

The one with a sharp point, and when you miss a trout charge your clumsiness to the hook and say you prefer some other make.

As conditions are innumerable, it is difficult to make rules to-day which will not fail to-morrow. My advice is—go often and visit many localities. Kill no more fish than you require for your own eating, and do that in the most scientific manner. A trout is a gentleman, and should be treated as such and lured with only delicate and humane weapons.

In 1961 a San Francisco hippie piled his wife and kid into a ten-year-old Plymouth wagon along with a Coleman stove, sleeping bags, diapers, and a portable typewriter and headed for the Snake River in Idaho. Setting up camp along streams, he began writing a novel that was rejected by a creelful of editors. When finally published in 1967, it sold over two million copies and a generation defined itself.
Only in America.
Only in *Trout Fishing in America*.

RICHARD BRAUTIGAN

The Hunchback Trout

The creek was made narrow by little green trees that grew too close together. The creek was like 12,845 telephone booths in a row with high Victorian ceilings and all the doors taken off and all the backs of the booths knocked out.

Sometimes when I went fishing in there, I felt just like a telephone repairman, even though I did not look like one. I was only a kid covered with fishing tackle, but in some strange way by going in there and catching a few trout, I kept the telephones in service. I was an asset to society.

It was pleasant work, but at times it made me uneasy. It could grow dark in there instantly when there were some clouds in the sky and they worked their way onto the sun. Then you almost needed candles to fish by, and foxfire in your reflexes.

Once I was in there when it started raining. It was dark and hot and steamy. I was of course on overtime. I had that going in my favor. I caught seven trout in fifteen minutes.

The trout in those telephone booths were good fellows. There were a lot of young cutthroat trout six to nine inches long, perfect pan size for local calls. Sometimes there were a few fellows, eleven inches or so—for the long distance calls.

64

I've always liked cutthroat trout. They put up a good fight, running against the bottom and then broad jumping. Under their throats they fly the orange banner of Jack the Ripper.

Also in the creek were a few stubborn rainbow trout, seldom heard from, but there all the same, like certified public accountants. I'd catch one every once in a while. They were fat and chunky, almost as wide as they were long. I've heard those trout called "squire" trout.

It used to take me about an hour to hitchhike to that creek. There was a river nearby. The river wasn't much. The creek was where I punched in. Leaving my card above the clock, I'd punch out again when it was time to go home.

I remember the afternoon I caught the hunchback trout.

A farmer gave me a ride in a truck. He picked me up at a traffic signal beside a bean field and he never said a word to me.

His stopping and picking me up and driving me down the road was as automatic a thing to him as closing the barn door, nothing need be said about it, but still I was in motion traveling thirty-five miles an hour down the road, watching houses and groves of trees go by, watching chickens and mailboxes enter and pass through my vision.

Then I did not see any houses for a while. "This is where I get out," I said.

The farmer nodded his head. The truck stopped.

"Thanks a lot," I said.

The farmer did not ruin his audition for the Metropolitan Opera by making a sound. He just nodded his head again. The truck started up. He was the original silent old farmer.

A little while later I was punching in at the creek. I put my card above the clock and went into that long tunnel of telephone booths.

I waded about seventy-three telephone booths in. I caught two trout in a little hole that was like a wagon wheel. It was one of my favorite holes, and always good for a trout or two.

I always like to think of that hole as a kind of pencil sharpener. I put my reflexes in and they came back out with a good point on them. Over a period of a couple of years, I must have caught fifty trout in that hole, though it was only as big as a wagon wheel.

I was fishing with salmon eggs and using a size 14 single egg hook on a pound and a quarter test tippet. The two trout lay in my creel covered entirely by green ferns, ferns made gentle and fragile by the damp walls of telephone booths.

The next good place was forty-five telephone booths in. The place was at the end of a run of gravel, brown and slippery with algae. The run of gravel dropped off and disappeared at a little shelf where there were some white rocks.

One of the rocks was kind of strange. It was a flat white rock. Off by itself from the other rocks, it reminded me of a white cat I had seen in my childhood.

The cat had fallen or been thrown off a high wooden sidewalk that went along the side of a hill in Tacoma, Washington. The cat was lying in a parking lot below.

The fall had not appreciably helped the thickness of the cat, and then a few people had parked their cars on the cat. Of course, that was a long time ago and the cars looked different from the way they look now.

You hardly see those cars any more. They are the old cars. They have to get off the highway because they can't keep up.

That flat white rock off by itself from the other rocks reminded me of that dead cat come to lie there in the creek, among 12,845 telephone booths.

I threw out a salmon egg and let it drift down over that rock and WHAM! a good hit! and I had the fish on and it ran hard downstream, cutting at an angle and staying deep and really coming on hard, solid and uncompromising, and then the fish jumped and for a second I thought it was a frog. I'd never seen a fish like that before.

God-damn! What the hell!

The fish ran deep again and I could feel its life energy screaming back up the line to my hand. The line felt like sound. It was like an ambulance siren coming straight at me, red light flashing, and then going away again and then taking to the air and becoming an air raid siren.

The fish jumped a few more times and it still looked like a frog, but it didn't have any legs. Then the fish grew tired and sloppy, and I swung and splashed it up the surface of the creek and into my net.

The fish was a twelve-inch rainbow trout with a huge hump on its back. A hunchback trout. The first I'd ever seen. The hump was probably due to an injury that occurred when the trout was young. Maybe a horse stepped on it or a tree fell over in a storm or its mother spawned where they were building a bridge.

There was a fine thing about that trout. I only wish I could have made a death mask of him. Not of his body though, but of his energy. I don't know if anyone would have understood his body. I put it in my creel.

Later in the afternoon when the telephone booths began to grow dark at the edges, I punched out of the creek and went home. I had that hunchback trout for dinner. Wrapped in cornmeal and fried in butter, its hump tasted sweet as the kisses of Esmeralda.

The search for Nelson Bryant's column in the sports section of the New York *Times* every week is akin to approaching an oasis in a sandstorm of statistics. You can smell the sweet water.

NELSON BRYANT

A Lovely Girl on a Lonely Stream . . .

A picture of a pretty girl in a bikini standing beside a glassy-eyed, 54-pound 8-ounce king mackerel was recently mailed to me by Lefty Kreh, manager of the annual Metropolitan Miami fishing tournament.

The girl, Mari Lawlor of 420 East Sixty-fourth Street, New York, says Lefty, will receive a citation for her catch.

After studying the fish for several minutes, I noticed Miss Lawlor and was reminded of my youth. In my salad days, when hope and judgment were equally green, I often thought of finding such a girl on a trout stream.

Those were the days, Lefty, the days when I said to myself, "Just around the bend in the stream where that big hemlock stretches out over Twin Rock Pool, she will be standing, clad in waders and a little suede jacket, with a pert hat on her lovely head. She will be watching a big brown trout rising behind the most distant rock, 'Hello,' she will say in a voice as melodious as water over smooth pebbles. 'See that big fellow over there? I'm resting him now. I've been trying to raise him for an hour.' "

In my daydream I picked a bit of fur and feathers from my fly box and said, "Try this. I tied it myself for this stream at this time of year."

Her clear, honest eyes measured me candidly. "Thank you," she said. "You're very kind. I like men who tie their own."

As she fastened the fly to her leader, I asked, "Do you fish this stream often?"

"This is my first time on it. I live in Wappingers Falls. But I'm coming back. It's a lovely stream. By the way, my name is Alison Anapest."

It seemed impossible that this lovely girl was the Alison Anapest from Wappingers Falls whose best-selling narrative poem, "Lover with Hard Hands," had left reviewers gagging on laudatory adjectives a month before.

She saw the question in my eyes.

"Let me love, let me kiss, let me dream," she began, and, overcome, I broke in, finishing the opening lines of her poem for her:

> Let my lover be strong,
>   let him ride
> Through the storm, through
>   the wind, in the sun,
> His hard, brown hands
>   gentle only for me.

We stood close. The big trout rose and hauled under a just-hatched mayfly. A hawk screamed high overhead, and the world was breathless and ours alone.

Well, Lefty, the nearest I ever came to such a confrontation was six years ago on Long Pond in Croydon, New Hampshire. I was struggling to load a huge old water-soaked 250-pound canoe on top of my car when a panel truck pulled up and a girl who weighed about what I do, two hundred pounds, climbed out. Her clear eyes—she was over six feet tall—looked down into mine.

"Let me give you a hand, Bud," she said and hoisted one end of the canoe over her head.

"Want help with yours?" I asked weakly after the canoe was on my car, but she seized her car-top boat, walked with it to the water, and set it down without a ripple.

"You ought to get a boat like this. You're gonna bust a gut one of these days," she said, hitching up her belt.

Snow, San Quentin, and bass. Russell Chatham compounds strange hues in his palette, dyestuffs charged with fluorescence and not easily subject to fading. For all the fishermen who fantasize of virgin pools in distant territories, he offers some rather unconventional wisdom.

RUSSELL CHATHAM

No Wind in the Willows

Outside a blizzard is raging. The familiar edges that normally define my yard, its fences, woodpile and barns, have long vanished beneath the snow. My house, the last on an unpaved road among aspen and pine forests along the northwestern perimeter of Montana's vast Absaroka wilderness, is well on its way toward becoming a smallish speck on the surface of a preposterous marshmallow.

Unable to go out, perhaps I will simply sit, reminisce and revisit. A word recurs, an idea, insisting itself upon the situation: *remoteness*. I moved to the Big Sky Country to get it. As an angler reflecting upon the fabric of American sport afield, I recognized the essential thread to be a romance with far places. In short, I'd identified the Mainstream and wanted in.

Early on, my fishing days were spent in a northern California cabin snugged against the hillside beneath stands of redwood. On a bookshelf beside its fireplace was a pile of old magazines, sporting journals, mostly, and some outdated tackle catalogs. It seemed fishing was more plain and intimate then. For example, the invocation, "Take a boy fishing!" required but a few Bass-O-Renos and perhaps a small outboard motor, called a "kicker," for immediate implementation.

This pastiche of allusions then, was rife with visions of adventure in which the canoe loomed large as a vehicle of escape. A guide, invariably of French descent, dressed appropriately in a red- and black-checked wool shirt, took us to lakes and rivers teeming with unusually large brook trout or northern pike somewhere in the vastness of the Canadian outback.

Portage! How much more a vision of unsoiled landscape this word promises than . . . ecology.

But before I founder completely in fatuous recall, it occurs that until very recently, among the hundred-odd thousand words placed by the Oxford Unabridged at my disposal, the adjective least correct as a predicate to my own angling past is *remote*.

San Francisco Bay: It is four-thirty in the morning on June 21, 1966. I am later than planned because of the time it took to clear myself with the policeman who pulled me over in San Anselmo for "suspicious behavior." Was it the generally fishy odor about the car that, in the end, convinced the law of my salient innocence? I don't know. In any case, we had parted amicably.

Now I am parking the car near a maintenance station on the Marin County end of the Richmond-San Rafael Bridge. I expect to be joined soon by an acquaintance but since he hasn't arrived I decide to walk out to the bridge itself for a quick preview.

On the way, rats scurry for cover behind a shabby row of shrubs. These would not be your big Norways, the kind you might see in the tropics sitting boldly in a palm while you sip your rum and tonic on the veranda below. No, the pusillanimous little rodents that people my morning are inclined to cower behind slimy rocks near the freeway, struggling on an equal footing with Marfak for control of the last strands of seaweed, or waiting in crevices for the next high tide.

I brush past the PEDESTRIANS PROHIBITED sign, jump the low guard rail and trot to the second light post. There is no visible traffic but from the north I hear a diesel truck shift down just before the crest that will bring him into view and then onto the bridge approach. He will be doing seventy when he reaches me so I hook one leg over the railing, grip the light standard and try to become inconspicuous. I would rather not be sucked under the rear wheels of a truck and trailer full of rutabagas. He goes by with a blast and the bridge vibrates ominously as I watch his lights diminish toward Richmond.

I run out to the next light and look down. As I'd hoped, half a dozen dark forms are finning in the shadow beneath the bridge. I am especially excited by the largest, which is a striped bass upward of thirty pounds. To my right, a pod of smelt moves near on a tangent certain to prompt an attack. The little fish are attracted by the brilliant light overhead. In their lack of purpose they seem ephemeral, like a translucent curtain quivering near a window, while the heavy predators lurking in the dark are deliberate and potent. In a moment the black shapes explode outward, sending the smelt showering away in a radius of flashing bodies.

Satisfied, I turn back toward the approach in time to see the California Highway Patrol car coming at me, its nose down under heavy braking.

"What are you doing out here, buddy?"

"Going fishing soon as it's legal time."

"Is that your car parked back at the maintenance building?"

"Yes."

"Well it's illegally parked. Better move it. Now get going and don't walk out here any more."

On my way to the car I see the patrolman who'd questioned me get out and look over the railing. Then the amber light is flashing and the driver is out too. Together they lean over the side, pointing.

I recognize Frank's blue sedan come down the off ramp and turn south. When I reach him he is untying his boat and I begin to do the same. In a few seconds we will have them in the water.

In order to launch we must trespass. The land belongs to the state of California and although I've never been verbally warned off, any number of KEEP OUT signs are posted.

For about eight years I kept a boat chained and locked behind a large sign reading CABLE CROSSING. Once a year they would repaint this sign getting white paint on the chain.

Some yards away in a square blockhouse belonging to San Quentin Penitentiary, trustees worked during the day. Each season they planted a handsome little vegetable garden that I was careful never to disturb.

I often talked to one convict in particular. After fishing it would take some minutes to put the boat behind the sign and then carry everything else up to the car. He would call a greeting and I'd perhaps comment on the progress in the garden. Then he'd ask, always rather plaintively, about the fishing. He said he liked to go fishing before he got "inside."

One December we had a severe storm, accompanied by especially high tides. Afterward, I went over to check the boat and all that was left was the chain. I was poking around the beach when I heard my friend's voice.

"Looking for your boat?"

"Guess it's gone," I replied sadly.

"No, I saw it break loose and caught it. Then I dragged it up there." He said, "Only thing I couldn't find was the seat."

Beyond the garden I could see the trim little *El Toro* upside down on a pair of two-by-fours.

In recent years there have been no inmates at the blockhouse and the garden lies fallow beneath wild anise. In a sense this has meant more license to trespass but I stopped keeping a boat behind the sign when I knew there would be no trustees to look after it.

It is a windless, overcast morning. Sunrise, such as it will be, is in an hour but the eastern horizon over San Pablo Bay is still dark. Bursts of flame glow against a cloudy ceiling above Point Molate, tangible evidence that behind the latter's headlands lies the Standard Oil Company of California's research center, in a bitter sense, petroleum's ode to the cubists with its sprawl of cylinders, cones, and rectangles.

At Point San Quentin, the flaring fires have become a familiar greeting like the dew on a chokecherry bush that starts off the trout fisherman's day in the Rockies.

"Did you look?" Frank asks.

"They're there."

We row around the tilted bow of a derelict tugboat, then past rotted pilings left from the ferryboat days. Over on the approach a yellow bridge patrol truck moves slowly, flashing its warning lights. Switching on a spotlight, the driver scans the water, catching sight of Frank and me. Then the light is off and the truck starts toward the toll plaza.

Unseen overhead, a black-crowned night hawk rasps its singularly forlorn call.

The smell of an institutional breakfast wafts unappetizingly across the water from San Quentin, an odor not unlike that of a cow barn in winter. No croissants and chilled grapefruit sections this morning, to be sure.

There is a fast tide and we must row smartly to pass beneath the bridge, where it is always dank and dripping. Sounds are magnified and echoed, especially that of wavelets slapping against pilings. Reflected light plays on the girders overhead, and just before we emerge I see several bass hovering at the edge, but Frank rows into the dark while I decide to try a few casts at the first light. The piling directly beneath the lamp attracts my attention so I drop the large bucktail fly where the current will swing it into the shadows.

Instantly there is a take and I set the hook twice. This is always the moment when you wonder if the bass will go under the bridge and break off on a sharp barnacle. But I've learned that initial light pressure generally encourages them to dive toward the boat.

Now my bass pulls around into the dark, and I try to gauge its size. It is, if nothing else, a stubborn fish that resolutely resists all the strain I can manage on a fifteen-pound tippet. Eventually, however, I land it and mentally record a weight slightly above twenty pounds.

Frank is anchored under the third light, where I see angular splashes as fish erupt under a school of bait.

It was Walt Mullen who showed me the bridge and how to fish it shortly after it was built. When we first met I was sixteen and he was more than eighty. Coincidentally, Walt had taken my father fishing and hunting back in the twenties when the latter was going to Stanford.

Mullen was an old sign painter, wiry and spry, surely no more than a hundred pounds soaking wet. I wanted to learn the sign business so I'd hang around his shop. But my patience proved short and my business acumen entirely nonexistent so we always ended up talking about fishing. He loved it more than anyone I'd ever met. In the front pocket of his coveralls he always had a tide book, dog-eared and paint-smeared.

"See here," he said one day, pointing out the numerals. "There's a good tide in three days. If the water's clear and it's not too windy, I'll take you out to the bridge."

At that point my own experience was primarily academic insofar as fly-casting for striped bass was concerned. Walt didn't fly-fish but he knew instinctively I would catch fish on the streamers I showed him.

I'd read about certain pioneer anglers on the East Coast who caught striped bass by fly-fishing. I knew also that Joe Brooks, the noted Virginian, was much interested in stripers and that he caught one of twenty-nine pounds six ounces in 1948 out of Coos Bay, Oregon. This fish was acknowledged as the fly-rod record.

For several years Walt and I fished together regularly. Then I married and became too busy and he closed his shop, moving the business to another county.

Occasionally I'd see him at the bridge. His eyes were failing and he didn't trust himself in a boat any more so he'd cast from the rocks, often a futile gesture since fish rarely fed close to shore.

One windy, choppy evening Bill Schaadt and I were in our boat at the third light.

"Look." Bill pointed.

On the bridge, hunched against the railing, oblivious to speeding traffic and thoroughly unable to distinguish Bill or me, was Walt clutching an enormous spinning rod. Cocking it back, he used it to drive his lure in a trajectory that carried it over a school of bass I'm sure he never saw. His face was locked in an expression of determination that did not make him look any less like an angling Ichabod Crane.

"Boy," Bill said, "now there's a guy who likes to fish!"

Then as we'd hoped and anticipated, Walt hooked a striper, whereupon he stalked grimly back to the rocks and landed it.

Several years passed during which time I did not see Walt Mullen. Then one cold spring morning I was out at the bridge alone. To avoid the noisome mob of trollers, with whom the bridge had become a favorite haunt, I'd begun going at odd hours and poorish tides. When it grew light I saw a figure on the rocks, casting. Walt! Excitedly I drew up my anchor and rowed in, circling widely so I wouldn't spoil anything. Close in, I turned but could no longer see anyone.

Going ashore, I called out with no response. I looked under the bridge and finally crossed the freeway to search the other side. There was no one. I felt a deep sense of loss, an uneasy melancholy. I went home.

Later I found out Walt had died earlier that spring.

I row around behind Frank. The bass are there and I see the heavy swirls as they feed.

Traffic on the bridge is picking up. Early commuters. They are too low in their cars to see us but the truck drivers give a wave or short blast of the horn. It is getting light, a gray dawn that I imagine could be heavily depressing to a man looking forward to eight hours on the production line.

"The coldest winter I ever spent," wrote someone, "was a summer in San Francisco." I wonder momentarily if this, in part, explains the high suicide rate and high alcohol intake for which the City on the Bay is known.

We are virtually within sight of well over a million people, yet alone. We are perhaps, out of step, ill placed, and ill timed, in a sphere where cogs must mesh and all parts syncopate to keep the system running smoothly. Even within the framework of angling as a popular endeavor, our methods are archaic: fly rods and rowboats. But we are touching something unrestricted, wild and arcane, beyond the reach of those who carefully maintain one-dimensional lives. There is, I tell myself, someone in the city nearby whose one contact today with unreconstructed nature will be to step into a diminutive pile of poodle excrement.

When I looked into the mirror during the late fifties I saw a striped-bass fisherman who often imagined, wrongly, that he was doing something remarkable and unique.

At the time an old gent by the name of Ellis Springer was pier keeper for the Marin Rod and Gun Club, which was situated only a few feet from the bridge. He let me use the club's launching ramp, dock, and fish-cleaning table even though I was not a member.

Ellis was never seen without a light-blue captain's hat and stubby cigar. He talked often of the days he'd spent in the Spanish-American War but his manner of speech was so unique that you could understand nothing of what he said. I didn't think he knew what fly-fishing was and wanting to let him in on my little discovery, I gave a demonstration one day off the dock. He looked properly astonished and when I showed him my flies, he became incoherently excited, exclaiming, "Yeeehhh! Hoopty poopty! Hoopty poopty!"

These exclamations became a permanent part of all subsequent conversations.

"Hi, Springer."

"Eeeeehhh! Hoopty poopty!"

I used to carry fish around in the back of my car the way other kids my age carried a six-pack of Country Club. I'd show Ellis and he'd become truly frantic.

"Yeeeehhh! Hoopty poopty! Hoopty poopty!"

Gradually I became aware of the fact he called everything that was not strictly a sardine fillet a hoopty poopty.

Frank hooks a bass. I put my anchor down out of his way but still close enough to reach the school. I see two powerful boils and cast the bulky fly on a slow loop toward the swirl closest to a piling. I overshoot so the fly tinks against the bridge hanging momentarily between the rail and roadway, then as it flutters downward I see the number 9 stenciled above on an abutment.

The take is authoritative and my response lifts the clearly visible fly line from the water, curving it abruptly to the left as a sheet of droplets limns the fish's first long run. It is not a frenetic contest as the striper stays deep far from the boat. But I am not inclined to carry out these contests gently and soon have the fish nearby. Once, glowering, he shoots away beneath a crescent of spray only to be turned in a verticle wallow. After all, nothing in their lives really prepares a fish to deal with the relentless affixation of being hooked.

Oddly, I am reminded of how Walt Mullen described playing a fish. "Then it fooled around and fooled around," he would say. And that is exactly it.

In the boat the fish is big.

"It's more than twenty-five," I say to Frank.

Earlier we had discussed a twenty-five-pound striper caught accidentally by a fly-fisherman in the Russian River. It seemed more appropriate that a fish taken by design should receive top honors for the season. Naturally, we both expressed the hope that one of us would catch such a fish.

Back at the beach we lay three large bass in front of the sign that reads CABLE CROSSING.

"That one's bigger than the one I caught last season," says Frank.

Getting his Polaroid camera, he takes a picture of me holding the fish, which comes out a minute later looking distant and journalistic. Then after promising to call him soon as I get the thing weighed, I head for San Rafael and he goes off to work in San Francisco.

Later, I call.

"It's big isn't it?" Frank asks right away. "I've been looking at this snapshot all morning."

"Yes. Thirty-six pounds six ounces."

The record Joe Brooks had held for eighteen years was broken. When I got to know Joe he would always introduce me as "a great salt-water fisherman," which was embarrassing because while he was alive he was so clearly one of the greatest. Now others have caught bigger bass, eliminating my personal stake in the matter. It is a relief to be reminded that competition in angling is entirely beside the point and that I'm simply an angler of average persuasion and ability who happened to cast a fly near a large, hungry fish one morning.

Besides, there are too many other things to think about, like a certain broad shovel on the porch. I finished all the Jack Daniel's last night and this morning we are hopelessly snowed in.

The evolution of the fishwife has never been as fully documented as in Cook's enduring series of classic case histories. Fortunately, the species faces no danger of imminent extinction; on the contrary, fresh sightings are reported almost daily. Exercising the most rigorous anthropological methodology, Cook explores the subculture as a participant-observer, the approach yielding insights of particular poignance.

BEATRICE COOK

A Worm's-eye View of Fishermen

I am a fishwife—or so it seems after being married over twenty years to a fishin' fool. I married one and raised two and claim to know more about fishermen than a salmon does, which is saying a lot, for fish are smarter than high school girls. I've shared a fisherman's life and therefore know the extremes of unreasonable exultation or blackest despair.

At the altar, I little realized I was pledged to love, honor, and obey three outboard motors, the ways of the river, the whims of the tide, and the wiles of the fish, as well as Bill, the man of my choice. Nobody told me I was to rear two babies with fish scales in their curls or that I would learn to change a diaper with one hand while keeping a steady tension on a spool reel with the other. I had to learn—or else.

Before our honeymoon was over, I was faced with a decision: I must become either a fishing-widow or a fishwife. If my husband chased salmon all over the Pacific Northwest without me, I would turn into a sad-eyed, introspective stay-at-home and, in time, resemble Whistler's Mother, who I've always suspected was patiently waiting for some fisherman to come home. So with a prayer in my heart to my new patron saint, Izaak Walton, I chose to become a fishwife, my husband's companion on all his trips. This is a role not to be undertaken lightly, for it requires the touch of a lady, the heart of a lion, and the constitution of a jackass.

Many brides here in the state of Washington have to make up their minds just as I did, for this is the fisherman's Promised Land, overflowing with salmon, bass, trout—and more salmon. Seattle bankers and brokers read the tide charts in the morning paper before turning to the Wall Street listings, and they'll skip dinner when an incoming tide in the evening assures good fishing. It's half an hour from office to rowboat, as Seattle's business section is only a Paul Bunyan fly cast from Elliott Bay, our semilandlocked harbor, which is teeming with salmon.

In books fishermen are referred to as dreamy, vacant-eyed philosophers who spend more time assembling tackle than they do in stream or boat. But anglers don't dream around here. They fish. The line on one reel or another is damp the year round, except perhaps in early December. At that time, just before the opening of the steelhead season, a kindly Providence planned to have most salmon leave shallow water and stay at sea. It's pure luck that the absence of fish corresponds to the Christmas season when fishermen-family acquaintanceship is renewed and Father is pleased to see how much the children have grown since he last noticed them. This is the time to give Mother the split bamboo rod he himself has wanted so long, and in this land of abundance, hip boots instead of Christmas stockings are hung by the fireplace on Christmas Eve. Chrome and shiny brass spoons make dandy tree ornaments, and a spool of Monel metal line has it all over glass balls.

Of course not everybody out here fishes. There are a few sane and sober merchants, manufacturers, and grocers needed to cater to the fishermen. But at some time during any party or gathering, you'll see a cluster of men hanging on each other's words and there is sure to be a glitter in their eyes. Hands grip an imaginary rod, which suddenly jerks upward to show how that thirty-pounder snapped the leader and made off with all gear. Everybody offers advice and tells how the same thing *nearly* happened to him—and would have, except for that little trick he knows. The tall tales have started.

All fishermen are liars; it's an occupational disease with them like house-maid's knee or editor's ulcers. Deacons and doctors alike enlarge upon "the one that got away," measuring off with ecclesiastical or surgical fingers the size of the mythical monster. At this point, the uninitiated fishing-widow yawns, but the fishwife nods understandingly. Save face, save the ego at any price—too often it's all a fisherman brings home. I've heard sterling characters swear to the most unlikely stories simply to cover their humiliation. For it *is* embarrassing to have a wee bass outthink you. I've seen a fifteen-pound salmon make a sucker out of a top-flight executive and a rainbow fool a psychology professor. Those big fish don't get that way by being dumb; a trout that doesn't think two jumps and several runs ahead of the average fisherman is mighty apt to get fried. With light tackle, fish get a fifty-fifty break and you don't need to pity them. The term "poor fish" may be based upon their uninteresting procreative habits, certainly not upon their intelligence.

Before you go with us up the Skagit River for steelhead or to the San Juan Islands for king salmon, I want to let you in on something. Did you know there's a roped-off, high priority section of Heaven exclusively reserved for the wives of fishermen? A celestial retreat uncluttered with leaky gas cans, rusty hooks, flooded motors, kinked wire lines, and mangy fishing hats? Here there will be no mention of incoming tides, three o'clock breakfasts, too much or too little feed. The baked ambrosia will not have to be cleaned and scaled first. In fact, the word "fish" never will be mentioned. This is a well-earned reward for those who, on earth, nursed husbands and sons through all the stages of fishing fever.

The symptoms? You know them well, no matter which creek or coast you fish. There are those moments of grandeur caused by a dozen twelve-inch trout, a mess of silvers or a tremendous king salmon, a string of sea bass or a couple of muskies. This is the time when Father is insufferable, little heeding the words of his wife—or Shakespeare, who reminds him that "Every braggart shall be found an ass." Nearly bursting at the seams, he phones all his cronies and they come on the run, flocking around the dinner table like flies at a Sunday school picnic. Father has his day; Mother, sagging arches; and the cat has the milt.

But days of deepest depression surely will follow when none of the hundred-thousand-dollars' worth of plugs he owns (a fishwife's loose estimate) has any appeal, when frozen herring are so soggy they fall off the hook, or the fish just aren't there anyway. This can drag on for weeks. Sympathy, liver pills, or even benzedrine slipped into coffee does no good. Nothing helps this blue funk but a few pounds of fishy protoplasm on the business-end of a line. However, this treatment must be continued to keep run-of-the-millstream anglers happy during the legal season.

Watch out! Even when lakes or streams are closed by law, a careless whiff of clam chowder will send the inveterate fisherman off again. 'Way off. Then he gets that mellow, faraway look in his eye which changes to a fanatic gleam as he dashes to the basement. Gear comes rattling out of closets, reels are unwound, and the place becomes an obstacle course with yards of line criss-crossed all over it for inspection. Rusty spark plugs are scraped, oiled—and left to drip on the ironing board. Children are threatened with double hernia as they tug and strain, trying to help Father pull rods apart. The mingled smell of varnish and reel oil acts as a come-on, and feverishly new hooks are tied to hallowed plugs, toothmarked veterans of many battles. These are crooned over while wife and children are forgotten. There's the pungent odor of rubber cement as boots are patched and the sharp ammoniac tingle of brass polish. And you can count on it: there will be a worse stench when Father accidentally—but perennially—drops that half-used jar of spoiled bait eggs or the bottle of home-preserved herring. Both smell higher than an Indian village at sundown. At a time like this, if I mention a social engagement, Father is sure to develop a touch of lumbago, or any other dreamed-up ailment serious enough to keep him home—in the basement. He might as well be fishing!

Just like measles, this sort of thing is expected all over the country in early spring, but it is indigenous to the Puget Sound region where there is no closed season for salmon. At any ungodly moment, winter or summer, a fishwife must be booted and spurred and ready to go. I'm grateful that no fish bites best in total darkness. Now I like to fish, but I'm a convert; I wasn't born that way. However, unlike the addict, I can take it or leave it, and I'd rather leave it at four in the morning when a January gale is strong enough to blow salmon scales backward.

The Pacific Northwest climate is mild and the seasons sort of run together, but an experienced fisherman can tell the time of year by noting what kind of fish tails the cat is chewing on. Winter king salmon are rich, oily, and the best of the year, but they have the nastiest dispositions—not quite so mean, however, as the spring steelhead well downstream and thus still in the full flower of fish-hood. April trout hate to leave home, and summer's silver and king salmon seldom give a novice an even break. Fall brings the mighty hook-nose silvers and cutthroat trout. You can see there's never a dull moment for fishermen out here.

Now I didn't know any of this—or suspect lots more—about a quarter of a century ago, when I was a girl and lived in Chicago. The state of Washington was just a half-inch pink square on the map and, like the rest of the Midwest and East, I thought Seattle had virgin forests running between First and Second Avenues. I was headed for a life on the prairie until I met Bill. He changed my plans in a hurry. He breezed in from the West with such a head of steam that I melted in my tracks. He was attending a medical convention and, after one disdainful look at the windy, dirty city, he began telling me about a glorious mountain world where one could go hiking, skiing, or fishing and get home again in time to make the gravy for the pot roast. He told of shooting the rapids in an Indian canoe and about his innumerable camping trips in the San Juan Islands. He spoke of majestic Mount Olympus and Mount Constitution as though they were personal friends, and he promised me a trip through the ice caves of Mount Rainier.

Of course he wedged in stories of fishing trips, so I knew he was a fisherman, but I little guessed all that this implied. He said I'd love it, too, and at the moment I didn't give it a second thought. Bill was so nice and big and brown, I would have been glad to go fishing for the rest of my life on the River Styx. And so, innocently, I rose to the fly and snapped at the lure.

He returned to Seattle. Mother and I followed him west soon after. I little guessed how ill-prepared I was for the life of a fishwife. I had been hand-raised by a widowed mother, definitely a member of the old school whose graduates have a Victorian hangover. To her, fish have intestines, not guts; stomachs, not bellies; and only female dogs are bitches. She thinks paper napkins and horsey women abominations unto the Lord. Well-bred and well-read, she taught me all the niceties of living, which proved slightly inadequate for my role of fishwife.

On the train, I reviewed all I knew about fishing. Terrapin was a member of the social set and salmon always canned. Herring were shirtsleeve fish, caught already smoked or pickled. I thought cod must be easy to catch—any fish would welcome death whose liver smelled so vile. Trout came from streams and whitefish from traps.

I remembered certain gatherings where, with a dab of caviar-smeared toast in one hand and something iced in the other, I innocently had joined in the song that sympathizes with the poor virgin sturgeon which needs no urgin'. Roe was sautéed or canned. In those sheltered pre-fishing days, I would have shuddered to my shoes had I seen "caviar" taken on the hoof. Even today, as an old fishhand, it makes my stomach revolve to watch Indians grasp a ripe, squirming female and hold it a few inches above their upturned mouths. Then they bring the red, gooey eggs directly from producer to consumer, by using a stroking motion of thumb and forefinger along the underside of the belly. Much lip-smacking ensues while they grab another salmon and toss the old one to the squaws. Thanks. I'll take my caviar salted, pickled, spiced, dyed, and spread very thin.

The train rolled on through the wheat belt. Everything I owned was with me. My trousseau frothed with satin and lace numbers such as one sees advertised in *Vogue*: shimmering bed jackets and cobwebby lingerie. This was the age of pale pink ribbon and I had enough woven in and out of my undies to foul the rudder of a battleship. This was just standard equipment for a bride, I thought. Now I know that the Better Business Bureau should force advertisers to put footnotes on such pages, saying, "Above items of no possible use to a fisherman's bride." Wiser still, there should be a companion page featuring such lovelies as fishwives need: flannel pajamas, wool socks and shirts, blue jeans, hip boots, and long underwear (drop seat).

The prairies stretched out in such vast, endless miles that I had plenty of time for premarital jitters. Bill was a physician by profession, a sports fisherman by preference, and just how would this double-threat deal work out for me?

But all my fears were forgotten, magically erased from my mind when the train began to curl and twist through the Cascade Mountains of Washington. We had passed through the Rockies at night so the Cascades were the first mountains I'd ever seen—honest-to-God ones, ripped right out of the *National Geographic* and practically at my fingertips! The sky was a blue dome over a world of jagged peaks crowned with snow. Misty falls dropped hundreds of feet to the timberline. I was enchanted with the queer little trees that had such sturdy, thick trunks compared with their height. Each mountain fir, with its short, downswept branches to shed the snow, was a miracle of symmetry. Some of them grew right out of crevices in the rock, and I wondered if their struggle for existence gave them that sober chrome green so unlike the frivolous yellow-green of the alders in the valley below, where soil was deep and life was easy.

Now the train was threading its way along a shelf cut from a mountain side, and we were in a great bowl of sky-touching mountains. Everything was sharp and clear: the river that sparkled a thousand feet below us, the snow fields ten miles away, and the track that glinted like silver wires behind us. How did the train ever get up here? There didn't seem to be a single break in the wall of mountains, and I pondered over the vision and skill of those first engineers who had plotted this pass.

The train nosed on, searching its way through a labyrinth of peaks, each curve opening up new wonders. Those thin white threads against the jumble of rocks must be water falls hurtling down through distance and the ages. Near us was a rushing stream, cloudy with glacial silt. It boiled and tumbled down a mile-square façade of naked rock, and its spray nourished rock gardens on either side.

As we worked slowly through the mountains, gradually the train lost altitude. Now we were in another world where everything was size forty-four. Only this time it was trees. I admitted to Mother that Bill's picture-postcards were not fakes—an automobile *could* drive through a tunneled-out fir. Where these giants thinned to just a scattering of hemlocks and spruce, there was a wild tangle of undergrowth. It was head high and I had a new respect for Lewis and Clark. Oregon is quite similar to Washington, and how could those intrepid explorers ever have cut through this to the coast?

Here a great fir had fallen, thundered to earth generations ago, and its flat, interlaced root structure stood up as tall as a one-story house. The trees dripped with yards of sage-green beard moss which added a sort of melancholy beauty. Everything—forests, mountains, vistas, trees, and sky—was scaled to majestic grandeur, and I wouldn't have been too amazed to see an armored dinosaur or mastodon peek around a cliff.

Regretfully, I said good-bye to my mountains. Then, with little time to get set for such a surprise, we were coasting beside Puget Sound, running just a few feet above high-tide level. Entranced, I gazed over the shimmering Sound toward the Olympic Mountains. They were taller and more splendid than the Cascades—and mine to love forever.

Mountains are good for the ego—they cut one down to size. Man's strivings seem so finite in a land of these proportions; the Empire State Building would look puny backed up against even a minor-league mountain. I didn't realize it then, but at that moment I was beginning to become a Westerner.

The sea gulls flew beside us all the way into Seattle. The cars hitched to a stop, each little bump jerking me back to reality. The depot platform was grimy, gray, and depressing, but suddenly it became a lovely place. Bill was there.

"Mother, Bill's terribly late. And for his own wedding!" . . .

At last—what every angler has waited for. An uncensored, blow-by-blow account of a great tench catch. With the historical record exhaustively searched and the following document uncovered, it is now time to reveal once and for all the heretofore covert modus operandi.

C. J. CORNISH

The Great Tench Catch

No one quite remembers who first started the idea that there were tench waiting to be caught in Colmere Lake. The time and place of its origin are, however, agreed upon. The time was shortly after the date when "coarse fishing" begins, and the place was in the smoking room, where we were planning how to kill time during the dullest part of the rural summer.

Colmere Lake is celebrated for its heronry, its flocks of wildfowl in winter, and for monster pike but not for summer fishing. Still it seemed unlikely that its deep waters did not hold other fish, and the theory that these existed in the form of tench explained everything. For tench are not only the shyest of all fishes, but have the longest memories. they will bite greedily once in ten years. Then every tench in the lake grows suspicious, and holds aloof from any form of bait. For any evidence to the contrary, they might have taken wings and flown off to other waters. That is why the notion of a huge tench population, thriving forgotten in the depths of the lake, "caught on" at once. In the course of the week the surmise hardened into a certainty. The doctor, who was a keen fisherman, had it directly from the lips of an old labourer whom he was attending for rheumatics, that he "minded" a huge haul of tench being netted in the lake some thirty years ago; and the curate, who was also an angler, was lucky enough to find an old woman who had fried some of the fish and corroborated the fact. But no recent record of a tench being caught was to be had in the neighbourhood.

From this, when we met next Saturday to compare notes, we formed two conclusions. First, that as no other fish ever kills a tench, some of those in the lake must be thirty years old; and secondly, that if they had bred at all, their number must be something quite beyond counting. Whoever first started the idea, to the doctor belongs the whole credit of the development to its legitimate conclusions. He "rose and addressed us," as the papers say, and put the case so well that we afterwards regretted we had not a shorthand writer within call to take it down. The substance of his remarks was as follows.

He reminded us that when once we had leave to fish (which we had not got, but no difficulty was apprehended), we were face to face with the chances of a lifetime. These tench were in the state of Adam before the fall—ignorant of guile, presumably very numerous, and of monstrous size. He deprecated all hurry and excitement, and begged us to show ourselves worthy of the occasion, and endeavour to realise our opportunities. It was not a chance to be thrown away by just going down to the lake and taking our luck with a rod and a worm. Something better than that was expected of us. He concluded by proposing that all action should be postponed for a fortnight and that meantime everyone there present should every evening collect worms on his lawn and, putting them into a common stock, send them to spots selected near the lake bank for advertisement by means of ground bait. At the end of the fortnight the attack was to be made early in the morning by our united forces, armed with two rods apiece. We all bound ourselves to adhere to this programme, and for the next ten days worm-catching by lamplight on our respective tennis lawns became a matter of conscience with us.

It is not generally known how difficult it is to catch worms. When realised, it increases one's respect for the early bird who does catch them. They shoot back into their holes like a piece of elastic, and have to be stalked with as much caution as rabbits. In time we got to like it. A lady who was among the keenest of the party said it *was* sport and was quite sorry when it was over.

Meantime we obtained leave to fish the lake, and fixed a Monday morning at six A.M. for the opening of the campaign. That Sunday night the rector, quite by accident, for we had kept our plans to ourselves, took for his sermon the text,—"I go a-fishing," and we hardly knew which way to look, for that is exactly what we were all thinking about.

We did not catch any worms that night (Sunday) as we were all in a highly nervous state, and painfully anxious not to do anything which might set Providence against us; besides we had an enormous stock accumulated in bags of moss. But we made the most elaborate preparations of rods, lines, floats, baskets, camp stools (for the grass was certain to be wringing wet with dew at six A.M.); and as the ladies were determined to be of the party, the arrangements for an early breakfast were more satisfactory and complete than is usual when sport is to begin before civilised hours.

The lake was nearly three miles off, and as we trotted off in our dog-carts in the fresh, clear morning, before the fields were well awake, along the roads all powdered with dust, edged by grass all sprinkled with dew, our hopes rose in spite of our natural misgivings. It is true that none of us had seen a single tench on our visits to the lake-side to deposit our ground bait. But that did not matter. We had evidence enough to satisfy ourselves that the fish *ought* to be there, even if they were not; meantime we had done all that we could to ensure success, and we felt that we deserved it.

The lake looked lovely. Herons slipped out of the big trees which fringed the side next us; the young wild ducks and their mammas were swimming quite tamely among the water lilies; crowds of rooks and jackdaws were chattering in the park, and where the shafts of sunlight struck the water or fell on the bank between the trees, little curling mists were drifting up from water and grass alike. The reed fringe at the lake head was broken in two or three places where our ground bait had been laid, and here on the dew-drenched grass we set up our rods, put on our baits, and cast the floats out into the lake.

We had not long to wait. In about thirty seconds or less—a shiver, then half-a-dozen little dips; then a steady rush of the floats was seen at the end of the doctor's line; and the next moment he was fast into something—a heavy fish not to be trifled with. We should all have rushed to see what he had got, and whether it were a tench or not, had not exactly the same thing happened to each and everyone of our floats in the next half minute. Then a splash and a cheer from the doctor showed us that it was as he expected. He was fast in a three-pound tench and was in the act of landing him. And we were all in the same case; each had a fish, and that fish was a tench, deep, broad, slab-sided, covered with tiny scales of dark gold and honey colour, and thickly lubricated with something like liquid glue. They came on solidly and stolidly, just waiting for one to be taken off the hook and a fresh worm put on, and then cruising off with bait and float, as if there were no such thing as a hook or a fish-rod in this wicked world.

In an hour there were four golden piles of fish lying on the bank, one by each rod, and the catch was going on as steadily as ever. We sent a boy up to the house to ask for a sack; filled it, and set to work to fill another. This we did by nine o'clock, and the tench were only just beginning not to be afraid of being caught—but to leave off feeding. We put our two sacks in the two dog-carts and drove home to our second breakfast. Then we sent the fish round to everyone in the little town to whom we could venture to offer them. In the poor people's houses the frying-pans were at work at luncheon, tea, and supper. Epicures stewed them with port wine sauce, and even we, who had had rather more than our share of tench in the uncooked state in the morning—for tench are, of fish, fishy—admitted that they were very fair eating. We caught another sackful next morning; and then the tench found us out. After eight A.M. not a fish would bite, and though several rods have visited the lake since, and caught roach, perch and pike, the remainder of the tench shoal will not look at a bait.

Perhaps in a dozen years they will have recovered from their fright.

Little is known of Davis's life, but we are sure of three things: he operated a tackle shop in olde London; he was not averse to a bit of jazzy self-promotion (as evidenced by the following advertising broadside); and he scared the living daylights out of kids in his neighborhood.

E. DAVIS

The Skeleton Angler

When the old clock in yon grey tower
Proclaims the deep, still midnight hour,
And ominous birds are on the wing,
I rise from the realms of the bony king.
My bonny elm coffin I shoulder and take
To fish in the blood-red phantom lake,
Where many a brace of spectral trout
For ever frisk, dart, and frolic about;
Then the hyaena's ravening voice
Gladdens and makes my heart rejoice.
The glow-worm and the death's-head moth
Are killing baits on the crimson froth.
For work-bench I've the sculptured tomb
Where tackle I form by the silent moon;
Of churchyard yew my rods I make;
Worms from the putrid corpse I take;
Lines I plait from the golden hair
Plucked from the head of a damsel fair;

Floats of the mournful cypress tree
I carve while night-winds whistle free;
My plummets are moulded of coffin lead;
For paste I seize the parish bread;
The screech-owl's or the raven's wing
For making flies are just the thing.
Should thunder roll, from the barren shore
I bob for eels in the crimson gore;
A human skull is my live-bait can;
My ground-bait the crumbling bones of man;
My lusty old coffin for punt I take
To angle by night in the phantom lake.
While Dante's winged demons are hovering o'er
The skeleton trout of the crimson gore,
To the blood-red phantom lake I go,
While vampire-bats flit to and fro.

SCENE THE SECOND (SUNRISE)

The owl is at roost in his ivy'd bower,
The bat hangs up in the old church tower,
The raven's head is beneath his wing,
The skeleton sleeps with the bony king,
The fierce hyaena has left the grave
To seek repose in his darksome cave.
The author of this piscatorial treat
Is the far-famed E. Davis, of King William Street;
Twenty-one is the number o'erlooking the Strand;
His prices are lowest of all in the land.

Outfit yourself with the identical tackle Izaak Walton used in the seventeenth century and follow his footsteps along the same rivers the master immortalized. As with all superb adventures, the impulse here is eloquently simple, lyrically resonant.

ROBERT DEINDORFER

Fishing Walton's Favorite Rivers

The fish jumped, a foot of gleaming silver, arched for a long moment in the soft, summery air, hit the surface hard in an effort to shake the feathered Judas lodged in its jaw. Quickly it drummed upstream, reaching for the fast water washing below a stone dam, where it jumped again, slim and perfect, a brown trout with an I-say-there English accent.

The brownie stunting in the picture river was not the biggest I have ever hooked, precise specifications of which I refuse to divulge for fear my career trophy might not sound as epic as it ought to, but it was not the smallest, either, especially after several seasons on the Battenkill in Vermont. Besides, the game was far from up. After all, I was fishing fairly fine, with a number 16 Cockwing Dun knotted to a twelve-foot 5x leader, which can add a shiver of suspense playing even small fish due to my boyish tendency to overreact before things have reached a proper boil.

For a change I managed to resist my customary manic impatience and let the trout gradually wear down, although there was an experience near a flat rock when it looked like more of the same old thing. In the end the fish slipped obediently into the net, quivering in the folds, went slack after a ritual blow with a staghorn priest, mine own, to lift a phrase from Izaak Walton, who was known to have lifted a few himself, the patron saint of angling, whose favorite waters I was sampling—something more than mine own, in fact, because that fourteen-inch brown trout happened to be the very first return in an intercentury challenge match I was personally conducting there on the Manifold River in Derbyshire.

The idea for such a match had evolved several weeks before during a long, hazy night with a British friend at a rural pleasure dome entitled Lords of the Manor. We talked motorcars, politics, literature, women, racehorses, the parlous state of the world, opening the catalog of our mutual interests, but mostly we talked fishing, which has both of us in its iron thrall.

"Of course you should fish at least one river exactly the way Walton used to fish, shouldn't you?" my friend Nigel said.

"What do you mean?"

"You know what I mean. I mean you should use kit straight out of the old fanatic's book—a rod six yards long, a line braided out of horsehair, genuine seventeenth-century kit."

Before a tolerant publican finally called Time, the two of us had improvised on that basic theme to a point where it sounded almost sane. According to the informal regulations we adopted, I was to work the Manifold with a good modern rod, reel, and flyline for an hour and a half, work the same stretch all over again with antique tackle, a close-up confrontation between now and then. The only slight cheat involved the choice of lures. Instead of fishing dry flies and nymphs with the flyrod and basic garden hackle with the blunderbuss rod, it seemed more equitable to use artificials with both rigs, despite Walton's chronic preference for live bait.

That fondness for back-to-nature lures shows through the pages of his classic work. "The trout is usually caught with a worm, or a minnow, which some call a penk, or with a fly, *viz.*, either a natural or an artificial fly," he wrote in *The Compleat Angler*. After tipping readers to the fact that trout feed by night as well as by day, Walton went into specific detail: "And the manner of taking them is, on the top of the water, with a great lob or garden worm, or rather two, which you are to fish with in a place where the waters run somewhat quietly." The amiable Royalist, while a wildly enthusiastic all-round fisherman, could by no stretch of the imagination be described as an expert with the fly, else he wouldn't have had to poach from others, as he did in the case of Thomas Barker, a retired cook, humorist, and outdoorsman, or fold in a long addendum specifically devoted to fly-fishing by his dear friend and adopted son Charles Cotton, beginning with the fifth edition of his dialogue.

If he amounted to no more than a recording secretary when it came to the fly, however, Walton cannot be faulted on his assessment of trout, including the demonstration model I had just landed. "The trout is a fish highly valued in this and foreign nations," Piscator-Walton advised his disciple during the course of their book-length rambles. "He is a fish that feeds cleanly and purely, in the swiftest streams, and on the hardest gravel; and . . . he may justly contend with all fresh-water fish, as the mullet may with all sea-fish, for precedency and daintiness of taste; and . . . being in right season, the most dainty palates have allowed precedency to him." In my own opinion, Walton, a didactic man who seldom had anything but the most lavish praise for particular fish, particular rivers, and attendant brothers of the angle, was putting it far too mildly in the case of trout. In my opinion, trout rank right up there with my wife and son, who need to be gently played on occasion, too.

After landing that inaugural trout on hard gravel in a swift stream, I continued on up the Manifold, fishing the likely spots with contemporary tackle that anglers more proficient than I could be proud of. I was using an eight-foot Leonard cane rod, a three-and-three-eighths-inch Hardy Perfect reel I uncovered with the help of an English town crier whose whirlwind lungs I hired to spread the word, and a double-taper floating Cortland line, which together had run me more than our hair-trigger family budget could stand, if only we were prudent enough to formulate one.

The dry flies and nymphs I was fishing, most of them, anyway, came from the Foster Sporting Services in nearby Ashbourne, established in 1763, as management generally reminds prospects in its literature, although the building on John Street, into which the firm had moved since my last visit six months before, was emphatically pre-Walton, the beamed front section where an assortment of flies was on display dating back to the ninth century. The fact that the flies were not only beautifully tied but came to merely twenty-five cents American, or half a bus token to the deadfall I generally patronize at home in New York City, put me in a mood so euphoric that I ordered far more than my usual ration.

A cheery man at Foster also sold me a cheap Severn-Trent Water Authority license good for seven days. The flip side of the ticket reminded everyone of the realities: "This license does not entitle the holder to fish in any private waters without permission of the owner." Since virtually all trout and salmon water in Britain is privately held, this meant I had to make some personal arrangements, which Foster Sporting Services completed on my behalf with its usual efficiency.

The blessings the proprietor had bestowed on me as I left the shop earlier that morning could hardly have been improved upon. "Tight lines," he said, "and if they're not as tight as you wish, you will have a memorable time of it all the same." A small trout boisterously rose, struck short, scudded away. I was fishing at no numerical profit now, but the whisper of the river, the soft green hills latticed with dry stone walls, some of them six feet high, and the cattle practically painted on the land already imprinted the gathering young day on what passes for my memory.

In a glossy run of water another small trout rose to the fly, a colorful blur in the sunshine. This one actually touched the fly, its jaws unhinged, reacting far faster than I, as frequently happens, the silence positively deafening. A galling amount of slack—"cumbered with too long a line," Piscator would probably have diagnosed it—allowed the fish to correct its tactical error before I could turn on some whiplash. It seemed almost blasphemous to expose my penny-ante reflexes there on one of the sainted rivers.

According to dated maps filed away in a local library, the Manifold follows much the same course it followed back in Walton's time, but the resident fish supply—like so much else—undoubtedly isn't what it used to be. More than three hundred years ago, for example, the abundance in England generally was so great that the maestro could admit to taking as many as twenty to forty trout at a standing. Several oak trees on adjoining fields go back to Walton or before, while the vicar swears that one public footpath pointed mostly east to west has been tramped ever since the fifteenth century.

Over a roll of many years, sights and sounds of modern times have intruded on the blissful old scene until, nowadays, the area in and around the village of Hartington looks much like any other part of rural England. But if cars drum up the narrow roadways, huge combine harvesters pick the fields clean of grain, and rude struts of television aerials rise like nightmares over the antique stone cottages, some of the pastoral scenes Walton portrayed with his normal relish still endure. Not the least of these are sheep, which graze the landscape in numbers so excessive that I literally found myself inundated in undergraduate lamb chops as I approached the Manifold by car. An alarming flow of sheep, patches of wool on their flanks stamped a proprietary red, driven by two small collies and a lank shepherd, covered the two-lane track.

"How many in this flock?" I asked.

"Approximately four hundred just now," the shepherd replied, his mouth a vacant wind tunnel suggesting that the state of British dentistry had not changed much since Walton's time, either.

The two-mile stretch of the Manifold assigned me for the day must have pleased the old boy beyond any singing of it. Like any river with real character to it, it varies considerably as it twines through the countryside, tumbling over stone dams, flattening in long slick runs, deepening in lovely pools, bending left and right, straightening briefly again, parts of it humped with rock, other parts shaded by beech or willow or oak.

Cursed with drought conditions, the water itself was not what it had been the season before, or the season before that. The blight had sunk the Manifold to vexing levels, thin and only ankle-deep in spots, and I do not suppose any of the stretch I fished ran to more than thirty feet across. What water there was was what Walton would have called silver and contemporary angling writers with a more jaded frame of reference invariably would describe as gin clear.

Despite the dry spell, however, which carried on for another few months, one long pool beyond a right turn in the river was four or five feet deep. Unfortunately, willow branches spread ominously close to the surface. After several tentative casts with a low sidearm motion, like Eldon Auker, who pitched for the Detroit Tigers in the 1930s, I climbed a ladder leaning against a steep bank, portaged through yellow musk around the frustrating pool, climbed back down into the Manifold a few yards upstream, where both the water level and the foliage along the bank were more to my taste, although I had no further success with my space-age rod and reel until I reached the tail of a more modest pool covered with nothing more than open sky.

A small trout was dimpling fairly close to the far bank, feeding on something I could not see, working a very small beat, sociable enough but never moving more than a rod length. The fish did not show the proper suicidal impulse when I cast over it first with an Upcher's Fancy and then with the Cockwing Dun, both in an eyesore size 16. But the first time I cast a British Oakden's Claret, the light sparse fly with the long tail was taken. There was a surge in the river, followed by a tantalizing pull. The trout had hooked itself, which was probably just as well, and from the feel it was no bigger than it had looked.

Whatever the actual size, I played the fish carefully on the light leader, mindful of the jangling warning Walton cast upon the centuries. "You may, if you stand close, be sure of a bite," he wrote of trout, a bit optimistically, I thought, "but not sure to catch him, for he is not a leather-mouthed fish." The soft gum tissues held while I slowly worked it in, a respectable brownie, eleven inches on the nose, a second vote for the status quo, no potential landslide, to be sure, but perhaps sufficient.

As things turned out, that was the sum of my experience with the Leonard rod: two trout, neither one especially big, not even for me. So much for modern times. In an hour and a half I had missed two other fish, cast to several more rising in the river, hooked a fly in the crotch of an oak tree, which water bailiff John Bonsall, who, at the age of eighty-five, followed me from along the bank, sort of, extricated with the crook of his walking stick.

Moments earlier, Bonsall had screwed his ruddy old face into a critical expression when I fished some open water without any cover. He didn't edit me by shouting across the Manifold, but it was perfectly clear that he didn't approve of my casting from a half crouch. If he had ever bothered to read the masterwork, of course, he must have covered the long swatch Walton's friend Cotton contributed, in which he specifically addressed himself to the plight of any brother of the angle fishing a shiny river on a sunny day. "And if you are pretty well out of sight, either by kneeling or the interposition of a bank or bush, you may almost be sure to raise, and take him too, if it be presently done," Cotton wrote. "The fish will otherwise, peradventure, be removed to some other place, if it be in the still deeps, where he is always in motion. . . ."

Since I was fishing a special Walton river for the first and only time, an eventual backache seemed a minimal price to pay. After all, whether Bonsall realized it or not, I conceivably might have gone to more elaborate lengths than a rheumatic crouch by way of camouflage. Among a number of artful ruses developed over the centuries, Dr. Thomas Birch, the Oxford scholar with the wonderfully telltale name, hit on what many anglers consider to be the most enterprising. Any time Birch set out to bamboozle the fish, he dressed as a tree—he would have been a smash at the Fancy Dress competitions that are such an integral part of British church and village fêtes—right down to an outercoating of branches, leaves, and even pine cones.

By the time Bonsall and I toddled back to the official starting point alongside a stone bridge and I assembled my blunderbuss rig, it was almost twelve of the clock, as Walton told time, which made me wonder whether the odds were not stacked against phase two of the competition between now and then. Fewer fish were rising in the river, the fly hatch had diminished, the speckled sunshine had given way to a bright cone beaming down from clear blue skies. In conditions like that, the long rod might cast a shadow roughly the dimensions of the Black Forest. Besides, I wasn't sure that I was up to doing the dated tackle justice, either, especially after the previous tour up the river had taken a bite out of my tired blood.

For a gaffer with so many years on him, John Bonsall expressed a bouncy curiosity in my tackle. Like a couple of strangers I encountered along the river later, he specifically wanted to know whether I had made the rod and line from scratch myself, which, mercifully, as I explained, I hadn't had to, thanks to a prominent British angling writer name of Dick Walker, who, when I phoned for advice on how to start braiding horsehair, kindly offered me the complete Walton kit he had concocted as a lark several years before. While the butt section of the three-piece, eighteen-foot rod was thick as the handle of a snow shovel, the tip thinned to a sporting size, live and supple, as I had learned on experimentally casting to, hooking, and landing an experimental trout on a reservoir in the Cotswolds the week before.

I have no way of knowing whether Walker laid on a troupe of Bavarian elves to help with the horsehair line or not, but, if he didn't he probably should have, at least if he followed the meticulous stricture Walton outlined in his dialogue. "First let your hair be clean washed ere you go about to twist it; and then choose not only the clearest hair for it, but hairs that be of an equal bigness, for such do usually stretch all together, and break all together, which hairs of an unequal bigness never do, but break singly, and so deceive the angler that trusts to them," Walton wrote without coming up for air. "When you have twisted your links, lay them in water for a quarter of an hour at least, and then twist them over again, before you tie them into a line: for those that do not so shall usually find their line to have a hair or two shrink, and be shorter than the rest, at the first fishing with it, which is so much the strength of the line lost for want of first watering it, and then re-twisting it." As a friend remarked on reading those stalwart directions, Walton could easily have moon-lighted turning out catch-as-catch-can bindings for pioneer bondage fetishists.

However Dick Walker had managed it, the line he sent me seemed more than adequate for my purposes, strong, loose, brunette in tone, free of the frets, unevenness, and scabs the father of us all had warned about. I knotted it directly to the tip of the rod in the seventeenth-century tradition—and, indeed, the tradition of my own faded youth, when modern engines such as reels were regarded as sissy stuff. In view of prohibitions up and down the Manifold, not to mention my own chronic sloth, certain modifications were in order in completing the kit I was to fish for the next hour and a half. Since the worms or penks Walton regularly fished were illegal despite my special pleading, I looped on a Cockwing Dun, a tiny number 16, with wings, a yellow body, and not much hackle. Instead of using the classic single strand of hair as a leader, or cast, I tied a length of 5x nylon to the braided horsehair line.

If my first few casts in a nice run where the river turned right were not an absolute disaster, they were enough to move Bonsall the water bailiff away from the bank where he had been leaning on his cane in a thicket of marguerite. A stand of birch trees close behind me rather restricted the movement of the epic tackle, but my own defective casting contributed to the basic problem too. Twelve feet of line tied to an eighteen-foot rod isn't my normal distance.

Still, the day thrummed with promise when a treeless stretch widened across to a steep rocky bank. Several fish—"a leash of trouts," as Walton would have said—fed in the sunshine, the rings of their rises enlarging, along with my hopes. Briefly, very briefly, I was fishing according to the code of British purists: I was casting only to rising fish. Swinging the rod with both hands, I dropped the Cockwing Dun lightly in the middle of a gathering ring, felt a slight but definite touch, pulled up too late, alas, an undeniable error I attributed to the long-range tackle. By the time the belated message finally reached me through a circuit of that total length, the fish undoubtedly had had time to read the fly-tier's signature.

After breaking the point of one hook on a flat rock, entangling another in a nest of stinging nettles behind me, and putting down more fish than I care to admit, I finally made what was, for me, a bull's-eye cast, three or four feet above a rising trout, in exactly the right longitude, in quiet water with no drag to it. The fish rose to the fly as if it had not eaten all day long. Once it engorged the lure, the trout showed no signs of being undernourished, however, running, running hard, stunting out of the water, abruptly doubling back, while I kept a bit of pressure on and wondered how to land anything with all that distance between us.

Eventually I was reduced to pulling in the rod, running it through my hands, foot by foot, trying to keep the tip elevated and giving no slack, until, with no more than five or six feet of it still before me, I reached far out and scooped my captive into the net. It was a reasonably good brown trout except for a slightly deformed right pectoral fin, nicely colored, fairly deep, breakfast size, all of eleven and three-quarters inches long, or more than enough to prove a point. Mark one up for old time's sake.

Given an open piece of water and an encouraging supply-demand factor, I saw no reason not to work the same arena after the remaining fish commenced feeding again. I humped down on the riverside, coating the walls of my lungs with the waste of another cigarette, pleased that Bonsall, who probably considered my antique fishing an American novelty item, had witnessed the encounter from the far side. It was pleasant sitting there smoking, making notes, confiding to a small tape recorder I packed along.

Yet it was even more pleasant when I started fishing that quiet flat water all over again. I took another trout, and another, ten inches and twelve and a half inches by my pocket measure, good fish, both of them, especially the biggest, far brighter than the usual brown, which would have looked magnificent hanging on my library wall if only it stretched a few more inches, three trout in thirty-five minutes of fishing with neo-Walton gear. Maybe the amiable old Royalist's primitive rig wasn't as quixotic as contemporary split-cane-and-floating-line anglers bluntly assume.

As I waded upstream toward the stone dam, a rumpled rustic walking a dirt track across the river paused to make some friendly noises. "If it's a few pounds of fish for dinner you want, I can nip back to the cottage for my spinning kit," he said, his voice stiff with a country accent. It was apparent that he didn't realize—perhaps because of my own formidable, no-nonsense tackle—that I was fishing for the sake of my soul instead of my stomach, the one being in greater need of sustenance than the other, and I declined his offer with appropriate thanks. Treating me to an encouraging thumbs-up signal I no longer felt any need for, he continued on up the river, a dwindling figure lighted in the sunshine, before he was finally lost to sight in a shelter of trees.

The brief encounter put me in mind of the touching misunderstanding an artist friend named John Groth experienced many years ago on a trip to Asia—Nepal or Afghanistan, I forget which. During a hike through the countryside,

Groth came upon a river so inviting that he could not resist the urge to joint up the Orvis Rocky Mountain Special rod he often packed along on trips in case he made a good connection. When several natives who spoke no more English than he spoke Urdu, or whatever, saw that Groth was having little or no success, they proceeded to rip limbs from nearby trees, string lines to them, bait primitive hooks, and start piling fish onto the bank. Smiling and pointing to the growing heap, they emphatically indicated that the fish were all for Groth, who, although he kept shaking his head, never quite managed to breach his sponsors' bedrock sense of pragmatism. In the evolving world out beyond God's back, as in Derbyshire, at least in the case of the countryman who had just passed by, anyone with a rod in his hands is regarded as a man in fundamental pursuit of fish to fry.

Up the river another few turns I missed a nice fish, the best of the day, no doubt about it, if only I had succeeded in landing it, which I did not when my leader snapped. But I took a small trout in the same run, nine inches, on an Oakden's Claret, fishing close against the leafy bank under a spread of willow. This latest captive, while it didn't make the competition a runaway, did make it fairly decisive, four fish to two, seventeenth century.

Swinging the triumphant long rod for a cast into some pocket water, I was transfixed by a cry from somewhere below me, a high, half-strangled sound, like the noise of an infant screaming for help. I peered back, searching for a stray child in trouble, and the cry rose again, not once but several times. Alarmed by the phantom noise, I looked quizzically over at Bonsall, whose broad face creased in a smile. "River hen, down under the trees, sounds like a tad of a boy, doesn't it?" he said.

At the deep pool that had given me such trouble on my previous tour with the Leonard rod, I sat in the grass pondering how to drift a fly onto the most likely part of it without hanging up on the foliage overhead. In the midst of my market research, I abruptly stiffened with excitement. There in the top of the pool lay an enormous fish, deep, husky as a fullback, occasionally twitching its tail. If it didn't quite measure up to Walton's extravagant description of "a trout that will feed six reasonable bellies," it was certainly big enough for a British family of four, to whom I was very much indebted for a splendid dinner party in my honor not long before.

Even Walton might have acknowledged that a prize so great as that called for extra precautionary measures, although he took a fairly stiff view of these matters. "And let not your line exceed—especially for three or four links next to the hook—I say, not exceed three or four hairs at the most, though you may fish a little stronger above, in the upper part of your line," Walton counseled with his normal bravado, "but if you can attain to angle with one hair, you shall have more rises, and catch more fish." In his hitchhike section of *The*

Compleat Angler, Charles Cotton was no less rigid on the subject of horsehair leader. ". . . he that cannot kill a trout of twenty inches with two, in a river clear of woods and weeds, as this and some others of ours are, deserves not the name of an angler," Cotton wrote. Not quite certain of my own name in these challenging circumstances, I replaced the 5x leader with stronger 4x, attached a size 14 Cockwing Dun, with which I had had most of my fish, and, almost magically, dropped the fly precisely where I hoped.

While a cast like that deserved something more, the big bull trout expressed no particular interest in my deceitful offering. It turned slightly in the water, regarded the fly as it passed over, fanned its fins, straightened out again, a demonstration of idle curiosity, nothing more. For fifteen minutes that ran my blood pressure up, I cast into the pool, as intended, or into the overhung foilage, as wasn't, changing flies every so often, revising the Blue Plate Special, trying Upcher's Fancy, Oakden's Claret, an import Hairwing Coachmen and Quill Gordon in size 14, all this without a flicker of genuine interest from my prospect out in the Manifold. Desperately I even tried an indigenous novelty nymph called the Derbyshire Belle, dark, bushy, and winged, two tiny red beads for eyes, ugly as sin, with the same response as I had been experiencing, meaning not much at all.

On my final cast of the intriguing day, from a few feet closer to the prize that had obviously resisted temptations far greater than mine during its long life, I slipped on a mossy stone. A perfectly good pair of patched corduroy pants and a sweater worn through at both elbows promptly flooded, which reminds me that American anglers are generally more informal in their dress, as well as their profanity.

On the better streams, our English brethren look like a full-page advertisement for Pickering and Hill, Ltd., of Old Bond Street, attired in tweed jackets and slacks, club neckties knotted against fresh shirts, under a grouse helmet, a deerstalker, or a twill cap, plus rainwear, of course, just in case. A friend with whom I fished some actually went so far as to change—he changed *upward,* mind you—after a cocktail party before we set off to fish the evening rise. Along with other differentials previously adumbrated herein, resident angling garb amounts to further culture shock for an outlander long accustomed to the easy informality of my home waters, the Neversink in New York, where participants dressed in anything more than denim shirts and rummage cords are suspected of putting on airs.

Despite the stiff upper British dress code, anglers are apt to belittle one another's general concept of fashion, especially in the matter of even more formal wear such as black ties. According to an especially sniffish member of the Fly-fishers Club of London, whose roll abounds with hyphenated names and pennywhistle titles, "Most of my fellow fishermen look as though they habitually catch fish in their dinner jackets." On the basis of two appearances at annual club dinners, I'm inclined to agree. Gentlemen anglers who invariably strike me as full-blown popinjays out on the riverbank gave off a rumpled, wrinkled, ill-fitting image of the South End social club in Aurora, Illinois, when they gathered for a hazy night of good company and good discourse, which Izaak Walton once identified as "the very sinews of virtue."

If the old prints are to be believed, Walton himself couldn't be charged with violating the local ordinance. A celebrated oil shows him seated against a tree along the Itchen, his rod, net, and wicker creel beside him, unmistakably a fop, wearing a vest, a waistcoat, a clean white bib, and white roll-back cuffs, looking for all the world as if he happened to be bound for a matins service at the nearest village—which might well have been the case a bit later, after he flogged the river some, because Walton was an all-rounder who took his religion every bit as seriously as the proper mix of groundbait.

I skinned down to nothing and wrung out my own wet down-home clothes before coiling the horsehair line and unjointing the eighteen-foot rod. John Bonsall hobbled over, turning his hearing aid on full throttle, for a last remnant of conversation.

"You did old Walton jolly proud, taking those fish on stroppy kit like his," he said.

Modesty prohibited me from responding in quite the boastful tone I felt entitled to employ.

The trip to a day of fishing is invariably a great pleasure, but in some ways the trip back after some successful sport is greater still. I was using a form of horsepower not known to Walton and those honest anglers he wrote of, six cylinders signed by Rolls-Royce instead of a live bay, but our sense of contentment teetered in a similar range. Six trout lay in the trunk of the car, memories, every one of them, moments to relive through the dark winter yet to come.

At the edge of a small stone village in Staffordshire, I heard the peal of church bells, just as Walton might have heard them, a lovely chord in the still day as some vagabond bell ringers took their turn, perhaps a complicated Cambridge Two or a Triple Bob Major, a sound reverberating through the centuries. The peal faded, I covered the narrow two-gauge road feeding on the memories I had scooped into the net, mourning the loss of that prize I hadn't.

After a number of reflective miles unwound, I decided that the bittersweet aspect of angling probably hadn't altered over the years, either. No matter how seldom he admitted in print to even a mild setback, the one and only Piscator, another of whose rivers I had just fished in his fashion, as well as my own, must have returned home every so often wondering why he had been repeatedly snubbed by a true beast of a trout, too.

Few people are aware that Charles Dodgson, at one time the world's leading authority on the topology of hypothetical constructs, rabbits, and the photography of little girls, was an avid fan of Izaak Walton. The evidence is contained in the following excerpt from a pamphlet published by the Oxford don. This stunning piece eerily reflects the brilliance of the writer who is perhaps better known as Lewis Carroll.

CHARLES DODGSON

A Conference

A conference betwixt an Angler, a Hunter, and a Professor; concerning angling, and the beautifying of Thomas his Quadrangle.

PISCATOR, VENATOR

PISCATOR. My honest Scholar, we are now arrived at the place whereof I spake, and trust me, we shall have good sport. How say you? Is not this a noble Quadrangle we see around us? And be not these lawns trimly kept, and this lake marvellous clear?

VENATOR. So marvellous clear, good Master, and withal so brief in compass, that methinks, if any fish of a reasonable bigness were therein, we must perforce espy it. I fear me there is none.

PISC. The less the fish, dear Scholar, the greater the skill in catching of it. Come, let's sit down, and, while we unpack the fishing-gear, I'll deliver a few remarks, both as to the fish to be met with hereabouts, and the properest method of fishing.

But you are to note first (for, as you are pleased to be my Scholar, it is fitting you should imitate my habits of close observation) that the margin of this lake is so deftly fashioned that each portion thereof is at one and the same distance from that tumulus which rises in the center.

VEN. O' my word 'tis so! You have indeed a quick eye, dear Master, and a wondrous readiness of observing.

PISC. Both may be yours in time, my Scholar, if with humility and patience you follow me as your model.

VEN. I thank you for that hope, great Master! But ere you begin your discourse, let me enquire of you one thing touching this noble Quadrangle,—Is all we see of a like antiquity? To be brief, think you that those two tall archways, that excavation in the parapet, and that quaint wooden box, belong to the ancient design of the building, or have men of our day thus sadly disfigured the place?

PISC. I doubt not they are new, dear Scholar. For indeed I was here but a few years since, and saw naught of these things. But what book is that I see lying by the water's edge?

VEN. A book of ancient ballads, and truly I am glad to see it, as we may herewith beguile the tediousness of the day, if our sport be poor, or if we grow weary.

PISC. This is well thought of. But now to business. And first I'll tell you somewhat of the fish proper to these waters. The Commoner kinds we may let pass: for though some of them be easily Plucked forth from the water, yet are they so slow, and withal have so little in them, that they are good for nothing, unless they be crammed up to the very eyes with such stuffing as comes readiest to hand. Of these the Stickleback, a mighty slow fish, is chiefest, and along with him you may reckon the Fluke, and divers others: All these belong to the "Mullet" genus, and be good to play, though scarcely worth examination.

I will now say somewhat of the Nobler kinds, and chiefly of the Gold-fish, which is a species highly thought of, and much sought after in these parts, not only by men, but by divers birds, as for example the King-fishers: And note that wheresoever you shall see those birds assemble, and but few insects about, there shall you ever find the Gold-fish most lively and richest in flavour: but wheresoever you perceive swarms of a certain gray fly, called the Dun-fly, there the Gold-fish are ever poorer in quality, and the King-fishers seldom seen.

A good Perch may sometimes be found hereabouts: but for a good fat Plaice (which is indeed but a magnified Perch) you may search these waters in vain. They that love such dainties must needs betake them to some distant Sea.

But for the manner of fishing, I would have you note first that your line be not thicker than an ordinary bell-rope: for look you, to flog the water, as though you laid on with a flail, is most preposterous, and will surely scare the fish. And note further, that your rod must by no means exceed ten, or at the most twenty, pounds in weight, for—

VEN. Pardon me, my Master, that I thus break in on so excellent a discourse, but there now approaches us a Collegian, as I guess him to be, from whom we may haply learn the cause of these novelties we see around us.

[Here PISCATOR and VENATOR meet with a PROFESSOR who, among other bits of wisdom, imparts the fact that "even an English book, worth naught in this its native dress, shall become, when rendered into German, a valuable contribution to Science!"

Next, a "conference with one distraught: who discourseth strangely of many things", i.e. a LUNATIC who "all the evening long saw lobsters marching around the table in unbroken order."

And, finally . . .]

VENATOR. Oh me! Look you, Master! A fish, a fish!
PISCATOR. Then let us hook it.
                          [They hook it.]

Once in a great while a first novel is published by a writer who, rather than standing on the shoulders of giants who came before, instead sort of squashes them.

DAVID JAMES DUNCAN

Dutch

There is a thing my father and his colleagues do that has always baffled me: whenever they find a good place to fish they return as soon as can be with a truckload of friends, take a hundred pictures, concoct descriptions intended to render it as alluring as possible, tell exactly how to fish it, and sell this veritable tourist brochure to the biggest publication they can find. Looking at the evidence, we can only conclude that they seek the prompt annihilation of their fishing grounds. This makes a kind of metaphysical sense: the metaphysicians, Titus tells me, say that Time is not *linear* but *cyclical*, and the unprecedented amount of chaos in our day and age is due to the fact that we are approaching the end not just of a Cycle of Time, but of a Cycle of Cycles. Now the fag ends of Cycles have always meant Bad Times, but compared to the end of a *Cycle of Cycles* they're almost mellow: someday soon, say the metaphysicians, so much cosmic havoc and hockey will hit the fan that the whole damned fan will short-circuit, Creation will go bideep, and Heaven will be forced to play the greatest Ace ever held in the hole to keep us all from biting the dust, which Ace will usher in the New Age. In the meantime, say the metaphysicians, if there's a Name of God that's dear to you, keep it on your lips and you'll be all right. Which is why what H2O and his colleagues do makes metaphysical sense: by ruining the fishing wherever they go, they speed us on toward the New Age; and by saying, "Jesus Christ! What happened to the fishing?" they keep a Name of God on their lips. My bafflement stems from the fact that H2O and his colleagues are adamant *non*metaphysicians and therefore neither perceive nor take pleasure in the esoteric wisdom of their actions. On the contrary, after spilling the beans in spades they return to the fishing hole, find a swarm of anglers, take pictures, write how rotten the fishing has become, concoct descriptions intended to make the place sound like a garbage heap, and get crocked when no publisher will touch this package with a ten-foot fly pole.

At the opposite extreme to this approach is (who else?) Ma and her backwoods buddies—who'd be hanged before they'd reveal the unpublicized and unfished-for anadromous runs they chase up local rivers. But the backwoods boys are schizoid, too, because they kill everything in sight till the fishing goes to pot, then they start cursing too. They curse the northward migration of retired Californians, the Fish Commission, the Army Corps of Engineers, the foreign fleets, and every other fisherman they see; they curse otters, mergansers, belted king-fishers, ospreys, eagles, raccoons; they curse Modern Times, logging companies, road builders, farmers who irrigate, factories that pollute (and for money they log, build roads, farm, and work in factories); they guzzle their booze, chew their chaws, look sadly at the river, and say, "They just don't make 'em like they used ta." To which Ma says, "But then they never did." And they nod, hangdog and brokenhearted.

It's a sorry fix for highbrow and lowbrow alike, and I've cursed and drunk many a time, in both camps. But the longer I waged war on the Wolf Clansman inside me, the more obvious the answers became: if you want a river full of fish, it won't help to advertise; it won't help to kill everything you catch; it won't help to work for a fish-killing industry; it won't help to curse and drink and lament. So I cut down on my killing; I tied more flies on barbless hooks; I built more fly- and fewer bait-rods; I told tales more than I gave tips; and I found myself loving rivers and fish and fishing more than ever before.

I'd learned, from Ma and the backwoods boys, of an unpublicized run of bluebacks on a stream not far from the Tamanawis; the same stream has a mediocre run of silvers that gets heavy pressure, but because of the salmon anglers' coarse gear and discommodious tactics the simultaneous superb run of sea runs moves upstream almost unscathed. It was on this creek (let's call it Shat Creek, in hopes that no one'll want to find it) that I encountered the more dangerous species of Notoriety:

It was late afternoon, mid-September; I'd driven to Shat Creek after a long stint of fly-tying and stopped on a one-lane bridge overlooking a deep pool. An old man stood at the head of the hole flinging a wobbler for salmon, but the water was so low and clear and the salmon so scarce he may as well have been fishing for Roosevelt elk. I didn't know it yet, but this man was my temptor; what I did know was that the slack water in the shadow of the bridge was lousy with fat bluebacks, lying deep, waiting for rain or darkness to move upstream.

The water was too quiet for fly-fishing, so I grabbed a light spinning rod and (alas, H2O) can of night crawlers, tied on a two-pound leader, crawled on hands and knees to the side of the pool, flicked in an unweighted worm and presto! I was into a seventeen-inch fish. When it jumped, the old man whoopied and came running, kicking rocks, stumbling, talking to himself, waving his arms—and boogering every blueback left in the hole. I landed my fish and killed it with a rock, then considered applying the same to the cranium of the old man, who was now trying to shake my hand while shouting what a nice jack salmon my trout was. But the fish were already spooked—right under a ledge at our feet—so in keeping with anti–Wolf Clan philosophy I tried to be friendly. It wasn't easy. While I tried to explain that the fish was a sea-run cutthroat, the old guy nodded like he'd never said it was a jack and sent his five-inch half-pound wobbler crashing into the center of the pool: a couple more bluebacks zipped under the ledge. I said, "What are you doin'?"

"Gettin' skunked, goddammit! Been fishin' my ass off all day and not a bump. Whatcha say ya got that jack on?"

I lit a cigarette and sucked it till my head rang while adrenaline and nicotine ran a footrace inside me: if nicotine won I'd have to sit down to keep from passing out; if adrenaline won I'd push the old fart in the creek. I sat down. Oblivious of nicotine's heroics on his behalf, the geezer kept strafing the pool with his B-52 wobbler. I watched him for a bit, then turned away to keep from having to light another cigarette: why should I die of cancer so he could keep spooking the fish?

I heard a sigh and a plunk and turned to see he'd thrown his pole in the sand; he sat on a rock, grimaced and said, "I'm plumb jinxed!"

"Or plumb dumb," I muttered, lighting another cigarette.

"Huh?"

"Nuthin'."

"Been here since early morning and nary a strike, and here you come for ten seconds and ZABBODABBO! ya nail a nice jack! How do you account for it?"

Between my nicotine and his zabbodabbo my head felt like it had a Liberty Bell in it. I stumped out the cigarette, caught my breath and said, "Lampreys."

"Huh?"

"Lampreys."

"Whatddya mean, 'lampreys'? What's lampreys got to do with it?"

I said, "Listen, Mr. Dabbo: you need lampreys out there, the way you fish. Lots of 'em."

"How come?"

"Because fish have an organ in their head which we scientists call a 'brain.' It's just a little brain, I'll grant you, but it's a brain nonetheless. But if a lamprey would latch onto a fish and suck its brain out, then the fish wouldn't mind if somebody kicked rocks at it and waved at it and threw a nuclear-powered wobbler on a transatlantic cable at it. So you ought to make it a rule of thumb always to fish where there's plenty of brain-sucking lampreys."

He said, "Oh," and lit a cigar. Then he sat and watched me. I watched him back. An inch down the cigar he asked, "Why'd ya stop fishin'?"

I nodded toward the water. "No lampreys. Just a lot of trout. In shock."

He said, "Oh," and watched me. I watched him back. Another inch down the cigar he said, "Sorry."

I liked him better then. I said, "That's all right. If we keep quiet a while maybe they'll hungry up."

We fell to gabbing and he turned out to be congenial enough. He knew an awful lot about the fishing around the state—and I mean "awful": everything he said was slightly askew, almost but not quite accurate, so that if you didn't know better you could spend a lifetime checking out his advice, and you'd find it just true enough to have an awful lot of awful fishing trips. When his cigar turned rasty he threw it in the creek (*zipzip* went two sea-runs, ssszft went the cigar), then asked if I knew anything worth telling about "our grand old sport." I said Yes. That was all I said. He waited and waited, then asked what it was I knew. I said I knew that if he wanted a grand old blueback he'd need lighter gear. He said, "I don't have lighter gear." And I amazed myself by saying "We can take turns with my pole." His face lit up like a chain smoker: he jumped to his feet, sent several chunks of basalt crashing into the pool, and *zipzipzipzipzipzipzip* went the bluebacks, back under the ledge. He cursed and apologized so profusely that I began to feel sorry for him; obviously the guy was a born oaf. I sat and pondered for a way to get this stumblebum into a sea-run . . . and had a brainstorm. I said, "Sit tight." He sat.

I went to a clay bank next to the bridge, grabbed a fistful of oozy gray clay, skewered a night crawler on my hook leaving lots to wiggle at each end, then squeezed the lump of clay gently around the worm. The old man marveled at my performance, pulled out a notepad, started to scribble and asked what I called this invention. I told him it was an old Estonian ploy the classical name of which I forgot, but that Estonian immigrants to America's fair shores had renamed it the Hostess Twinkie. He carefully recorded this flubdub on his pad. I waited for him to put his pen away, then handed him my pole.

We crawled to the ledge on hands and knees (I didn't trust him to walk); I flipped the bail on the reel and set the drag so loose that he couldn't break the leader no matter how hard he struck; then I lowered the Twinkie by hand down to the spooked cutthroat in the undercut; when the Twinkie touched bottom I said, "Get ready!"

We lay on our bellies, watching: the clay around the worm began to dissolve and crumble away; the ends of the night crawler emerged, writhing like a stripper coming out of a cake . . . the sea-runs went nuts! Four of them assaulted the Twinkie and the biggest swallowed it, mud and all, gulping it so deep that even Mr. Zabbo Dabbo couldn't manage to lose it. It was a nice trout, almost twenty inches; when we landed it he was ecstatic, literally jumping for joy— and sending another avalanche into the pool. But now it didn't matter: we had the formula. Two more Twinkies got us two more fish, then I said, "That's two apiece. That's enough."

He said, "You're right! Anyhow, I gotta rush back to town and write all this up for tomorrow's paper!"

I nearly choked. "Tomorrow's *What?*"

"Tomorrow's Oregon *Reporter.*" He beamed and held out his hand. "I'm Dutch Hines. The 'Fishing Dutchman'!"

Holy Hostess Hohos. Dutch Hines! He was so much more wrinkled and klutzy looking than the picture at the head of his biweekly column. He said, "You said your name was Gus, didn't you?"

"Huh? Who? Me? Gus? Oh, well, that's just a nickname."

"Well I'd like to interview you, Gus. By golly I would! Haven't had a better day's fishin' since I lost nine steelhead in one morning, on the Kilchis it was, two winters ago, with Fuzz Gramsay."

I told him I remembered that trip. Did I ever—he'd written twelve columns about it! Pen and pad in hand, he said, "So how 'bout that interview?"

Cripes! Dutch Hines. I didn't know what to do. All my life I'd marveled at his prose, amazed that any man could say so much about catching so few fish; even more amazed by his stubborn use of the editorial "we." He reminded me of a kid in my first-grade class, Mikey. Mikey used to talk about his pencil at Show'n'Tell. It was a fat green pencil with the school's name and district number stenciled on it. Every kid in the class had an identical pencil. But that didn't stop Mikey. He would hold it up for us to see, read the stenciled name and number to us, tell us it was a gift from his grandma, or his dad, or his uncle, tell us how green it was, and how fat, tell us how we must be sure to turn the dial on the pencil sharpener to the very biggest hole before attempting to sharpen such a pencil, point out to those who'd just joined us that yes it was a pencil, and yes wasn't it a fat one, and wasn't it green, and he'd show it and tell it and tell it and show it till children of frailer constitution started passing out from ennui and the teacher would have to carry him by his belt,

telling all the way, to his desk. The Dutchman's fishing trips were his green
pencil; the *Reporter* was his Show'n'Tell; and the addiction of America's eyeballs to newsprint constituted the invisible walls of an inescapable first-grade
classroom. . . . Dutch Hines! Crikeys. What to do? This bozo had easily three-
quarters of a million readers. That's 1.5 million eyes, barring cyclopses. And
he wanted to interview *me!* My brain began to lurch and flutter like a moth
toward the flame that will cook it. I knew his writing habits; I knew about
the Green Pencil Syndrome; I knew he would be show'n'telling about this
afternoon on Shat Creek, about the bluebacks, about the Twinkie, about *me,*
for many a column to come if nothing distracted him: And nothing *would*
distract him, because it would be weeks, maybe months, before he caught
another fish. I knew he'd made Fuzz Gramsay a rich man by endorsing him,
and that if I told him that I'd built the rod he'd just used he would do the same
for me; I knew that if he endorsed me I'd get a thousand rod orders before the
month was out; I knew that even if I lowered my prices, even at a meager ten
dollars profit per rod, that was ten thousand smackers; I knew that with profits
from that first burst of orders I could advertise in every major sporting magazine
in the country, could hire a half-dozen peons to do my rod-building and fly-
tying for me while I became a designer, an organizer, an entrepreneur; I could
open a tackle factory and warehouse in Fog; I could hire salesmen and financial
advisers and marketing experts; I could automatize and computerize and expand; I could spend my days inventing prototype rods and flies and let the
local peasantry hunch over vises, squinting their eyesight away and snorting
rod varnish; I could shunt Gus Orviston Autograph rods off to every corner of
the trout-infested world; I could put Fleas and Headless Hunchbacks and Bermuda Shorts on the map; I could buy a floatplane, a fleet of jet-boats, start a
guide service, take fat cats to all the great sport-fishing grounds on earth; I
could buy a jet, make connections in high places, hire politicians, hire accountants, secretaries, research assistants—all of them women, sleek-thighed
and soft-bosomed; I could open a chain of Trusty Gus's Custom Rods and Flies
that circumscribed the continent; I could invest, get into real estate, play the
stock market, cruise Tahoe and Vegas, start chains of Cutthroat Gus's Seafood
Restaurants, Cutthroat Gus's Riverside Fishing Schools, Cutthroat Gus's Trout-
er's Resorts; I could buy myself a harem to forget Eddy with; I could catch
(or buy the proof and claim I caught) record-breaking fish to heighten my repute;
I could speculate in land and lumber, subdivide the Coast Range, build private
solar-powered hatcheries and surround them with resorts; I could build a geo-
desic dome over the Tamanawis and control its ebbs and flows with a push-
button control panel by my half-acre bed where I'd loll with my harem, dic-
tating fish stories into computers that edited and polished and sold them for
national syndication; I could buy myself a nuclear aircraft carrier with built-

in spas and woods and trout ponds and sail out to sea to escape the rabble on weekends; I could make H2O look like a hick with a cane pole and bobber compared to me; I could buy the whole blasted coast of Oregon, name it Gussica, secede from the Union, start my own space program, make Titus my Lieutenant Spock and me the Captain of an Intergalactic Winnebago and blast away into space to search out potential trout planets and go where no fisherman had gone before; I could stock my new planets with Donaldson Rainbows, Montana Black-spotted Cutthroat, or the Salmo-Gussious Titantrout I'd have developed by then in Gussica's solar hatcheries; I could spread my name, face, rods, and flies all through the fish-infested heavens, and every resource and river, every hidden treasure and tree, every huge fish and alien queen and natural and unnatural wonder would spread itself before me . . . and so on.

"Well," said Dutch. "What do you say?"
I said, "Sure, Dutch. I'll do the interview."

The following day the Oregon *Reporter*'s three-quarters of a million readers found the following special double-sized column ensconced in their sports sections:

THE FISHING DUTCHMAN

Dutch Finds Redhot Cutthroat Fishin' on Shat Creek!

Well, we learned yesterday afternoon that there's nothing to the old saw that says "You can't teach an old dog new tricks." By a stroke of dumb luck this old dog learned a bagful of tricks from a young buck he bumped into who just might be the finest fisherman this Great Northwest of ours has seen in many a decade. We were trying for silvers on Shat Creek, but the run isn't what it once was, nor will it ever be until something is done about a problem this writer has pointed out again and again. We do not refer to pollution, overfishing, poaching, clear-cutting, bad management, or any of the things the ecology boys keep raising such a stink about. No, the culprit behind all the lousy fishing is, in our opinion, sea lions. That's right. Sea lions. And here's proof: just twelve years ago we were fishing with Jocko Dreyfus, who runs the excellent charter service out of Yaquina Bay, when we got into a school of silvers, and this writer had hooked a dandy when—you guessed it! A sea lion ate our lunker right off the line! We think every saltwater angler ought to carry a rifle and shoot these creatures on sight. Why, the blubbery monsters are so fat and active, one can easily guess how many salmon they swallow in a single day!

But getting back to the old dog and the young buck, his friends call him Gus, but he told us this is just a nickname and he doesn't know where it came from.

His real name is Antoine Chapeau, and he hails, believe it or not, from Palm Springs, California, where he used to manage a beauty salon. In yesterday's exclusive interview, Antoine told us,

"I got awful tired of looking at women's hair all day, Dutch. Most of 'em had hair just the color of monofilament, you know. The healthy ones reminded me of eight-pound test and the ones who wore wigs, once you pulled the wig off, reminded me of 5x tippet or algae or something. I got to thinking, 'This can't be healthy!' So I sold out, pulled up stakes, headed for Oregon, baited my hook, and started fishin'!"

And fish he does! With a passion and a skill he claims he learned in the desert around Palm Springs. Chapeau told us he learned to fish by studying books on mesmerism, Indian mythology, behavioral psychology, and by working with a fly rod out in the wastelands. Throughout his youth he diligently practiced an art he calls "Dry Fishing," and it is this that taught him both the incredible patience and the "shamanistic" approach to the sport that characterizes him today. Chapeau told us,

"After a day spent casting hookless flies into mirage creeks among the arid dunes, one begins to sense an order of things imperceptible to those whose minds are unaffected by extreme heat and dehydration. You see, Dutch, fish live in water. If one understands water one understands fish. And it is by craving water that one comes to understand it. Hence, to learn to fish, go to the desert and stay there. When the seizures and hallucinations start, you'll be amazed at what you'll learn!"

Sounds odd to us, too, but you should see the results! One trick he learned in the desert from an aged Estonian immigrant is called a "Twinkie." When the big sea-runs we were after shied under a rock ledge, Chapeau wrapped a wad of clay around a night crawler and lowered it down. As soon as the worm started poking out of the clay the big cuts smashed the "Twinkie," and did they ever put up a fight! We caught four in minutes, all fifteen- to twenty-inchers, then Chapeau made us stop. A true sportsman, he didn't want to deplete the supply. While we cleaned the dandies he talked about some of the desert lore he uses to take lunkers by surprise:

"In the first place, Dutch, you got to be superstitious as h—ll. You got to think like a witch doctor. There's too much science in people's approach to fishing nowadays. Fish don't understand science. But they worship magic!

"Take a trick I use on chinooks. (By the way, Dutch, not many know this, but the best runs of chinooks anywhere are in northern California, not in Oregon. You might go try it come November.) Anyhow, what I do when the chinook run is late is I get out my knife and carve a little salmon out of driftwood, then hook it on my line, cast out and reel it upriver. I do this seven times each in seven different places, and all the while I recite a Nootka Indian incantation, part of which, roughly translated, goes:

> Getting strong now.
> Time to spawn now.

Time to throng now.
Won't be long now.
Getting high now.
Time to die now.

When I finish this ritual I reel in, replace the totem fish with a conventional lure, cast back into the same water, and before long BINGO!"

Sounds strange, we realize, but Chapeau showed us the very knife he uses to carve those totem salmon! If more proof than this is needed, go try that Twinkie method on bluebacks!

Another interesting technique of Chapeau's is not for the modest! When he knows there are salmon or steelhead in a hole and they just aren't biting, he walks up to the edge of the water where the fish can all see him, props up his pole, pulls out a little line, places his lure on the ground a few feet from the pole, lays his landing net beside it, then retires into the bushes. In the bushes he strips naked, then he moves back toward the water, puffing his cheeks and writhing his nude body in a fishlike manner; he pretends to swim up to the lure, grabs it, pretends to be hooked, struggles for a while, then throws the landing net over his head and cries out in a loud voice so the fish can hear, "OH! WHAT HAS HAPPENED! OH! OH! I FEAR I AM CAUGHT!"

This sophisticated psychological pantomime serves to condition the behavior of the spectator fish, so that when he sneaks away to the bushes, resumes his clothing and casts his lure back into the pool they mimic his every action to a "T," and a limit is soon lying on the bank!

Sounds a bit weird, we admit, but don't scoff till you've tried it. Antoine showed me how he puffs his cheeks and "swims," and even with his clothes on it was very convincing. Besides, if the Twinkie worked (and did it ever!), why shouldn't these others?

Chapeau promises to share more angling secrets when we meet next week provided we print a message for him here. We don't understand the message, but we can't wait to hear those tips, so here goes!

Will the girl who ran from the guy who recited Izaak Walton in the tree please contact Gus on the other river he named. He has your rod and fish and wants to return them. He is totally harmless, but urges you to bring a loaded gun if frightened, as long as you come. Thank you.

Two days after a rash of irate letters poured into the *Reporter* offices accusing Dutch of senility, insanity, homosexuality, communism, and other perversions, demanding a new fishing editor and generally raising a stench. Perhaps the most eloquent of these epistles was from one Henning Hale-Orviston. Dutch quoted the least insulting part of H2O's letter in his next column, along with an apology to the makers of Hostess products, and in conclusion admitted that he may have been hoodwinked in part but that skeptics simply *must* try the fabled Twinkie. The same day I received a telegram from Ma. It read,

EVER HEAR OF A FELLA NAME OF CHAPEAU STOP
SOMETHING ABOUT HIM REMINDED ME AWFUL MUCH
OF A SON OF MINE STOP HIGH TIME SOMEBODY
PULLED RUG FROM UNDER THAT OLD FART HINES
STOP NICE GOING BOY STOP LOVE MA

Even after three hundred years, poor old Franck still hasn't been forgiven for calling Izaak Walton a "scribbling putatationer," a "mudler," and part cribber of *The Compleat Angler*. But you have to give Franck credit for declining the manicured charms of England in favor of fishing the moors of savage Scotland. No milkmaids there, Izaak; real anglers don't eat quiche.

RICHARD FRANCK

The Salmon and the Trout

As the salmon is a monarch and king in the freshes, so he is the ultimate result of the angler's conquest. This royal game (all the summer-time) has his residence in the rapid and forcible streams in rivers; but the sea is his sanctuary most months in the winter: So that a man may rationally conclude, without a parenthesis, that he is always to be found, though not always in season. Besides, the salmon is incident, as other fish are, to various accidents; more especially if we consider the female fish, who in the spring (as other females do) drops her eggs (but some call it *spawn*) which makes her infirm: and if it so happen that she lags behind her natural mate in the fall of the leaf, she is then prohibited the benefit of salt-water to bathe her fins, and carry off her slimy impurities, which is the natural cause of her kipperish infirmity, that alters her delicate proportion of body, and blots out the beautiful vermilian stain and sanguin tincture of blood, which vividly and transparently shines through her rubified gills; so that now she begins to look languid and pale, her fins they fag, and her scales by degrees lose their natural shining brightness; as also her regular and well-compos'd fabrick of body, looks thin, lean, and discoloured: and her head that grows big and disproportionable, as if distemper'd and invaded with the rickets; over whose chaps hangs a callous substance, not much unlike to a falcon's beak, which plainly denotes her out of season, and as plainly as any thing demonstrates her kippar.

Now I come to nominate some eminent rivers in England, that accommodate the angler with the race of salmon. First, therefore, I prefer the river Trent, because of her rapid and oriental streams, that never sully themselves, till arriving near to the shores of Gainsborough, where Trent oft washeth her banks with the Eagre, so glides immediately into the arms of Humber. Next unto Trent, we present you with the translucid glittering streams of Severn, that not far from Bristol mingle themselves with the ocean. Nor shall we omit those torpid and melancholy streams of Owse, that gulph themselves into Trent-fall. But of all rivers that glide through the cultivated fields in England, the bountiful, beautiful, and most illustrious Thames has the soveraignty of the rest; because her streams influence not England only, but all the banks and shores in Europe; and is without precedent, because of the excellency and delicacy of her fish, more especially below Bridg; where the merchants turn anglers, and throw their lines as far as both Indies, Peru, the Ganges, Mozembique, Barbary, Smirna, Alexandria, Aleppo, Scandaroon, and all the wealthy ports in the universe. These are the fish that feast the nation; otherwise England would be unlike it self, if unhappily wanting such provident anglers.

But Scotland has already received a character of most of her eminent rivers and rivulets, that wash and moisten her sandy shores; nor have I nominated more than four metropolitan rivers in England, that bathe her fertil and florid banks; because having a mind to step into Wales, or the suburbs of it, to discover there a singular curiosity, which probably may puzzle the opinion of artists and others. Now one of these rivers is called Wye, but the other is known by the name of Usk; both which rivers, as I am told, incorporate themselves on the southside of Monmouth. But the reason why I mention these two eminent rivers, is only in regard of their various entertainments, by reason the salmon there are always in season; for the one supplies the defects of the other. As thus for example; if when to consider Wye flourisheth with salmon, Usk, as if no river, is rarely discours'd of. On the contrary, when as Usk sends her supplies to the bordering inhabitants, then is Wye as little as any thing thought of. By this contrariety and diversity of nature, the natives may conclude that winter and summer give not only the season to salmon, but rather that they have laws from the streams they glide in; or Wales differs from all the world.

The next thing that falls under the angler's consideration, is the bait or charm for the royal race of salmon; which I reduce under the classis of two generals, viz. the fly for frolick, to flourish and sport on the surface of the streams; and the ground-bait for diversion, when designing to drag at the bottom. But what if I direct you a central way, that in my opinion, upon approved practice will intice him ashore in mid-water. Now if the angler design that for his exercise, (in such case) let him make provision of fair and large minews, small gudgeons, or a diminutive dace, (with the artificial use of the swivel to flourish his bait) the brightness or gloominess of the day considered: But if the ground-bait be intended, which always succeeds best in discoloured waters; then in such case, prepare for him a well-scoured lob-worm, or knotted dew-worm, drag'd forth of the forest, or any other sterril or barren soil, which as soon as any thing (with dextrous management) will compel him ashore though it cost him his life. I write from experience, for I am not unacquainted with the multiform variety of terrene animals; as you may read more at large in my following appendix: more especially of those worms that are taken and drag'd forth out of a hard and skirrous earth, which ought to be well depurated (or scoured) two or three days in the finest, cleanest and sweetest moss that fastens it self to the root of the ash-tree; sprinkling it first with new and sweet ale; afterwards remember to squeeze it forth, so operate like an artist: but that which is better, and more concordant to my approbation, is fleeted cream, from the benevolence of the dairy; which to admiration, makes your worm become viscous and tough; and that which yet is more to be admired, they also become bright, and almost transparent: for that end I counsel and advise the angler, when designing to approach the deeps for diversion, that he take some always with him to heighten his exercise, or influence and inamour his game. It is not so difficult to put some in a box made of wood called *lignum vitae,* perforated with holes, besmearing or anointing it over first with the chymical oil of bays, sulphur, Barbadoes tar, ivy, *cornu-cervi;* or indeed almost any other oil that has but a strong and fœtid empyruma, will serve well enough, where the oil of oesprey is generally wanting.

With these requisite circumstantials we approach the deeps, and the strongest descents and falls in the stiffest streams; the like we do in eddies, and turns in back-waters; for the salmon you must know loves a solitary shade. Arm well be sure, and fish as fine as you can, (*Isaac Owldam* used to fish with but three hairs at hook) and forget not the swivel, as above precautioned; and the running line be sure you remember. Stand close I advise you, and keep your distance, especially when approaching the rapid fords, because there, for the most part, the streams run clear, and you with design come on purpose to destroy him; as it's probable you may, provided your art, skill and ingenuity do but serve to manage so eminent an encounter. Now give me leave but to step from the water-side to numerate and describe the various brood of salmon; so to distinguish them according to mode, or as some will have it, the custom of the country. Where note, in the south they call him *samlet;* but if you step to the west, he is better known there by the name of *skeggar;* when in the east they avow him *penk;* but to the northward, *brood* and *locksper,* so from thence to a *tecon;* then to a *salmon.*

Now to recreate with the fly, (meaning the artificial) that's another sort of exercise for the angler's diversion; which ought to be considered, and diversely consulted, in regard of so great variety of form, lustre, beauty and proportion. For that end let me advise you, that the ground of your fly be for the most part obscure, of a gloomy, dark and dusky complexion; fashioned with tofts of bears-hair, blackish or brownish discolour'd wool, interwoven sometimes with peacocks feathers, at otherwhiles lap'd about with grey, red, yellow, green, or blewish silk, simple colours, or colours sometimes intermingled. For instance, black and yellow represent the wasp or hornet; and a promiscuous brown the flesh fly; so of the rest. For that end consult the humour of the fish, who to humour your exercise puts himself out of humour, chiefly and principally when he parts with his life. These requisite precautions ought to be the study of every studious and ingenious angler, together with the knowledg of time and season, when to resort to the river for recreation. The next thing necessary is the shape of your rod, which ought in all respects to represent the rush in its growth; for that end we call it rush-grown: and be sure it be streight and plient. Your line also that must be accurate and exactly taper'd; your hook well compassed, well pointed, and well barbed: and be mindful that your shank exceed not in length; I mean not so long as when you drag with the ground-bait. Nor is it proper for the artist to court a stream, except he be always provided of his dubbing bag, wherein are contained all sorts of thrums, threads, silks, moccado-ends, silver and gold twist; which are of excellent use to adorn your fly, and in a great measure quicken the sight of your game; provided the day be promiscuous and dark, occasioned by smooty and discoloured clouds.

Now should I enumerate the multiform variety of animals, the various colours and proportion of insects, with the diversity of flies, it would but redouble my labour and trouble; since already I have discoursed them in another place; where the artist also, if he be ingenious, may consult and examine the methods of experiments, so make himself master of this solitary mystery; otherwise let him remain silent among proficients, and a profest ignoramus among practitioners. And among the variety of your fly-adventurers, remember the hackle, or the fly-substitute, form'd without wings, and drest up with the feather of a capon, pheasant, partridg, moccaw, phlimingo, paraketa, or the like, and the body nothing differing in shape from the fly, save only in ruffness and indigency of wings. Another necessary observation, is the wing of your fly, which ought to proceed from the teal, heron, malard, or faulcon. The pinion and wing thereof ought to lie close, and so snug as to carry the point exactly downward. But the last thing material is, the moderate stroak, which always proves mortal, and best succeeds if used without violence; the line also, keep that streight as occasion requires, so that nothing be remiss, nor any thing wanting; and the necessity of the wheel be sure you remember.

The salmon loves those rapid rivers, where
The craggy rocks above the streams appear.
In deepest waters, and in strongest streams
He lives; yet like a martyr sometimes dies in flames.

I have already told you that the salmon is king in the freshes: And now I must tell you that the princely trout has his residence and principality in the same fluctuating element, partaking very much of the nature of salmon, admiring stiff and rapid streams in the vernon ingress; but he accosts the solitary deeps most months in the winter. In the spring, you shall observe this active animal scud to the fords, where he flutters his fins at every silly fly; for that's his rendezvouz, and there you'l find him, picking and gliding against stones in the bottom, to scour off, if possible, the slimy substance and scurf from his sickly sides, frequently occasioned through want of motion. So that when the sun vegetates and invigorates the creation, then is he invigorated with motion and activity, which argues a very great and unpardonable absurdity in the ignorant and incredulous angler, to fancy that peregrination debilitates and weakens him, when apparently it adds an additional strength, not well considering they were only told so; or peradventure they had read it in some printed book, concluding from thence an infallibility in the press.

But as I intend not to burden you with circumlocutions, for brevity sake, I shall range the trout under the consideration of the first classis of fish. For that end, I must signalize his vivacity and vigour, his activity and courage, how naturally they spring from the nature of this fish, till age or accident indispose and deprive him, not only of activity, but of natural ability; who struggles with himself to out-do motion, and out-live, if possible, the law of his life. So that to prohibit him travel, you totally destroy him; since he is a fish that can't live under confinement. And thus it happens to the race of salmon, for nature's laws are alike to both. In the summer's solstice he accosts the fords, making inspection and inquisition after the variety of emmits and

insects, hovering his fins in every murmuring purling stream in rivers and rivulets, which not only puts a spur to the angler's exercise, but his expectation also: and this, if any thing, is the angler's Elizium, which I shall not insist upon here, because having inlarged upon it sufficiently already. In this place I shall only treat of the ground-bait, which most commonly is a knotted or budled dew-worm; much of the nature and kind of the former, but not usually so large as that we procure for the salmon.

Now as every angler concludes the trout a delicate fish for diversion, so others, as artists, consult him a delicious entertainment. But the trout to entertain himself, as eagerly sucks in a well-scour'd red-worm, as the wide-mouth'd Humber swallows up a full spring-tide. For that end, grudg him not what he loves, and give him time to digest it. Your business is only to stand sentinel, and to keep a vigilant eye and a diligent hand over him; for patience is not only an exercise but an excellency in anglers, provided they fall not asleep at their exercise; especially when angling or troling with the ground-bait, which upon probate proves most profitable after gluts of rain and dis-coloured waters. Nor is this ground-bait otherwise than a worm, variously discours'd by me at several times, and in sundry places. For that end (to avoid repetitions) where the worm fails of success, make trial of the minew, in sharps or scours, by dragging at the bottom, or in mid-water; which if dextrously performed (with the swivel) by the hand of an artist, he shall seldom or rarely fail of success.

But for the fly-fishing, if that be the artist's intention, let me soberly advise him to solicite moderate winds, rather than intemperate and violent gusts. Rally my reasons, and sum them up; you will find them more copious in my former conference, where at large I discourse and decipher both the shape, colour, and the proportion of flies; for I hate tautologies, because hateful in themselves; and there's nothing more troublesom to an ingenious artist, than to be glutted by telling a story twice. The trout, therefore, judicially considered, his mouth is not by much so large as the salmon's, nor requires he so copious nor so large a hook, nor need his tackle be so robust and strong. But for the rod and line, take care, that they in all respects be exactly tapered. And to hit the mark as near as may be, let care be taken that the line in every part be equally stretch'd, and the steel of your hook of an even temper; nor matters it how light you are arm'd at the hook; so that on the surface, when you flourish your fly, be sure that you gain the head of the stream; and if possible, the wind, to facilitate your cast. But if the ground-bait be your exercise, then let the length of your line seldom or rarely exceed the rule of your rod: whilst the fly-diversion grants a larger charter, distance and dimension also come under the consideration of every artist that is mindful to measure exact pro-portion, by concealing himself from the streams he sports in. So that if at any time the fly fails of success, as frequently it has happened to my self and others, let the angler then have recourse to the ash-tree-grub, the palmer-worm, caterpillar, green or gray drak, the depinged grasshopper, or that truculent insect, the green munket of the owlder-tree. But if none of these baits presented, succeed to profit, and the water, as we apprehend, to remain discoloured, let him then assault the trout at the bottom, with that mortal allurement which I call the gild-tale; for that of all worms allures him ashore.

> The generous trout to make the angler sport,
> In deep and rapid streams will oft resort.
> Where if you flourish but a fly, from thence
> You hail a captive, but of fish the prince.

At first glance this appears to be a typical "Me 'n' Joe" story, nothing more than a historical curiosity written in 1899. Then comes that chilling last line.

WILLIAM FREED

Fishing in the St. Vrain

"HELP! Help! Help! Come quickly. I can hold on no longer."

This call, uttered in a piercing shriek, came from our companion, Bert Andrews, who at the moment was holding on with fingers and toes to the crevices in the great wall of perpendicular rock that lined the St. Vrain cañon. Below his feet rushed the mad waters of the river, the bed of which was strewn with great boulders. To fall into the swift cataract of water meant certain death. This was known to every venturesome fisherman, and as the only route through the dangerous cañon was obtained by holding on with foot and hand to the seams in the side of the rock, very many were deterred from undertaking the passage.

To go through the cañon was, however, the supreme test of courage and every sportsman visiting this picturesque section of the Rocky Mountains aspired to the honor of having successfully accomplished the dangerous feat.

Andrews was a genuine sportsman and no obstacle, however great, could stand between him and the game he was pursuing; but he was in failing health at the time of this, his first attempt to go through the perilous passage, and his failure was due to exhaustion.

His cry for help reverberated through the cañon and mingled with the sound of the waters as they rushed madly among the great mass of fallen rock. It was heard by his four companions, each of whom was in precisely the same perilous position, but they immediately responded to the call and in a few moments strong arms were assisting him to a place of security.

We had left Camp Billings, which is situated on the St. Vrain River a few hundred yards west of the old Long's Peak trail, at the first break of dawn of a beautiful July day. Under the guidance of our host, Josh Billings, who, assisted by his wife, furnished the entertainment for the tramp. We struck out over the range in a southwesterly direction for a distance of five or six miles. The journey was accomplished without feeling fatigue, although the grade was oftentimes steep and the sun scorching hot. Killing a couple of rattlesnakes, which were found disporting themselves on a flat rock in the sunlight, proved an exciting diversion and relieved the monotony of the tramp through sage, cacti, scrub-oak, and mesquite.

At the point where we entered the river, a magnificent view of the range was obtained, with Fremont's and Long's peaks in the foreground. There was the charm of snow-capped peaks on that summer day that words cannot express. The enjoyment which such a sight affords is as pleasant in retrospection as it was in reality.

To reach the river we had a hard climb, downwards of fully half a mile; then a plunge, a cast into the stream and zip! the first trout. We found the water icy cold and between two and four feet in depth along its entire course. The cold water produced a severe shock and our pocket flask came in opportunely. The fish were abundant, small in size, though we caught some trout that measured twelve to fifteen inches, but the greater number were much smaller.

After lunch, the pipe, and then the stories of former fishing trips. On this day the topic of conversation was the cañon of the St. Vrain, which we were approaching, and the large trout that frequented the pools and deep holes beyond its precincts. Josh Billings confirmed every story of the big trout taken on former occasions, and succeeded in working the entire party into a condition of mind that can be best described as a frenzy of enthusiasm, by the recital of a recent, big catch where the fish taken would tip the scales at three pounds. These stories settled the question about making the trip through the cañon for the entire party, and reduced the danger to be encountered to the minimum. No other member of the party was more enthusiastic over the prospective landing of the "big fellows" than was Bert, who was enjoying his first fishing in the Rockies.

The St. Vrain at the entrance to the cañon has a fall of about twenty feet to the mile. Great walls of rock rise above the river on either side and nowhere is there a safe foothold. Around and over the rocks in the river bed the water rushes and swirls, and he must be the possessor of a stout heart who does not shrink from the dangers so vividly apparent.

But there are big fish in the pools beyond the danger point, and this fact puts courage and strength into the sportsman and eliminates all fear from his mind.

It was the expectation of taking some of these big trout that brought our friend into the dangerous position in which he is found at the opening of this story. He was assisted through the perilous passage by two of his companions, and after regaining sufficient strength proceeded to whip the pools down stream.

It so happened that on this occasion Bert was the only one to take a large fish. He was a "whopper," to use Bert's expressive language, and never was a fisherman so fully compensated as was this fellow who a few hours before had expected to meet a horrible death in the waters from which he had taken so much pleasure.

On reaching the camp, Bert, although nearly exhausted, held his two-and-a-quarter-pounder before the members of the party for their admiration, his face reflecting the pleasure that welled up within him.

A few months later I visited Bert in Denver. Consumption had wrecked his body and he was about to die. While seated beside his bed one night he suddenly exclaimed: "Say, do you remember that big trout that I caught after going through the St. Vrain cañon?"

The memory of taking that fish was the last pleasure in this life enjoyed by Bert Andrews.

You've seen how the Yanks handle match fishing (see the piece by Roy Blount, Jr.); now read how the Brits do it. Granted, it's not quite cricket—more maggot than anything—but Gammon's title says it all. Here truly is a strange and fairly disgusting fish story.

CLIVE GAMMON

A Strange and Fairly Disgusting Fish Story

The first thought to strike one—and it turns out to be monstrously unfair—is: Hey, this must be where all those English soccer hooligans go when there's no game, no storefronts to smash, no foreign fans to beat up.

It's 7 A. M. in Scunthorpe, a large town a few miles south of the vast shipyards of Hull on England's North Sea coast. Milling about in the bright sunlight on the grounds of Quibell Park, a pretty little stadium, is a crowd maybe 2,000 strong. If one looks hard, one can pick out a few men in their fifties wearing blazers and carrying clipboards, but the great majority is younger and affects studded leather belts, lank hair worn long, and meticulously filthy jeans. They appear to be the rabble one might run into—and maybe away from—at Wembly or Indy or on the infield at Churchill Downs on Derby Day, the kind that give the distinct impression they're looking for something to molest, stab, or burn down.

But what these lads have very seriously on their minds is going fishing. At least that's what the 960 of them who constitute the eighty teams of a dozen anglers each (the other 1,000 or so chaps are spectators) are concentrating on as they prepare to compete for the 1981 National Championship of England, a title that in one form or another has been awarded annually, except in wartime, since 1903.

To an American angler, the style in which these Englishmen will fish, the equipment and baits they will use, in fact almost every aspect of the day's fishing would be as alien as cricket would be to a Little Leaguer. Yet cricket, a sport molded by the English upper classes, draws in some ways an inapt analogy, because match angling, as this sort of fishing is called, is strictly working class. It was originated by the men who toiled in the ironworks of the Industrial Revolution, who flooded in from the countryside to labor in the dark Satanic mills of Manchester and Sheffield and to live packed into grim terraces of tiny houses.

With the advent of the railroad in the mid-nineteenth century, such laborers found a degree of liberation. On weekends they would buy cheap excursion tickets back to the countryside and fish. The pellucid streams of the North and the West Country, where the laborers' ancestors might have cast, were now reserved for their "betters," because in those streams swam the game fish, the salmon and trout. But relatively close to the great industrial cities, fishing of a kind was available. There, in the sluggish, already polluted rivers of the middle of England, were what the gentry contemptuously labeled "coarse" fish—small, slimy species, for the most part inedible.

So match angling was born. If the fish were nothing to write home about, why not make a competition of it, have a bit of a gamble? Skittles alfresco, as it were. The anglers would divvy up a riverbank into short sections called beats, marked by numbered stakes, and then draw lots to decide who fished where.

At first it was a rough-and-ready pastime. In 1953 J. W. Martin, a noted angler, wrote sniffily of a competition held in 1918: "This particular match had only about fifty contestants but they must have been selected from the very scum of the Sheffield dregs . . . the very lowest of the low grinders, men whose every word was an oath; men who exchanged compliments so painful and free that I should have thought would have blistered the tongues that uttered them. Those men consumed more beer and tobacco than was good for them, and in short conducted themselves in such a manner that any respectable angler who was looking on felt ashamed. . . . Every now and then one of the competitors would yell at the top of his voice to another fifty yards away to inquire in language more forcible than polite if he had 'copped owt yet' and that one would reply in still more forcible terms, 'Ave I. . . .' "

Match angling has come a long way since, spreading right through Europe, including the Eastern bloc countries, but the sport is still resolutely working class in England as elsewhere. Archie Bunker would definitely be into the sport, though a little past his prime now. British environmentalists have been ecstatic since the Atlantic salmon started to make a comeback in rivers like the Thames about six years ago, but matchmen, as these fishermen call themselves, have been conspicuously unmoved over the news.

Nothing, short of a groundwater sump, could be less like a salmon river than the body of water where the 1981 National Championship match was to be fished: a ten-mile-long canalized section of the Ancholme, a narrow, almost featureless waterway that is, therefore, ideal for match angling, the aim of the sport being to give every competitor an equal chance to catch fish.

But the Ancholme has a drawback. Roving in it are bream, some of them grotesquely large by matchmen's standards, three-, even four-pounders. They aren't there in great numbers, but a few anglers are undoubtedly going to draw positions where they will catch one or two, thereby turning the whole damn thing into a lottery. It seemed that luck, not skill, would prevail this day.

And even though on this sunny morning at Quibell Park there was a real lottery, on the National Championship, with a first prize of £2,000 (about $3,700) available, most everybody would rather employ his wits and back his favorite with Billy Knott, Jr., the Angler's Own Bookie. Even before the draw for beats is made and the star anglers' positions are known, Knott is shouting the odds on crack teams like the Barnsley Blacks.

"Should've got in when Pete did," mutters a disgruntled bettor with ROTH-ERHAM RAIDERS emblazoned on the back of his jacket. "Pete got 10s. Now it's gone down to bleedin' three to one. Three to one in a field of eighty bloody runners? That ain't no bloody bet."

Scunthorpe is a steel town, savagely hit in the present recession with a 25 percent unemployment rate. Yet one has to fight to give his money to Knott. He has brought along two assistants to count the notes that are filling up deep plastic tubs. He also has employed Dennis the Minder, a heavy gentleman with the look of an ex-pug, who never strays more than a foot away from the tubs. A plunger elbows through the knot of bettors and slaps £1,200 down at one hundred to one on the unfancied team from Derby. Knott takes the bet at those odds, but he quickly turns, scrubs his blackboard and revises the odds on Derby to twenty-five to one. The Angler's Own Bookie will take bets on individual fishermen as well as on teams, but there are too many to post. One has to accept a whispered quotation.

The draw is at 8 A.M. The Ancholme has been divided up into thirteen lengths labeled A through M, and each length has within it eighty beats, marked off by numbered stakes some forty-five feet apart. When the Barnsley captain steps up and draws number 35, it means that one of his men will fish at Section A, Stake 35, the next at B-35, and so on up the river. Thus each angler is far enough from his nearest teammates so that, in accordance with the rules, no communication is possible.

After the draw, there's a glacial Le Mans start. Buses have been chartered to take the contestants and their equipment as close to their stakes as possible, and one after another they lumber off. The match itself won't start until 11 A.M., but every moment of that will be needed for the competitors to get their equipment properly set up.

Among the match anglers' gear are things most fisherman are acquainted with, like rods, but there also are wagglers, sticks, bombs, feeders, micromesh keep nets, slingshots, and, of course, plentiful supplies of cloud bait, squatts, gozzers, jokers, and bloodworms, the last having nothing to do with the marine worm that is commonly used as saltwater bait in the United States. Rather, bloodworms are the larvae of the gnat.

The sheer bulk of a matchman's equipment is daunting. Most of it is carried in what looks like a small steamer trunk and in a rack holding as many as seven or eight rods. Altogether, the weight of a properly outfitted angler's tackle is rarely less than forty pounds, but the matchman's caddie is a figure who has yet to evolve.

Nor has anyone ever worked out with precision just how much match angling costs. It's safe to say, however (leaving boats out of it), that the investment is rather more to set oneself up as a perfectly equipped matchman than as a marlin fisherman. No marlin fisherman, for instance, has to pay £900 for his rod. Just *one* of his armory of rods, that is. Matchmen do.

Opening day of the match season is June 16, and on its eve, one of the extraordinary sights of the London year is at Don Neish's Tackle Shop in Edmonton, in the northeastern part of the city. A line of matchmen stretches way down the block, the anglers waiting patiently to make bulk purchases of gozzers, jokers, squatts, and the like (patience, all will be made clear soon). It's not the sort of day on which to inspect Neish's stock of rods, although if he has a second he may recount to you the legend of the first high-priced Japanese graphite match-fishing pole that he placed on display.

That was six years ago, and the price then was a mere £860. Neish didn't expect to sell it—"Costs more than me bleedin' motorbike" was a typical remark of his clientele—but it brought people into the shop. The problem was that they all wanted to hold the rod.

In a flash Neish saw a way to cash in on the rod. He announced, "Ten pence a hold," which was not quite as avaricious as it may sound because each time the rod was held, Neish reduced its price by 10p. Roughly 500 holds later, Neish sold it for £800.

To understand why a matchman pays as much as £900 for a rod, one must understand that match fishing involves catching very small fish at very high speed. And also that a lot of money may be on the line, so to speak.

The now-standard graphite match rod is thirty-three feet long when fully extended—the better to fish far from one's stake—and on the Sunday before the National Championship just such a rod was used to excellent effect by Dickie Carr, a thirty-five-year-old truck driver from north London, on a canal in the sheep pastures of Romney Marsh in Kent. His line was a two-and-a-half-pound-test wisp; his hook a number 26, which is about the size of this "j"; and he was catching fish whose average weight was a half ounce. He had no reel, the thirty-three feet of graphite making it unnecessary to cast, and he was using a "wobbler," a type of bobber, of which a moderately well-equipped matchman will have sixty to seventy. This one was a sliver of balsa wood, of which perhaps only a sixteenth of an inch floated above the water's surface. Carr's movements were close to automatic. First he threw out a tiny ball of finely ground cereal that contained a sample of two sorts of hookbait, squatts, and pinkies (I swear an explanation is coming in a minute). Occasionally, when he needed more distance, he wielded a slingshot to fire his bait out into the water. Carr quickly flipped his hook, baited with a single pinkie, into the milky chum slick. The float tip moved fractionally. Or Carr said it did, and it must have, because immediately thereafter a tiny silver fish was swung out of the water and dropped in the net—the eleven-foot-long keep net that holds the catch alive until it is weighed at the end of the match. Then Carr began the procedure all over again. He hit at a rate of about one fish every two minutes—and no other rod material but enormously expensive graphite is light enough to make a thirty-three-foot pole that one could hold outstretched for long periods of time. "Won about £6,000 with that rig so far," Carr said. Hence the second reason for the £900 rods.

Carr hadn't been as happy the previous day when he fished in a match on the Thames at Goring. It was an idyllic scene out of *The Wind in the Willows*: plum brick Queen Anne houses for a backdrop; fair-weather cumuli floating overhead; wild roses and elderflower in full bloom; all the birds in full voice. The peace was disturbed only by a floating gin palace called *Rive Gauche* that could well have been steered by Mr. Toad.

Carr didn't appreciate that setting because the little fish weren't cooperating. The match was won by an angler who waded out over a shallow cattle run and pulled out a thirty-pound-chub, a carplike fish. That is a fair-size fish by most standards, enormous by a matchman's. And he wasn't even using gozzers, let along pinkies.

Well, no longer can it be avoided. We must come forth with a recognizable definition for this bait. Here goes: pinkies, gozzers, squatts are all maggots; politer folk sometimes use the word "gentles." Without them, match fishing would scarcely exist.

To most people, the larvae of bluebottle and greenbottle flies, maggots, are simply disgusting. To coarse fish, they are the staff of life. Gozzers, often specially bred on decaying chickens or pigeons, are particularly succulent and thin-skinned. Squatts are small, used mainly as chum, and pinkies are just ordinary pink maggots. They can be dyed orange and bronze, ostensibly for attracting fish, but actually for attracting fishermen. Disused military airfields are frequently used as maggot factories for sanitary reasons: Both the smell— maggots are bred on carrion—and the working conditions are appalling. But maggot raising is highly profitable; Neish sells almost 500 gallons, at £20 per gallon, on opening day. The maggot breeder can also be stricken by sudden disasters, as when refrigeration fails or when high-quality flies, as valuable to maggot breeders as good studs are to horsemen, die and have to be replaced, at famine prices, by stock from rival owners.

There are dark stories of feuds among breeders, tales of powerful insecticides being let loose on stud flies, of electric cables cut. It's hard to get confirmation, though. The maggot industry, thankfully, is very secretive.

As is the bloodworm biz. Bloodworms are a lot more expensive than maggots. A pint can cost £13, and that measure includes the damp peat the worms are kept in. One gets about 1,000 bloodworms to a pint, some so tiny—jokers, they're called—that one has to use a hook as small as a 24 to present one. Normally, though, bloodworms are used as chum.

There are no bloodworm factories. They are collected by individual entre- preneurs from the mud of stagnant ponds, and especially in winter. The life of a bloodworm man is a hard one. He wades up to his armpits in icy water, toting a scythelike implement, called a scraper, that he draws through the silt when he gets down to business. If all goes well, bloodworms by the dozen will be draped over the edge of the scraper when it emerges. The bloodwormer also has to protect his patch, physically if necessary, from poachers.

Naturally, in a sport where the financial rewards can be considerable (though not overwhelming—prize money, plus backing oneself with a bookie, plus endorsing fishing tackle can earn an angler as much as $9,500 a year), a certain amount of sharp practice goes on, but it usually takes the form of gamesman- ship rather than cheating.

"Say I get a fish early on," one prominent matchman says. "If there's some- body sitting alongside me I want to aggravate, I take the hook and make sure it's well into the fish and slip the fish into the water again so it swims out a little way. Then I catch it again and again and again, and by this time the bloke next to me is redoing his rig, getting nervous, spilling his shot (sinkers). He feels unreal.

"But there's illegal things, as well. People carry small live fish to matches in the butt section of those 10-meter poles. It's a nice, long, cylindrical con- tainer, and you can fill it with water. You might be in such a bad stretch that one little fish could be the winner.

"It only has to be a *fish*, remember, and alive. It only has to have fins on. I've dragged my keep net through the weeds in some places and got fourteen little fish that I would be happy to have swimming around in my keep net at some matches."

Match fishing, like any professional sport, also has its star system. It can be as difficult to get a phone call through to a master angler like Ivan Marks of the Barnsley Blacks as to a star quarterback, and sometimes when he fishes in a match, Marks, forty-four, has a gallery that many a golf pro would envy.

"What will happen on Saturday," said Marks, a week before the National Championship, "is that the Barnsley lads will guard me like I was God. They'll smuggle my tackle separately onto the bus. I won't have a name on my jacket, nothing, because if the fans know where I am, if I get a couple of hundred people watching me, then I can't control them. And they cause vibrations. There might be just one fish around my stake, and that fish will get the vibrations and he'll be gone."

One tiny fish can be that important because under the scoring system, the angler who has the top weight in a section gets a point for everyone he beats. The second highest gets the same score minus one, and so on down to zero. But if one catches no fish, one gets no points, so if you have a half-ounce fish and thirty anglers in your section get nothing, that lone minnow is worth thirty-one points toward your team's total.

There was an extraordinary example of that, Marks related, in 1972, when he was a member of the Leicester team. Leicester won the National that year simply because in a particularly bad section the Leicesterman caught a *quarter-ounce* fish and collected sixty points for it.

The whole sport of match angling seems cold, technical, and money-obsessed at times. Marks himself will tell you that he gets no thrill from ordinary fishing—which matchmen call, with contempt, pleasure fishing—"unless they pay me, too, for the TV. If I just happen to be out with a friend, a good friend I laugh and joke with, then I've got to fish him for *something*—a cup of tea, a stick of chewing gum, a cigarette. And then I become a nasty enemy. I have to win. I have to say, 'I am the best today.' "

Even so, Marks confesses that as a member of that winning Leicester team he was crying like the others when they went up to get their trophy in front of 6,000 or 7,000 fans. "Tell me," he said suddenly, "are there places in the States where you could catch four or five fish a minute? I wonder if there's anyone who'd take me on there. On my own terms, of course."

He'd become intrigued by the fact that his business partner and erstwhile Leicester teammate, Ray Marlow, had recently been on a fishing trip to Key West, where the charter boat captain had told him it would take an hour to get the pinfish they needed as bait for amberjack fishing. "Give me ten minutes," Marlow had said, producing his match-angling gear, which he's never without. And, lo, the bait well had been filled with pinfish in just that time.

On the same trip, Marlow also organized evening matches—a Florida first, no doubt—outside his motel to catch mangrove snapper, sophisticated ones that ignored the locals' heavy gear. "Two-pound-test and a 14 hook," Marlow said proudly, "and I murdered those Yanks."

On the Ancholme, on the day of the National, Marlow's luck doesn't hold; with five and a half ounces of fish, at least he isn't dry-netted, as are many others who fish under the blazing sun. Afterward, some of the anglers would describe how, as they walked upriver to their respective stakes, they would see a mass of bream, stolid, indifferent, moving ahead of them all the time. Spectators could stand on one of the bridges over the Ancholme and see the water black with fish, but under the rules of the National, no stakes are placed within fifty yards of a bridge.

The pattern is as expected. Most anglers catch very little. A few of them find the bream—the slabs, the dogs, as matchmen call them—unimpressive fighters but good enough to win the individual championship for David Steer from Surrey, who weighs in with twenty-one and a half pounds, and for the team championship to go to Essex, which finished up on Knott's board at twenty to one. Unhappily, Essex failed to bet on itself, although Steer, a bit more self-confident, did so, and collects £3,000 from the bookies.

The Barnsley Blacks end up eighteenth. Marks, limping disconsolately back to the bus, caught precisely a quarter of an ounce of fish. "An' then I put me tackle on the wrong bus," he says.

Only a bit less dismayed is Tony Davis, who landed a total catch of one ounce in the same section as Marks, but who was disqualified for leaving his stake—to pick up litter, he claims. "I thought Hitler died in 1945," Davis says bitterly, "but I see he's a steward in C Section."

By now, though, the beer tent is open, the atmosphere relaxed. "If anybody's lost his wallet, it's lying on the bar," crackles the P.A. system. Any body of men who can be as honest as that can't be all bad.

You could razor-cut every page of a telephone book in tiny pieces, toss the whole confetti mess in a dead calm, and still not drop as many names as Gingrich does hitting his stride. The founding editor and publisher of *Esquire* fished with everybody who was anybody. He'd have fished with you even if you were dead, if you were good. His angling library was probably the finest ever assembled in private hands. Pick up Gingrich and you're in good company.

ARNOLD GINGRICH

Mr. Hewitt and His Water

He was pushing eighty-nine, that first time I met him, and though he could still thread a fly without glasses, he didn't hear everything you thought he heard. I was fishing at the Big Bend Fishing Club, which held a lease on Mr. Hewitt's water on the Neversink, as the guest of Charles Kerlee. It was the second time I'd fished there, Charlie having had me up once before as his guest during the previous season, when we'd had wonderful fishing and he had suggested that I might join the club if I wanted to. It hadn't worked out that year, but circumstances had changed and Charlie had renewed the invitation. So we had fished the stream again today, this time without a strike, and had come in, skunked, and sat down for dinner at the cabin that the Kerlees had built on the Neversink's bank just above the spot known as Theodore Gordon's favorite pool.

Vivian Kerlee had said what a shame it was that we hadn't had a fish between us, and I'd said that it couldn't matter less, and what a thrill it was for me just to be on Hewitt's water and to be sitting in sight of Gordon's pool, when there was a sliding rattling noise outside. It sounded like a minor avalanche.

"That must be Mr. Hewitt," said Vivian.

And it was. At last I was to see him plain.

He had come down off the mountain, like Zeus from Olympus, and at something of the speed and noise of a thunderbolt in his antique high-sprung sedan with holes bored in the top to poke rods through. Incredibly small and ancient, he and his car alike, but they were equally spry for their years, and he looked as perky as one of the seven dwarfs. He had come down from his home up above to bring a reel he had made the previous winter to give Charlie as a present. On it he had graven Charlie's name, and his own, and the date. (I have since seen one other like it which he made for Ellis Newman, and I would give all but two of the twenty best reels I own to have either of them.)

They asked him to sit down to dinner, after the reel had been sufficiently praised and admired, and he did. He couldn't believe that we hadn't moved a fish. That is, he could well believe that I hadn't, because he didn't know me from the nearest rhododendron, but he couldn't believe that Charlie, whom he obviously respected and admired as an angler, could have failed to cause a fish to stir on this fabled water.

"Did you try the iron blue dun?"

"Yes, we did, Mr. Hewitt."

"Did you try one of my nymphs?"

"Yes, we did."

"The one with the dirty white belly?"

"Yes, and the yellow one, too."

"But was it size 14?"

"Yes, and we tried the 10 and the 12, too."

"Did you fish 'em upstream, and let 'em bump?"

"Yes, we did, Mr. Hewitt. And downstream, too."

"Ah, but you didn't wrap those little bits of lead fuse wire around your leader!"

"But we did, Mr. Hewitt."

And we had, much as I had disliked the idea at the time.

"Well, did you let 'em dead-drift, too? You never can tell, you know."

"Yes, we tried 'em every which way."

"Hmm. Well, I never fish this water before May tenth, myself."

He was very positive in all his pronouncements, and he tended to make a pronouncement out of almost everything he said. But sometimes he'd forget a name, and other times you could only assume that he might not have heard correctly. Talking about flies, he tried to remember the name of "that fellow out west."

"Could it have been Dan Bailey?" I suggested.

"Yes, I believe that's the fellow."

But when we were talking about the known tendency of big browns to be cannibalistic, he said: "I've never known one to be." That was directly contrary

to what he had written more than once in more than one of his books, including
the last, where revised versions of *Telling on the Trout* and *Secrets of the
Salmon* had been incorporated into *A Trout and Salmon Fisherman for Seventy-five Years*. But Charlie Kerlee, who knew him much better than I—who
had only just met him and whose name he didn't catch—seemed disinclined
to argue, so I contented myself with telling them about the two dead rainbows
I had found on the Esopus, one stuck halfway inside the other, which I had
carefully pried apart and measured. A ten-incher had tried to swallow an eight-
incher, and had halfway made it before dying in the attempt. Again, Mr. Hewitt
professed never to have seen the like, in eighty years of fishing, man and boy.
But I couldn't be sure whether he hadn't fully heard me or was just trying to
be polite.

Though I did join the club that year, and fished the Hewitt water at least
once a week that season and the next, I wasn't to meet him again. But I did
see him again on the stream. He was fishing in its upper reaches, with Herman
Christian, who for years played Sancho Panza to his own Quixote, and instead
of going on to another spot I shamelessly stayed behind some bushes, to eaves-
drop and eyedrop. After all, he had turned ninety by then, and I can always
have the dubious pleasure of my own company wherever there's water for me
to fish, but how many times more might I have the privilege of watching one
of the sport's acknowledged masters?

The only thing I heard him say was that Herman Christian ought to be using
a nymph, as he was. Christian was too far away for me to see, even if I had
had binoculars—exactly what he was using—but even from twice the distance
I could have deduced that he was fishing a "ladder" of three flies. When he
made his lazy cast it was as casual as—and indeed that's what it resembled—
the motion of a farmer tossing aside a rake or even a pitchfork. He jerked his
rod constantly, and more often than my eyes could credit he would give a
sudden upward hoist, as he set one of the flies in a fish. I must have seen him
peel off a dozen trout in the course of a hundred yards as he stomped and
splashed downstream. His every motion seemed awkward, and I would have
thought that the manner of his wading, high-stepping and as forthright as the
goosestep of troops passing in review, would have been enough to scare away
all the trout and most of the suckers, but he seemed to be attracting them like
the Pied Piper.

Mr. Hewitt, meanwhile, appeared to be working on one fish. He cast with
elaborate caution, peering ahead and crouching, as if casing the water like a
burglar. Working upstream, he rarely moved, and then barely, while Christian
crashed on downstream like a brass band on parade. But though I watched for
better than half an hour, I never saw Mr. Hewitt get a strike, whereas whenever
I looked at Christian, as long as he was in sight, he was prying a hook out of

the mouth of another trout. I wish I could report that Hewitt seemed the picture of grace, that the movements of his rod were poetry in motion. They weren't. But then what kind of figure would you cut when you're ninety?

The one thing I got out of two years' membership in the Big Bend Club, aside from the privilege of being able to say that I had fished Mr. Hewitt's water and that I had seen him fishing it himself, was my first acquaintance with the Midge rod, and though membership in the club was not cheap, it would have been cheap at many times the price if I might not otherwise have met the rod that entirely transformed my fishing life. Charlie had got one from Paul Young in Detroit, where he often went in his work as a professional photographer, and had bought it with no intention of using it himself, as he is over six foot, with the build of a tackle. But Vivian is small, and he wanted a light little rod that she could use without arm fatigue.

The morning after the night that Hewitt came to dinner, Vivian let me try it, and the very first cast was a revelation. I had been using an Edwards, eight feet and four and a quarter ounces, and liked it. I still have it, and it's all right in its way, as such rods go. But the Midge, at six feet three inches and weighing just 1.73 ounces, made a bum out of it, and giving it back was like giving back a piece of my arm. I wrote a check for one that same day. They cost only $65 at that time, but I'd have paid five times as much, if that had been the price. I never wanted anything more avidly in my life.

Once I got it, I used no other rod, except another one like it, and then another and still another, until finally I had acquired a dozen in the same general category. But more about that later on.

The Neversink trout were wary, and they grew to impressive size. But with Mr. Hewitt fishing fairly infrequently, and with only a half dozen members in the Big Bend Club, they were less often fished over than those at Suffolk Lodge, and hardly at all, compared to those in the Esopus. The other members had built cottages along the upper half of the Hewitt water, and while I was entitled to do the same it never worked out for me to do it, so I kept on going to Kahil's Rainbow Lodge on Friday nights, fishing the Esopus through Saturday. Then, getting up early Sunday morning, I would drive on the back road over the mountain from Big Indian, coming down at Claryville, which was hardly more than a minute or so from the covered bridge that led to the rudimentary road, facing a schoolhouse, which curved around to the Hewitt water in the Neversink Valley. Thus I would get one full day on the Neversink each week. And I would leave after dark on Sunday nights to head back for my work week in New York.

Mr. Hewitt was always experimenting with the stocking and the feeding of fish on his water. He had even tried bringing over salmon from Scotland. The construction of the big dam had made the lower mile of his three-mile stretch too deep to permit wading any more, completely obliterating the place where his own old camp had been, and the creation of this little ocean at the foot of his water led him to attempt to introduce into it all sorts of seagoing specimens. He kept U.S. Customs in New York in an uproar, those last years of his life. They never knew what live thing, short of the Loch Ness monster itself, he might be trying to import.

Once, peering down into the sun-illumined waters at the big bend in the river from which the club took its name, I saw or thought I saw something hugely white, looking almost man size, even after making due allowance for the magnifying effect of the water. What it was I'll never know, nor do I think any of the other members ever found out, but of an evening, from the porch of the nearest cottage, we occasionally heard splashes exceeding anything that could have been caused by a 200-pound policeman taking a bellywhopper.

The Atlantic salmon experiment was a fizzle, so far as I know, but Charlie Kerlee more than once pulled out landlocks, and some of the twenty-four- and twenty-five-inch rainbows he consistently raised on a Quack Coachman and returned to the water were kissing cousins for steelheads. Charles Kerlee was one of the two fishermen I've ever known whose lives I truly envied. The other one, of course, is Al McClane, but perhaps that should be thrown out because he's a professional, one of the rare types who succeed in merging their work and their fun. When he shows up in his office they say: "Why aren't you out fishing?" so about three hundred days a year he is. Why couldn't I, with about a fifteen-year head start on him, ever find an office like that? Charles Kerlee never fished for a living, or ever studied ichthyology and all that, as McClane did, to prepare for a career in any aspect of fishing. But with a cabin on the Neversink, and another on the Southwest Miramichi, and still another in the Bahamas, he can legitimately be at ease with himself and in the bosom of his family, fearing and beholden to nobody, in the right place at the right time, very nearly all around the calendar.

There is the consideration that he's one hell of a photographer, and those fellows are notoriously well paid, while I never got beyond a 2A box Brownie, and can't even master a Polaroid. There is the further consideration that he is now avowedly at least semiretired, but even when I was wholly retired, as I was for the last three of my four years in Switzerland, I never had sense enough to arrange myself a setup like that. There is the one additional consideration that he has a wife who not only loves to have him fish but loves to fish herself, and is actually a member of something that is known, in what my own experience would have branded a contradiction in terms, as The Ladies' Fly Fishers.

There, perhaps, is the rub. Still, I too had a wife—for eight months—who loved to fish, and my angling life was never more wretched.

My first wife, whom I had married twice in youth and who was the mother of my three sons, had before she died become my third wife, or fourth, depending on whether those first two weddings are counted as one or as two. She was the eldest of four children whose father was an avid fisherman and a rabid hunter. He was the kind who wants "a little pal," and God help the little pal if he's a she. He made her fish and shoot and ride before he could have been any too sure she could walk, with the perhaps not entirely surprising result that a more vigorously anti-sports-minded female never grew up. When she went to girls' camp in Maine, she begged to be allowed to curry the horses, if only she could be excused from riding any of them. As for rods and guns, she'd seen enough of them to last her a lifetime before she was able to read *Elsie Dinsmore* or the Oz books.

My present wife, on the other hand, whom I hesitate to identify as fifth except that she has herself been married four times and a man must try any way he can to assert rank, was riding and showing horses in Madison Square Garden before she was knee-high to them, and had shot elephants and rhino in Tanganyika and Kenya with Philip Percival before Hemingway had ever heard of him, and had her own boat on the blue water, from which Ernest helped her pioneer the Cuban big game fishing, before he did. She could well have been one of those whom Scott Fitzgerald had in mind when he said that Ernest was always ready to lend a helping hand to the one on the rung above him. She shot two elephants so big that their tusks comprise the posts of a monumental four-poster bed, and a rhinocerous that was the biggest of its year, and while she never held any big game fishing record, she has insisted that every trout I ever caught was smaller than something she had once used for bait, and it is a matter of record that while fishing with her second husband she tried to throw back a nine-pound smallmouth as an object that nobody could conceivably want to keep. With a sporting background, but one devoted to the cult of bigness, she can no more understand my passion for trout than if I were, instead, to develop a mania for collecting broken milk bottles. Or just possibly she might understand it if I were to get completely hipped on collecting mushrooms, because I suspect that the only form of the chase that she really respects is one where the quarry has something like an even chance of getting back at you.

Though these two women, in their attitude toward sports, were alike only in the way the extremes of hot and cold are alike, both being equally painful to the touch, it was only between the death of one and my marriage to the other that I managed to sneak in two seasons of membership in the Big Bend Club, after which I had to explain to Charlie Kerlee why I could no longer be a member, and never hope to have a cabin, like his, on the Neversink. I told him I envied him his freedom to fish when and where he liked, but I consoled myself with the recollection of that passage in D. H. Lawrence's *Studies in Classic American Literature*, which reads—when looked up, for I had only recalled its gist: "Men are not free when they are doing just what they like. The moment you can do just what you like, there is nothing you care about doing. Men are only free when they are doing what the deepest self likes."

The consummate angler Theodore Gordon introduced more than the dry fly to America. His heady manifestos set standards of excellence; his gift is a perfection of grace. There was fishing before him. There was better fishing after.

THEODORE GORDON

A Reply to Mr. Denmead

Mr. Denmead's defense of bait-fishing, in the last issue of *Forest and Stream*, reminded me of the brook in which I caught my first trout with a worm. But it was not just a common worm, because I was chaperoned on that memorable afternoon by Docky Noble, and he had great faith in scented baits.

After digging his baits in the garden, Docky would proceed to the drug store and invest several coppers in a good big bunch of asafetida. The worms were placed in a dirty sock, and in their midst a piece of asafetida, which is very good for nervous people, as well as to attract fish. My family always knew when I had been fishing with Docky, because on my return I perfumed the whole house.

Bonnie Brook was a perfect trout brook, flowing in part through sweet meadows and in part through a swampy woodcock covert, where one or two broods of cock were always bred, and where a few flight birds could usually be found in October. Bonnie Brook had many deep holes, and there were great cavities under banks where huge trout lurked. How many these were we never knew, until a miscreant in the disguise of a fish culturist set his nets and secured great numbers of splendid *fontinalis* (native brook trout) from one-half pound to a noble specimen of two and one-half pounds.

We had killed one now and then of one pound or better, but it was difficult to get the worm to work four or five feet under a bank covered with rank grass or overhung with bushes. The water in Bonnie Brook was clear as crystal and ran over either clay or clean bright gravel. It was a fascinating little stream, and the man or woman who named it in the early days of the first settlers knew quite well what he or she was about. It was a favorite haunt of our friend Docky—his fourteen-foot fly rod was rather long for a such a stream—but he was a dyed-in-the-wool bait-fisher, although he always carried a tangled mass of flies on gut in his pocket book and could cast them lightly with his big rod when he wished. But Docky was a bit lazy and very fond of whiskey, so he found worms on an easy open stream more agreeable to his taste than fly-fishing. He rarely entered the tangle of vegetation in the woodcock covert, but fished the water in the open meadows. I recognize the type of trout stream described by Mr. Denmead, and hope that he does not fish the little brooks in which we put the fingerlings. (We have put out 10,000 recently.) Men and boys do fish these nurseries and kill great numbers of baby trout, which are placed there to feed and grow big enough to afford sport in the main stream.

Of late there have been signs of a reaction against the cult of the dry fly. In this country we can do nothing quietly or in moderation, and for about two years the floating fly had a tremendous "boom." It was advertised so much that many people were impressed with the idea that the dry fly was a dead sure thing at any old time anywhere and would always lure big trout, while wet fly and bait-fishers could do nothing at all except sit around and admire. I love floating fly and fish it often in early spring when I know quite well that I could kill more trout with wet flies properly fished. But the floating fly affords the maximum of sport upon the waters suited to it, and we are not after records or thinking of the cook.

I know the streams described by Mr. Denmead, and quite understand that the large trout in them can only be secured by bait-fishing, which requires good and patient work. At one time I used all kinds of baits and flies also, and punished the streams I fished to the best of my ability, but there is one deadly bait which I never used and never mention, as it seemed to madden the trout. A very few fish content me nowadays if they are large enough to afford really exciting sport. I have fished the dry fly for more than twenty years, at first only to trout that I saw rising at natural flies. If one can fish for large trout in sight, sport becomes most exciting, and the next best is a rise that one knows must be a big fish. The greatest good for the largest number is conserved by fly-fishing only, as one can follow many fly-fishers and still have sport. The angler's chances are reduced to a minimum when he is compelled to follow a minnow fisher, who scores the trout and puts them down. Worms are not so injurious and grasshoppers do not interfere much if they are fished by a decent man who has some regard for those who follow him. In a large body of flowing water the trout are less easily alarmed and come on the feed again sooner than in small streams. When a club is formed to fish a bit of leased water, one of the first rules to be adopted is "fly-fishing only," and this is for the good of the stream and the members. One greedy angler might ruin the sport for a dozen men who only had a day or two to spare for fishing.

We do not care for preserved waters unless they are hard fished and hold wild trout. Who cares much for trout that will rise freely at almost any fly and can be taken without effort? . . .

If I needed fish for food I would use bait if it was necessary. As for wet and dry flies, it is, I think, true that there are more dry-fly fishers than really scientific wet-fly men. I know a few of the latter and we have fished together wet versus dry. They are quite equal to taking care of themselves.

Let us be liberal and kind to one another, trying to smother prejudice and cultivating a spirit of peace and good will among the brethren of the angle rod. We can have a good stock of trout in free waters—that are pure and well stocked with food—if we are not too greedy and obey the laws.

A few ultra dry-fly men may assume airs of superiority, but they are mostly good fellows. I have never known one of them to kill too many trout. To be able to meet difficulties successfully, yet stick to the artificial fly in all trout waters, we feel that the American angler should thoroughly understand the dry, the wet, and the sunk fly.

Most people know Zane Grey as the man who wrote *Riders of the Purple Sage*, one of a string of phenomenally best-selling Westerns that earned him more than $37 million (most of that pulled in before the imposition of income tax set creel limits). You might think he could afford the best tackle engineers could design, the world's ultraexotic fishing holes to dip a line, and the most lavishly equipped yachts to transport him there. He could and he did.

Here he begins to reach his form, going after that slightly oversized herring, a.k.a. the tarpon.

ZANE GREY

Rivers of the Everglades

Next morning we were up even earlier, and on the fishing ground where we had located the tarpon, just a little after dawn. None of us really expected the tarpon to be there. But they were. We heard them splashing, sousing, and puffing before we could see them in the dim gray light.

Morning came quickly, a soft, sweet, balmy spring morning, with music of awakening birds all around us and the fragrance of blossoming vines or trees somewhere near. The sun heralded his coming by a pink effulgence in the sky, and soon rose red and gold. The water shimmered like a stream of molten jewels; and everywhere we looked its surface was rippled or broken by rolling tarpon.

An early start and a later tide made conditions better for us than they had been the day before. In fact, the tide had just begun to rise. Only one factor remained to make the experience perfect—and that was for the tarpon to bite.

R. C. was located near a small island where the channel appeared to form a deep eddy. Here dozens of tarpon were rolling. And very soon R. C. called out sharp and clear, "Something doing!"

That was a fair promise for the morning's luck. Fishermen never outgrow their superstitions regarding chance.

A moment more and a splendid tarpon cleared the air, so brilliant and beautiful in the early morning sunlight that he seemed to come from some unreal and fairy-like world. When he crashed down, to leap again on a tight line, R. C. let out a cry that meant the tarpon had not thrown the hook. In and out, up and down, this silver fish flashed until at last, halfway across the channel he wagged out and plunged back. I did not see him again for half an hour when he rolled his head out near R. C.'s boat. He was a big fish and required careful handling.

"Well, what you doing over there?" called R. C.

"We constitute your audience," I replied.

R. C. had scarcely settled down to a comfortable seat when he had another strike. I saw it before he whistled. An instant later my line started out slow, strong, steady. As I picked up my rod Captain Thad said: "By gosh! There's a bite on your other rod!"

That seemed a superfluity of good fortune. But presently it did not look so good. The line on my extra rod was crossing the one I held. I felt the contact. My line ceased to pay out—then it whizzed off the reel. There followed a tremendous splash and a huge tarpon leaped so close to us that he made a great black blur against the sky. As he obscured the sun he actually looked black. But I saw the marvelous outline and the incredible action. The tussle he made somewhat resembled the action of a horse shaking off dust which he had gathered rolling. With a loud live crash he disappeared. And my line was limp! I stared at it.

"Just as well that happened. You've still got another bite," said Captain Thad, handing me the other rod.

I had again the same thrill of expectancy, the same tingling, breathless curiosity. When I struck hard and felt the heavy weight, the sudden lunge on the line, I stared as if fascinated at the space of water where the tarpon should show.

"Shark," said Thad. "Too bad! He ran across your other line and made the tarpon throw the hook. He sure made a flop."

Before a sickening disappointment quite seized upon me I heard the unmistakable rapid flopping of a fish half out of the water. I had forgotten R. C. Wheeling, I was just in time to see a tarpon in a beautiful headlong dive. The next leap was a twisting somersault. After that the fish stayed down. I watched R. C. working on him, bending the little rod. The fish was away fully two hundred yards and fighting doggedly.

"Do you fellows ever follow a tarpon?" I called, sarcastically.

"Reckon we'll wait till we hang a buster. This one'll only go aboot hundred forty-five," replied King, cheerily.

I was certainly delighted to see my brother so fortunately engaged and so blithe about it, but I did not think any too favorably of his risking so much on the light tackle.

"Say, R. C.," I yelled, finally, "if you'd fall overboard what do you suppose you would come up with?"

"Cheer up. You'll catch one some day, maybe," he replied. "Watch me pull this bird's head off."

He did not quite literally succeed in accomplishing his boast, but he managed to whip that tarpon and pull him in, without moving the boat.

Contrary to what we naturally expected, the tarpon continued to roll and sport on the surface.

"You can never tell," said Thad. "Look how they acted yesterday morning. We'll ketch another one, sure, before they work off on the flats."

"That lucky redhead may, but I've a feeling of disaster," I replied.

In truth, I was two persons, a composite of a watcher by the sea, reveling in the glancing, mysterious water as every instant it gleamed here or there with a bar of silver, and an angler glad to be alive, grateful to be there, happy at my brother's good luck, and very peevishly anathematizing my own miserable fortune.

"Hey! Come over here and take my rod," R. C. called, gayly.

I turned to see him standing in the skiff, bending forward, rod extended, in that familiar and thrilling pose I had seen him assume thousands of times since boyhood.

"What for?" I yelled, as if I did not know.

"I just got a bite . . . Watch me hand it to this one!"

I did watch him then, and every instant for a while. I saw him hook and begin to play a still larger tarpon. It made seven leaps clear to the surface, and then, after surging this way and that, turned toward our boat. I got ready with the camera. I was facing the sun, and that was bad for picture taking. The tarpon appeared so active that I was certain he would leap again.

"Get ready to beat it away from there," called King, warningly.

Captain Thad wound in our lines, and was hauling on the anchor when the tarpon broke close to us. It was like the explosion of a shell. Then he slapped his gills in loud cracks. And that same shuddering, convulsive shaking noise filled my ears. I snapped a picture with the camera focused for one hundred feet when the tarpon had leaped scarce twenty-five feet from us. Swiftly I changed focus. He came out again, farther away, and again I was wrong. The best jump occurred while I was winding a new number into place. I did not see it, but I heard it and the shouts of my comrades. When I faced around the tarpon was down. I saw the line and tried to judge where the fish would again appear. But he fooled me. I figured between fifty and a hundred feet. He split the water close to us again and shot up in a perfect action, a clean-cut leap without wagging, shaking, or cracking his gills. When he went down he was headed for our boat. R. C. was yelling. So was King. Captain Thad shouted warnings—I could not hear what. And I was frantically changing my focus. I just had it done when the tarpon burst out of a caldron of flying white spray, and carrying up a wreath of foam and a rainbow mist, and myriads of diamond drops, he went into the air until his tail was as high as my head. My camera snapped too late.

That appeared to be the end of his aerial performances. But we got out of his way, and standing off at a safe distance we watched R. C. handle him in masterly fashion and at length bring him in. Captain King had to gaff this fish, as manifestly he was too heavy to take care of otherwise. Both he and R. C. disappeared in spray, and most certainly received a good wetting. I could hear King talking to the wrestling tarpon.

"Didn't I tell you we'd ketch you?" he demanded. Captain King was nothing if not a real fisherman.

Biggest one yet!" called R. C. as he looked over at me, with the light flashing on his face.

That ended our fishing in the channel. The tide was rising fast and with it the tarpon were drifting toward the bays and coves and creeks.

I did not see another tail or break for three hours. Captain Thad kept poling along, into every likely nook he espied. R. C. and King had returned to the launch.

The day had grown still and warm, drowsy, with the breath and fragrance of summer. Birds, turtles, fish, were out of sight.

"Mebbe we'll find some up this cove," offered Thad, hopefully.

The water was clear and shallow, not more than three feet deep. Thad poled and paddled very cautiously along the overhanging banks of green.

"There goes one," he called, pointing to a swell on the surface. It traveled out into the cove. "Where there's one there's more."

Soon he pointed out a tarpon lying motionless half a foot under the surface, a long gleaming bar golden in hue through the amber water.

"He'll go less than a hundred," said Thad. "I believe I could make him take a bait. Shall I try or will we hunt for a big one?"

I was sorely tempted, but yielded to the suggestion in his last words. Then we glided slowly along, sometimes in the shade, but for the most part just outside the spreading foliage. It grew to be a fascinating game. I sighted several tarpon that Thad missed or did not point out. They did not move even a fin, though we passed so close I could have touched them with an oar. Asleep! Thad assured me this was the case, and I believed him.

We came to a narrow lane or rather opening in the green bank. Two tarpon were lying on the surface, one with fins out. They appeared to be moving very slightly. Thad stuck his oar in the mud, and taking up my rod he cast the bait right at the very nose of the big tarpon. I watched with immense eagerness and curiosity. And just what I had expected really happened. Roar! Smash! Both tarpon plunged away from there, spreading huge furrows and raising the mud.

"That fellow wasn't asleep," averred Thad. "He was scared. But if he'd been asleep he'd taken the bait for a mullet hopping close. An' he'd sure have hopped it."

"Well!" I ejaculated. "Then you must call this method casting for tarpon?"

"Yes. An' it's the best way, at times like this."

We glided into the opening, to find it a small cove, shallow and quiet, where the wind could not ruffle the water. The bottom appeared to be clean sand.

"I see a buster, over there," said Thad.

"I see one, over here," I replied.

"Yes. There's another in the middle—good big one, too. All asleep! We'll sure hang one of these birds, as R. C. says. Be careful not to make any noise."

Very slowly he moved the boat, in fact so slowly that suspense wore on me. Yet I tingled with the pleasure of the moment. Nor was it all because of the stalking of big game! The little round cove was a beautiful place, resposeful and absolutely silent, lonely, somehow dreamy. A small blue heron flew away into a green aisle where the water gleamed dark in shade.

Not for moments did I espy the big tarpon Thad was gliding so carefully toward. When I did see him I gasped. He lay close to the bottom in several feet of water. But I could see every detail of him. He shone brighter, a little more silvery gold than those we had seen out in the larger cove. His back looked black. I could scarcely believe this enormous shadow was really a fish, and a tarpon.

Thad halted about twenty-five feet distant, and with slow deliberation gently pushed his oar down into the sand. The boat had not made even a ripple.

"Now I'll hit him right on the nose," said Thad, with the utmost satisfaction.

He wound up the line until the leader was within a few inches of the tip; then he carefully balanced, and swung the bait.

"Watch. I'm bettin' he takes it," said Thad.

I was all eyes, and actually trembling. But only with the excitement of the place and the fish. I had not the remotest idea that the tarpon would do any more than wake up and lunge out of there.

Thad cast the bait. It hit with a plop and a splash, not right over the tarpon, but just in front of his nose. It certainly awoke him. I saw him jerk his fins. A little cloud of roily water rose from behind his tail.

Then, to my exceeding amaze, he moved lazily and began to elevate his body. It shone gold. It loomed up to turn silver. His tail came out and flapped on the surface. What a wonderful tail! It was a foot broad.

"He's got it," said Thad, handing the rod back to me.

"No!" I ejaculated, incredulously.

"Sure. I saw him take it in his mouth . . . So far so good. Now if he doesn't get leary!"

"Oh, he's moving off with it," I whispered, breathlessly. Indeed,that seemed the remarkable fact. The long, wide, shadowy shape glided away from the edge of the shade. I hoped it would move away from the boat. But he was going to pass close.

A triangular wave appeared on the water. It swelled. I heard the faint cut of my line as it swept out. I saw it move. My eyes were riveted on it. I pulled line off the reel and held my rod so it would run freely through the guides. What an impossible thing was happening! My heart felt swelling in my throat. I saw that great tarpon clearly in sunlit water not over three feet deep. I saw the checkerboard markings of his huge scales. I saw his lean, sharp, snub-nosed face and the immense black eye. All as he reached a point even with me!

Then he saw the boat, and no doubt Thad and me standing almost over him. Right before my rapt gaze he vanished. Next I heard a quick deep thrum. I saw a boiling cloud of muddy water rising toward the surface.

"He saw the boat!" yelled Thad. "He's scared. Soak him!"

But swift though I was, I could not throw on the drag, and reel in the slack line, and strike in time to avert a catastrophe. I seemed to freeze all over.

The very center of that placid cove upheaved in a flying maelstrom and there followed a roaring crash. A grand blazing fish leaped into the sunlight. He just cleared the water, so heavy was he, and seemed to hang for an instant in the air, a strange creature of the sea. Then the infinite grace and beauty of him underwent a change. His head suddenly became deformed. The wide gill-covers slapped open, exposing the red. He shook with such tremendous power and rapidity that he blurred in my sight. I saw the bait go flying far. He had thrown the hook.

With sounding smash he fell back. The water opened into a dark surging hole out of which flew muddy spray. With a solid, heavy thrum, almost like a roar of contending waters, the tarpon was gone. He left a furrowed wake that I shall never forget.

Slowly I reeled in, unmindful of the language of the usually mild Captain Thad. On the moment, as I recovered from what seemed a stunning check to my emotions, I did not feel the slightest pang. Instead, as the primitive thrills of the chase and capture, and the sudden paralyzing shock of fear and loss, passed away together, I experienced a perfect exhilaration.

Something wonderful had happened. I had seen something indescribably beautiful. Into my memory had been burned indelibly a picture of a sunlit, cloud-mirroring green-and-gold-bordered cove, above the center of which shone a glorious fish-creature in the air, wildly instinct with the action and daring of freedom.

Just then, before the exultation vanished, I felt as if I had been granted a marvelous privilege. Out of the inscrutable waters a beautiful fish had leaped, to show me fleetly the life and spirit of his element. And I had sought to kill!

When I laid my rod down and took my chair, motioning Captain Thad that we would go, I knew I had reached the end of this fishing trip. There is always an end to everything, even the longest lane. There is always a place for a story to end.

If I fished only to capture fish, my fishing trips would have ended long ago.

At nineteen and restless, Haig-Brown left England in search of the perfect river. He found the Campbell in British Columbia, wooed and then married it. For the rest of his life he shared his love with his readers.

RODERICK HAIG-BROWN

To Know a River

I have written in this book nearly always of rivers—occasionally of lakes or the salt water, but nearly always of rivers and river fishing. A river is water in its loveliest form; rivers have life and sound and movement and infinity of variation, rivers are veins of the earth through which the life blood returns to the heart. Rivers can attain overwhelming grandeur, as the Columbia does in the reaches all the way from Pasco to the sea; they may slide softly through flat meadows or batter their way down mountain slopes and through narrow canyons; they may be heavy, almost dark, with history, as the Thames is from its mouth at least up to Richmond; or they may be sparkling fresh on mountain slopes through virgin forest and alpine meadows.

Lakes and the sea have great secret depths quite hidden from man and often almost barren of life. A river too may have its deep and secret places, may be so large that one can never know it properly; but most rivers that give sport to fly-fishermen are comparatively small, and one feels that it is within the range of the mind to know them intimately—intimately as to their changes through the seasons, as to the shifts and quirks of current, the sharp runs, the slow glides, the eddies and bars and crossing places, the very rocks of the

151

bottom. And in knowing a river intimately is a very large part of the joy of fly-fishing.

One may love a river as soon as one sets eyes upon it; it may have certain features that fit instantly with one's conception of beauty, or it may recall the qualities of some other river, well known and deeply loved. One may feel in the same way an instant affinity for a man or a woman and know that here is pleasure and warmth and the foundation of deep friendship. In either case the full riches of the discovery are not immediately released—they cannot be; only knowledge and close experience can release them. Rivers, I suppose, are not at all like human beings, but it is still possible to make apt comparisons; and this is one: understanding, whether instinctive and immediate or developing naturally through time or grown by conscious effort, is a necessary preliminary to love. Understanding of another human being can never be complete, but as it grows toward completeness, it becomes love almost inevitably. One cannot know intimately all the ways and movements of a river without growing into love of it. And there is no exhaustion to the growth of love through knowledge, whether the love be for a person or a river, because the knowledge can never become complete. One can come to feel in time that the whole is within one's compass, not yet wholly and intimately known, but there for the knowing, within the last little move of reaching; but there will always be something ahead, something more to know.

I have known very few rivers thoroughly and intimately. There is not time to know many, and one can know only certain chosen lengths of the few. I know some miles of the Dorsetshire Frome and of the little river Wrackle that cuts away from the Frome by Stratton Mill and rejoins it farther down, because I grew up with them and had all the quick instinctive learning power of the very young when I fished there. It was a happy and proud thing to know those streams, and the knowing paid great dividends in fish; it paid even greater dividends in something that I can still recapture—sheer happiness in remembering a bend or a run or the spread below a bridge as I saw them best, perhaps open in sunlight with the green weeds trailing and a good fish rising steadily, or perhaps pitted by rain under a gray sky, or white and black and golden, opaque in the long slant of the twilight. I knew those streams through fishing them, through cutting the weeds in them, through shooting ducks and snipe all along them, through setting night lines in them, through exploring them when the hatches were down and the water was very low. I carry them with me wherever I go and can fish them almost as well sitting here as I could were I walking the meadow grass along their banks six thousand miles from here.

I learned other waters almost as easily, though more superficially, when I was very young. The lower reaches of the Frome, between Wool and Wareham, where we used to fish for salmon, were harder to know than the best of the trout water because the river was deeper and darker and slower down there, more secret within itself. But I fished with a man who knew all the secrets, and we used the prawn a lot, fishing it deep down and slow, close to bottom and close under the banks. Fish lay where he said they should lie and took hold as he said they would take, and one remembered and fished it that way for oneself until the knowledge was properly one's own. I think I could still start at Bindon Mill and work on all the way down to the Salmon Water without missing so very many of the good places. And then, perhaps, I could walk back along the railroad track toward evening with a decent weight of salmon on my back.

I knew the little length of narrow carrier in Lewington's field by the bakery at Headbourne Worthy; it was so small and clear that one couldn't help knowing it and so difficult that one had to know it. I knew where each fish lay and why, how he would rise and when, what chance of ground would hide me during the cast, what tuft of grass would probably catch my fly on each attempted recovery. And Denis and I knew the narrow part of Avington Lake where the great pike lay under the shadow of the rank weeds; we knew the schools of roach and rudd and the few solitary trout; we had seen the big carp and the slow black tench; we knew, almost, where each little one- or two-pound pike had his hunting ground.

The winter days at Avington, under the tall bare beeches and ashes and sycamores, were very good. There were always mallard to be seen in hundreds, always herons, sometimes a peregrine falcon chasing the mallards; the cock pheasants were richer, burnished gold against the gold of fallen beech leaves, and rabbits sometimes rustled the leaves softly, unaware that we were fishing near them. The rank thick weed banks of the bottom showed clearly, green through the shallow water of the narrow part of the lake. We cast our big spoons and phantoms and wagtails far out, letting them into the unrippled water as gently as we could, then brought them twinkling back over the dark mystery of the weed beds. Sometimes a big pike was lying out over the weeds, and we tried and tried to tempt him. Sometimes one appeared suddenly behind the spoon, followed it and took or turned away. Sometimes—and this was best and surest of all—there was a heavy flash and a swirl as the spoon passed over a known lie, then the pull and the lunging fight.

The first western river I learned was the Nimpkish, the seven twisting miles of it that lie between the lake and the sea. I learned the best of the trout pools first, wading the round and slippery rocks in an old pair of calked shoes, letting the swift water climb up to the pockets of my shirt and sometimes letting it knock me down and carry me half the length of a pool before I could find a way out of it. Then I learned the tyee pools and the cutthroat trout runs of the tidal reaches. Taking the canoe up to go over the traps, lining the big skiff through to the lake, fishing for steelhead, watching the salmon runs, I learned more of it and felt it my own. But I never really knew the river as one can know a river. I don't know, even today, just how and when the steelhead run there, nor more than a fraction of their lying places. And I never could solve the secrets of Ned's Canyon and Wright's Canyon or that third one of the long, slow, deep pools on the river; they were so big, and I knew so many other places to catch fish that it was hard to give them time. But I once wrote a book that had the Nimpkish for a heroine and I saw and learned so much of her for myself through five or six years that I feel my faulty knowledge has given me a full love of her. Whenever I think of a western fishing river, one typical of all the best things that western fishing can offer, I think of the Nimpkish; and I expect I always shall.

The Campbell I know almost as a man should know a river. I don't know the whole story, or anything like the whole story; but the outlines of plot and characterization are clear and definite, much of the detail is filled in and each new detail fits neatly into an appointed place as I learn it. The Campbell is a little like the Nimpkish, yet most unlike it. Both rivers are broad and clear and swift, with broken, white water, rare, smooth pools and rocky beds. But the Campbell runs only three or four miles to salt water from the foot of its great Elk Falls, beyond which salmon and steelhead and cutthroat trout from the sea cannot pass. The Nimpkish is a highway to all the miles of Nimpkish Lake and the Kla-anche River and Woss Lake, to the Hustan River and the chain of lakes beyond that, and to all the tributary streams of the watershed. The Campbell draws to itself a noble run of winter steelhead, a run of fine cutthroats, a queer little run of small summer steelheads; it has its great tyees, its dying run of humpbacks, a fair run of cohos and dogs in some years, but no more than an occasional sockeye, probably a stray from some other parent stream. The Nimpkish has all the runs that the Campbell has in fullest strength and adds to them a fine run of true summer steelheads, a wonderful sockeye run and a fabulous dog-salmon run. The Campbell is the simpler river of the two, easier to know and understand for all those reasons. Nimpkish is more wonderful, more impressive, more beautiful; but Campbell—and not simply because I live within sight and sound of her—is the better of the two to love.

I can mark the months on the Campbell and tell myself, at least to my own satisfaction, what will be happening in the river during each one of them: In January the steelhead are running well; in February the cutthroats are spawning; in March and April the winter steelheads spawn; in May the little summer steelhead should be in the Island Pools, most of the humpback fry will already have found their way to the sea and the flying ants will hatch out; in August it is time to go to the Canyon Pool and look for the big cutthroats; in September the tyees are in the river; during October the cohos will come; in December the steelhead again. I know the mayfly and stone-fly nymphs that I will find under the rocks and the caddises that will crawl over the bottom in the different months; I know the rocks that the net-winged midges will blacken with their tiny cases, the places where the bright-green cladophora will grow richly, and where and when the rocks will be slippery with brown diatom growth. Some of these things, perhaps, are not important to know if one only wishes to catch fish; but they have their part in the pleasure of fishing.

I find I am quite often wrong about the Campbell even now. I may say that it is too early for the fish to be in, then go up and find them there. I can't always judge when the freshets are coming, but that, perhaps, is no more than saying I'm not an infallible weather prophet. Perhaps it is truer to say that I often find new things about the river than that I am often wrong about her; and sometimes I suddenly realize things that I have known for quite a long time almost unconsciously. It is years, for instance, since I first knew that I could kill fish well in August with the fly I call the Silver Brown. I tied the fly to imitate coho fry, which are the only numerous salmon fry in that month. In spring, when the river is full of many kinds of fry, the Silver Brown does not do so well for me, and I use the Silver Lady, which has a paler wing and a more complicated tying. I changed over with comparatively little thought, and the true inference of the change only came to me this year—trout may at times feed rather selectively on fry of different species.

Apart from bullheads and sticklebacks, one can expect some five or six different species of fry in the Campbell. Cutthroat fry and coho fry are so much alike that no sensible fish would bother to distinguish between them; it is reasonable to use the Silver Brown as an imitation of both. But humpback fry are like no other fry, trout or salmon; they are, for instance, quite without parr marks, their bellies are brightest silver, their backs generally bluish. I remember that I have fished a fly with long blue hackles for wings and often killed well with it during the humpback run. From there it is only a step to the making of a special humpback imitation; I think I shall start with something of this sort: tail—green swan, body—flat silver tinsel, hackle—scarlet and quite small, wing—blue hackles, back to back, enclosing a white strip and perhaps a strand or two of blue herl, cheeks—pale-blue chatterer. When I fish the river again in springtime, I shall use that fly.

If a coho-cutthroat imitation and a humpback imitation, why not imitations of the others in their days and seasons? The Silver Lady, perhaps, is sufficiently like spring salmon and steelhead fry. Yet the spring salmon fry has a light brown in his back and an impression of palest pink about him which the steelhead fry has not. It might make all the difference one day. So I shall build a fly with a tail of pink swan, a silver body and wings of barred summer duck enclosing yellow swan; and if that isn't good, I shall try grizzled hackles, preferably from a Plymouth cock with a touch of Red Game in him, set back to back with light-red hackles between them.

None of that is desperately important or highly significant, and I suppose I should feel ashamed of having waited ten or fifteen years to think of it. What I really feel is a good measure of gratitude to the Campbell for having at last brought home to me the rather obvious point that, if it is worth trying for exact imitation of sedges and mayflies, it is worth trying for reasonably exact imitations of salmon and trout fry. In time I shall think of dressings for the green color that is dominant in the backs of dog-salmon fry and the olive-grass green of the young sockeye's back. I may catch very few more fish through my efforts than I should have caught without them, but it's going to be fun.

I fish the Campbell with a sense of ownership fully as strong as that of any legitimate owner of fishing rights in the world, not because I do own any part of the river, nor even because I should like to or should like to keep other people away from it; I should not care to do either of these things. The sense of ownership grows simply from knowing the river. I know the easiest ways along the banks and the best ways down to the pools. I know where to start in at a pool, where to look for the fish in it, how and where I can wade, what point I can reach with an easy cast, what lie I can barely cover with my strongest effort. This is comfortable and pleasant and might well begin to seem monotonous sooner or later were it not something of an illusion. I have a fair idea of what to expect from the river, and usually, because I fish it that way, the river gives me approximately what I expect of it. But sooner or later something always comes up to change the set of my ways. Perhaps one day, waiting for a friend to fish down a pool, I start in a little farther up than usual and immediately hook a fish where I had never been able to hook one before. A little more of the river becomes mine, alive and productive to me. Or perhaps I notice in some unusual slant of light what looks to be a glide of water along the edge of a rapid; I go down to it and work my fly through, and whether or not a fish comes to it, more of the river is known and mine.

For years I have promised myself to fish through the sort of half pool below the Sandy Pool. It starts almost opposite my own line fence and is little more than a smoothing off of the long rapid that runs right down to the Highway Bridge; but there are many big rocks in it and—I can say this now—some obvious holding water. I fished it twice this spring. On the first evening I caught two or three fair-sized cutthroats, and once a really good fish broke water at the fly. I went down earlier on the second evening. A three-pound cutthroat came to my first cast. There was a slow silver gleam as the fly came around on the second cast, a solid heavy pull and the 2x gut was broken. I put up heavier gut and hooked a clean steelhead that ran me almost to the end of the backing. I hooked two others along the pool that evening, both of them too close to their spawning; but the pool is the Line Fence Pool now, something so close to home and so obvious that I took ten years to learn about it, a discovery as well worthwhile as any I have ever made.

One discovers other things than new pools and new fish lies in old pools. One learns to mark one's casts by such things as the kidney stones and the flat rock in General Money's Pool in the Stamp, one learns to hope for the sight of a pileated woodpecker crossing the river in swooping flight at this place, a flock of mergansers at that place, a dipper against black rocks and rippled water somewhere else, deer coming down to eat the moss on the rocks at the water's edge in hard weather. All these things are precious in repetition and, repeated or no, they build the river for one. They are part of the background of knowing and loving it, as is every fish hooked, every cast fished through, every rock trodden. And men and women come strongly into it. Here, I can remind myself, was where Ann sat that first day we came up the river together, and here it was that she loved the September sun the year before Valerie was born. Here we stopped and Letcher made us an old-fashioned before we went on to the Canyon Pool that day. Here Buckie brought his first fish to the bank, here I gaffed Sandy's first steelhead for him, here Tommy hooked one last winter, there it was that the big fish took Reg's line across the roots of the cedar tree. . . .

I still don't know why I fish or why other men fish, except that we like it and it makes us think and feel. But I do know that if it were not for the strong, quick life of rivers, for their sparkle in the sunshine, for the cold grayness of them under rain and the feel of them about my legs as I set my feet hard down on rocks or sand or gravel, I should fish less often. A river is never quite silent; it can never, of its very nature, be quite still; it is never quite the same from one day to the next. It has its own life and its own beauty, and the creatures it nourishes are alive and beautiful also. Perhaps fishing is, for me, only an excuse to be near rivers. If so, I'm glad I thought of it.

It was bound to happen. The doilies dusted. The tea service removed. The gaslights dimmed and the doors eased shut. At last! Murder was gently ushered from the paneled drawing room and dragged, screaming, into the fresh air. Some would say it belonged there all the time.

In the complete novel Hare plays fair—no easy task in whodunits. But don't be shocked to examine his creel and discover a glistening brace of red herring lying in a bed of damp moss.

CYRIL HARE

The Polworthy Arms

Shortly after the signature of the Treaty of Versailles, four businessmen, who had made enough money during the war to be able at last to attend to the really important things in life, formed a syndicate among themselves and bought the fishing rights of a reach of the River Didder. They were fortunate, for fishing on that famous chalk stream is, as all the world knows, hard to come by and the properties along its banks are tightly held. From the village of Didford Parva down to the estuary it is reputed that few below the standing of a millionaire can afford to cast a fly upon those limpid waters. None of the four who composed the syndicate was a millionaire, or anything approaching it, and they counted themselves lucky to be able to secure the little-known stretch that goes with the Polworthy property, upstream from Didford Magna.

Didford Magna, as its name implies to anyone familiar with English topography, is a very small place. An eighteenth-century Act of Parliament, empowering certain turnpike trustees to build a road bridge across the river at Didford Parva, six miles lower down, effectually diverted thither the traffic and the trade of the valley, and the only relics of Magna's old superiority are its name, its vast church—which is the despair of the Rector—and its tithes—which are (or, until the recent legislation, were) his consolation. Apart from the Rectory itself and Didford Manor, nearly two miles away, the whole village comprises no more than two farms, a dozen laborers' cottages, the post office, and the "Polworthy Arms." This last, standing at the corner of the lane that leads down through lush water meadows to the old ford, became the unofficial headquarters of the syndicate. For seven months of the year an undistinguished and not very prosperous public house, it blossomed out in the summer, and at weekends in particular, into the semblance of a fishing hotel. Two things it had in common with all such establishments—a pervasive smell of damp waders, and an extreme irregularity as to mealtimes. The landlady had in all probability never even noticed the first, and had certainly learned in the course of time to accept philosophically the second.

At about a quarter to ten on a warm Friday evening in June, when the murmur of voices from the bar was rising to a throaty *crescendo*, two fishermen were just sitting down to their supper in the parlor. Neither was an original member of the syndicate. Since its formation death had claimed one member and the crisis of 1931 another. A third, crippled with rheumatism, had resigned his membership only when his fingers could no longer be forced to tie a fly. Their places had been filled. The first newcomer was Stephen Smithers, who now sat at the head of the table. His bland, round face concealed a lively intelligence and a particularly crusty temper. He had used the former to advantage in his profession of a solicitor, and it was common knowledge that only an unwise display of the latter had prevented him from having been long since elected president of the Law Society. This evening, with a brace of two-pound trout to his credit, he was, for him, in an agreeable mood.

"Did I ever tell you, Wrigley-Bell," he said to his companion, "how I came to be a member of this outfit?"

"No," said the other, "I don't think you ever did."

"You'd have remembered it if I had. It was when old Lord Polworthy died and the executors sold the Manor to your friend Peter Packer."

"He's not my friend," Wrigley-Bell put in emphatically. His heavy brows came down in a frown as he spoke.

"I apologize. Your business rival, Sir Peter Packer, baronet, I should have said. The estate was split up, you may remember. The farming tenants—poor devils—bought the freehold of their farms, and Peter took the house and demesne land only. Well, the farmers gave no trouble, but the purchaser of the Manor claimed that the fishing rights were not a covenant running with the land, but merely an easement terminable with the death of the grantor, if you can understand that—"

"Put into plain English, you mean that Packer claimed he had bought the fishing with the estate?"

"For a businessman you show unusual intelligence. That is just what I do mean. His property only affects a bit of our water, of course, from the road corner to the willow tree pool, but it's the very heart of the fishing, and naturally if he established his claim, the other owners might have done the same, and there would be an end of the syndicate. Matheson, who was then as now the secretary of the syndicate, came to see me about it. The fellow who drew up the original agreement, like more than half of my profession, hadn't known his business, and it looked as if Packer had a case. I examined the papers and said to Matheson, 'I can get you out of this difficulty, but my fee will be the next available vacancy in the syndicate.' I'd wanted to fish the Didder all my life, you see, and I knew Hornsby was due to go bankrupt, so I shouldn't have to wait long."

"And Matheson agreed?"

"He had to. I told him that if he didn't like my terms he could go elsewhere, and he didn't care to take the risk."

Wrigley-Bell laughed.

"And I always thought you liked the old guv'nor," he said.

"I do," answered Smithers unexpectedly. "Unfortunately, he doesn't like me. Why, I can't for the life of me imagine."

The other found it prudent to make no comment. He helped himself largely to potatoes and then endeavored to change the subject.

"I wonder why Packer has set up that sawmill by the road corner?" he remarked.

"Because he's the kind of beast who can't resist the temptation of spoiling anything he gets his hands on," was the reply. "Because he's so rich that he must take the chance of making a little money out of the estate wherever he sees it. Because he knows that the road corner is the best bit of our water and he hates us like poison for having it. By putting up the sawmill he manages three things at once—he destroys the prettiest beech copse in the country, makes a little profit for himself, and makes life a hell for the unfortunate who happens to be trying to fish the road corner pool."

"It's easy to see that you don't like Packer," said Wrigley-Bell with a smile. He was much given to smiling, and unfortunately his smiles were not attractive. They began and ended with the lips, and were invariably coupled with a quick glance upward from beneath his thick brows. The effect was oddly disturbing, a mixture of humility and defiance. It was a kind of propitiatory snarl.

Smithers looked at him as though he were seeing him for the first time.

"Like him?" he repeated. "No. No more than anybody likes him, so far as I know. I could forgive him if he were a self-made man, as his father was, but he isn't even that. For Sir Peter Packer, second baronet, I have no use at all. Why, even you are no friend of his. You've just said so."

"Good gracious no! Not a friend," Wrigley-Bell protested. "But in business, you know, one has to keep on decent terms." He smiled again. "I certainly don't feel any better disposed toward him after suffering from that sawmill today."

"Yes. It has spoilt the second beat altogether. You'll be happier tomorrow in the peace and quiet of beat three. The guv'nor will be the sufferer tomorrow."

"Only in the morning. I suppose they knock off work at midday on Saturdays."

"Then you suppose wrong. Our beloved Peter is so anxious to make the most of the fine weather that he is paying overtime to keep the men on all day."

Wrigley-Bell spluttered in indignation.

"Really, that is most—most inconsiderate," he exclaimed. "Are you sure?"

"Perfectly. Jimmy Rendel said so, and he ought to know."

"I don't see that Rendel knows any more about it than the rest of us."

"Don't you? Really, even for a businessman you are remarkably obtuse. Hasn't it occurred to you that Jimmy and Marian Packer are—shall we say—somewhat closely acquainted?"

"Rendel and Lady Packer? You astonish me, Smithers, you really do!"

"Well, don't be so old-maidish about it. You can ask him about it tomorrow when he comes, if you like. Let us hope Peter is as slow on the uptake as you are."

"But Rendel!" Wrigley-Bell protested. "Why, he's only a boy!"

"I agree. Just the age for a romantic and hopeless love. Hopeless it is, mind you. I fancy that Marian Packer has her head screwed on the right way. But it can be no joke being married to Peter, and I expect she gets some fun out of Jimmy's attachment."

"Certainly, now I come to think of it, Rendel has been behaving rather strangely lately. He has scarcely caught a fish this season."

"As to catching anything, he's a rank bad fisherman. What can you expect from a lad of his age? The Didder is no place to learn the game on. We had to let him in, of course, because old Rendel had paid his shot before he crocked up, and Matheson insisted that he had a right to name his successor. But he's too young. This isn't a place for boys—or for women either. And talking of women," he added, as quick footsteps sounded in the passage outside, "that must be the fair Euphemia."

Euphemia Matheson was a woman of thirty-five or so, who, without being in the least degree stout, contrived to give a general and decidedly pleasing impression of roundness. Her cheeks were plump, her lips full and delicately curved, her brown eyes large and liquid, and she walked with a spring that was just not a bounce. Though dressed for the country in tweeds that admirably set off her really beautiful figure, she scarcely seemed to belong to the dingy inn parlor. Her careful make-up and reddened fingernails contrasted too sharply with the untidy paraphernalia of rods, nets, and fly boxes that encumbered it, and with the shabbily attired men at the table.

"Good evening!" she exclaimed in her rich contralto.

"Good evening, Mrs. Matheson," said Wrigley-Bell. "Are you coming to join us?"

"Good heavens, no! I had my dinner at a Christian hour, ages ago. I've been out for a walk. It's such a delicious evening. What I came to ask for was news of my truant husband."

"Your husband is still flogging the unresponsive waters of beat one, so far as I know," said Smithers.

"The poor lamb! He'll be dead when he comes in! Why are you such brutes to him? It's the worst beat on the whole river. Couldn't one of you have changed with him?"

Smithers grinned and, rising, walked over to the mantelpiece, above which hung a green baize notice board. On the board was displayed a large card, setting out the names of the members of the syndicate and the beats that were assigned to them throughout the fishing season, in strict rotation. With great solemnity, he consulted a pocket calendar.

"Friday the 17th of June," he announced, and studied the card. The relevant part of it was to this effect:

	17th June	*18th June*	*19th June*
R. MATHESON	1	2	3
T. WRIGLEY-BELL	2	3	4
S. F. SMITHERS	3	4	1
J. RENDEL	4	1	2

"I find that your husband was fishing on beat one according to the rules," he said, going back to his chair. "They are somewhat Draconian, I agree, but after all, he made them, so he should be the last to complain. Every man has to take each beat in turn, and it's as much as our lives are worth to try to change them. Now, for instance, I was on beat three today, and beat four, at the top of the water, was empty. There was a good fish rising fifty yards above the boundary post, but do you think I could have come home and confessed to him that I had caught one outside my beat? I shouldn't have dared."

Mrs. Matheson shrugged her shoulders.

"I think men are perfectly ridiculous," she said with an adorable pout. "You simply make rules for the sake of rules. Why should you take so much trouble to spoil your own pleasures?"

"Women are lawless cattle by nature," observed Smithers. "Our ancestors were sensible enough to recognize it. The ridiculous modern idea that they can be treated like reasonable beings—"

Mrs. Matheson, who was looking out of the window, paid no attention.

"It's pitch dark outside," she declared. "The rise must have been over ages ago. What can he be doing?"

"I shouldn't worry," said Wrigley-Bell. "He's probably investigating the domestic habits of a brown owl, or something of the kind."

"Now then, Wriggles, you're not to laugh at my dear old man."

"Oh, but I wasn't, Mrs. Matheson, I assure you, I wasn't. I think his enthusiasm is wonderful, at his age. I only wish I had it."

"Thank you, Wriggles. You don't mind my calling you Wriggles, do you?"

"Not in the least."

"Your husband is very lucky," observed Smithers, "to have ornithology to fall back upon when fishing fails. We less fortunate ones, when we have a blank day, are unable to plead what American boxers—inaccurately—call an alibi. If I don't catch anything, it is obvious that it was because I couldn't. He always has the excuse that he was so busy looking at a three-toed flycatcher that he forgot to put up his rod. I've noticed that the excuse grows on him with advancing years."

"You are a jealous brute, Smithkins. You know that he is still the best fisherman of the lot of you. He can catch as many fish as he wants to, any time."

"Even on beat one, Mrs. Matheson?"

"Even on beat one, Smithkins. You don't mind my calling you Smithkins, do you?"

"I do, very much indeed. I think I have said so before."

Euphemia grinned at him without a trace of malice.

"Sweet Smithkins, I really believe you have," she said, and then, at the sound of the front door opening and closing behind an incomer, ran from the room. The two men heard her voice in the passage raised in affectionate remonstrance: "Robert, you're to change your socks before you do anything else! No, never mind about drying your line, that can wait. Come upstairs at once, you bad old man!"

"She is a wonderful wife to him, is she not?" said Wrigley-Bell. His smile seemed at once to apologize for her and his own temerity in defending her.

"Wonderful is the word, no doubt," grunted the other. "I never cease to wonder that any woman should marry a man old enough to be her own father. But it continues to happen."

"I didn't mean it in that sense exactly. I only meant that she is such a splendid wife for him, looks after him, makes such a success of marriage, and so on."

"As to the marriage being a success, I have only outward appearances to go on, and they are apt to be deceptive, in my experience. But that doesn't concern me. Whether he likes it or not, whether she adores him or finds life a hell, is their affair, unless and until they get to the point of calling me in professionally. What does concern me, and what I do wonder at is the fact that for the last year or two she should have insisted on coming down here with him. She doesn't fish—thank God! She doesn't even care for the river. She has nothing to do down here except moon about the countryside and incidentally spoil what used to be a very agreeable bachelor party with her feminine imbecilities. What does she want to do it for?"

"But that's just my point," protested Wrigley-Bell, "it's just because she's such a wonderful wife to him. Obviously she comes down to look after the old fellow, see that he doesn't get overtired or wet through, for instance."

"Rubbish! The guv'nor is as strong as a horse. He doesn't need any looking after. And if she really wanted to do it, she'd be out on the water with him, making sure he came home in good time, instead of going for long walks by herself after dinner."

"Then what do you think is the reason?"

"I haven't got one. It's not my business to find reasons for other people's behavior. But if I were asked for an explanation, I should be tempted to say—"

His explanation, whatever it was, was cut short by the reappearance of Mrs. Matheson, accompanied by her husband.

Robert Matheson, everybody who knew him agreed, was a remarkable man for his age. How remarkable might be judged from the fact that it was only within the last few years that his age had come into consideration at all when he was being discussed. His lean, erect form had seemed to ignore the passage of time, his movements had remained as vigorous, his voice as firm as those of a man in the prime of life. When, twelve years previously, already well over sixty, he had married a young woman, nobody had seen in it anything extraordinary, or been moved to make the usual comments which the alliance of age and youth provoke. But nature cannot be defied forever. Long days of hard exercise had begun to take their toll, and those who knew him best and studied him most closely could see that the tremendous nervous energy which had sustained him so long was beginning to droop. Just now, as he came through the door, a heavy fishing bag in one hand and a rod case in the other, he looked an old, tired man, and the contrast between him and his vivid, vital wife was only too evident.

Matheson dropped into a chair with a sigh of relief, and, rummaging in the bag, produced a reel.

"Well, well!" he exclaimed. "It's been a long day. I shall be glad of something to eat."

"They are just heating up some soup for you, darling," put in his wife.

"Good." He began pulling the line off the reel. "Well," he went on, turning to the other two, "and how did you get on? There was quite a useful hatch of fly this evening, wasn't there?"

"I didn't do too badly," answered Smithers. "I got two and a grayling, and returned two."

"Splendid! Where did you get them? In the Alder Pool?"

"One in the Alder Pool and the other just below the weed-rack. Did you—?"

"Just below the weed-rack, eh? Excellent! I always said there would be good lying for a fish there once we had the bottom muddied out. That proves I'm right."

"It certainly does. And did you catch anything?"

Matheson did not hear, or at all events did not answer, the question. Instead, he said to Wrigley-Bell:

"Did you do any good on your water?"

"Not very much," grimaced the other. "I got one just above the bridge, one pound six ounces, and then at the road corner I hooked a big fish. He got me into the weeds and broke me."

"Hard lines! Very hard lines! What was the fly, by the way?"

"The little hackle blue I told you about the other day."

"I wish you'd let me have one or two. It seems to be a very taking fly."

"I only wish I could, Matheson. But unfortunately that was my last. I shall have to write for some more."

"A pity. It's always the fly you most want that you run short of, isn't it?"

"You haven't told us yet what luck you had on beat one," Smithers pointed out, somewhat aggressively.

"Oh, everybody knows what beat one is like," put in Wrigley-Bell, with a propitiatory smirk. "Nobody expects much there."

At this moment a diversion was effected by the entrance of the disheveled maid of all work, carrying a steaming plate of soup.

"Ah, thank you, Dora!" said Matheson, settling himself at the table. "Beat one?" he went on, spooning the soup into his mouth. "It's not so bad as all that, you know. There are some good fish there, though they take some getting."

"Did you get any of them this evening?" asked Smithers.

"Oh, I wasn't fishing. As a matter of fact I—"

"But I noticed you were drying your line just now," the solicitor persisted. "Why was that, if you hadn't been fishing?"

"I took a cast or two early on in the evening," Matheson admitted in some confusion. "But that isn't what I meant to tell you about. It's really most interesting, and I've had a delightful evening. Listen. You know that tree creeper that is always about on the elms by the bottom of the lane?"

"I know that you have often mentioned it," said Smithers. "I can't say that I have the pleasure of the bird's acquaintance. I don't even know what a tree creeper looks like, for that matter."

"My dear Smithers! What on earth do you do with your eyes? I see that tree creeper every time I go down to the river. But what has always puzzled me till this evening has been, *where does the bird roost?*"

Matheson delivered the question with profound emphasis. In the enthusiasm of the subject, he looked almost young again. His eyes sparkled, his cheeks glowed, and his spoon swung forgotten in midair.

"Robert, dear," cooed his wife. "Your soup is getting quite cold."

"Thank you, I've had all I want. Perhaps if you would cut me a little ham. . . . Thank you. You see the importance of the question," he went on. "It is well established now that the tree creeper prefers to roost in the trunk of some soft-barked tree, such as the sequoia, digging himself into the bark for shelter. Now there are no sequoias near here except up at the Manor. (I wish Packer would let me go up there and examine his trees, by the way.) So this evening I made a careful examination with my torch of every place that seemed likely, and where do you think I found him?"

"Where, darling?" asked Euphemia from the sofa in the corner. Neither of the other two seemed in the least interested. Wrigley-Bell was staring up at the ceiling from under his eyebrows, Smithers was ostentatiously fluttering the pages of the *Fishing Gazette*.

"In a holm-oak!" cried Matheson triumphantly. "It is most interesting— probably unique! I shall send word to the editor of *British Birds* about it. I'm quite sure it has never—but am I boring you?"

"Not a bit, darling," exclaimed Euphemia before Smithers could open his mouth. "Do go on."

He went on.

Nick Adams caught trout with grasshoppers. Hemingway caught a Nobel Prize with *The Old Man and the Sea*. It was a long but rich time in between. In this extraordinary letter first published in *Esquire*, we are treated to a glimpse of the novella in a protean state.

ERNEST HEMINGWAY

On the Blue Water

Certainly there is no hunting like the hunting of man, and those who have hunted armed men long enough and liked it never really care for anything else thereafter. You will meet them doing various things with resolve, but their interest rarely holds because after the other thing ordinary life is as flat as the taste of wine when the taste buds have been burned off your tongue. Wine, when your tongue has been burned clean with lye and water, feels like puddle water in your mouth, while mustard feels like axle-grease, and you can smell crisp, fried bacon, but when you taste it, there is only a feeling of crinkly lard.

You can learn about this matter of the tongue by coming into the kitchen of a villa on the Riviera late at night and taking a drink from what should be a bottle of Evian water and which turns out to be *Eau de Javel*, a concentrated lye product used for cleaning sinks. The taste buds on your tongue, if burned off by *Eau de Javel*, will begin to function again after about a week. At what rate other things regenerate one does not know, since you lose track of friends and the things one could learn in a week were mostly learned a long time ago.

The other night I was talking with a good friend to whom all hunting is dull except elephant hunting. To him there is no sport in anything unless there is great danger and, if the danger is not enough, he will increase it for his own satisfaction. A hunting companion of his had told me how this friend was not satisfied with the risks of ordinary elephant hunting but would, if possible, have the elephants driven, or turned, so he could take them head-on, so it was a choice of killing them with the difficult frontal shot as they came, trumpeting, with their ears spread, or having them run over him. This is to elephant hunting what the German cult of suicide climbing is to ordinary mountaineering, and I suppose it is, in a way, an attempt to approximate the old hunting of the armed man who is hunting you.

This friend was speaking of elephant hunting and urging me to hunt elephant, as he said that once you took it up no other hunting would mean anything to you. I was arguing that I enjoyed all hunting and shooting, any sort I could get, and had no desire to wipe this capacity for enjoyment out with the *Eau de Javel* of the old elephant coming straight at you with his trunk up and his ears spread.

"Of course you like that big fishing too," he said rather sadly. "Frankly, I can't see where the excitement is in that."

"You'd think it was marvelous if the fish shot at you with Tommy guns or jumped back and forth through the cockpit with swords on the ends of their noses."

"Don't be silly," he said. "But frankly I don't see where the thrill is."

"Look at so and so," I said. "He's an elephant hunter and this last year he's gone fishing for big fish and he's goofy about it. He must get a kick out of it or he wouldn't do it."

"Yes," my friend said. "There must be something about it but I can't see it. Tell me where you get a thrill out of it."

"I'll try to write it in a piece sometime," I told him.

"I wish you would," he said. "Because you people are sensible on other subjects. Moderately sensible I mean."

"I'll write it."

In the first place, the Gulf Stream and the other great ocean currents are the last wild country there is left. Once you are out of sight of land and of the other boats you are more alone than you can ever be hunting and the sea is the same as it has been since before men ever went on it in boats. In a season fishing you will see it oily flat as the becalmed galleons saw it while they drifted to the westward; white-capped with a fresh breeze as they saw it running with the trades; and in high, rolling blue hills the tops blowing off them like snow as they were punished by it, so that sometimes you will see three great hills of water with your fish jumping from the top of the farthest one and if you tried to make a turn to go with him without picking your chance, one of those breaking crests would roar down in on you with a thousand tons of water and you would hunt no more elephants, Richard, my lad.

There is no danger from the fish, but anyone who goes on the sea the year around in a small power boat does not seek danger. You may be absolutely sure that in a year you will have it without seeking, so you try always to avoid it all you can.

Because the Gulf Stream is an unexploited country, only the very fringe of it ever being fished, and then only at a dozen places in thousands of miles of current, no one knows what fish live in it, or how great size they reach or what age, or even what kinds of fish and animals live in it at different depths. When you are drifting, out of sight of land, fishing four lines, sixty, eighty, one hundred, and one hundred fifty fathoms down, in water that is seven hundred fathoms deep, you never know what may take the small tuna that you use for bait, and every time the line starts to run off the reel, slowly first, then with a scream of the click as the rod bends and you feel it double and the huge weight of the friction of the line rushing through that depth of water while you pump and reel, pump and reel, pump and reel, trying to get the belly out of the line before the fish jumps, there is always a thrill that needs no danger to make it real. It may be a marlin that will jump high and clear off to your right and then go off in a series of leaps, throwing a splash like a speedboat in a sea as you shout for the boat to turn with him watching the line melting off the reel before the boat can get around. Or it may be a broadbill that will show wagging his great broadsword. Or it may be some fish that you will never see at all that will head straight out to the northwest like a submerged submarine and never show and at the end of five hours the angler has a straightened-out hook. There is always a feeling of excitement when a fish takes hold when you are drifting deep.

In hunting you know what you are after and the top you can get is an elephant. But who can say what you will hook sometime when drifting in a hundred and fifty fathoms in the Gulf Stream? There are probably marlin and swordfish to which the fish we have seen caught are pgymies; and every time a fish takes the bait drifting you have a feeling perhaps you are hooked to one of these.

Carlos, our Cuban mate, who is fifty-three years old and has been fishing for marlin since he went in the bow of a skiff with his father when he was seven, was fishing drifting deep one time when he hooked a white marlin. The fish jumped twice and then sounded and when he sounded suddenly Carlos felt a great weight and he could not hold the line which went out and down and down irresistibly until the fish had taken out over a hundred and fifty fathoms. Carlos says it felt as heavy and solid as though he were hooked to the bottom of the sea. Then suddenly the strain was loosened but he could feel the weight of his original fish and pulled it up stone dead. Some toothless fish like a swordfish or marlin had closed his jaws across the middle of the eighty-pound white marlin and squeezed it and held it so that every bit of the insides of the fish had been crushed out while the huge fish moved off with the eighty-pound fish in its mouth. Finally it let go. What size of a fish would that be? I thought it might be a giant squid but Carlos said there were no sucker marks on the fish and that it showed plainly the shape of the marlin's mouth where he had crushed it.

Another time an old man fishing alone in a skiff out of Cabañas hooked a great marlin that, on the heavy sashcord handline, pulled the skiff far out to sea. Two days later the old man was picked up by fishermen sixty miles to the eastward, the head and forward part of the marlin lashed alongside. What was left of the fish, less than half, weighed eight hundred pounds. The old man had stayed with him a day, a night, a day and another night while the fish swam deep and pulled the boat. When he had come up the old man had pulled the boat up on him and harpooned him. Lashed alongside the sharks had hit him and the old man had fought them out alone in the Gulf Stream in a skiff, clubbing them, stabbing at them, lunging at them with an oar until he was exhausted and the sharks had eaten all that they could hold. He was crying in the boat when the fishermen picked him up half crazy from his loss, and the sharks were still circling the boat.

But what is the excitement in catching them from a launch? It comes from the fact that they are strange and wild things of unbelievable speed and power and a beauty, in the water and leaping, that is indescribable, which you would never see if you did not fish for them, and to which you are suddenly harnessed so that you feel their speed, their force and their savage power as intimately as if you were riding a bucking horse. For half an hour, an hour, or five hours, you are fastened to the fish as much as he is fastened to you and you tame him and break him the way a wild horse is broken and finally lead him to the boat. For pride and because the fish is worth plenty of money in the Havana market, you gaff him at the boat and bring him on board, but the having him in the boat isn't the excitement; it is while you are fighting him that is the fun.

If the fish is hooked in the bony part of the mouth I am sure the hook hurts him no more than the harness hurts the angler. A large fish when he is hooked often does not feel the hook at all and will swim toward the boat, unconcerned, to take another bait. At other times he will swim away deep, completely unconscious of the hook, and it is when he feels himself held and pressure exerted to turn him, that he knows something is wrong and starts to make his fight. Unless he is hooked where it hurts he makes his fight not against the pain of the hook, but against being captured and if, when he is out of sight, you figure what he is doing, in what direction he is pulling when deep down, and why, you can convince him and bring him to the boat by the same system you break a wild horse. It is not necessary to kill him, or even completely exhaust him, to bring him to the boat.

To kill a fish that fights deep you pull against the direction he wants to go until he is worn out and dies. It takes hours and when the fish dies the sharks are liable to get him before the angler can raise him to the top. To catch such a fish quickly you figure by trying to hold him absolutely, which direction he is working (a sounding fish is going in the direction the line slants in the water when you have put enough pressure on the drag so the line would break if you held it any tighter); then get ahead of him on that direction and he can be brought to the boat without killing him. You do not tow him or pull him with the motor boat; you use the engine to shift your position just as you would walk up or down stream with a salmon. A fish is caught most surely from a small boat such as a dory since the angler can shut down on his drag and simply let the fish pull the boat. Towing the boat will kill him in time. But the most satisfaction is to dominate and convince the fish and bring him intact in everything but spirit to the boat as rapidly as possible.

"Very instructive," says the friend. "But where does the thrill come in?"

The thrill comes when you are standing at the wheel drinking a cold bottle of beer and watching the outriggers jump the baits so they look like small live tuna leaping along and then behind one you see a long dark shadow wing up and then a big spear thrust out followed by an eye and head and dorsal fin and the tuna jumps with the wave and he's missed it.

"Marlin," Carlos yells from the top of the house and stamps his feet up and down, the signal that a fish is raised. He swarms down to the wheel and you go back to where the rod rests in its socket and there comes the shadow again, fast as the shadow of a plane moving over the water and the spear, head, fin, and shoulders smash out of water and you hear the click the closepin makes as the line pulls out and the long bight of line whishes through the water as the fish turns and as you hold the rod, you feel it double and the butt kicks you in the belly as you come back hard and feel his weight, as you strike him again and again, and again.

Then the heavy rod arc-ing out toward the fish, and the reel in a band-saw zinging scream, the marlin leaps clear and long, silver in the sun long, round as a hogshead and banded with lavender stripes and, when he goes into the water, it throws a column of spray like a shell lighting.

Then he comes out again, and the spray roars, and again, then the line feels slack and out he bursts headed across and in, then jumps wildly twice more seeming to hang high and stiff in the air before falling to throw the column of water and you can see the hook in the corner of his jaw.

Then in a series of jumps like a greyhound he heads to the northwest and standing up, you follow him in the boat, the line taut as a banjo string and

little drops coming from it until you finally get the belly of it clear of that friction against the water and have a straight pull out toward the fish.

And all the time Carlos is shouting, "Oh, God, the bread of my children! Oh look at the bread of my children! Joseph and Mary look at the bread of my children jump! There it goes the bread of my children! He'll never stop the bread the bread the bread of my children!"

This striped marlin jumped, in a straight line to the northwest, fifty-three times, and every time he went out it was a sight to make your heart stand still. Then he sounded and I said to Carlos, "Get me the harness. Now I've got to pull him up the bread of your children."

"I couldn't stand to see it," he says. "Like a filled pocketbook jumping. He can't go down deep now. He's caught too much air jumping."

"Like a race horse over obstacles." Julio says. "Is the harness all right? Do you want water?"

"No." Then kidding Carlos, "What's this about the bread of your children?"

"He always says that," says Julio. "You should hear him curse me when we would lose one in the skiff."

"What will the bread of your children weigh?" I ask with mouth dry, the harness taut across shoulders, the rod a flexible prolongation of the sinew pulling ache of arms, the sweat salty in my eyes.

"Four hundred and fifty," says Carlos.

"Never," says Julio.

"Thou and thy never," says Carlos. "The fish of another always weighs nothing to thee."

"Three seventy-five," Julio raises his estimate. "Not a pound more."

Carlos says something unprintable and Julio comes up to four hundred.

The fish is nearly whipped now and the dead ache is out of raising him, and then, while lifting, I feel something slip. It holds for an instant and then the line is slack.

"He's gone," I say and unbuckle the harness.

"The bread of your children," Julio says to Carlos.

"Yes," Carlos says. "Yes. Joke and no joke yes. *El pan de mis hijos.* Three hundred and fifty pounds at ten cents a pound. How many days does a man work for that in the winter? How cold is it at three o'clock in the morning on all those days? And the fog and the rain in a norther. Every time he jumps the hook cutting the hole in a little bigger in his jaw. Ay how he could jump. How he could jump!"

"The bread of your children," says Julio.

"Don't talk about that any more," said Carlos.

No it is not elephant hunting. But we get a kick out of it. When you have a family and children, your family, or my family, or the family of Carlos, you do not have to look for danger. There is always plenty of danger when you have a family.

And after a while the danger of others is the only danger and there is no end to it nor any pleasure in it nor does it help to think about it.

But there is great pleasure in being on the sea, in the unknown wild suddenness of a great fish; in his life and death which he lives for you in an hour while your strength is harnessed to his; and there is satisfaction in conquering this thing which rules the sea it lives in.

Then in the morning of the day after you have caught a good fish, when the man who carried him to the market in a handcart brings the long roll of heavy silver dollars wrapped in a newspaper on board it is very satisfactory money. It really feels like money.

"There's the bread of your children," you say to Carlos.

"In the time of the dance of the millions," he says, "a fish like that was worth two hundred dollars. Now it is thirty. On the other hand a fisherman never starves. The sea is very rich."

"And the fisherman always poor."

"No. Look at you. You are rich."

"Like hell," you say. "And the longer I fish the poorer I'll be. I'll end up fishing with you for the market in a dinghy."

"That I never believe," says Carlos devoutly. "But look. That fishing in a dinghy is very interesting. You would like it."

"I'll look forward to it," you say.

"What we need for prosperity is a war," Carlos says. "In the time of the war with Spain and in the last war the fishermen were actually rich."

"All right," you say. "If we have a war you get the dinghy ready."

While scores of presidents have fished holding the office, fewer than a dozen were skilled enough to do it holding a rod. None has been more candid in expressing his angling opinions than Hoover. This piece was published a year before he died.

HERBERT HOOVER

Fishing Presidents and Candidates

There are a dozen justifications for fishing. Among them is its importance to the political world. No political aspirant can qualify for election unless he demonstrates he is a fisherman, there being twenty-five million persons who pay annually for a license to fish.

In Roman times the people formed their political auguries by observing the flights of birds and the entrails of dead sheep. I have recently been fishing. In the long time between bites I have come to the firm conclusion that today fish take the place of the flight of birds and the entrails of sheep.

Also, I should inform you that from an augury point of view, there are two kinds of fish: there are the host of species of common or garden fish, which are the recreation of the common man. There are also the rare species of fish sought by the aristocracy of fishermen. They require more equipment and more incantations than merely spitting on the bait. Politically speaking, these fish can be ignored since they are only landed the hard way and have no appeal to most voters.

A few years ago a press photograph showed my friend, the late Senator Taft, awkwardly holding a common fish. It was taken from many angles for all the common men to see. I knew without other evidence that he was a candidate.

Some years ago my friend, General Eisenhower, burst into photographs from all angles, gingerly holding three very common fish. The augury was positive.

The political potency of fish is known to presidents as well as candidates. In modern times all presidents quickly begin to fish soon after election. I am told that McKinley, Taft, Wilson, and Harding all undertook fishing in a tentative way, but for the common fishes.

President Coolidge apparently had not fished before election. Being a fundamentalist in religion, economics, and fishing, he began his fish career for common trout with worms. Ten million fly-fishermen at once evidenced disturbed minds. Then Mr. Coolidge took to a fly. He gave the Secret Service guards great excitement in dodging his backcast and rescuing flies from trees. There were many photographs. Soon after that he declared he did not choose to run again.

President Franklin Roosevelt caught many common fish from the military base of a battleship.

President Truman, prior to his 1948 election, appeared once in a photograph somewhere in a boat gingerly holding a common fish in his arms. An unkind reporter wrote that someone else had caught it. I can find no trace of the letter that the reporter must have received. It is also reported that Mr. Truman was fishing somewhere north of Key West when his boat was surrounded by sharks. But sharks are always a bad augury. Mr. Truman did not run for a third term.

President Theodore Roosevelt, President Cleveland and myself—with a slight egotism!—I think, are the only presidents who had been lifelong fly-fishermen before they went to the White House.

Everyone knows of the first Roosevelt that he was a valiant hunter of big animals, and generally an evangel of the strenuous life—which included fishing. He relates an adventure with an Adirondack stream when he was twelve years old:

> After dinner all of us began to "whip" the rapids. At first I sat on a rock by the water but the black flies drove me from there, so I attempted to cross the rapids. But I had miscalculated my strength for before I was half way across the force of the current had swept me into water which was above my head. Leaving the pole to take [care] of itself I struck out for a rock. My pole soon stuck and so I recovered it. I then went half wading, half swimming down stream, fishing all the time but unsuccessful.

President Cleveland is author of a delightful little volume called *Fishing and Hunting Sketches*, in which he sets forth his ideas on the beatitudes of those sports. As a fisherman, he preferred small-mouthed black bass to trout, and in this respect claimed kinship to another political fisherman, Daniel Webster, from whose history he draws this interesting example of the interrelation of fishing and politics:

> Perhaps, [writes President Cleveland] none of Mr. Webster's orations were more notable or added more to his lasting fame than that delivered at the laying of the cornerstone of the Bunker Hill monument, and it will probably be conceded that its most impressive and beautiful passage was addressed to the survivors of the War for Independence then present, beginning with the words "Venerable Men."
>
> This thrilling oratorical flight was composed and elaborated by Mr. Webster while wading waist deep and casting his flies in Mashapee waters. He himself afterwards often referred to this circumstance; and one who was his companion on this particular occasion has recorded the fact that, noticing indications of laxity in fishing action on Mr. Webster's part, he approached him, and that, in the exact words of this witness, "he seemed to be gazing at the overhanging trees, and presently, advancing one foot and extending his right hand, he commenced to speak—*Venerable Men . . .*"

Mr. Cleveland says that he got this story from Webster's guide, who told him that the Massachusetts Senator frequently prepared his orations in this wise, and was in the habit of addressing "mighty strong and fine talk to the fish." President Cleveland adds:

> It is impossible to avoid the conclusion that the fishing habit, by promoting close association with nature, by teaching patience and by generating or stimulating useful contemplation, tends directly to the increase of the intellectual power of its votaries and through them to the improvement of our national character."

That presidents have taken to fishing in an astonishing fashion seems to me worthy of investigation. I think I have discovered the reason: it is the silent sport. One of the few opportunities given a president for the refreshment of his soul and the clarification of his thoughts by solitude lies through fishing. As I have said in another place, it is generally realized and accepted that prayer is the most personal of all human relationships. Everyone knows that on such occasions men and women are entitled to be alone and undisturbed.

Next to prayer, fishing is the most personal relationship of man; and of more importance, everyone concedes that the fish will not bite in the presence of the public, including newspapermen.

Fishing seems to be one of the few avenues left to the presidents through which they may escape to their own thoughts, may live in their own imaginings, find relief from the pneumatic hammer of constant personal contacts, and refreshment of mind in rippling waters. Moreover, it is a constant reminder of the democracy of life, of humility and of human frailty. It is desirable that the president of the United States should be periodically reminded of this fundamental fact—that the forces of nature discriminate for no man.

There may be stranger ways to find companionship on a river, but none comes to mind. Hoyt's detective novel begins with a cast and a rather startling drift.

RICHARD HOYT

I Wish Zane Grey Had Been There

I wish Zane Grey had been there. Maybe he would have known what to make of it all.

We were fishing at Steamboat on the North Umpqua River. Steamboat is one of the most famous steelhead drifts in the West. Zane Grey fished at Steamboat. Every summer fishermen gather there with their chest waders and ease out from the south shore to try their luck.

It is there, at Steamboat, that the big steelies lay.

It was there that I found a naked girl floating ass up at twilight.

Now it wouldn't be especially shocking to find a corpse in the Monongahela at Pittsburgh or the Anacostia at the District of Columbia. Dead people, after all, are the jetsam of cities and civilization. We love cities and we hate them. We say they are doomed yet we embrace them. The North Umpqua is different. It has a purity that makes a floating corpse especially ugly, an affront to decent people and a violation of propriety.

The inhabitants of Ernest Hemingway's Left Bank may change from generation to generation, twisted by history and fashion, but not the Douglas fir of Zane Grey's river. The North Umpqua is permanent, immutable. The evergreens still smell the same as they did in 1927. The mosquitoes slap the same.

It's hard to imagine any water being clearer or colder than the North Umpqua in the springtime. The drift itself—located downstream from the creek of the same name—is more than a hundred yards long and tails dogleg left into a series of swift channels as it moves downriver. The water in the drift is deep and rolling; it wells up from primal sources of the river. It's best fished from a shelf on the south bank that varies from fifteen to thirty yards wide. The water that sweeps across the shelf is waist-deep and so cold it takes your breath away.

Fishing at Steamboat is for those who know how. It's a privilege and a pleasure, a lovely memory for old men facing the long nights of December.

The road to Steamboat flanks the north bank and follows the twists and turns of the river higher and higher into the Cascades, deeper and deeper into forests of virgin Douglas fir. A few tourists on their way to Crater Lake use the highway, turning east from Roseburg at the interstate. But mostly it is used by fishermen and by loggers with strapping suspenders and too many Y chromosomes. The loggers horse their big Whites and Macks down the highway at breathtaking speeds. They own the highway by right of mass and muscle.

I don't know what I was doing there in the first place. I'm the kind of guy who wades around in shorts and tennis shoes trying to go one-on-one with hypothermia. Nobody wears tennis shoes at Steamboat, except maybe an escapee from a farm pond. It isn't done. So I borrowed a pair of chest waders from my brother-in-law, a surgeon who has a few bucks. I was entertaining one of his colleagues, a man from Chicago who specialized in diseases of the rich. I even brought along my Irish walking hat—a real prize—so that I looked like a mannequin at Norm Thompson's in Portland. My companion, whose name was Floyd, walked into Norm's and bought a pair of $80 waders, the kind that float if you slip in the water. He also bought himself a $180 carbon fly rod, the kind the professionals use in the *Field and Stream* stories.

Let it be said that on this occasion he didn't catch any more steelhead than I did. Part of the reason was he didn't know a whole lot about steelhead. I tried to help him out, but he wouldn't listen; some people are like that. What do you do?

What he needed to know is that steelhead don't eat when they make their spawning runs. They're said to strike at something just because it's there and annoying. That accounts for steelhead lures being particularly obnoxious— colored silver and gold and fluorescent green and orange. Steelhead flies are likewise large, gaudy, and often wrapped with silver thread.

He also should have known that steelhead won't hit a lure or a fly, but instead will mouth it and spit it out. So you get a nudge and not a hit. You have to pay attention. I think Floyd expected a fish to hit his fly like a shark and take off for parts unknown while he posed, extra cool in his expensive outfit, and played the fish like he'd been doing it all his life.

You fool a trout with a fly that looks like the real thing. A trout will hit it and catch himself.

But steelhead are mean and wary. If they see your line, they won't even go through their mouthing routine. So you have to use tackle that's light for the size of the fish.

When I fish a place like Steamboat, I know there're fish in the water. There has to be or else all those grown men wouldn't gather there with their expensive gear.

I approach a drift like Steamboat with expectations of catching a trophy. I have great patience. I can nurse my fantasy for an entire day when it's obvious to all but fools that the fish aren't hitting. But I never give up. So it was on this day. For hours I sent those great bright flies tumbling into the rich green of Zane Grey's drift.

Nothing.

So there I was. I stood for hours in the cold water of the North Umpqua, feeling awkward and pretentious in my fancy borrowed boots. I sent that fly out there again and again and again, until my shoulder sagged from the effort, hoping against hope that a steelhead would take it and set out on one of those heart-thumping runs that sets the reel drag screaming and the blood surging.

When darkness settled over the river, I stayed with it, hoping that perseverance and blind luck might make up for skill. My friend and the fishermen with good sense had long since retreated to the warmth of the café above the tail of the drift. I was alone with the night sounds and the brooding shadows of Douglas fir on the sides of the river.

There was no traffic on the highway above the north bank. Just me and the bugs. Me and the mosquitoes. Me and the slight breeze that kicked up from the west. Me and Zane Grey's phantom fish. Me with my brother-in-law's waders cinched up tight around my chest. Me and the cold. Damned fool me.

I saw a log enter the head of the drift, riding in the water, turning slowly this way and that. I watched the log pause for a moment at an eddy before it continued to glide silently down the drift.

I saw that the log had buttocks, legs, and a spine.

It was the North Umpqua that offered me the log's foot.

But it was me, jackass that I am, who stepped forward to accept it.

It was also me who stepped off the ledge and into the icy depths of the drift.

And it was me who held stubbornly onto the foot and forgot about the waders and forgot about the current.

My brother-in-law is not a bad sort, but his boots were not $80 jobs that float no matter what. Fill them up with water and they're like columns of concrete. He is a medical doctor, a surgeon. Why hadn't I complained? Why hadn't I invoked the name of my sister and forced him to buy better boots for me to borrow?

Too late.

When the water got by the belt cinched around my chest and under my armpits, it entered the waders like a sheepherder in a whorehouse. I let go of the log's foot and sank to the bottom like a sack of sand. It happened so fast that I hadn't let go of the made-in-Korea fly rod I had bought on sale in a supermarket. Corned beef hash in one aisle, fly rods the next. I let go of the rod with some regret—it had cost me twenty bucks—and attacked the snaps around my chest with a vengeance while I rolled and tumbled lazily along the bottom of Zane Grey's famous drift. I wriggled free at last and shot upward with pain shooting through my lungs.

I came up under the log, which seemed to be waiting for me in the darkness.

I hooked my arm around it, discovering in the process that it was a young woman, and headed for the lights of the café above the tail of the drift. Sensible men were up there drinking coffee and eating enormous chiliburgers heaped with grated cheese and chopped raw onions.

The coffee was farther away than I thought. As I got within twenty feet of the shore, I could feel the current take control. It was a masterful, sure current and would have its way. I struggled for a better grip on the body, which turned faceup. I could see her face as we swept past the lights of the café. I could have let go and should have, but I was momentarily confused. I clung stubbornly to her corpse as the two of us were carried silently and swiftly toward the terror of the rapids at the tail of the drift.

She was a brunet. Her shoulder-length hair floated back from a widow's peak in great, black, undulating folds. She had a slender face with a fine nose and full lips, parted slightly in death. Her eyes, separated by a neat bullet hole, were closed—a blessing the movies would have us believe is usual. The closed eyes gave her the appearance of being asleep. It is one of life's sweetest, most private, and most remembered moments to wake in the early hours of the morning and see a woman sleeping by your side. The quarrels and the hard times are past and she is there, trusting. The innocence is special.

That's how it was with the girl on the North Umpqua. I swallowed. I felt like a voyeur. If I could have apologized, I would have. But she was dead. I watched her and maybe fell a little in love.

It had begun to rain. The rain felt good. It was then that I realized that I wouldn't be making it to shore. Falling in love and feeling the rain were two pleasures I was to be denied. No man could survive the rapids in the dark. In the daytime when you could see the rocks up ahead, maybe. That was a fact that I assessed without emotion as the savage current tightened its grip on me. It was pulling. Pulling tighter. Pulling me to the rocks as we are all pulled from the moment of conception. Most people aren't aware of the current until they're in their mid-thirties and begin divorcing their spouses, turning to drink, worshiping strange gurus, or generally screwing up their lives.

There on the North Umpqua the years turned into seconds. There was no use getting excited; that wouldn't do any good. The end was near; it was as simple as that. I welcomed it, maybe—who knows? I was also trying to figure a way out. There had to be a way.

There was a way.

The body.

The corpse was buoyant. It apparently had air trapped in its lungs. I shifted the body underneath me and spread-eagled her so she wouldn't roll. I spread her arms and gripped each wrist. I pinned her legs together with my own and locked my feet beneath her ankles. I clutched her as tightly as I could and held my head to her chest for maximum protection. If it worked, it would result in life. My own.

And so it began.

Immediately below the drift the current quickens and the river splits into a series of channels that weave in and out like a tangle of roots. The channels are separated by narrow islands of jagged basalt. The river turns sharply to the left. After another hundred yards the current swings right again and the channels come together for the run at the narrows. Here the riverbed takes a precipitous thirty-degree drop and the water is forced through a chute no more than fifteen yards wide and bordered by rock walls.

The narrows and the channels are the reasons why the fishing is good at Steamboat. The fish rest in the drift after their struggle up the falls and white water.

A white-water enthusiast with the best equipment might test the channels were it not for the narrows. The narrows were out of the question.

The dead girl rode low in the water and was awkward to maneuver, but she was better than nothing. I peered over her forehead searching for basalt. The channels narrowed as the current quickened. My eyes were accustomed to the darkness by now. I saw a flash of white. Ahead and to the left. Water against stone. I let go with my right arm. Stroked hard and deep.

Rock zipped by.

Couldn't think. More rocks. Her skull snapped. Long hair in my eyes. I couldn't see. Her body shuddered.

Rock.

Rocks on either side.

The roar.

I could hear the awful roar.

The narrows.

I adjusted myself on the girl's torso. Her body was cold to the touch.

I held on.

The roar was louder.

The water swifter.

We were into it.

She rolled.

I held.

Again.

I held.

It was over.

We were plunging deep, deep into the head of another drift. It was finished. I was alive. I didn't know who she was, had never met her, but felt as close to her as I had to any woman in my life. I took her by the hair and, stroking with my left hand, pulled her to the highway side of the river.

The rain had increased to a downpour when I pulled her body onto the rocky shore. I turned her over. Her skull was split wide open in the back. Her rib cage was caved in and her spine was twisted at an odd angle. I squatted there in the rain and examined the girl I had met in the drift and had embraced in the face of death. There had been no formal introductions as at a church, cocktail party, or bar. The river had introduced us. She, a silent form in the North Umpqua. Me, a jerk who didn't know when to give up. She had asked me and I had stayed. Then she had protected me. I was alive.

It's not easy to explain how I felt. It was a matter of honor and of being civilized. What would one of Zane Grey's heroes have done?

He would have done what I now had to do. The right thing.

I stood up and took the long walk to the café at Steamboat.

There are some writers who weave spells, methodically, strands thatched by hand. Humphrey forgoes the labor and casts them, effortlessly. He possesses that rarest of qualities—empathy—tempered by craft. When he goes down to the sea we follow, bidden.

WILLIAM HUMPHREY

Great Point

When the alarm clock went off at half past four I was awake and waiting for it, wishing for it, that nightlong, fitful southwest wind having made my sleep fitful—that, plus my anticipation, mixed with some misgiving, over the coming day. The place was Nantucket, the month September, the day the last one of my two weeks' stay on the island.

Disgruntled with freshwater fishing, with drought and pollution and crowds on the streams, I had heeded the advice given me by a famous fisherman, now dead, and had turned to the ocean, expecting to find it teeming with trophies and to have, if not all of it to myself, at least a sizable private portion of it. During my time on Nantucket I had seen more fishermen than fish. The striped bass and the bluefish had shunned its accessible shores. In the tackle shops, fishermen reported daily on conditions at Surfside, Smith Point, Tom Nevers Head, and the story was everywhere the same: high tide or low, daylight or dark, using this bait or that lure—nothing.

Such conversations, however, often ended on a note intriguing to a newcomer like me. "Catching them out at Great Point," one man would observe with a sigh. To which another man would give a snort and say, "Oh, sure! There!" After that, there was nothing more to be said, it seemed. I ventured a time or two to wonder aloud, why not try at Great Point, then, if that was where the fish were? What I got by way of reply was the dampening look of an old salt for a rank apprentice, of an islander for an off-islander.

Now surfcasters are men of stamina, rugged and adventurous, ready for anything. Theirs is not a gentle and contemplative recreation. They rise in darkness, drive distances, fish in the worst weather. Of all the many subspecies of fishermen, they take the greatest risks; in fact, they are downright reckless, even foolhardy. A few of them, breasting the breakers, invading the surf, seeking to extend their casts a few feet to reach schools of feeding fish, are swept to sea and lost each year, leaving widows and orphans to mourn them. What was there about Great Point that deterred these old-time surfmen whose scuttlebutt I overheard at Bill Fisher's Tackle Shop? And who were those fools who rushed in where others feared to tread, the ones who were out there catching the fish?

These questions were to be answered today. I had been joined on the island by my friend, the dauntless Al Clements, a man whom nothing can discourage or deflect, or even distract, wherever there is water with possible sport in it, who groans at the thought of fishes being changed into loaves. Al would stop at nothing. Knowing this was the cause of my misgiving, and my anticipation. He had arrived in his four-wheel-drive Scout—the indispensable conveyance for the trip to Great Point. Now as I dressed in the predawn darkness to the lost-soul wailing of the wind, I felt a bit like Melville's Ishmael, accosted on another Nantucket morning by Elijah, crazed survivor of a voyage aboard the *Pequod* with that maniacal fisherman Captain Ahab: "Shipmates, have ye shipped in that ship? Anything down there about your souls?"

Today's Nantucket fishing fleet is not made up of square-rigged whalers with longboats on davits ready for lowering at the cry of "Thar she blows!" It is an even more numerous fleet of four-wheel-drive vehicles bristling with surf rods the length of harpoons, ready-rigged for the signal that sweeps over the island with the wind—"Bluefish in!" You can see them coming off the ferryboats from Hyannis, bouncing over the cobblestones of Main Street, parked outside the A & P, rods riding flat in racks on the roof or else upright, like lances, in a row of sockets bolted to the front bumper so that the riders look through them as through bars. In the darkness of early morning and early evening, from May to November, they ply the sand-swept island roads, bound for the beaches. For although the books tell you that bluefish are mainly daytime feeders, the ones that vacation around Nantucket have not read the books. They are as independent and set in their ways as the islanders themselves; they dine at dusk, they breakfast by the light of the moon.

It was dark but moonless when we set off that morning from Madaket, on the west side of the island, with Al, pipe in mouth, at the wheel. The treeless, featureless, flat landscape might have been the sea and we in the cabin of a boat. We were to traverse the length of the island. A strong starboard wind opposed us as we tacked toward Nantucket town. Sanguine as always, Al said, "Today, Bill, we're going to kill them." Doubtful as always, I grunted.

Our course took us around the town and out east toward Siasconset. We veered from that route shortly to go northwest toward Polpis. Long, narrow, nearly enclosed Nantucket Harbor was off our portside.

At the coastal settlement of Wauwinet, the paved road ended. It seemed that the world ended there. We stopped and got out, and, by flashlight in a hurricane wind, deflated our tires. For not even a four-wheel-drive vehicle, even in low, low gear, can get through deep sand with its tires inflated. We reduced the pressure to ten pounds, making certain by the gauge that it was the same in all four tires. The least imbalance—as little as a pound's difference—can cause one wheel to dig into the sand and spin uselessly. You do not want to be stuck on a narrow beach with the tide rising or a line storm coming on. A fisherman-conscious community has provided an air compressor and hose at that jumping-off place for the use of those returning from the Point and resuming travel on the paved road—a reassuring thought, and one that I, buffeted by the wind and blinded by the darkness, grasped at uncertainly but eagerly.

There we left behind us the last long human habitation, and entered upon Great Point, a narrow spit of sand extending five miles into Nantucket Sound. Instantly we learned why all but the most determined—some might say, the most demented—fishermen avoid Great Point. It was as though we had launched a small craft upon a stormy sea and in a raging gale.

On either side of the land, which rose barely above water level, the ocean heaved and swelled. The spit seemed to undulate upon it. Running more or less down the middle of this ribbon of sand was a road of sorts—a track about as permanent as the wake of a boat. Ruts made in it by previous vehicles lasted little longer than a trail in water, buried within minutes in drifts, dunes, waves of sand. You had to cut your own path through them. No caution could be observed, for to pause was to sink, so we went at breakneck speed—I know of no stretch of road anywhere that restores that tired expression to more vivid life. As in a small boat at sea, we pitched, we tossed, we yawed, almost plunging into the water on one side and the next moment into that on the other side. We rolled, we crested, we bottomed. We were jolted in all directions, now against the roof and now against the doors and now against the dashboard and now against each other. His pipe removed from his mouth for safety, Al clung to the wheel. I clung, when I could, to my door handle.

The five-mile drive took twenty minutes; it seemed longer. After about the first mile of it I began to laugh. I was laughing at my own madness in going to such lengths in pursuit of fish. After that, I laughed because I didn't know what else to do. Then I laughed to keep myself from crying. Finally, I laughed because I was enjoying myself. So was my friend. There comes a time in life when, because you are on an adventure, even an uncomfortable one, you enjoy yourself. It is not the old routine, whatever it may be, and there is no knowing how many more chances life will bring you to do something madcap. Living over just such experiences as you try to fall asleep at the end of yet another day, you are reassured that you have lived.

It was just over a year earlier, shortly before his death, that the world-renowned fisherman Charles Ritz had said to me, "Our kind of fishing, yours and mine, fly-fishing for trout and salmon, is coming to an end. The habitat of these fastidious fish has been tampered with too much. Their range has shrunk steadily and, despite the efforts of a few concerned people, will continue to shrink. The future of sport fishing is in the ocean. Only it—up to now—has been big and mighty enough to withstand man's mistreatment of it." His prediction was being realized faster than he had foreseen, if my experience the past couple of seasons was indicative. So, late in life, I had faced about and gone to encounter the ocean.

To get here I had come a long way—not in distance so much as in attitude, orientation—and I had arrived as ignorant as an immigrant. Born and brought up on the prairies, I had remained a landlubber. Oh, I had crossed the Atlantic more times than I could remember, both by boat and by plane, but once safely on either of its shores I had headed inland instinctively. No beachcomber I. That was not my element. So much water seemed too much for me. Now, a latecomer to the ocean, I felt as though I were the first, as though I had discovered it. From this desolate outpost, in the nacreous light just breaking, it looked as though the ocean were being seen for the first time, just emerging from the primal void.

A fierce wind was blowing—just how fierce we would learn when, battered and bruised from our wild ride, we stepped out into it. From off the Point it blew to sea laden with sand, a veritable sandstorm, making the waves look like windswept desert dunes. Arrested upon the wind, hundreds of gulls and terns hung low over the water, screaming incessantly. The waters off the Point—treacherous waters where many a shipwreck lies—matched the wind in their convulsions. Heaving and seething, hissing loudly, the waves dashed against the spit, each lapping higher than the last on the rising tide, each undertow capturing and carrying back with it more of the shrinking shoreline. They seemed at war among themselves, wave rearing and crashing against wave, roller chasing roller.

I was, of course, far from the first ever to see it. From this very island, so changed since his time, Herman Melville once looked to sea, and it appeared the same to him as it does now to us—about the only thing that does. Arresting thought! We have polluted it, depleted it, we have all but exterminated the leviathans Melville fished for in it, yet it endures, outwardly unchanged. Of little on land can it be said that we see it now as it has always been seen. The ocean withstands our imposition. In its ceaseless motion lies its permanence.

No wonder we invest it with prodigies, with sea serpents and monsters, for not even its real and observable wonders, its whales and its great sharks, its giant squid and octupuses, seem commensurate with its vastness, the mysteries of its depths, its tremendous pressures, its titanic moods. No wonder we fancy it to contain a Bermuda Triangle into which all who venture disappear, with a lost Atlantis, with legends such as that of the *Flying Dutchman* doomed to wander eternally over its wastes. The imagination is unmoored by it and drifts without landmarks on its limitless expanses, over its fathomless profundities.

Was it hereabouts, on Nantucket, perhaps, that Melville first had his thought: meditation and water are wedded forever?

At first the doors of the Scout could not be opened. They were unlocked, yet they could not be opened. When finally one was, the wind took it, wrenched it half off its hinges, slammed it against the front fender and sprung it so it could not be closed again until after a visit to a body shop.

Outside, you could not see your feet: they were lost in the driven sand. It seemed that the entire spit was being blown away; we wondered whether by the time we were ready to leave we could be able to get back overland. There was no looking into the wind—no facing it, even. Wherever you were exposed to it, your skin smarted and stung, even the palms of your hands. It was a moving wall. It doubled you over, knocked out your breath, rocked you on your heels. It threatened momentarily to blow just a pull harder and pick you up and hurl you out to sea. The sand filling it was coarse, all finer stuff having long since been winnowed out, rated as shotgun pellets, it would have been about number 9, the size for quail. With that blast you could have frosted glass, removed house paint, scoured brick buildings, engraved—or effaced—tombstones. Luckily for us the wind was at our backs as we faced the water, otherwise we could not have fished. Had we had to cast into the wind, it would have flung our big, heavy lures, treble hooks and all, right back at us.

The sea surface erupted regularly in a fine spray as though a shotgun had gone off underwater. Then birds dropped to the water as though shot. They rose again with baitfish wriggling in their bills. An instant later the same spot erupted again, this time with heavier ammunition. Out of the water and into the air leaped fish a yard long, missile-shaped, metal-colored, glistening bluefish of twelve to fifteen pounds. It was these that had driven the baitfish inshore and made them leap out of the water in terror and desperation. The baitfish drew the gulls and the terns. Now these were drawing other fishermen besides us.

Here was one of the differences I was discovering between freshwater and saltwater fishing. One of the principal charms of trout fishing, at least for me, is the solitude, one of my disappointments in it recently had been the growing crowds on my favorite streams. Now expecting to find myself alone somewhere on the long Atlantic coast, I found myself on one of its most inaccessible points fishing in a crowd, at times even tangling lines with my neighbor on one side or the other, and finding this a key element of the excitement. Just seeing so many fish caught was exhilarating. There were times when every man on the beach was tugging at a rod bent nearly double. To be one among them elevated the blood pressure—*not* to be one among them did, too. Then you cast even faster, even farther.

There was, I was learning, a pattern, a rhythm to the waves—a different one each day, even at different hours of the same day, and even on adjacent stretches of the same beach. I was learning, too, that you must observe this rhythm and conform to it, else you may feed the fish instead of their feeding you. Even then you must be alert, for the sea is capricious and can slip in a breaker out of step. Already in my brief experience I had had unlooked-for waves take the sand from under my feet, drop me in a hole, sweep me up and draw me in.

That morning off Great Point it was twin breakers succeeded by the undertow. In tandem they slammed the shore, then withdrew deeply to gather themselves for another assault. By waiting out the breakers, then sprinting after the tow, I could lengthen my cast by a good thirty feet. Then, while my plug was still traveling through the air, I scurried up the strand, sandpiper-quick, to escape the incoming breaker, meanwhile leaving open the bail of my reel and letting out line. In effect, I was casting my lure in one direction and myself in the other. I had to propel myself backward, for the wind was not to be faced. Such was its force and the steadiness with which it blew that the sand was driven into everything. It grated in the gears of reels designed to keep it out. It spoiled a can of beer before I could down it. I had later to be shoveled from the Scout. I was to find on returning after four hours exposure to it that my pants pockets contained enough sand to fill a large hourglass. My hair and scalp could have furnished enough for several egg timers. Five showers later, I would still be picking grains from my ears.

I would backpedal up the strand and retrieve my lure. That may sound like a leisurely enough exercise to someone whose fishing has been confined to freshwater ponds. In surf casting for bluefish, using a big, long, heavy rod, a big reel, and big, heavy plugs, you retrieve as fast as you possibly can. Seeing it done for the first time, you will think those maniacs on the beach reeling so frantically away are not trying to catch fish but to rescue their lures from them. They are doing what you must do. When baitfish find themselves in the vicinity of bluefish they flee fast, your imitation baitfish has got to do the same. So you reel until you pant, until your hand is stiff, your arm trembling with the strain. And as soon as you have recovered your lure you hurl it back out as fast as you can get rid of it. As in all fishing, you will catch nothing with your bait out of water, but in fishing for bluefish you cannot rest for a minute. For, just as capriciously as they appear offshore, they are gone again. You fish for them while they are there, before they consume all the baitfish and depart. That does not take them long, for they are a gluttonous fish, equipped with a mouthful of teeth that could shred a truck tire. They will redden the surf with the blood of their prey. When they have gorged themselves, they vomit and start all over again. Although it is grueling and you are aching all over, especially on Great Point after that ride to get there, you are too absorbed to notice.

You crank as fast as you can, and with today's fast-ratio spinning reels, each turn of the handle recovers nearly a yard of line: that will give you an idea of the speed of your lure on top of the water. The first time it is stopped dead as though hooked to a pier, you will have an idea of the speed of a big bluefish frenziedly on the feed. Casting a minute dry fly to a finicky, mistrustful, one-pound trout is no preparation for it. No caution in bluefish. They are greedy, undiscriminating, and seem never to have been warned against fishermen. My first one that day nearly yanked the rod from my hands.

The fish and I were both stunned and disbelieving to find ourselves connected by a line. The fish did not panic and bolt. It just stopped where it was like a balky mule with all four feet dug in. The fish was not to be budged from the spot where, mistaking my lure for the real thing on which it had been feasting, it bit my barbed plug and found itself being pricked and tugged at. I could feel its bafflement and indignation through the line. I could feel it toss its head as it tried impatiently to shake the hook. Then it made a run; the drag of my reel was loosened to give it its head. One hundred yards it went before I could rein it in. I was using twenty-pound-test line, and the odds were long that my fish weighed much less than that, yet, fresh-hooked and full of fight, it easily had the power to break the line. I lowered my rod tip and pumped. I gained line, the fish took it. For a quarter of an hour this tug-of-war went on. At the end I was almost as spent as the fish.

I coaxed my fish in at last on an incoming wave and beached it. I knew not to put my hand in its mouth to free my plug. Its teeth can take off fingers. Nor did I pick it up by the tail while it was still alive. Bluefish are limber, like sharks, able to bend double and bite you. I beat my fish to death with a billy club.

Unlike freshwater fish, solitaries that drive others of their kind out of their territories, saltwater fish school. Where you catch one you are apt to catch more. Bluefish hunt in packs, like wolves. Sometimes these packs fill acres of water. (When that happens you are in for an added sensation, unless, as we had that day at Great Point, you have a steady, strong wind at your back: you can smell them. The smell is that of a ripe melon.) It was plain that we were into such a school, and, there being no legal limit on the catch of bluefish, nor any prohibition against their sale, as there is against the sale of a few saltwater fish and all freshwater game varieties, fish were now accumulating on the beach behind each man. These were soon covered with sand.

There was no time to put them in cars, no time even to shoo away the gulls that alighted to peck at their gills.

The frenzy with which the fish were foraging was imparted to us. Add to this the pounding of the surf, the wind, the screaming birds, and now the sun rising red and swollen, possibly portending an early end to the fishes' feeding and to our sport. Meanwhile, on every other cast you hooked one. You grew impatient with the time it took to subdue and land it before you could catch another. Down the line one man was setting his hook, another pumping his bent rod, another clubbing one. Seeking to cast farther, I stood in the surf now, wet to my chin. All caution was thrown to that wild wind. The teeming ocean was casting up its bounty to us. It was shortly to prove too much of a good thing.

I was trying to untangle a frantic tern I had caught on the wing. Beside me, Al was fighting a fish. I heard a twang, like the crack of a rifle, audible above the wind. When I had freed the bird I turned and found Al reeling in a slack line. It had broken and he had lost his fish and with it his lure and wire leader. A moment later the same thing happened to another fisherman. On my next cast it happened to me.

We tied on longer leaders. When, even with these, we lost lures, we reasoned that our lines had been frayed on submerged rocks.

Our school of fish had multiplied and, their numbers goading them to competition among themselves for the baitfish, they were feeding more voraciously than ever. Baitfish exploded everywhere from the water. The birds collided with one another in falling upon them.

Now on every cast you hooked a fish, only to lose it. I watched one man alone lose what he told me were twenty-two plugs, costing $3 to $4 apiece. Such was the spell of the place, with the waves and the wind and the clamorous birds and the frenzied fish and the very frustration of it goading you on. The more of them you lost the more determined you were to land this one. And you would think you were going to. You would regain the line, feel the fish finally tire, its will and its resistance weaken, walk it down the beach to somewhat quieter water. Then it was gone like all the others, taking with it yet another of your lures. Al had been cleaned out, was using mine and losing them.

All were mystified by what was happening to us. It was the man at the body shop who later enlightened us. A native Nantucketer and a fisherman himself, he explained that our trouble had been simply too many fish. When a bluefish, one of a large school such as we had run into, is hooked, he told us, the others bite the line, the swivels, even bits of weed caught on the line, mistaking the motion these make in the water for that of a baitfish.

By ten o'clock the other fishermen, out of lures, or out of patience, or both, had departed, leaving the beach to us; Al had gone through his half of my lures; finally I lost my last one. We exhumed our fish, and I began to recover from the spell I had been under.

I was not sorry to quit, though I had had to be forced to do it. Only then did I realize how tired I was—contented but tired, and sore all over—and I had yet to fillet and freeze my share of all those fish as soon as I got them home.

And before I could do that, as I remembered only now, I had to make the return trip over that road.

It would be taxing enough for most anglers to name two or three kinds of bliss, let alone five. Jeffries describes seven and you can call it what you like.

NORMAN JEFFRIES

Ketchin' Pick'rel

Some people call it pick'rel and some others call it pike.
That is all the same to me, they can call it what they like.
The name don't cut no figger; all I care about is this:
That when you git one on your line it's seven kinds of bliss.

I don't want to ketch no tarpon that weighs a half a ton.
And feedin' clams to sheepshead isn't just what I call fun.
Of salmon when it's boiled or baked I'll say that I am fond—
But when I'm after sport I fish for pick'rel in a pond.

I don't use no fuss and feathers tied on those little hooks,
All red and white and green and blue that come in fancy books.
And multiplyin' reels and sich don't cut no ice with me
Or dinky castin' rods that land your tackle in a tree.

A chunk of pork or old red shirt, a minny or a frog;
A corncob pipe, some good black jack, a dry seat on a log.
Just give me those old-fashioned tools is all I ask or wish
Then if you'll come along with me I'll show you how to fish.

If you let your frog drift over beneath that lily pad
Some old pick'rel there may see it who wants his breakfast bad.
You don't have to do no trampin', or cussin' sky blue flies,
That you slam in all directions but never git a rise.

Let the pick'rel do the guessin' while you squat there and think
And fill the corncob pipe again and take another drink.
There ain't no call for hurry, you don't have to ketch no train,
For if there's nothin' doin' you kin hit the jug again.

By-and-by your float will wiggle and then go out of sight
That's the time you git a move on and soak that pick'rel right.
When you've got him on the bank you'll agree with me in this:
That ketchin' pick'rel in a pond is seven kinds of bliss.

It seems odd that more existentialists have not offered us a critical study of the act of angling. Suppose, in the most extreme case, a groom is forced to choose between the hand of a devoted, ardent bride in the bloom of youth and, well, a fish. A tough choice. Make it a seventy-pound salmon fresh from the sea and Andrew Lang gives us a truly classic dilemma.

ANDREW LANG

The Lady or the Salmon?

The circumstances that attended and caused the death of the Hon. Houghton Grannom have not long been known to me, and it is only now that, by the decease of his father, Lord Whitchurch, and the extinction of his noble family, I am permitted to divulge the facts. That the true tale of my unhappy friend will touch different chords in different breasts, I am well aware. The sportsman, I think, will hesitate to approve him; the fair, I hope, will absolve. Who are we, to scrutinize human motives, and to award our blame to actions that, perhaps, might have been our own, had opportunity beset and temptation beguiled us? There is a certain point at which the keenest sense of honor, the most chivalrous affection and devotion, cannot bear the strain, but break like a salmon line under a masterful stress. That my friend succumbed, I admit; that he was his own judge, the severest, and passed and executed sentence on himself, I have now to show.

I shall never forget the shock with which I read in the *Scotsman*, under "Angling," the following paragraph:

Tweed.—Strange Death of an Angler.—An unfortunate event has cast a gloom over fishers in this district. As Mr. K——, the keeper on the B—— water, was busy angling yesterday, his attention was caught by some object floating on the stream. He cast his flies over it, and landed a soft felt hat, the ribbon stuck full of salmon flies. Mr. K—— at once hurried upstream, filled with the most lively apprehensions. These were soon justified. In a shallow, below the narrow, deep and dangerous rapids called the Trows, Mr. K—— saw a salmon leaping in a very curious manner. On a closer examination, he found that the fish was attached to a line. About seventy yards higher he found, in shallow water, the body of a man, the hand still grasping in death the butt of the rod, to which the salmon was fast, all the line being run out. Mr. K—— at once rushed into the stream, and dragged out the body, in which he recognized with horror the Hon. Houghton Grannom, to whom the water was lately let. Life had been for some minutes extinct, and though Mr. K—— instantly hurried for Dr. ——, that gentleman could only attest the melancholy fact. The wading in the Trows is extremely dangerous and difficult, and Mr. Grannom, who was fond of fishing without an attendant, must have lost his balance, slipped, and been dragged down by the weight of his waders. The recent breaking off of the hon. gentleman's contemplated marriage on the very wedding-day will be fresh in the memory of our readers.

This was the story which I read in the newspaper during breakfast one morning in November. I was deeply grieved, rather than astonished, for I have often remonstrated with poor Grannom on the recklessness of his wading. It was with some surprise that I received, in the course of the day, a letter from him, in which he spoke only of indifferent matters, of the fishing which he had taken, and so forth. The letter was accompanied, however, by a parcel. Tearing off the outer cover, I found a sealed document addressed to me, with the superscription, "Not to be opened until after my father's decease." This injunction, of course, I have scrupulously obeyed. The death of Lord Whitchurch, the last of the Grannoms, now gives me liberty to publish my friend's *Apologia pro morte et vita sua*.

Dear Smith [the document begins], Before you read this—long before, I hope— I shall have solved the great mystery—if, indeed, we solve it. If the water runs down tomorrow, and there is every prospect that it will do so, I must have the opportunity of making such an end as even malignity cannot suspect of being voluntary. There are plenty of fish in the water; if I hook one in the Trows, I shall let myself go whither the current takes me. Life has for weeks been odious to me; for what is life without honor, without love, and coupled with shame and remorse? Repentance I cannot call the emotion which gnaws me at the heart, for in similar circumstances (unlikely as these are to occur) I feel that I would do the same thing again.

Are we but automata, worked by springs, moved by the stronger impulse, and unable to choose for ourselves which impulse that shall be? Even now, in decreeing my own destruction, do I exercise free will, or am I the sport of hereditary tendencies, of mistaken views of honor, of seeming self-sacrifice, which, perhaps, is but selfishness in disguise? I blight my unfortunate father's old age; I destroy the last of an ancient house; but I remove from the path of Olive Dunne the shadow that must rest upon the sunshine of what will eventually, I trust, be a happy life, unvexed by memories of one who loved her passionately: Dear Olive! How pure, how ardent was my devotion to her none knows better than you. But Olive had, I will not say a fault, though I suffer from it, but a quality, or rather two qualities, which have completed my misery. Lightly as she floats on the stream of society, the most casual observer, and even the enamored beholder, can see that Olive Dunne has great pride, and no sense of humor. Her dignity is her idol. What makes her, even for a moment, the possible theme of ridicule is in her eyes an unpardonable sin. This sin, I must with penitence confess, I did indeed commit. Another woman might have forgiven me. I know not how that may be; I throw myself on the mercy of the court. But, if another could pity and pardon, to Olive this was impossible. I have never seen her since that fatal moment when, paler than her orange blossoms, she swept through the porch of the church, while I, disheveled, mud-stained, half-drowned—ah! that memory will torture me if memory at all remains. And yet, fool, maniac, that I was, I could not resist the wild, mad impulse to laugh, which shook the rustic spectators, and which in my case was due, I trust, to hysterical but *not* unmanly emotion. If any woman, any bride, could forgive such an apparent but most unintentional insult, Olive Dunne, I knew, was not that woman. My abject letters of explanation, my appeals for mercy, were returned unopened. Her parents pitied me, perhaps had reasons for being on my side, but Olive was of marble. It is not only myself that she cannot pardon, she will never, I know, forgive herself while my existence reminds her of what she had to endure. When she receives the intelligence of my demise, no suspicion will occur to her; she will not say "He is fitly punished"; but her peace of mind will gradually return.

It is for this, mainly, that I sacrifice myself, but also because I cannot endure the dishonor of a laggard in love and a recreant bridegroom.

So much for my motives: now to my tale.

The day before our wedding day had been the happiest of my life. Never had I felt so certain of Olive's affections, never so fortunate in my own. We parted in the soft moonlight; she, no doubt, to finish her nuptial preparations; I, to seek my couch in the little rural inn above the roaring waters of the Budon.[1]

> Move eastward, happy earth, and leave
> Yon orange sunset fading slow;
> From fringes of the faded eve
> Oh, happy planet, eastward go,

I murmured, though the atmospheric conditions were not really those described by the poet.

---

[1] From motives of delicacy I suppress the true name of the river.

> Ah, bear me with thee, smoothly borne,
> Dip forward under starry light,
> And move me to my marriage morn,
> And round again to——

"River in grand order, sir" said the voice of Robins, the keeper, who recognized me in the moonlight. "There's a regular monster in the Ashweil," he added, naming a favorite cast; "never saw nor heard of such a fish in the water before."

"Mr. Dick must catch him, Robins," I answered; "no fishing for me tomorrow."

"No, sir," said Robins, affably. "Wish you joy, sir, and Miss Olive, too. It's a pity, though! Master Dick, he throws a fine fly, but he gets flurried with a big fish, being young. And this one is a topper."

With that he gave me good night, and I went to bed, but not to sleep. I was fevered with happiness; the past and future reeled before my wakeful vision. I heard every clock strike; the sounds of morning were astir, and still I could not sleep. The ceremony, for reasons connected with our long journey to my father's place in Hampshire, was to be early—half-past ten was the hour. I looked at my watch; it was seven of the clock, and then I looked out of the window: it was a fine, soft, gray morning, with a south wind tossing the yellowing boughs. I got up, dressed in a hasty way, and thought I would just take a look at the river. It was, indeed, in glorious order, lapping over the top of the sharp stone which we regarded as a measure of the due size of water.

The morning was young, sleep was out of the question; I could not settle my mind to read. Why should I not take a farewell cast, alone, of course? I always disliked the attendance of a gillie. I took my salmon rod out of its case, rigged it up, and started for the stream, which flowed within a couple of hundred yards of my quarters. There it raced under the ash tree, a pale delicate brown, perhaps a little thing too colored. I therefore put on a large Silver Doctor, and began steadily fishing down the ash tree cast. What if I should wipe Dick's eye, I thought, when, just where the rough and smooth water meet, there boiled up a head and shoulders such as I had never seen on any fish. My heart leaped and stood still, but there came no sensation from the rod, and I finished the cast, my knees actually trembling beneath me. Then I gently lifted the line, and very elaborately tested every link of the powerful casting line. Then I gave him ten minutes by my watch; next, with unspeakable emotion, I stepped into the stream and repeated the cast. Just at the same spot he came up again; the huge rod bent like a switch, and the salmon rushed straight down the pool, as if he meant to make for the sea. I staggered on to dry land to follow him the easier, and dragged at my watch to time the fish; a quarter to eight. But the slim chain had broken, and the watch, as I hastily thrust it back, missed my pocket and fell into the water. There was no time to stoop for it; the fish started afresh, tore up the pool as fast as he had gone down it, and, rushing behind the torrent, into the eddy at the top, leaped clean out of the water. He was seventy pounds if he was an ounce. Here he slackened a little, dropping back, and I got in some line. Now he sulked so intensely that I thought he had got the line round a rock. It might be broken, might be holding fast to a sunken stone, for aught that I could tell; and the time was passing, I knew not how rapidly. I tried all known methods, tugging at him, tapping the butt, and slackening line on him. At last the top of the rod was slightly agitated, and then, back flew the long line in my face. Gone! I reeled up with a sigh, but the line tightened again. He had made a sudden rush under my bank, but there he lay again like a stone. How long? Ah! I cannot tell how long! I heard the church clock strike, but missed the number of strokes. Soon he started again downstream into the shallows, leaping at the end of his rush—the monster. Then he came slowly up, and "jiggered" savagely at the line. It seemed impossible that any tackle could stand these short violent jerks. Soon he showed signs of weakening. Once his huge silver side appeared for a moment near the surface, but he retreated to his old fastness. I was in a tremor of delight and despair. I should have thrown down my rod, and flown on the wings of love to Olive and the altar. But I hoped that there was time still—that it was not so very late! At length he was failing. I heard ten o'clock strike. He came up and lumbered on the surface of the pool. Gradually I drew him, plunging ponderously, to the graveled beach, where I meant to "tail" him. He yielded to the strain, he was in the shallows, the line was shortened. I stooped to seize him. The frayed and overworn gut broke at a knot, and with a loose roll he dropped back toward the deep. I sprang at him, stumbled, fell on him, struggled with him, but he slipped from my arms. In that moment I knew more than the anguish of Orpheus. Orpheus! Had I, too, lost my Eurydice? I rushed from the stream, up the steep bank, along to my rooms. I passed the church door. Olive, pale as her orange blossoms, was issuing from the porch. The clock pointed to 10:45. I was ruined, I knew it, and I laughed. I laughed like a lost spirit. She swept past me, and, amidst the amazement of the gentle and simple, I sped wildly away. Ask me no more. The rest is silence.

Thus ends my hapless friend's narrative. I leave it to the judgment of women and of men. Ladies, would you have acted as Olive Dunne acted? Would pride, or pardon, or mirth have ridden sparkling in your eyes? Men, my brethren, would ye have deserted the salmon for the lady, or the lady for the salmon? I know what I would have done had I been fair Olive Dunne. What I would have done had I been Houghton Grannom I may not venture to divulge. For this narrative, then, as for another, "Let every man read it as he will, and every woman as the gods have given her wit."[2]

---

[2] After this paper was in print, an angler was actually drowned while engaged in playing a salmon. This unfortunate circumstance followed, and did not suggest the composition of the story.

Nick Lyons has probably had more fishing books dedicated to him than anyone except Izaak Walton. And for good reason. An indefatigable editor, he has spawned, nurtured, and godfathered the best of modern American angling literature. When he finds time to write, fishermen read.

NICK LYONS

Bright Rivers

Rivers.

Bright green live rivers.

The coil and swoop of them, their bright dancing riffles and their flat dimpled pools at dusk. Their changes and undulations, each different flowing inch of them. Their physics and morphology and entomology and soul. The willows and alders along their banks. A particular rock the size of an igloo. Layers of serrated slate from which rhododendron plumes like an Inca headdress, against which the current rushes, eddies. The quick turn of a yellow-bellied trout in the lip of the current. Five trout, in loose formation, in a pellucid backwater where I cannot get at them. A world. Many worlds.

> . . . oft, in lonely rooms, and 'mid the din
> Of towns and cities . . .

as Wordsworth said in "Tintern Abbey," about a nature he felt but never really saw,

> . . . I have owed to them
> In hours of weariness, sensations sweet,
> Felt in the blood, and felt along the heart. . . .

Yes, I owe rivers that. And more. They are something wild, untamed—like that Montana eagle riding a thermal on extended wings, high above the Absaroka mountain pasture flecked with purple lupine. And like the creatures in them: quick trout with laws we can learn, sometimes, somewhat.

I do not want the qualities of my soul unlocked only by this tense, cold, gray, noisy, gaudy, grabby place—full of energy and neurosis and art and antiart and getting and spending—in which that business part of my life, at this time in my life, must of necessity be lived. I have other needs as well. I have other parts of my soul.

Nothing in this world so enlivens my spirit and emotions as the rivers I know. They are necessities. In their clear, swift or slow, generous or coy waters, I regain my powers; I find again those parts of myself that have been lost in cities. Stillness. Patience. Green thoughts. Open eyes. Attachment. High drama. Earthiness. Wit. The Huck Finn I once was. Gentleness. "The life of things." They are my perne within the whirling gyre.

Just knowing they are there, and that their hatches will come again and again according to the great natural laws, is some consolation to carry with me on the subways and into the gray offices and out onto upper Broadway at night.

Rivers have been brought to me by my somewhat unintelligible love of fishing. From the little Catskill creek in which I gigged my first trout to the majestic rivers of the West—the Madison, the Yellowstone, the Big Hole, the Snake—fishing has been the hook. And in the pursuit of trout I have found much larger fish.

"Must you actually *fish* to enjoy rivers?" my friend the Scholar asks.

It is difficult to explain but, yes, the fish make every bit of difference. They anchor and focus my eye, rivet my ear.

And could this not be done by a trained patient lover of nature who did not carry a rod?

Perhaps it could. But fishing is *my* hinge, the "oiléd ward" that opens a few of the mysteries for me. It is so for all kinds of fishermen, I suspect, but especially so for fly-fishermen, who live closest to the seamless web of life in rivers. That shadow I am pursuing beneath the amber water is a hieroglyphic: I read its position, watch its relationship to a thousand other shadows, observe its steadiness and purpose. That shadow is a great glyph, connected to the darting swallow overhead; to that dancing cream caddis fly near the patch of alders; to the little cased caddis larva on the streambed; to the shell of the hatched stone fly on the rock; to the contours of the river, the velocity of the flow, the chemical composition and temperature of the water; to certain vegetable life called plankton that I cannot see; to the mill nine miles upstream and the reservoir into which the river flows—and, oh, a thousand other factors, fleeting and solid and telling as that shadow. Fishing makes me a student of all this—and a hunter.

Which couldn't be appreciated unless you fish?

Which mean more to me because I do. Fishing makes rivers my corrective lens; I see differently. Not only does the bird taking the mayfly signify a hatch, not only does the flash of color at the break of the riffle signify a fish feeding, but my powers uncoil inside me and I must determine which insect is hatching and what feeding pattern the trout has established. Then I must properly equip myself and properly approach the fish and properly present my imitation. I am engaged in a hunt that is more than a hunt, for the objects of the hunt are mostly to be found within myself, in the nature of my response and action. I am on a Parsifalian quest. I must be scientist, technician, athlete, perhaps even a queer sort of poet.

The Scholar smiles wanly and says, "It all sounds like rank hedonism. And some cultism. With some mumbo jumbo thrown in."

Yes, I am out to pleasure myself, though sometimes after I've been chewed by no-see-ums until I'm pocked like a leper you wouldn't think that. There is a physical testing: the long hours at early morning, in bright sun, or at dusk; casting until your arm is like lead and your legs, from wading against the stiff current, are numb. That is part of the quest: to cleanse through exertion.

And the cultism and mumbo jumbo?

Some of trout fishing has become that, perhaps always was that. It is a separate little world, cunningly contrived, with certain codes and rules and icons. It is not a religion, though some believers make it such, and it is less than an art. But it has qualities of each. It touches heart and head; it demands and builds flexibility and imagination; it is not easy. I come to rivers like an initiate to holy springs. If I cannot draw from them an enduring catechism or from their impulses even very much about "moral evil and of good," they still confer upon me the beneficence of the only deity I have been able to find. And when the little world becomes *too* cunningly contrived? Wit helps.

My friend the Scholar says he is not a puritan or a moralist but that it seems to him it would be more satisfying to make something that would last—a book, a poem, a cabinet, a wooden bowl—than merely to fish well. He quotes Cézanne, from a letter, after a day of fishing: "All this is easier than painting but it does not lead far."

Not hardly. Not very far at all. Except that this may be precisely where I want it to lead. Let the world lead far—as one should frame it to do; let art last long and lead far and to form. Let a few other human activities lead far, though most of them lead us up a tree or up the asshole of the world. Let fly-fishing be temporary and fleeting and inconsequential. I do not mind.

Enough. Enough.

Too much theory and this pleasant respite from the north Broadway renaissance and gray offices will become an extravagant end that leads too far. Fishing is nothing if not a pastime; it would be hell if I did it all the time.

Beyond the dreams and the theories, there are the days when a close friend will pick me up at dawn on my deserted city block and we will make the long drive together, talking, connected, uncoiling, until we reach our river for the day. It is a simple adventure we are undertaking; it is a break from the beetle-dull routine, a new start, an awakening of the senses, a pilgrimage.

Flooded with memories and expectations, we take out our rods, suit up in waders and vest, special fish hats and nets, arrange flies and leaders, and take to the woods. Each article of equipment, each bit of gear in our ritualistic uniform, is part of the act. The skunk cabbage is thrusting up, lush and green-purple out of the moist brown mulch of last year's leaves; we flush a white-tailed deer that bounds off boldly; we see the pale-green buds pressing out of the birch branches. "Spring has come again," says Rilke. "The earth is like a little child who knows poems by heart—many, so many." We wonder whether the Hendricksons will or will not hatch at midday. We have our hopes.

With rivers as with good friends, you always feel better for a few hours in their presence; you always want to review your dialogue, years later, with a particular pool or riffle or bend, and to live back through layers of experience. We have been to this river before and together. We have much to relive.

Then we are on the river. It is still there. So much is perishable, impermanent, dispensable today, so much is gobbled up by industry and housing and the wanton surge of people, we half thought it might be gone, like that river we used to fish in Dutchess County, now bludgeoned by tract homes and industrial plants and trailers, now littered and warm and dead. Trout are yardsticks; they are an early warning system like the canary in the mine—when they go, what will happen to the rest of the planet, to the quality of life?

Yes, this river is still there, still alive, still pregnant with possibility.

"There's a swirl," I say, pointing.

"I saw one upstream, too."

"A few flies are coming off, see?"

"Yes, we're going to make a day of it."

My pulse quickens, the long gray city winter vanishes. In a moment we separate and belong to the river and to its mysteries, to its smooth glides and pinched bends, to the myriad sweet problems that call forth total concentration, that obviate philosophy.

Yes, these are Hendricksons, *Ephemerella subvaria*, and the hatch, on schedule, is just beginning. I am by profession neither an angler nor a scientist but there's always more pleasure in knowing than in not knowing. I take the lower pool and spot four good trout, poised high in the clear, flat water, waiting for the duns to hatch in the riffles and float down. By tilting my head close to the surface, I can see them, like little sailboats, drifting down. Two, three, there's another. Not many yet. A couple of birds are working, dipping and darting; against the light sky above the treeline I pick out one mayfly, watch it flutter, watch a swallow swoop, hesitate, and take it. What looks so pastoral is violent; it is, only on a smaller, more civilized scale, a horde of bluefish slashing a bunker school to bits, leaving blood and fin and head everywhere, to be picked up by the ravenous sea birds. The bites are cleaner here: the birds and trout take a whole creature in one mouthful.

Then back to the river. There are circles below me; the fish are feeding steadily. Shall I fish above or below them? They are so still, so firmly established in an irregular row across the channel in that clear flat water, that I elect the road less traveled and decide to fish down to them on a slack line—this way I won't have to cast over their backs.

It is delicate work, but I know that this year I have an excellent imitation of the natural fly, that my 5x leader is light enough, and that I've done just enough slack-line downstream casting to manage. Fishing is cumulative, though you don't learn all of it, ever.

I position myself carefully on the bank—it would be fatal to wade above such fish—strip about forty feet of line from my reel, and false-cast twice.

My rod jerks backward. I've hung my fly in that low brush.

The interruption of the music, like the needle hitting a scratch on a recording of the Brandenburg Concerto, irritates madly but is not final.

When I return, the fish are still feeding, more steadily now, even rhythmically.

My cast lands well above the fish, and my fly floats without drag a few feet short of their feeding station before the line tightens; a little V forms behind the fly and it goes under.

I retrieve the fly slowly, unwilling to ruffle the surface until there are no more than ten feet of line still in the water, then cast again. The fly floats freely and I hold my breath. This time it will go far enough. It's two feet upstream of the first fish; I'm still holding my breath; the snake in the line unwinds and begins to straighten, slowly, then faster; I lean forward to give it another foot, another few inches; I watch the fish move slightly, turn toward the fly, inspect it, nose up to it, and then the fly drags and the fish turns away.

A deep breath.

Two more casts: one that quarters the river too amply and causes the fly to drag within two feet; another that floats properly but gets there a second after the trout has taken a natural. Then a good cast, a good float, and the fish pivots and takes, feels the hook, jumps twice, and burrows across and upstream. It's thirteen inches and not strong enough to cause much mischief; anyway, after the strike, after I have successfully gulled this creature from another element, linked my brain to its brain, I am less interested. After a few minutes I have the fish near my bank, lean down and twitch the hook free, and it is gone, vigorously—sleek and spotted and still quick.

When I've taken the slime off the fly and air-dried it, I notice that most of the fish have left their stations; only one fish is working in the pool now, across the main current, in a little backwater. It will require a different approach, a different strategy. I take fully five minutes to work my way downstream along the bank, into the water, and across to the other side, moving slowly so as not to disturb the life of the river. I am only its guest. The fish is still working when I get there.

I am directly below the trout now and can see only the periodic circles about forty feet above me. I don't want to put the fly line over it, and I know its actual feeding position in the water will be at least several feet above the mark of the rise form, which is floating downstream and is the final mark of his deliberate inspection ritual. I elect to cast into the edge of the main current above the fish and hope the fly will catch an eddying current and come down into the trout's position. The cast is good. Squinting, I watch the fly float down, then free of, the fast center current and my fly line hug the nearly dead water. There is an electric moment when the circle forms. My arm shoots up. The fish has taken the fly solidly and feels like a good one. It does not jump but bores into its little pool, then into the current; then it gets below me. I slip, recover, and begin to edge downstream, the fish stripping line from the reel now, boiling at the surface twice, then coming upstream quickly while I raise the rod high and haul in line to keep the fish from slipping the hook.

A little later I release the fish from the net, turning it out—a beautiful seventeen-inch brown.

I take two more fish, smaller ones, in the riffle below the pool, then head upstream again to where the first fish were feeding, approaching the spot from below. The hatch has peaked and is tapering now; the late-afternoon chill of late April has set in and I feel it for the first time. One fish is still feeding but I cannot, in six or seven casts, raise it, and finally it stops.

I breathe deeply and take out a pipe. There may be a spinner fall in another hour but I am exhausted. The river is placid, calm now. No fish are rising. The drama is over; the actors have retired to the wings. I have been caught for two hours in an intensely sensual music, and I want to stop, perhaps for the day— to smoke the pipe now, watch that squirrel in the oak, look for deer tracks and chipmunk holes. The city has become a bad dream, a B movie I once saw that violates my imagination by returning at odd moments. Most of the world would be bored by these past two hours. Most of the world? Most of the world is polluting the rivers, making the worse appear the better cause, peacocking, grating on each other's ears, gouging, putting their fingers on others' souls or their hands in the wrong pockets, scheming, honking, pretending, politicking, small-talking, criticizing.

"Is that *all* you find?" I hear the Scholar ask me.

"Nope. But there's a damned lot of it."

"You're a misanthrope, a hater of cities," he says. "You claim to love gentleness but . . ."

I don't especially want to answer his questions now so I look back at the river. We invented the non sequitur for just such moments.

Yes, we have made a day of it. Two, three hours sandwiched in. Little enough. But deep. And durable. And more than a day's worth. We've earned memories—full and textured—that live now in our very marrowbones, that make us more alive. Our thoughts will be greener, our judgments perhaps sharper, our eyes a bit brighter. We live day to day with little change in our perceptions, but I never go to a river that I do not see newly and freshly, that I do not learn, that I do not find a story.

On the way home I still feel the tug of the river against my thighs, and in my mind's eye I can see that largest rising trout, the neat circle when it took a natural, the quick dramatic spurt—electric through my whole body—when it took my fly and I felt its force. And I wondered why I had not raised that last fish.

It was not the ultimate river, the ultimate afternoon; it was not so exquisite as a Keatsian moment frozen and anguished because it would not last. There will be others—never equal, always discretely, sharply different. A thousand such moments. Days when, against all expectation, the river is dead; days when it is generous beyond dreams.

A luxury? A mere vacation?

No, those rivers are more. They are my Pilgrim Creek and Walden Pond, however briefly. Those rivers and their bounty—bright and wild—touch me and through me touch every person whom I meet. They are a metaphor for life. In their movement, in their varied glides, runs, and pools, in their inevitable progress toward the sea, they contain many of the secrets we seek to understand about ourselves, our purposes. The late Roderick Haig-Brown said, "Were it not for the strong, quick life of rivers, for their sparkle in the sunshine, for the cold grayness of them under rain and the feel of them about my legs as I set my feet hard down on rocks or sand or gravel, I should fish less often." Amen. When such rivers die, as so many have, so too dies an irretrievable part of the soul of each of the thousands of anglers who in their waters find deep, enduring life.

Fact or fiction?—nowhere else but in angling literature is the distinction so irrelevant. It is the memory that is important, a tale recalled by the teller. When the story happens to be your own life, so much the better. It is Maclean's.

NORMAN MACLEAN

A River Runs Through It

In our family, there was no clear line between religion and fly-fishing. We lived at the junction of great trout rivers in western Montana, and our father was a Presbyterian minister and a fly-fisherman who tied his own flies and taught others. He told us about Christ's disciples being fishermen, and we were left to assume, as my brother and I did, that all first-class fishermen on the Sea of Galilee were fly-fishermen and that John, the favorite, was a dry-fly fisherman.

It is true that one day a week was given over wholly to religion. On Sunday mornings my brother, Paul, and I went to Sunday school and then to "morning services" to hear our father preach and in the evenings to Christian Endeavor and afterward to "evening services" to hear our father preach again. In between on Sunday afternoons we had to study *The Westminster Shorter Catechism* for an hour and then recite before we could walk the hills with him while he unwound between services. But he never asked us more than the first question in the catechism. "What is the chief end of man?" And we answered together so one of us could carry on if the other forgot, "Man's chief end is to glorify God, and to enjoy Him forever." This always seemed to satisfy him, as indeed such a beautiful answer should have, and besides he was anxious to be on the hills where he could restore his soul and be filled again to overflowing for the evening sermon. His chief way of recharging himself was to recite to us from the sermon that was coming, enriched here and there with selections from the most successful passages of his morning sermon.

Even so, in a typical week of our childhood Paul and I probably received as many hours of instruction in fly-fishing as we did in all other spiritual matters.

After my brother and I became good fishermen, we realized that our father was not a great fly-caster, but he was accurate and stylish and wore a glove on his casting hand. As he buttoned his glove in preparation to giving us a lesson, he would say, "It is an art that is performed on a four-count rhythm between ten and two o'clock."

As a Scot and a Presbyterian, my father believed that man by nature was a mess and had fallen from an original state of grace. Somehow, I early developed the notion that he had done this by falling from a tree. As for my father, I never knew whether he believed God was a mathematician but he certainly believed God could count and that only by picking up God's rhythms were we able to regain power and beauty. Unlike many Presbyterians, he often used the word "beautiful."

After he buttoned his glove, he would hold his rod straight out in front of him, where it trembled with the beating of his heart. Although it was eight and a half feet long, it weighed only four and a half ounces. It was made of split bamboo cane from the far-off Bay of Tonkin. It was wrapped with red and blue silk thread, and the wrappings were carefully spaced to make the delicate rod powerful but not so stiff it could not tremble.

Always it was to be called a rod. If someone called it a pole, my father looked at him as a sergeant in the United States Marines would look at a recruit who had just called a rifle a gun.

My brother and I would have preferred to start learning how to fish by going out and catching a few, omitting entirely anything difficult or technical in the way of preparation that would take away from the fun. But it wasn't by way of fun that we were introduced to our father's art. If our father had had his say, nobody who did not know how to fish would be allowed to disgrace a fish by catching him. So you too will have to approach the art Marine- and Presbyterian-style, and, if you have never picked up a fly rod before, you will soon find it factually and theologically true that man by nature is a damn mess. The four-and-a-half-ounce thing in silk wrappings that trembles with the underskin motions of the flesh becomes a stick without brains, refusing anything simple that is wanted of it. All that a rod has to do is lift the line, the leader, and the fly off the water, give them a good toss over the head, and then shoot them forward so they will land in the water without a splash in the following order: fly, transparent leader, and then the line—otherwise the fish will see the fly is a fake and be gone. Of course, there are special casts that anyone could predict would be difficult, and they require artistry—casts where the line can't go over the fisherman's head because cliffs or trees are immediately behind, sideways casts to get the fly under overhanging willows, and so on. But what's remarkable about just a straight cast—just picking up a rod with line on it and tossing the line across the river?

Well, until man is redeemed he will always take a fly rod too far back, just as natural man always overswings with an ax or golf club and loses all his power somewhere in the air; only with a rod it's worse, because the fly often comes so far back it gets caught behind in a bush or rock. When my father said it was an art that ended at two o'clock, he often added, "closer to twelve than to two," meaning that the rod should be taken back only slightly farther than overhead (straight overhead being twelve o'clock).

Then, since it is natural for man to try to attain power without recovering grace, he whips the line back and forth making it whistle each way, and sometimes even snapping off the fly from the leader, but the power that was going to transport the little fly across the river somehow gets diverted into building a bird's nest of line, leader, and fly that falls out of the air into the water about ten feet in front of the fisherman. If, though, he pictures the round trip of the line, transparent leader, and fly from the time they leave the water until their return, they are easier to cast. They naturally come off the water heavy line first and in front, and light transparent leader and fly trailing behind. But, as they pass overhead, they have to have a little beat of time so the light, transparent leader and fly can catch up to the heavy line now starting forward and again fall behind it; otherwise, the line starting on its return trip will collide with the leader and fly still on their way up, and the mess will be the bird's nest that splashes into the water ten feet in front of the fisherman.

Almost the moment, however, that the forward order of line, leader, and fly is reestablished, it has to be reversed, because the fly and transparent leader must be ahead of the heavy line when they settle on the water. If what the fish sees is highly visible line, what the fisherman will see are departing black darts, and he might as well start for the next hole. High overhead, then, on the forward cast (at about ten o'clock) the fisherman checks again.

The four-count rhythm, of course, is functional. The one count takes the line, leader, and fly off the water; the two count tosses them seemingly straight into the sky; the three count was my father's way of saying that at the top the leader and fly have to be given a little beat of time to get behind the line as it is starting forward; the four count means put on the power and throw the line into the rod until you reach ten o'clock—then check cast, let the fly and leader get ahead of the line, and coast to a soft and perfect landing. Power comes not from power everywhere, but from knowing where to put it on.

"Remember," as my father kept saying, "it is an art that is performed on a four-count rhythm between ten and two o'clock."

My father was very sure about certain matters pertaining to the universe. To him, all good things—trout as well as eternal salvation—come by grace and grace comes by art and art does not come easy.

So my brother and I learned to cast Presbyterian-style, on a metronome. It was mother's metronome, which father had taken from the top of the piano in town. She would occasionally peer down to the dock from the front porch of the cabin, wondering nervously whether her metronome could float if it had to. When she became so overwrought that she thumped down the dock to reclaim it, my father would clap out the four-count rhythm with his cupped hands.

Eventually, he introduced us to literature on the subject. He tried always to say something stylish as he buttoned the glove on his casting hand. "Izaak Walton," he told us when my brother was thirteen or fourteen, "is not a respectable writer. He was an Episcopalian and a bait fisherman." Although Paul was three years younger than I was, he was already far ahead of me in anything relating to fishing and it was he who first found a copy of *The Compleat Angler* and reported back to me, "The bastard doesn't even know how to spell 'complete.' Besides, he has songs to sing to dairymaids." I borrowed his copy, and reported back to him, "Some of those songs are pretty good." He said, "Whoever saw a dairymaid on the Big Blackfoot River?

"I would like," he said, "to get him for a day's fishing on the Big Blackfoot—with a bet on the side."

People generally take up angling for contemplation, fun, and genial companionship. Then there are midge fishermen. Their terminal tackle is "something invisible attached to nothing." They take up angling for the same reason blind swordsmen take up the blade in samurai films.

VINCENT MARINARO

Small Fly: Big Fish

It is a hot day in September, the season called the doldrums when the water is low and clear and the overhead sun makes the sweat run into your eyes. You have come to the quiet meadow stream to capture a big handsome trout, bull-shouldered from spring and summer feeding.

The bold, slashing trout strikes of spring have died with the big mayflies. The trout is now a furtive creature who makes leisurely, inconspicuous rises, sometimes so fleeting and insignificant as to be almost invisible. He is the smart trout of late summer and early fall, feeding on the millions of tiny insects that now crowd the stream.

In your hand you have the most graceful and delicate of modern sporting weapons: a light, dainty fly rod (preferably of split bamboo) that may weigh as little as one ounce. Brilliantly conceived and executed, the rod has the romantic appeal and appearance of an ancient Toledo blade, responsive to your slightest wish, nodding and trembling with every movement of your hand. Yet, it can be powerful, capable of hurling a long cast, and conquering a creature a hundred times its weight.

Attached to that rod there should be as fine a reel as you can afford, with tension adjustments and a silky smooth operation. You will depend heavily on this reel for the delicate give-and-take required to protect the leader's end, a fine strand called a tippet with a diameter as little as .0033 inch—as fine as human hair—and a breaking point of only three-quarters of a pound.

To the tip of that leader is attached a dry fly so tiny the complete rig is often referred to as "something invisible attached to nothing."

There is no precedent for this minute artificial. We inherited our angling techniques from an older generation devoted to larger dry flies, 12, 10, 8, even larger. Number 16 flies have long been considered "small" and number 18, "tiny." But the flies for what I call midge fishing are much smaller—sizes 22, 24, 26, and 28. A number 28 dry fly is to a number 12 as a mosquito is to a large grasshopper.

One of my most exciting experiences with this sort of tackle was on a stifling day in late August. I prowled one of the long meadows of the beautiful Letort River near Carlisle, Pennsylvania, pausing now and then to cool off under a shady tree, but always looking keenly for some sign of a rise. Then I saw it, a faint wrinkle in the glassy surface that was gone in a flash. It happened on the outside edge of a little backwater near my bank.

Up to this point I had stayed well back from the water's edge, looking from a safe distance (in smooth, clear water a trout can see you at least thirty feet away when you stand at water level—farther if you are on the bank). I knew I must avoid wading if at all possible, so I began to stalk the fish on hands and knees. Presently I could peer at him through streamside weeds from no more than five or six feet.

That fish was magnificent, and when I got my first glimpse of him I gasped a little. He was big-shouldered and heavy-girthed, with a broad tail that undulated with easy power every time he rose to take an insect. I estimated this brown trout to be between three and four pounds and more than twenty inches long. Every time he rose he drifted backward and lifted in that languid manner that often characterizes a big trout. At the end of each drift he turned away from me and faced the far bank as he picked off the insect. The interval between rises was something like one minute.

I backed off until I was at a safe distance from the water, then sat down to ponder the situation and check my tackle. I peeled off fifty feet of line and quickly respooled it to make sure there were no kinks. My leader was a modern no-knot, continuous taper to 6x to which had been connected a thirty-inch tippet of 7x testing about one pound. After seeing a trout I promptly broke the 7x and replaced it with thirty inches of 6x, testing perhaps two pounds. I felt that I needed an extra margin of safety. (The no-knot leader is necessary on weed-filled streams like the Letort, as a conventional leader's several big knots pick and hold weed balls that are heavy enough to break a fine tippet.)

My rod was a seven-and-one-half foot, three-ounce bamboo on the stiff side.

At that time of the year I needed length and stiffness to hold up my backcast above meadow weeds higher than my head. I tied on a number 20 black beetle and hurried downstream to get below my fish, then approached the bank, crawling until I was about thirty feet below the trout.

Still crouched, I shook out the leader and some line to make sure everything was free and easy, then waited for the rise. Shortly it came and I marked its position in relation to a clump of grass on the bank. Now I began to extend line and leader until I had enough to make a pitch to the far bank, opposite the rise. Another pitch and shoot adjusted the length to put the fly two feet in front of the trout and a foot to his right, plus a float of at least six feet.

I slammed my pitch high and hard, deliberately overshooting so when the cast recoiled it came down just right, the loose, snaky 6x tippet settling softly on the surface. I could barely discern the little hump created by the tiny fly and noted with satisfaction it was floating freely on a true course. Now I saw the shadowy form of the trout beginning to lift, slowly undulating backward and upward, then turning to the right, and finally the little sip and the faint dimple on the surface.

The suspense created by the slow, deliberate, and visible rise of a big trout to your fly is agonizing. Only age and experience prevented me from jerking that fly from his open jaws or smashing the fine tippet with a violent strike.

Trembling, I lifted the rod gently and softly flexed the tip. Nothing happened and for a few long seconds time stood still. Suddenly the trout exploded in a furious dash upstream, plowing a long furrow in the water while my little reel chattered and whined. There were agonizing moments until he stopped short of a fallen willow. I looked down at my reel and noted with alarm that only a few turns of line were left on the drum, for I had no backing. (It would not have mattered anyway since there is no way to stop a big fish with midge tackle.)

I had put the rod tip down during that run and now I kept it low with the line hanging loosely. There was no pressure on the fish but he was still nervous, his head shaking in an effort to dislodge that passive but nagging irritation in his jaw.

Within a few minutes the trout became calm and I began the most delicate, tricky operation in midge fishing. I had to bring that fish back downstream, recover my line, and get him away from that fallen willow. One mistake and he would be into the willow with a jump.

I started by pinching the line with the thumb and forefinger of my free hand, drawing backward until I barely felt the fish. Then, increasing the pull slightly, I began to ease him toward me. I got him back a few feet before he realized what was happening to him. He got nervous again and I promptly released the line. When he had calmed I pinched the line and resumed; with several stops and starts, I got him back to his original position. But this was only the beginning.

I knew his kind—strong, wild, full of tricks. A smart trout that knew his ground better than I. His next maneuver was a familiar one that had lost me some fish in former years: he began swimming in a tight circle, slapping the leader hard with his tail. There is only one way to stop this—you must lift the rod high and parallel to the water, and with as much bend as possible.

When the trout found he could no longer slap the leader he became panicky, streaked downstream a short distance, turned upstream, and slithered into a big weed bed. I groaned. This is the safest refuge for a big meadow-stream trout and he knows it. It would be a grueling contest after all.

I hurried downstream to get below him, put the rod low and to one side with as much bend as possible short of breaking that 6x point. You cannot drag a big trout out of a weed bed; you must hold him with a light but constant downstream pressure until he tires and backs out of his own volition. Sometimes this takes many minutes. It worked for me on this occasion and the trout did what I expected—he ran downstream again and burrowed into another weed bed.

Through sweat-blurred eyes I suddenly noticed that one of the dreaded weed balls was draped over my leader. A weed ball the size of your fist is surprisingly heavy; it can pop a fine tippet if the fish moves before you can free the weeds. I hurried downstream below the resting fish, plunged my rod tip into the water to force the floating line below or at least level with the weed ball, and swished the rod tip from side to side. Soon I had the weed ball slipping toward me, pushed along by the current and the rod movement. I quickly removed it.

The dive-into-weeds maneuver was repeated over and over, each stop becoming a little shorter. The contest was going my way and I felt good about it until the trout suddenly bolted downstream and started around a bend. Between me and the fleeing trout was a swampy section that I could not negotiate. I ran backward and headed for high ground, the rod held high to clear the meadow weeds, and dashed in a circular route after the trout.

We arrived at the end of the bend neck and neck, the trout still racing. Now I saw a final hazard that I did not anticipate—a small, midstream logjam with a clear channel on both sides. If he headed through the far channel, all would be lost.

He headed for the far channel. There was hardly time to think and my next act was pure instinct. I lifted the rod high with a lot of line bellying from the tip, then drew the rod back and hurled a high loop over the logjam. It cleared beautifully and fell in the far channel, running freely with the trout down the straightaway.

That was really the end of the fight. The trout's final defiant gesture was to push his head into a patch of watercress near my feet, leaving his body exposed. I netted him and carried him to a clear, shallow channel near the bank, then sat down to stroke him and help him recover.

What I said to this gallant fish during that rest period he probably never understood. If he had, I am sure we would have parted friends when, with a flick of his broad tail, he shot back into the safety of the Letort—after a contest that had lasted an hour and five minutes and had covered a quarter of a mile of stream.

When an angler new to midge fishing sees me land a trout like this, and I show him what I caught it on, the inevitable reaction is: "I don't believe it!" Not because the tackle is so delicate but because the fly is so tiny as to appear inconsequential.

Midge fishing differs from ordinary dry-fly fishing in two ways. Instead of doing everything possible to make one of the tiny flies float high by spraying it with a silicone solution and carefully snapping the water droplets from it, the fly is cast *into the surface film* so as to float flush like a drowning insect. This is a radical departure from standard practice. Also, you must never strike a fish in the conventional way with a sharp lift of the rod.

The bite of the tiny hook is only about one-sixteenth of an inch, microscopically enhanced by bending the hook so the point is slightly offset to one side. As a result of this small bite, a midge fly is tricky to lodge in a trout's mouth, as I relearned one day last October when I located a really big trout feeding on tiny *Caenis* flies. I watched as the old boy tipped up and down with that easy, rocking-chair motion a big trout uses during a heavy hatch.

After surveying the situation I decided that the only spot where I could pitch to him without causing the fly to drag was directly across from him. I didn't like this, but I had no choice. Eventually I got a good pitch in front of him that he took. I lifted the rod gently. The hook, a number 24 on a one-pound tippet, held momentarily, then popped out of his jaws.

I renewed my casting. Again he took my little *Caenis*. I lifted as gently as before and again the hook came out. Bitterly disappointed, I sat there berating myself for botching it. Then, to my amazement, that big trout began to feed again.

I made a good pitch and watched breathlessly as he tipped and sucked the fly. For the third time, so help me, the little fly came out of his jaws. When I lifted the rod to make a fourth try I couldn't get the cast away; my hand shook and I had to let the cast die.

Curious now, I crossed the stream below the trout and came back up, crawling close to his position. What I saw startled me—he was a hook-billed male with a big gap in his jaws! The fly had merely scraped past his teeth.

You must get that little hook into the soft, tough tissue in the corner of a trout's mouth. Once embedded, the fly will stay there and nothing can shake it loose. To accomplish this you must cast either upstream or across at a fish that turns away on the take so the fly catches at the jaw hinge. Then all you need do is tighten the line gently to sink the barb.

What makes midge fishing exciting is the challenge and the variety; each trout stalked poses different problems. One trout last season seemed almost impregnable, since his lair was only a yard beyond a hot cattle fence.

Cows had cropped the grassy banks as close as a putting green and there was no cover. Yet there was this eighteen-incher sipping *Caenis* spinners and there was that dreadful fence. I knew the trout would bolt downstream under the fence the moment he felt the hook.

I made a desperate plan. I put my landing net on the bank near a large bed of watercress. Then I crawled under the fence well away from the stream and inched toward it, pulling myself along by my elbows.

In position at last and still prone, I raised my right arm and cast. The trout took and shot under the fence. Keeping the rod low, I lurched up and ran to the fence and poked the throbbing rod under it. I was just able to reach across the fence and grab the rod with my other hand. Then I hurled the rod at the watercress thirty feet downstream.

Again I crawled under the fence. When I had dashed to the watercress and retrieved my rod, the trout was still on. I picked up my net, for the campaign was won. Some say trout fishing is a contemplative sport, but it never is when you stick a tiny fly into a big unsuspecting trout.

It takes two to angle—fish and fisherman. The addition of a third party introduces the problem of etiquette. The French take these things seriously. Very seriously.

GUY DE MAUPASSANT

The Hole

CUTS AND WOUNDS WHICH CAUSED DEATH

That was the heading of the charge that brought Leopold Renard, upholsterer, before the Assize Court.

Round him were the principal witnesses, Mme. Flamèche, widow of the victim, Louis Ladureau, cabinetmaker, and Jean Durdent, plumber.

Near the criminal was his wife, dressed in black, a little ugly woman who looked like a monkey dressed as a lady.

This is how Renard described the drama:

"Good heavens, it is a misfortune of which I am the first and last victim and with which my will has nothing to do. The facts are their own commentary, Monsieur le Président. I am an honest man, a hard-working man, an upholsterer in the same street for the last sixteen years, known, liked, respected, and esteemed by all, as my neighbors have testified, even the porter, who is not *folâtre* every day. I am fond of work, I am fond of saving, I like honest men and respectable pleasures. That is what has ruined me, so much the worse for me; but as my will had nothing to do with it, I continue to respect myself.

"Every Sunday for the last five years my wife and I have spent the day at

218

Passy. We get fresh air, not to say that we are fond of fishing—as fond of it as we are of small onions. Mélie inspired me with that passion, the jade; she is more enthusiastic than I am, the scold, and all the mischief in this business is her fault, as you will see immediately.

"I am strong and mild-tempered, without a pennyworth of malice in me. But she, oh la la! She looks insignificant, she is short and thin, but she does more mischief than a weasel. I do not deny that she has some good qualities; she has some, and those very important to a man in business. But her character! Just ask about it in the neighborhood; even the porter's wife, who has just sent me about my business—she will tell you something about it.

"Every day she used to find fault with my mild temper: 'I would not put up with this! I would not put up with that.' If I had listened to her, Monsieur le Président, I should have had at least three bouts of fisticuffs a month."

Mme. Renard interrupted him: "And for good reasons too; they laugh best who laugh last."

He turned toward her frankly. "Oh! very well, I can blame you, since you were the cause of it."

Then, facing the president again, he said:

"I will continue. We used to go to Passy every Saturday evening, so as to be able to begin fishing at daybreak the next morning. It is a habit that has become second nature with us, as the saying is. Three years ago this summer I discovered a place, oh! such a spot! There, in the shade, were eight feet of water at least and perhaps ten, a hole with a *retour* under the bank, a regular retreat for fish and a paradise for any fisherman. I might look upon that hole as my property, Monsieur le Président, as I was its Christopher Columbus. Everybody in the neighborhood knew it, without making any opposition. They used to say: 'That is Renard's place'; and nobody would have gone to it, not even Monsieur Plumsay, who is renowned, be it said without any offense, for appropriating other people's places.

"Well, I went as usual to that place, of which I felt as certain as if I had owned it. I had scarcely got there on Saturday when I got into *Delila*, with my wife. *Delila* is my Norwegian boat which I had built by Fourmaise and which is light and safe. Well, as I said, we got into the boat and we were going to bait, and for baiting there is nobody to be compared with me, and they all know it. You want to know with what I bait? I cannot answer that question; it has nothing to do with the accident; I cannot answer, that is my secret. There are more than three hundred people who have asked me; I have been offered glasses of brandy and liquors, fried fish, matelots,[1] to make me tell! But just go and try whether the chub will come. Ah! they have patted my

---

[1] A preparation of several kinds of fish with a sharp sauce.

stomach to get at my secret, my recipe. Only my wife knows, and she will not tell it any more than I shall! Is not that so, Mélie?"

The president of the court interrupted him:

"Just get to the facts as soon as you can."

The accused continued: "I am getting to them; I am getting to them. Well, on Saturday, July eighth, we left by the five-twenty-five train, and before dinner we went to grind bait as usual. The weather promised to keep fine, and I said to Mélie: 'All right for tomorrow!' And she replied: 'It looks like it.' We never talk more than that together.

"And then we returned to dinner. I was happy and thirsty, and that was the cause of everything. I said to Mélie: 'Look here, Mélie, it is fine weather, so suppose I drink a bottle of *Casque à mèche.*' That is a little white wine we have christened so because if you drink too much of it it prevents you from sleeping and is the opposite of a nightcap. Do you understand me?

"She replied: 'You can do as you please, but you will be ill again and will not be able to get up tomorrow.' That was true, sensible, prudent, and clear-sighted, I must confess. Nevertheless, I could not withstand it, and I drank my bottle. It all comes from that.

"Well, I could not sleep. By Jove! It kept me awake till two o'clock in the morning, and then I went to sleep so soundly that I should not have heard the angel shouting at the Last Judgment.

"In short, my wife woke me at six o'clock and I jumped out of bed, hastily put on my trousers and jersey, washed my face and jumped on board *Delila.* But it was too late, for when I arrived at my hole it was already taken! Such a thing had never happened to me in three years, and it made me feel as if I were being robbed under my own eyes. I said to myself, 'Confound it all! Confound it!' And then my wife began to nag at me. 'Eh! What about your *Casque à mèche!* Get along, you drunkard! Are you satisfied, you great fool?' I could say nothing, because it was all quite true, and so I landed all the same near the spot and tried to profit by what was left. Perhaps, after all, the fellow might catch nothing and go away.

"He was a little thin man in white linen coat and waistcoat and with a large straw hat, and his wife, a fat woman who was doing embroidery, was behind him.

"When she saw us take up our position close to their place she murmured: 'I suppose there are no other places on the river!' And my wife, who was furious, replied: 'People who know how to behave make inquiries about the habits of the neighborhood before occupying reserved spots.'

"As I did not want a fuss I said to her: 'Hold your tongue, Mélie. Let them go on, let them go on; we shall see.'

"Well, we had fastened *Delila* under the willow trees and had landed and were fishing side by side, Mélie and I, close to the two others; but here, monsieur, I must enter into details.

"We had only been there about five minutes when our male neighbor's float began to go down two or three times, and then he pulled out a chub as thick as my thigh, rather less, perhaps, but nearly as big! My heart beat and the perspiration stood on my forehead, and Mélie said to me: 'Well, you sot, did you see that?'

"Just then Monsieur Bru, the grocer of Poissy, who was fond of gudgeon fishing, passed in a boat and called out to me: 'So somebody has taken your usual place, Monsieur Renard?' And I replied: 'Yes, Monsieur Bru, there are some people in this world who do not know the usages of common politeness.'

"The little man in linen pretended not to hear, nor his fat lump of a wife, either."

Here the president interrupted him a second time: "Take care, you are insulting the widow, Madame Flamèche, who is present."

Renard made his excuses: "I beg your pardon, I beg your pardon; my anger carried me away. . . . Well, not a quarter of an hour had passed when the little man caught another chub and another almost immediately and another five minutes later.

"The tears were in my eyes, and then I knew that Madame Renard was boiling with rage, for she kept on nagging at me: 'Oh, how horrid! Don't you see that he is robbing you of your fish? Do you think that you will catch anything? Not even a frog, nothing whatever. Why, my hands are burning just to think of it.'

"But I said to myself: 'Let us wait until twelve o'clock. Then this poaching fellow will go to lunch, and I shall get my place again.' As for me, Monsieur le Président, I lunch on the spot every Sunday; we bring our provisions in *Delila*. But there! At twelve o'clock the wretch produced a fowl out of a newspaper, and while he was eating, actually he caught another chub!

"Mélie and I had a morsel also, just a mouthful, a mere nothing, for our heart was not in it.

"Then I took up my newspaper, to aid my digestion. Every Sunday I read the *Gil Blas* in the shade like that, by the side of the water. It is Columbine's day, you know, Columbine who writes the articles in the *Gil Blas*. I generally put Madame Renard into a passion by pretending to know this Columbine. It is not true, for I do not know her and have never seen her, but that does not matter; she writes very well, and then she says things straight out for a woman. She suits me, and there are not many of her sort.

"Well, I began to tease my wife, but she got angry immediately and very angry, and so I held my tongue. At that moment our two witnesses, who are present here, Monsieur Ladureau and Monsieur Durdent, appeared on the other side of the river. We knew each other by sight. The little man began to fish again, and he caught so many that I trembled with vexation, and his wife said: 'It is an uncommonly good spot, and we will come here always, Desiré.' As for me, a cold shiver ran down my back, and Madame Renard kept repeating: 'You are not a man, you have the blood of a chicken in your veins'; and suddenly I said to her: 'Look here, I would rather go away, or I shall only be doing something foolish.'

"And she whispered to me as if she had put a red-hot iron under my nose: 'You are not a man. Now you are going to run away and surrender your place! Off you go, Bazaine!'

"Well, I felt that, but yet I did not move while the other fellow pulled out a bream. Oh! I never saw such a large one before, never! And then my wife began to talk aloud, as if she were thinking, and you can see her trickery. She said: 'That is what one might call stolen fish, seeing that we baited the place ourselves. At any rate they ought to give us back the money we have spent on bait.'

"Then the fat woman in the cotton dress said in turn: 'Do you mean to call us thieves, madame?' And they began to explain, and then they came to words. Oh Lord! those creatures know some good ones. They shouted so loud that our two witnesses, who were on the other bank, began to call out by way of a joke: 'Less noise over there; you will prevent your husbands from fishing.'

"The fact is that neither of us moved any more than if we had been two tree stumps. We remained there, with our noses over the water, as if we had heard nothing; but, by Jove, we heard all the same. 'You are a mere liar.'

" 'You are nothing better than a streetwalker.'

" 'You are only a trollop.'

" 'You are a regular strumpet.'

"And so on and so on; a sailor could not have said more.

"Suddenly I heard a noise behind me and turned round. It was the other one, the fat woman, who had fallen on to my wife with her parasol. *Whack! whack!* Mélie got two of them, but she was furious, and she hits hard when she is in a rage, so she caught the fat woman by the hair and then, *thump, thump.* Slaps in the face rained down like ripe plums. I should have let them go on—women among themselves, men among themselves—it does not do to mix the blows, but the little man in the linen jacket jumped up like a devil and was going to rush at my wife. Ah! no, no, not that, my friend! I caught the gentleman with the end of my fist, *crash, crash,* one on the nose, the other in the stomach. He threw up his arms and legs and fell on his back into the river, just into the hole.

"I should have fished him out most certainly, Monsieur le Président, if I had had the time. But unfortunately the fat woman got the better of it, and she was drubbing Mélie terribly. I know that I ought not to have assisted her while the man was drinking his fill, but I never thought that he would drown and said to myself: 'Bah, it will cool him.'

"I therefore ran up to the women to separate them, and all I received was scratches and bites. Good Lord, what creatures! Well, it took me five minutes, and perhaps ten, to separate those two viragoes. When I turned around there was nothing to be seen, and the water was as smooth as a lake. The others yonder kept shouting: 'Fish him out!' It was all very well to say that, but I cannot swim and still less dive!

"At last the man from the dam came and two gentlemen with boat hooks, but it had taken over a quarter of an hour. He was found at the bottom of the hole in eight feet of water, as I have said, but he was dead, the poor little man in his linen suit! There are the facts, such as I have sworn to. I am innocent, on my honor."

The witnesses having deposed to the same effect, the accused was acquitted.

What would you do with half a million trout? A lot of anglers wish they had that problem. Few could propose so tasty a solution as A. J. McClane.

A. J. McCLANE

Blue Trout

I have probably caught at least a half-million trout in my lifetime. While the greatest percentage were released to lend themselves to other anglers, it still adds up to many meals from Alaska to New Zealand and across to the Arctic barrens of Finland. Trout in a collective sense are not my favorite fish at table. There are more degrees of quality than species; certainly the pink-fleshed brook trout of central Labrador and Quebec, and the crimson-meated rainbows of southern Chile and Argentina, or for that matter a fresh-run steelhead from Oregon's Rogue River, are without peer. The native cutthroat trout of the Rocky Mountains and the golden trout are especially memorable and made even more so when cooked at a campfire among the craggy peaks of the Jim Bridger Wilderness. For my part, brown trout usually rate well down the list comparatively, although the unique sea-run form taken in the frigid rivers of Iceland and Norway has an ocean-firm musculature and a flavor superior to Atlantic salmon. The Sheriff House at Stockbridge can make brown trout from the weedy Test River taste like no other fish, but that is kitchen magic and perhaps a dollop of nostalgia for Hampshire's waters. In the same genre I recall those little Catskill brook trout of my boyhood, delicate and as gaily colored as butterflies; pan fried with crunchy skins, one could eat them heads and all. It was a morning ritual with a steaming mound of hot cakes splashed with
224

butter and homemade maple syrup, but *that* appetite is as distant now as the old wood-burning stove that worked its daily miracles.

Trout are the most universally cultured fish both for the purpose of angling and for the commercial market. Their domestic propagation began in the fourteenth century when a French monk, one Dom Pichon, discovered that trout eggs could be artificially impregnated. During the next 400 years there were some minor individual contributions to trout culture, but the science did not gain momentum until 1852 when the first public-owned trout hatchery was constructed in France. The alarming decrease of trout in America due to the industrialization of our river valleys soon required their production by artificial methods here, and in 1864 Seth Green built a hatchery at Mumford, New York. Jordan and Evermann in *American Food and Game Fishes* (1902) quote a Reverend Myron Reed "... a noble man and excellent angler ..." as seeing that era as the terminal point in the history of our angling. "This is the last generation of trout fishers. The children will not be able to find any. Already there are well trodden paths by every stream in Maine, New York, and Michigan." The good reverend went on to say that "... trout will be hatched by machinery and raised in ponds, and fattened on chopped liver, and grow flabby and lose their spots. The trout of the restaurant will not cease to be; but he is no more like a trout of the wild river than the fat and songless reed-bird is like the bobolink. Gross feeding and easy pond life enervate and deprave him."

Seth Green was a pioneer fish culturist; he helped to construct private and state hatcheries throughout New England and the Middle Atlantic states. Although he initially reared our native eastern brook trout, then the hardier rainbow trout of our West Coast, in 1886 a German fish culturist, Von Behr, sent the first brown trout to the United States. It was during this period that immigrants to New Zealand brought Atlantic salmon from England by ship and, failing to establish that species, began the importation of Pacific salmon and rainbow trout from California. To this day, the generic American Indian *quinnat*, which is simply the collective name for all salmon, is used in New Zealand for the chinook. The trainbow trout, however, was a phenomenal success and by the turn of the century the fish was being shipped all over the world ultimately to thrive in countries where natural populations of salmonids were unknown. Transplanted into ecological voids such as New Zealand, Tasmania, temperate South America, and the high country of South Africa, the red-sided rainbow is today internationally esteemed. The species is farmed throughout Denmark, for example, where the commercial production of trout is that nation's second largest industry.

From a culinary standpoint I feel the same way about trout recipes as about salmon recipes—the simplest methods are best. My first choice is blue trout. During the summer of 1948 I made a tour of the trout streams in Normandy with that *grand hôtelier* Charles Ritz. Automobiles were still scarce in postwar

France but the resourceful Monsieur Ritz borrowed an open touring car of 1924 or 1925 vintage which had originally belonged to the French police. Among other things, its brakes were virtually worthless. The car didn't have a horn, so Charles simply leaned out over the door and yodeled when we approached a busy intersection. This had a miraculous effect on otherwise indifferent citizens, and especially on the livestock in rural areas. In Niederwald, Switzerland, one learns to yodel at an early age, and the Ritz family held many local honors. Driving with Charles was a hair-raising experience even when he had a horn to blow, but the frenzied activity of motoring from river to river was assuaged by some of the finest dry fly-fishing I have ever enjoyed. The trout taken from cold cress-filled waters provided many memorable meals. Among other delights I was introduced to *truite au bleu*, a dish of European origins that only found its way to American tables in recent years.

The organoleptic appreciation of trout begins with a fish done in the blue style. This dish is the pure unadulterated essence of trout. If a salmonid has any ambition whatsoever, it is to expire in a metallic burst of blue. When you achieve a *limon bleu*, a touch of the fork will loose rivulets of ambrosial nectar, clear and heady as a summer brook. The very color tells you that the sweets of the river are locked in the fish. Its belly skin may be the shade of a blushing cardinal, or yellow spring butter, but once the trout enters the court bouillon, its mayfly fat is sealed under the regal robe. Since the day Philogenes of Leucas recited the ground rules of purist cookery, the trout has worn this color with unparalleled majesty. Ernest Hemingway, who was a man of lusty appetites, described it best in one of his columns for the Toronto *Star Weekly (Dateline: Toronto*, edited by William White, Charles Scribner's Sons, 1985) written while he was fishing in Switzerland:

> It is not a well-known dish at the hotels. You have to go back in the country to get trout cooked that way. You come up from the stream to a chalet and ask them if they know how to cook blue trout. If they don't you walk on a way. If they do, you sit down on the porch with the goats and children and wait. Your nose will tell you when the trout are boiling. Then after a while you will hear a pop. That is the Sion being uncorked. Then the woman of the chalet will come to the door and say, "It is prepared, Monsieur."
>
> Then you can go away and I will do the rest myself.

Blue trout recipes invite a turgid flow of metaphor from European cooks, but they always fail to explain where the color originates. There are no plums in plum pudding, no duck in Bombay duck, and no blue coloring in a trout's skin. The color comes from the same lubricant that makes a fish slippery—the film that keeps our trout waterproof. Without it he would drown and without it there can be no blue. Consequently, the idea has existed that the trout must be cooked alive. Something is always lost in translation, but this calculated sadism grew out of the French phrase, "in a live condition," meaning that the trout should *not* be washed or scaled before going into the vinegar bath. A fish that is handled too much or one that has been frozen will not color, simply because the slime has been removed. Bear in mind that all trout have almost microscopic scales and the skin is an important source of flavor as well as nutrition, which we try to preserve in all cooking methods; it is removed usually for decorative purposes in preparations such as trout in aspic. Actually, your fish should be quite dead, but killed and gutted an instant before bluing. All good restaurants that serve this have a holding pool in the dining room from which the trout are removed with a dip net. Part of the dogma handed from kitchen to kitchen also reveals that more than one restaurant has made a practice of using trout that are not exactly fresh. Numerous recipes suggest running a cord through the trout from mouth to tail, or piercing the fish's head with a toothpick and trussing him tail to head. The idea is to serve curved trout, but the final gesture of a *freshly killed* trout is to curl, and he will do this with no help from the chef. String and toothpicks are dubiously necessary only when the fish has been dead for many hours and the muscle tissue will no longer contract. The actual preparation of the fish is easy.

Virtually all blue trout recipes require that the fish be cooked in what amounts to vinegared water; this inevitably results in a trout that tastes like vinegar. To retain a delicate flavor I prefer a two-step procedure which produces instant bluing and more aromatic poaching.

COURT BOUILLON FOR BLUE TROUT

2 quarts water	1 onion, quartered
1 cup dry white wine	a few parsley sprigs
1 tablespoon lemon juice	1 tablespoon
2 celery ribs,	fresh tarragon,
cut into small pieces	or 1 teaspoon dried
large fistful of	3 bay leaves
celery leaves	6 peppercorns, bruised
1 large carrot,	salt
cut into chunks	

Put all the ingredients in a large kettle, bring to a boil, and let it bubble merrily for 30 minutes. Strain to remove the solid parts, and return the liquid to the kettle. Bring again to a boil.

tarragon vinegar
water
trout

In another kettle mix one-third tarragon vinegar with two-thirds water and bring to a boil. With large kitchen tongs grasp each trout firmly by the lower jaw and lower it into the hot vinegar mixture. When properly blue, place the trout in the boiling court bouillon. The bouillon will cease bubbling for a few minutes, but when it comes to a boil again, remove the pot from the heat and cover. Let this stand for 15 to 20 minutes and your trout are cooked. Remove the fish carefully with a large spatula, and drain them.

Classically, blue trout are served with marble-size new potatoes bathed in butter and garnished with parlsey. There should also be a side dish of garden-fresh asparagus smothered in mousselin sauce (hollandaise mixed with an equal part of stiffly whipped cream). After the cream has been added to the hollandaise, heat it very carefully and stir until the sauce is hot. A dry white wine would be the proper mate to such rich fare. A watercress salad is a must.

The way they did trout in the old days out of Willie Pollock's Antumalal Lodge on the Trancura River in Chile would be hard to duplicate but it should be recorded before the formula is lost. You would begin at dawn when snow-capped Andean peaks gleamed like helmeted sentinels, with a skilled *botero* maneuvering the craft over foaming rapids. Wherever he gentled the double-ender into smooth currents behind piano-sized boulders you could make a few casts to the rainbow trout that lay in these calm eddies. Often as not, a fish would rush the fly, then you bounced down through swift water following its furious leaps. By noon on a good day the count was forty or fifty released fish. The *botero* always saved two of a size suitable for his grill. Then, he would pull up on a gravely bank in the shade of the forest and begin his ritual by chilling the wines behind a cofferdam of river stones. While you gathered dry wood, he spitted a lamb on a long iron rod. After much calculation with respect to its position over the fire, the rod was angled into the ground, and the grill balanced on rocks of a proper height below the lamb. When the flame seared its fat, the crimson-fleshed trout, now in fillets, were laid skin side down on the grill where the lamb sprayed hot droplets over the fish like an atomizer until a golden crust sealed their juices inside. The trout was served first, washed down with a cold *vino blanco*. Next came the pink lamb with a pot of brown rice and crisp green asparagus followed by those incredible succulent pears that grow only in Chile. One could also pick the huge blackberries growing profusely in the volcanic ash along the stream bank. Soon it was siesta time and you dozed by the sound of the Trancura's rapids before getting on with the fishing.

Big fish, little fish—what's the difference? If you don't know, you have never fished. McDonald offers this exquisitely crafted essay, straight from the pen of angling's quintessential scholar.

JOHN McDONALD

All the Big Ones Got Away

Every day I see the head of the largest trout I ever hooked, but did not land.
—Theodore Gordon

Of course all the big ones got away, and we all know why. Lies, delusions. And, in violation of the law of sufficient reason, it's plausible. That's how the big ones got big. But see how the old story goes when you try to put it down chapter and verse.

To start, you have to untangle the question: What's a big fish? Every angler has his private scale. On mine, thinking of good, not big, fish which I have actually caught, I can say roughly that a fourteen-inch trout in a Catskill creek equals a two-pounder on the Yellowstone River equals a seventeen-pound salmon on the Restigouche. On the same scale, a two-pounder in a stream equals a much larger one in a lake; and a two-pounder caught on a fly representing an insect equals a much larger one caught on a streamer fly representing a minnow—all quite arbitrary according to one's own game rules and values. "Big" before fish is a peculiar word, suggesting, I imagine, for many anglers

229

something outlandish in relation to the circumstances. I have seen Lee Wulff, who has taken the biggest fish in the world on the lightest tackle, catch a ten-inch trout on the Battenkill with sewing thread, to his evident pleasure. Joan Miller, who once caught a 900-pound swordfish off Cape Cod with spear and barrel, yelled "Oh my God!" when she hooked her first trout later in the Yellowstone—a nine-incher on a tiny Gray Wulff dry.

When I say that all the big ones got away, however, I have in mind for the occasion a formidable minimum on an objective scale: a four-pound trout caught on fly in a stream. The scale was set by Dan Bailey for the walls of his Fly Shop in Livingston, Montana. You can put a tracing of the outline of your trout on the wall if it meets these conditions, and few anglers who have qualified have disdained the invitation. Bailey set the scale remarkably well for that country, whose streams yield an extraordinary number of trout below four pounds and relatively few above, so that a four-pounder or better is an event to bring everyone running. Some anglers around there have caught numerous wall fish, and since so many are on the wall now, the rule is that a fisherman can add a new one only if it is larger that the one he has already put up, in which case the old one must come down. This rule can give the angler a tough choice: Does he want to take down his five-pounder caught on a big streamer fly and put up a four-pounder caught on a number 16 Quill Gordon? I have not had to face such problems; after more than twenty years of visiting the Fly Shop and fishing the Boulder, Yellowstone, Gallatin, Madison, Big Hole, and many other rivers, streams, brooks, spring creeks, and ditches of Montana, I am not on that wall.

I regret the omission for all the obvious reasons, and for another more obscure personal one. When Bailey and I shared a cabin beside a creek in the Catskills in the 1930s, we casually put our larger trout on the cabin wall. We traced the shape of the trout on a piece of paper and took it off in a line drawing in ink on the old faded wallpaper, writing in the name of the one who had caught it and the date, and attaching the fly to the nose of the outlined trout. Bailey put up the first one on July 14, 1935, a fifteen-inch brown which really looked impressive coming out of that creek; and we made a rule that the next one would have to be larger. It was two years before another went up, a sixteen-incher of mine, and thanks to Bailey's emigration to Montana, I had the honor of putting up the rest. There were only four in all—the largest one eighteen inches—when I abandoned the cabin in 1941, carved the whole thing out of the wall, and took it to New York to be framed.

That I never put a trout on the wall in Montana was not for lack of expert teachers. I have fished under the aegis of some of the best and most dedicated fishermen since Gordon. I have seen Bailey catch wall fish without particularly trying, that is, while fishing wet or dry, with tiny delicate flies or large Muddlers. Phil Fjellman, a habitué of the Yellowstone with whom I often fished, put fifteen trout on the wall while I went blank. Joe Brooks (*Trout Fishing*, 1972) a fabulous fisherman in all styles and a specialist in power fishing, a style he popularized for catching big fish in Montana, said to me one day in the Fly Shop, "I think you ought to be on the wall. Come with me."

Power fishing, or perhaps more correctly, power casting, is a mode of fishing that grew out of tournament techniques for casting long distances. It is widely practiced in San Francisco and around Miami. Some tournament casters never actually go fishing, but many do. Their techniques are now standard practice in steelhead fishing and saltwater fly-fishing. Visiting fishermen brought the techniques to Montana, and Joe Brooks had a lot to do with demonstrating that they paid off in big fish. Since then the style has become a vogue with a number of good Montana fishermen.

Power fishermen discard the old casting styles, familiar to Easterners, of holding the arm to the side. The key to the power style is the "double haul." If you are right-handed, you work your line with your left hand, giving it impetus with a sharp stripping motion when picking the fly off the water and again in the forward cast. The equipment includes the "shooting" or "torpedo" line, which weighs more near the forward end. When you go over to power fishing, you have to give up the versatility of traditional delicate styles for working varieties of water with small flies. And if you fish in the traditional style, you have to give up a lot of big fish, which you will see others taking in the big-fish season (September and October in Montana) with rods that are eight and a half feet, five and a half ounces or larger.

On the rivers I have fished, power fishing appears to be almost exclusively a man's sport. Yet this kind of casting does not take unusual strength with a floating line, and tournament-casting women—Joan Wulff, for one—get considerable distance. Perhaps one difficulty is the strength needed to stay at it with streamer flies for hours on end. Another is the real power it takes to drag a long sinking line out of the water.

In any case, this circumstance has not worked altogether to the disadvantage of women. Their mastery of the dry fly followed on its invention. And although far fewer women than men fish fly, six have put stream trout on the Fly Shop wall since 1958. Debie Waterman, of the fishing team of Debie and Charles Waterman of De Land, Florida, is represented with a seven-pound brown from the Missouri, caught on a Silver Outcast or Renegade (an outcast from the Silver Doctor Salmon fly), and a four-pound, one-ounce brown from the Yellowstone, caught on a Muddler. As she had to choose one to stay up, I asked her which it would be. She replied without hesitation, "The four-pounder. The Yellowstone is more of a challenge." This preference reflects the impression that big browns are comparatively easy to find and catch in the rich trout grounds at the confluence of the Missouri and Beaver Creek near Helena, where they come down from the lakes to spawn. Consider also a further complexity in fishing values. Debie Waterman says, "I come to Montana to fish dry fly. The greatest catch of my life in salt or fresh water was a three-and-a-half-pound brown on Nelson's Spring Creek [a tributary of the Yellowstone] with a number 16 [fairly small] Cahill on a 6x [extremely fine] tippet."

Mary Brooks, of the far-ranging fishing team of Mary and Joe Brooks of Richmond, Virginia, is on the wall with a four-pound, fourteen-ounce brown from Yellowstone, caught on a Muddler. Sue McCarthy of Daytona, Florida, displays a five-pound, four-ounce brown from the Missouri, caught on a Muddler. Ann Prickett has a five-pound, thirteen-ounce brown from the Yellowstone, caught on a Muddler. Mrs. Winston Dine-Brown is represented by a four-pound, twelve-ounce brown from the Yellowstone, caught on a Dark Spruce streamer. And Patricia O'Neill has hung a six-pound, one-ounce brown from the Madison, caught on a Salmon fly (mysteriously named, as it represents rather realistically a large natural stone fly). Perhaps someone can figure out why four of the six caught their trophy trout on a Muddler. Although it is a big-fish fly, on one wall panel displaying sixty-three four- and five-pounders caught by men and women, only twelve were caught on a Muddler; on another panel containing six-pounders and better, very few were taken on a Muddler.

Joe Brooks and I went out together on a great pool of the Yellowstone, once called Paine's Pool—the only time I recall going out especially to try for a big trout. Joe lent me a powerful rod, a shooting line, and some large, bright-blue streamer flies from the Argentine, along with a couple of dark-brown patterns. A master of casting who has written authoritative books on the subject, he showed me how to get the wind-resisting streamers out to the edge of the fast water on the far side of the pool, where big trout often lie. I didn't catch anything worth talking about, but Joe, illustrating his teaching, brought in and released a great trout which he denied would go four pounds, though I knew better. The kick in this kind of fishing is in the great expectations and the suspense. But I had to say that I found it too repetitive, and Joe agreed with that. He is a generous and versatile fisherman who likes to work the water.

Certainly fishing in traditional ways excuses no one for failing to catch big trout; anyone who fishes long enough should get at least a few. But as it was, I amassed a record collection of ways to lose the big ones. Of course there are the routine ways of striking too soon or too late (these account for a normal number of my losses), inattention to damaged tackle (quite a few), entanglements in moss and other flora of the watery depths (quite a few), buck fever while casting to a big rise (a few), and the like. Altogether these mount up, but come to no more than most fishermen have experienced. Indeed, there is no normal way for me to account for all the big ones getting away. I like to think that I am absolved because the really big ones got away by being inspired and superbrilliant tacticians. I give just three examples, from the Madison River.

Here I was in the Bear Trap stretch of the Madison, a wilderness area where the great river narrows and the water crashes through a gorge—unfishable except in side pockets and eddies. I hooked a trout on a number 10 Bailey Grizzly in a large pocket and saw him only in the shape of the swirls he made before he plunged recklessly into the gorge and—upstream! It made as much sense for fish to go upstream in that water as it would for one to climb Niagara Falls. However, the maneuver gave me the advantage of holding for a moment. He then turned and raced down twenty yards or so with the torrent and should have kept on going. But he didn't seem to want to leave the neighborhood. Against the laws of nature, he turned again and streaked upstream through the middle of the gorge. Then this old Greek fish-god settled to the bottom under a great rock in front of me. I sat there above him for a long time before I concluded that he would outwait me. I then broke him off and went on my way looking for more natural fish.

Doubt unsettled me. How can one have an experience with nature contrary to its laws? Could the fish have been a phantom of my imagination? Did the swirls of its rise actually belong to a whirlpool in the pocket? Were line and fly dragged by an unseen current into the maelstrom, where one or the other caught on a rock at the bottom? Was the dash upstream my own doing as I raised the rod to get a tight line, and the dash down a result of my yielding to the pressure of the heavy rushing water? Was the return to the rock my return to a tight line? Descartes's aphorism, "I think therefore I am," ran through my head, and I wondered whether my doubt about the existence of the Bear Trap trout did not attest to *my* existence—a consolation of angling that I believe has heretofore gone unnoticed.

Again, I stood in late afternoon on the east bank of the Cameron stretch of the Madison—several miles of flat prairielike rocks and sagebrush cut through with winding roads, near the town of Cameron. I left my companions and went downstream, casting from the bank into the swift runs that pushed up and around protruding rocks close by. I caught several ten- and twelve-inch rainbows on a small, slender wet fly, which suggested that the fishing might be very good. The Madison here is wide, straight, and powerful, strewn with open and slightly submerged rocks. A fisherman in these parts usually keeps restlessly moving down or up, and on occasion across, if the opportunity appears. But crossing the Madison is a considerable undertaking when its depth ranges from knee to waist. Only in a few spots can it be done at all, and the angler can never be sure of making it all the way. I began to have eyes for better water on the other side, however, and looked for a possible crossing.

Presently I found one that seemed feasible. Holding the rod high, I fished across inch by inch, the pressure of the current just short of carrying me away.

For this heavy water I had put on a number 10 Trude (a down-wing hair fly looking rather like a wet Royal Coachman), which tended to float a little before sinking. Three good strikes came, and though none held, I concluded that I had the right fly (no insect hatch was visible). When I reached the other side, I fished down again through some long streamy runs, and the fishing was beautiful. Cutthroats. Good ones, never jumping (they almost never do), but fast, hard runners. I lost track of time and distance, until the water turned black and its whitecaps crystal in the twilight. I looked for a ford, found none, turned back, and tried to remember the landmarks of the crossing: a fallen aspen on my side, a clump of willows standing alone on the other. Here they were. I relaxed and started carefully fishing across.

About a third of the way, balanced on my left foot against the force of the water and casting straight ahead, I let the Trude fall over the bulge of a submerged boulder, lifted the rod, and—it stopped. It seemed that a full minute passed, during which the powerful water rushed on while the fly stood still below the bulge. Then it started moving away from me at a right angle to the current, toward the other bank. I held the rod high with the line running and edged forward while I tried to find footing. But it wasn't necessary to follow, for the trout changed course in a sweeping, arc-shaped run downstream and back toward the middle of the river. At the end of the run he came out high and twisting, a great rainbow, I judged, from the way he danced on his tail. I stood still as he went under, moved slowly up against the current, leaped again and again, and rolled away, tearing the river into swirling black and white designs.

He was one of those trout over whom the fisher has at this stage no control whatever—every move an awesome phenomenon. He held again, and neither trout nor angler moved in the deep dusk, all but night. It was a long hold, giving me time to ponder a question. This was a very big fish—pounds greater, I imagine, than the wall's minimum. (I say that now, though the wall was not in my head then.) It was the kind of fish I would stay there all night with. If luck favored me I would eventually catch him somewhere downstream along the bank I had come from. But if I did that, I would be marooned in darkness on the west bank, with several square miles of rangeland around me. My companions would be at the car on the east bank, waiting, knowing nothing of this adventure. If only I had carried a flare! (The thought of carrying a flare had never occurred to me before that moment.)

I came to understand that I had no choice; I had to cross. I began a maneuver to get below him, but when I moved down, so did he, maintaining the same angle. We must have been together about a half hour when I took the only way out. I started moving across upstream from him, the worst position for an angler; but as long as I was on either side of him, I could go with him and turn him so that he couldn't break away. The critical point would come when I passed directly over him. I hated to reach that point; I felt like an astrologer before an eclipse. Would he know what I knew?

He knew. As the line came parallel to the main current straight above him, he rose, not forty feet away, carrying the entire line into the air. Against the white water I saw him full and entire, the biggest thing imaginable in the whole river. Wise old trout, like all my big friends and antagonists in the water, he came down, a launched torpedo, and shot straight downstream. I let the line run freely into the backing, knowing he was gone before he was off. As the line ran out, I pointed the rod down and straight after him, in a sign of resignation, for the snap which came in due course. So I wound up with the story and without the fish and did the talking at supper that night.

It is twenty years since I first met the king of the Madison trout, a brown, at Papoose Creek—the best-known big fish not on the wall at the Fly Shop. It was a clear August morning, too clear to be promising, and the salmon-fly hatch for which the Madison is celebrated—its great stone fly that brings up the big fish—was long past, when Pat Barnes, Dorothy McDonald, and I set out to float the river. The practice of floating the Madison has been criticized because thoughtless boatmen pass through water being fished by wading or bank anglers, and some of them are fish hogs. We felt innocent enough, since Pat is a scrupulously courteous as well as skillful boatman (and angler), and we were not out to kill many fish. Pat grew up fishing the Madison, taught school until recently in Helena, and spends all his summers in West Yellowstone, tying flies and running an elegant fishing shop with his wife Sig, and guiding, not to speak of fishing. He knows the Madison the way a deer knows its woods.

We launched the boat about thirty miles downstream from the river's start in Hebgen Lake. It was a McKenzie River boat made to run rough water, with eight-and-a-half-foot oars for control among rocks. In the bow was a sort of pulpit against which one could lean and cast without losing balance. These features were a necessity, as we were soon running through rapids and around submerged rocks.

Of the hundred or so flies in my fly box I picked out a number 12 Royal Wulff dry, a variation on the classic Royal Coachman. Theodore Gordon never liked the Royal Coachman; indeed, he was positively irked by it. He knew of it as a renowned killer, but he considered it a lure and could not understand what its attraction could be when fished dry. His best guesses were that it resembled a "glorified ant" or that its colors aroused the trout's curiosity. "One thing sure," he conceded, "the trout can scarcely fail to see it." He had in mind the quieter waters of the East, where this fly might be seen too well. I have often found it an effective dry fly in fast, splashy water, where it throws off distinct glints of light—not, I imagine, with the effect of a lure but with that of some brilliant spinner. Fishing dry in the absence of a hatch, especially on Western waters, I sometimes begin the day by experimenting with the light effects of fancy flies.

As it turned out, the Royal Wulff was the only pattern I needed to use all day. Standing in the bow, I cast to one side or the other, twenty to fifty feet and slightly ahead of the boat. All day I saw that sparkling fly bobbing or gliding through marvelous waters. Floating the Madison introduces one to every conceivable kind of fishing water. It was a much better day than we had expected, and we began catching and releasing quite a few fish—Dorothy and I alternating with the rod. After awhile we approached the little tributary, Papoose Creek, which comes down from the east out of the Madison Range.

We left the main current for a channel between an island and the east bank, and with Pat braking the boat, I dropped the fly into a deep, slow run along the bank. At the confluence with Papoose Creek I saw a shallows, and beyond it the incoming flow of the creek. I dropped the fly just inside the flow, with some slack leader curled behind it. The fly moved naturally with the flow; and disappeared. I drew up and the line tightened. Pat held the boat. The king came straight up, clear of the water, framed against the bushes on the other side of the creek: a yellowing brown trout of enormous dimensions. We had a long time to look at him as he hung, seemingly weightless, at the peak of his jump. He fell back with a great splash and circled around the same point several times, while Pat maneuvered the boat backward and toward the bank. Then he came up again, giving us another full view as he turned completely over and dived nose first, with only a swish, into the water. I was so spellbound that, although I automatically held the line tight, I forgot I was fishing.

Two things then happened almost at once. Pat, who had kept his head, jumped into the deep water, clothes and all, to drag the boat to shore. Had I not been distracted, I should have followed him. In the next instant the king rose again sidewise, throwing himself out into the river. I came to, and saw I had to make a choice. Pat had assumed that I would play the fish from the shore, which would have been a sound move if I had left the boat when Pat did. But now the fish was off and running downstream, and in the split second of decision I yelled to Pat to come back in. The old king had benefited by the spell he had cast which put Pat in the water and left me in the boat. Pat was back in the boat in another moment and we were soon after him, but he had taken a lot of line. He was fairly far out and going swiftly downstream before we were moving with him and I was taking in line. Some 300 yards downstream were two boulders, the larger one about 100 feet offshore. But for those boulders the course of my angling life would be quite different—I should not be writing this story. The king knew his territory well. I had recovered a good deal of line when he went outside the big boulder and circled it. We couldn't make it quickly enough, and as we circled it the line slacked. When I reeled in, the fly was still on and the hook was bent straight.

We crossed to the other side. I listlessly dropped a new fly along the edge of a wide pocket. It disappeared and I drew up. A trout came out into the river; about five minutes later I lifted him out of the water and, deciding to keep him along with a couple of others, knocked him on the head and tossed him into the boat. That evening when we beached the boat seventeen miles downstream from where we had started, I laid our fish on the bank. Dorothy looked at them and said, "That last one was pretty good." I took out a pocket scale and weighed him: three and three-quarter pounds. With the Papoose measure in my mind, I hadn't thought much of him for size. Yet he was the largest trout I have ever caught.

The next day when I came into the Fly Shop, I looked at the wall for the largest stream trout caught on dry fly. There it was—a rainbow, ten pounds, three ounces, caught by a Livingston fisherman, Roy Williams, on a Grey Hackle Yellow dry fly in the Yellowstone River in October 1950 (a record that still stood in the spring of 1972). I studied this fish and compared him in my mind's eye with the lost king. Needless to say . . .

During the next two years, I went back to Papoose Creek several times with different companions. On one occasion Dan Bailey went along, only because he was willing to humor me. We got into the water a couple of hundred feet above the confluence of creek and river and waded out to the shallows. Dan started fooling around a boulder below the island, waiting while I waded down the shallows and fished back in toward the bank until I came to Papoose. When I reached the creek, I heard a shout from Dan that told me he had a strike. I found him a few minutes later, aghast. "The waters parted," he said, holding his arms wide and laughing, "I was catching some little fish on a small Grizzly Wulff and this fine leader, not expecting anything else, when he rose beside that rock. All around, the river went dry behind his rise. He went straight across to the end of my line and never stopped."

McGuane certainly isn't the first to seize the dialectic of sport and worry it to the bone. But he may be the best. And if he exposes a few nerves along the way, it's only to let you know that Novocain is not his favorite prescription.

THOMAS McGUANE

Skelton's Party

"Ma'am, you want to hand me that lunch so I can stow it?" Skelton took the wicker basket from Mrs. Rudleigh; and then the Thermos she handed him. "I've got plenty of water," he said.

"That's not water."

"What is it?"

"Gibsons."

"Let me put them in the cooler for you then—"

"We put them in the Thermos," said Rudleigh, "so we don't have to put them in the cooler. We like them where we can get at them. In case we need them, you know, real snappy."

Tom Skelton looked up at him. Most people when they smile expose a section of their upper teeth; when Rudleigh smiled, he exposed his lower teeth.

"Hold the Thermos in your lap," Skelton said. "If that starts rolling around the skiff while I'm running these banks, I'll throw it overboard."

"An ecologist," said Mrs. Rudleigh.

"Are you sure Nichol cannot appeal his sentence, Captain?" asked Rudleigh.

"I'm sure," said Skelton.

Mrs. Rudleigh reached out one hand and bent it backward so her fingernails

238

were all in display; she was thinking of a killer line but it wouldn't come; so she didn't speak.

Skelton knew from other guides he could not let the clients run the boat for him; but he had never expected this; now all three of them were glancing past one another with metallic eyes.

Mrs. Rudleigh came and Skelton put her in the forward chair. Rudleigh followed in squeaking bright deck shoes and sat aft, swiveling about in the chair with an executive's preoccupation.

"Captain," Rudleigh began. Men like Rudleigh believed in giving credit to the qualified. If an eight-year-old were running the skiff, Rudleigh would call him "Captain" without irony; it was a credit to his class. "Captain, are we going to bonefish?" Mrs. Rudleigh was putting zinc oxide on her thin nose and on the actual edges of her precise cheekbones. She was a thin, pretty woman of forty who you could see had a proclivity for hysterics, slow burns, and slapping.

"We have a good tide for bonefish."

"Well, Missus Rudleigh and I have had a good deal of bonefishing in Yucatán and we were wondering if it mightn't be an awfully long shot to fish for permit . . ."

Skelton knew it was being put to him; finding permit—big pompano—was a guide's hallmark and he didn't particularly have a permit tide. "I can find permit," he said though, finishing a sequence Rudleigh started with the word "Captain."

Carter strolled up. He knew the Rudleighs and they greeted each other. "You're in good hands," he said to them, tilting his head toward Skelton. "Boy's a regular fish hawk." He returned his head to the perpendicular.

"Where are your people, Cart?" Skelton asked to change the subject.

"They been partying, I guess. Man said he'd be late. Shortens my day."

Skelton choked the engine and started it. He let it idle for a few minutes and then freed up his lines. The canal leading away from the dock wandered around lazily, a lead-green gloss like pavement.

"Ought to find some bonefish in the Snipes on this incoming water," Carter said. Skelton looked at him a moment.

"We're permit fishing, Cart."

"Oh, really. Why, permit huh."

"What do you think? Boca Chica beach?"

"Your guess is as good as mine. But yeah okay, Boca Chica."

Skelton idled on the green tidal gloss of the canal until he cleared the entrance, then ran it up to 5,000 rpm and slacked off to an easy plane in the light chop. He leaned back over his shoulder to talk to Rudleigh. "We're going to Boca Chica beach. I think it's our best bet for permit on this tide."

"Fine, fine."

"I hate to take you there, a little bit, because it's in the landing pattern."

"I don't mind if the fish don't mind."

Skelton swung in around by Cow Key channel, past the navy hospital, under the bridge where boys were getting in some snapper fishing before it would be time for the military hospitals; then out the channel along the mangroves with the great white wing of the drive-in theater to their left, with an unattended meadow of loudspeaker stanchions; and abruptly around the corner to an expanse of blue Atlantic. Skelton ran tight to the beach, inside the boat-wrecking niggerheads; he watched for sunken ice cans and made the run to Boca Chica, stopping short.

The day was clear and bright except for one squall to the west, black with etched rain lines connecting it to sea; the great reciprocating engine of earth, thought Skelton, looks like a jellyfish.

"Go ahead and get ready, Mr. Rudleigh, I'm going to pole us along the rocky edge and see what we can see." Skelton pulled the pushpole out of its chocks and got up in the bow; Rudleigh was ready in the stern behind the tilted engine. It took two or three leaning thrusts to get the skiff under way; and then they were gliding over the sand, coral, sea fans, staghorn, and lawns of turtle grass. Small cowfish, sprats, and fry of one description or another scattered before them and vanished in the glare. Stone crabs backed away in bellicose, Pentagonian idiocy in the face of the boat's progress. Skelton held the boat into the tide at the breaking edge of the flat and looked for moving fish.

A few small sharks came early on the flood and passed down light, yellow-eyed and sweeping back and forth schematically for something in trouble. The first military aircraft came in overhead, terrifyingly low; a great delta-winged machine with howling, vulvate exhausts and nervous quick-moving control flaps; so close were they that the bright hydraulic shafts behind the flaps glittered; small rockets were laid up thickly under the wings like insect eggs. The plane approached, banked subtly, and the pilot glanced out at the skiff; his head looking no larger than a cocktail onion. A moment after the plane passed, its shock wave swept toward them and the crystal, perfect world of the flat paled and vanished; not reappearing until some minutes later and slowly. The draconic roar of the engines diminished and twin blossoms of flame shrank away toward the airfield.

"It must take a smart cookie," said Mrs. Rudleigh, "to make one of those do what it is supposed to."

"It takes balls for brains," said Rudleigh.

"That's even better," she smiled.

"Only that's what any mule has," Rudleigh added.

Mrs. Rudleigh threw something at her husband, who remained in the stern, rigid as a gun carriage.

Skelton was so determined that this first day of his professional guiding be a success that he felt with some agony the ugliness of the aircraft that came in now at shorter and shorter intervals, thundering with their volatile mists drifting over the sea meadow.

The Rudleighs had opened the Thermos and were consuming its contents exactly as the heat of the day began to spread. Skelton was now poling down light, flushing small fish; then two schools of bonefish, not tailing but pushing wakes in their hurry; Rudleigh saw them late and bungled the cast, looking significantly at Mrs. Rudleigh after each failure.

"You've got to bear down," she said.

"I'm bearing down."

"Bear down harder, honey."

"I said: I'm bearing down."

Now the wading birds that were on the flat in the early tide were flooded out and flew northwest to catch the Gulf of Mexico tide. Skelton knew they had about lost their water.

"It's kind of slow, Captain," said Rudleigh.

"I've been thinking the same thing," Skelton said, his heart chilling within him. "I'm going to pole this out and make a move."

A minute later, he was running to Saddlebunch and got there in time to catch the incoming water across the big sand spot; he hardly had a moment to stake the skiff when the bonefish started crossing the sand. Now Mrs. Rudleigh was casting, driving the fish away. Rudleigh snatched the rod from her after her second failure.

"Sit down!"

Rudleigh was rigidly prepared for the next fish. Skelton would have helped him but knew in advance it would make things worse. He felt all of his efforts pitted against the contents of the Thermos.

"You hawse's oss," said Mrs. Rudleigh to her husband. He seemed not to have heard. He was in the vague crouch of lumbar distress.

"I can fish circles around you, queen bee," he said after a bit. "Always could."

"What about Peru? What about Cabo Blanco?"

"You're always throwing Cabo Blanco in my face without ever, repeat, ever a word about Tierra del Fuego."

"What about Piñas Bay, Panama."

"Shut up."

"Seems to me," she said, "that Raúl commented that the señora had a way of making the señor look real bum."

A small single bonefish passed the skiff. Rudleigh flushed it by casting right into its face. *"Cocksucker."*

"That's just the way you handled striped marlin. Right there is about what you did with those stripes at Rancho Buena Vista."

Rudleigh whirled around and held the point of his rod under Mrs. Rudleigh's throat. *"I'm warning you."*

"He had a tantrum at the Pez Maya Club in Yucatán," Mrs. Rudleigh told Skelton.

"Yes, ma'am. I see."

"Uh, Captain—"

"I'm right here, Mr. Rudleigh."

"I thought this was a permit deal."

"I'm looking for permit on this tide. I told you they were a long shot."

"Captain, I know about permit. I have seen permit in the Bahamas, Yucatán, Costa Rica, and at the great Belize camps in British Honduras. I know they are a long shot."

Skelton said, "Maybe your terrific familiarity with places to fish will tell us where we ought to be right now."

"Captain, I wouldn't presume."

A skiff was running just off the reel, making sheets of bright water against the sun.

"Do you know what today's tides are?" Skelton asked.

"No."

"Which way is the Gulf of Mexico?"

Rudleigh pointed all wrong. Skelton wanted to be home reading Proudhon, studying the winos, or copulating.

"Is that a permit?" Mrs. Rudleigh asked. The black fork of a large permit surfaced just out of casting range: beyond belief. Rudleigh stampeded back into position. Skelton slipped the pole out of the sand and began to ghost quietly toward the fish and stopped. Nothing visible. A long moment passed. Again, the black fork appeared.

"Cast."

Rudleigh threw forty feet beyond the permit. There was no hope of retrieving and casting again. Then out of totally undeserved luck, the fish began to change course toward Rudleigh's bait. Rudleigh and Mrs. Rudleigh exchanged glances.

"Please keep your eye on the fish." Skelton was overwhelmed by the entirely undeserved nature of what was transpiring. In a moment, the big fish was tailing again.

"Strike him."

Rudleigh lifted the rod and the fish was on. Skelton poled hard, following the fish, now streaking against the drag for deep water. The same skiff that passed earlier appeared, running the other direction; and Skelton wondered who it could be.

"God, Captain, will I be able to cope with this at all? I mean, I knew the fish was strong! But honest to God, this is a nigger with a hotfoot!"

"I'm still admiring your cast, darling."

Skelton followed watching the drawn bow the rod had become, the line shearing water with precision.

"What a marvelously smooth drag this reel has! A hundred smackers seemed steep at the time; but when you're in the breach, as I am now, a drag like this is the last nickel bargain in America!"

Skelton was poling after the fish with precisely everything he had. And it was difficult on the packed bottom with the pole inclining to slip out from under him.

His feeling of hope for a successful first-day guiding was considerably modified by Rudleigh's largely undeserved hooking of the fish. And now the nobility of the fish's fight was further eroding Skelton's pleasure.

When they crossed the edge of the flat, the permit raced down the reef line in sharp powerful curves, dragging the line across the coral. "Gawd, gawd, gawd," Rudleigh said. "This cookie is stronger than I am!" Skelton poled harder and at one point overtook the fish as it desperately rubbed the hook on the coral bottom; seeing the boat, it flushed once more in terror, making a single long howl pour from the reel. A fish that was exactly noble, thought Skelton, who began to imagine the permit coming out of a deep-water wreck by the pull of moon and tide, riding the invisible crest of the incoming water, feeding and moving by force of blood; only to run afoul of an asshole from Connecticut.

The fight continued without much change for another hour, mainly outside the reef line in the green water over a sand bottom: a safe place to fight the fish. Rudleigh had soaked through his khaki safari clothes; and from time to time Mrs. Rudleigh advised him to "bear down." When Mrs. Rudleigh told him this, he would turn to look at her, his neck muscles standing out like cords and his eyes acquiring broad white perimeters. Skelton ached from pursuing the fish with the pole; he might have started the engine outside the reef line, but he feared Rudleigh getting his line in the propeller and he had found that a large fish was held away from the boat by the sound of a running engine.

As soon as the fish began to show signs of tiring, Skelton asked Mrs. Rudleigh to take a seat; then he brought the big net up on the deck beside him. He hoped he would be able to get Rudleigh to release this hugely undeserved fish, not only because it was undeserved but because the fish had fought so very bravely. No, he admitted to himself, Rudleigh would never let the fish go.

By now the fish should have been on its side. It began another long and accelerating run, the pale sheet of water traveling higher up the line, the fish swerving somewhat inshore again; and to his terror, Skelton found himself poling after the fish through the shallows, now and then leaning over to free the line from a sea fan. They glided among the little hammocks and mangrove keys of Saddlebunch in increasing vegetated congestion, in a narrowing tidal creek that closed around and over them with guano-covered mangroves and finally prevented the boat from following another foot. Nevertheless, line continued to pour off the reel.

"Captain, consider it absolutely necessary that I kill the fish. This one doubles the Honduran average."

Skelton did not reply, he watched the line slow its passage from the reel, winding out into the shadowy creek; then stop. He knew there was a good chance the desperate animal had reached a dead end.

"Stay here."

Skelton climbed out of the boat and, running the line through his fingers lightly, began to wade the tidal creek. The mosquitoes found him quickly and held in a pale globe around his head. He waded steadily, flushing herons out of the mangroves over his head. At one point, he passed a tiny side channel, blocking the exit of a heron that raised its stiff wings very slightly away from its body and glared at him. In the green shadows, the heron was a radiant, perfect white.

He stopped a moment to look at the bird. All he could hear was the slow musical passage of tide in the mangrove roots and the low pattern of bird sounds more liquid than the sea itself in these shallows. He moved away from the side channel, still following the line. Occasionally, he felt some small movement of life in it; but he was certain now the permit could go no farther. He had another thirty yards to go, if he had guessed right looking at Rudleigh's partially emptied spool.

Wading along, he felt he was descending into the permit's world; in knee-deep water, the small mangrove snappers, angelfish, and baby barracudas scattered before him, precise, contained creatures of perfect mobility. The brilliant blue sky was reduced to a narrow ragged band quite high overhead now and the light wavered more with the color of the sea and of estuarine shadow than that of vulgar sky. Skelton stopped and his eye followed the line back in the direction he had come. The Rudleighs were at its other end, infinitely far away.

Skelton was trying to keep his mind on the job he had set out to do. The problem was, he told himself, to go from Point A to Point B; but every breath of humid air, half sea, and the steady tidal drain through root and elliptical shadow in his ears and eyes diffused his attention. Each heron that leaped like an arrow out of his narrow slot, spiraling invisibly into the sky, separated him from the job. Shafts of light in the side channels illuminated columns of pristine, dancing insects.

Very close now. He released the line so that if his appearance at the dead end terrified the permit there would not be sufficient tension for the line to break. The sides of the mangrove slot began to yield. Skelton stopped.

An embowered, crystalline tidal pool: the fish lay exhausted in its still water, lolling slightly and unable to right itself. It cast a delicate circular shadow on the sand bottom. Skelton moved in and the permit made no effort to rescue itself; instead, it lay nearly on its side and watched Skelton approach with a steady, following eye that was, for Skelton, the last straw. Over its broad, virginal sides a lambent, moony light shimmered. The fish seemed like an oval section of sky—yet sentient and alert, intelligent as tide.

He took the permit firmly by the base of its tail and turned it gently upright in the water. He reached into its mouth and removed the hook from the cartilaginous operculum. He noticed that the suddenly loosened line was not retrieved: Rudleigh hadn't even the sense to keep tension on the line.

By holding one hand under the permit's pectoral fins and the other around the base of its tail, Skelton was able to move the fish back and forth in the water to revive it. When he first tentatively released it, it teetered over on its side, its wandering eye still fixed upon him. He righted the fish again and continued to move it gently back and forth in the water; and this time when he released the permit, it stayed upright, steadying itself in equipoise, mirror sides once again purely reflecting the bottom. Skelton watched a long while until some regularity returned to the movement of its gills.

Then he cautiously—for fear of startling the fish—backed once more into the green tidal slot and turned to head for the skiff. Rudleigh had lost his permit.

The line was lying limp on the bottom. Why didn't the fool at least retrieve it? With his irritation, Skelton began to return to normal. He trudged along the creek, this time against the tide; and returned to the skiff.

The skiff was empty.

All sciences require specialized languages, lingos to expedite thought; angling is no exception. Fortunately McManus has compiled an armchair lexicon of the essential terminology, common and uncommon.

PATRICK McMANUS

Fish Poles, and Other Useful Terminology

I have long held the opinion that a person should know the jargon of any activity in which he professes some expertise. A writer, for example, should not refer to quotation marks as "those itty-bitty ears." It is unsettling to hear the carpenter you have just hired refer to his hammer as "a pounder." A mechanic tinkering in the innards of your car arouses anxiety by speaking of a pair of pliers as his "squeezer." Similarly, it would be disconcerting to have a doctor tell you he had detected an irregularity in your "thingamajig." (If you're like me, you're composed almost entirely of the thingamajigs, some of which you value a good deal more than others.) Ignorance of proper terminology often leads to confusion, alarm, and panic, especially when one talks about the sport of fishing.

I recently met a man and his son out bass fishing. The father was making superb casts with what was obviously a new rod.

"Is that a boron you've got there?" I asked.

The man turned and looked at his son. "Well, he ain't too bright, that's for sure," he said.

Here was a case where a man had mastered the art of fishing, but had failed to keep up on recent nomenclature. I could hardly blame him. I now spend so much time learning all the new fishing terms that I scarcely have time to fish.

Nonanglers think fishing is easy. Well, just let them spend a day poring over one of the new fishing catalogs and memorizing the terms. One 1982 catalog, for example, contains such terms and phrases as "fiberglass integrated with unidirectional graphite," "silicone carbide guides with diamond polished silicone carbide guide rings," "Uni bent butt," that sort of thing. I'm just lucky I didn't ask the man fishing with his son if he had a Uni bent butt. I might have come home with a Uni bent head.

Consider just a few of the terms you now must learn in order to go out and catch a few bass: *structure, isolated structure, sanctuary, stragglers, breakline, suspended fish, pattern, holding area, riprap, point, scatter point, contact point, cheater hook, buzz bait, Texas rig, crank bait, triggering, flippin', pH, jig and pig, spinnerbait, fly 'n' rind.* The aerospace industry requires less technical jargon than the average bass fisherman.

When I was a youngster, my friends and I could get by on fewer than a dozen fishing terms. No doubt we could have expanded our angling vocabulary by going to the county library and checking out a book on fishing techniques. The problem was that if one of the gang showed up at the library to check out a book, Miss Phelps, the librarian, might have suffered a heart attack on the spot. Enlarging our fishing vocabularies didn't seem worth the risk of taking a life. We chose to get by on the few fishing terms we knew.

Although our fishing terminology was limited, it was not without its own peculiar complexity. Take the word "keeper" for example. The first fish you caught was always a keeper. This was not the result of outrageous coincidence, but of definition. The first fish was interpreted as a keeper merely by having a mouth big enough to stretch over the barb of a hook.

There were several advantages to this definition of keeper applying to the first fish. Suppose the first fish you caught during the day was also the only fish, and you had released it. That would mean you would have to go home skunked, an angling term every bit as significant then as it is today. Calling the first fish a keeper often prevented the emotional damage which resulted from going home skunked.

Furthermore, if someone later asked you if you had caught any fish, you could reply, in reference to a fish no longer than a pocketknife, "Just one keeper." The phrase "just one keeper" implied, of course, that you had caught and released numerous *small* fish, thereby contributing to one's reputation as a "sportsman."

If the first fish was particularly small, it did not always remain a keeper. A larger fish, when caught, became a keeper and the small first fish became a *badly hooked* one. You always explained, with a note of regret in your voice, that you had kept the badly hooked fish because it would have *died anyway*.

Proper fishing terminology even in the time of my youth was extremely important, both socially and psychologically.

Although some of our terms might seem simple by today's standards, they were not without their subtle shades of meaning. Take the word "mess" for instance, which was the word used to denote your catch while telling someone about your day of fishing. "Mess" used without modifiers usually meant two fish—a keeper and a badly hooked. A "small mess" referred to a single keeper. A "nice mess" meant three fish, excluding any badly hooked. Any number of fish over three was, naturally, a "big mess." To ask for specific numbers was considered rude when someone told you he had caught a big mess of fish.

Today, the phrase "a mess of fish" is seldom heard, probably because anyone uttering it would instantly be identifying himself as a fish glutton. Quantity of the catch is now always referred to by specific numbers, although a certain element of deception is still retained. An angler who has spent twelve hours flailing a trout stream and managed to land a total of three fish, responds to a question about the number of fish caught by saying "I only *kept* three." If asked exactly how many he caught and released, he will be overcome by a coughing fit and have to rush from the room. Now, as always, it is considered poor form to lie about the number of fish caught, unless, of course, the angler has not mastered the technique of the coughing fit.

It took me fifteen minutes the other day to memorize the name of my new casting rod, and I've already forgotten it. When I was younger, we didn't have to memorize the names of our rods because we didn't have any. We had what were called fish poles. Even now, after nearly forty years, I will still occasionally refer to a three-hundred-dollar custom-built fly rod as a fish pole.

"That's a nice fish pole you've got there," I'll say to the owner of the rod.

He will go white in the face, shudder, twitch, gurgle, clench his hands, and lurch toward me. "Wha-what d-did you s-say? F-fish pole? FISH POLE! Y-you called my three-hundred-dollar rod a FISH POLE?"

I will back away, hands raised to fend him off, and explain that I have never shaken a bad habit picked up in my childhood.

"Fish pole," in the old days, was a generic term for any elongated instrument intended for the purpose of propelling hook, line, sinker, and worm in the general direction of fish-holding water, and then wrenching an unlucky fish to the bank with as little fuss as possible. Some fish poles were made from cedar trees that had been rejected as too short or too slender for use as telephone poles. A few fortunate kids owned metal telescoping fish poles. My first fish pole was a single-piece, stiff metal tube about six feet long. There was a wire that could be pulled out of the tip if you wanted "action." I never pulled the wire out. Action, in my fishing circles, was not considered a desirable characteristic in a fish pole. It merely complicated the process of wrenching the fish from the water, or *landing it.*

Landing, by the way, consisted of whipping the fish in a long, high arc over your head and into the branches of a tree, which you usually had to climb in order to disengage both line and fish. Sometimes the fish would come off the line right at the peak of the arc and whiz away toward the state line like a stone loosed from a sling. These fish were later referred to as badly hooked.

"Forked stick" is a term seldom heard among anglers nowadays, which is too bad, because the forked stick once served to enrich both fishing and conversations about fishing.

"I prefer the forked stick to a creel for carrying fish," a kid would say. "The creel is too bulky and keeps catching on brush. It gets in your way when you're casting, too. Most creels are too small for a really big fish anyway. Give me a forked stick to a creel any time." This statement actually meant "Give me a forked stick any time until someone gives me a creel. Then I'll prefer a creel."

There was much discussion about the kind of tree or bush that produced the best forked sticks for carrying fish. In theory, the way you selected a forked stick was to seek out a good specimen from the preferred species of bush or tree, cut it off with your pocketknife, and neatly trim it to appropriate and aesthetically pleasing dimensions. Ideally, there would be a fork at both ends, one to keep the fish from sliding off and the other to be hooked under your belt, thus freeing both hands for the business of catching fish.

The theory of the forked stick didn't work out in practice, because the kid never even thought about cutting a forked stick until he had caught his first fish. To cut a forked stick prior to catching a fish would have been presumptuous and probably bad luck to boot. (Also, few things look more ridiculous than an angler walking around with a empty forked stick.) Once a fish had been caught, the youngster, in his excitement, would instantly forget the aesthetically pleasing proportions prescribed for the forked stick. He would twist off the nearest branch with a fork on it, gnaw away any obstructing foliage with his teeth, thread the fish onto it, and get back to his fishing. When you are catching fish, you didn't have time to mess with aesthetics.

The forked stick contributed much excitement to our fishing. Since a double-forked branch or willow was almost never available when needed, the forked stick could not be hooked under your belt but had to be laid down somewhere while you fished. Once or twice every hour, a panicky search would begin for a string of fish left on a log or rock "just around that last bend." Approximately 30 percent of your fishing time was spent trying to catch fish and 70 percent looking for fish you had already caught.

Thus, the term "forked stick" denoted not merely a device for carrying your catch, but a whole mode of fishing that the boy who grows up owning a creel can never come to know or appreciate. He should consider himself damn lucky for it, too.

There were a few other terms that filled out our fishing vocabulary. "Game warden" is one that comes to mind. I don't know if any state still has game wardens. Most have wildlife conservation officers or persons of similar sterile title to enforce fishing regulations. Somehow it doesn't seem to me that *Wildlife Conservation Officer* has the same power to jolt a boy's nervous system as does *game warden*. How well I remember a fishing pal once exclaiming, "Geez, here comes the *game warden*!" We jerked our lines from the creek, sprinted up the side of a steep, brush-covered hill, threw our fish poles and and fork sticks under a log, and tore off across the countryside. And we hadn't even been violating any of the fishing regulations. The term "game warden" just had that sort of effect on you.

There is at least one indication that many terms and phrases closely associated with fishing may soon be made obsolete. A new reel on the market is reputed to virtually eliminate backlash, that wonderfully intricate snarl of line that has served to enrich the vocabularies of anglers ever since reels were invented. It seems likely the eradication of backlash could mean the end of such colorful expressions as "bleeping bleep of a bleep bleep." Truly, the language of fishing will be the less for the absence of backlash.

And it's about time, if you ask me.

When a reporter forsakes the *Wall Street Journal* for angling, you figure he's dedicating himself to writing a lifetime of hair-raising adventures. Unless, of course, the reporter is the infamous Sparse Grey Hackle. In which case we are quite content to settle for first-rate adventures.

ALFRED MILLER

The Perfect Angler

I never saw him; if anyone else ever did, it has not been reported. I don't believe he exists. But if he did, what would his attributes be?

If we accept the little girl's statement that piano playing is easy—"you just press down on those black and white things"—and apply it to trout fishing, all it involves is:

1) finding a fish
2) deceiving it into taking an imitation of its food
3) hooking, playing, and landing it.

The first requirement is the most important; my guess is that finding a fish is anywhere from 50 percent to 80 percent of catching it. Overwhelmingly, the reason why so many experienced and well-equipped fishermen catch so few trout is that most of the time they aren't fishing over fish.

Bill Kelly, a research aquatic biologist and a skillful, experienced angler, says I should specify a *feeding* fish. If he means a big fish, I agree. "To catch a five-pounder, you must be there when he's feeding," Ed Hewitt once told me. And experts like Herman Christian agree that a good hatch of big flies must be on for about half an hour before the larger fish, over sixteen inches, will come on the feed.

Also, if Bill means the rich Pennsylvania limestone streams or the lush British chalk streams, I agree. But most of our eastern trout waters are hungry streams in which the smaller fish, up to maybe twelve inches, tend to harbor between hatches close enough to a feed lane to seize anything edible that may come riding down the current.

Anyway, finding a fish is the problem; the rest is patience.

Fish finding is done by sight; by knowing the kinds of places in which fish harbor or feed; or by the simple hammer-and-chisel process of fishing one stretch so often that eventually one learns where the fish are, without knowing or caring why. The first method is the rarest, the second the most difficult, and the third the easiest but most limited.

Really fine fishing eyesight is a gift of the gods, the rarest and most enviable attribute a fisherman can possess, and I have never known a truly great angler who did not have it. Edward R. Hewitt had the eyes of an eagle, right up to his death; so did George M. L. LaBranche. And Ray Bergman's ability to see fish was so instinctive that he never could understand why everyone couldn't do it.

The hawk-eyed angler sees not only the fish themselves but the faint, fleeting signs of their presence—the tiny dimple in the slow water next to the bank, which indicates a big fish sucking down little flies; the tiny black object momentarily protruded above the surface, which is the neb of a good, quietly feeding fish; the slight ruffling of the shallows by a school of minnows fleeing from the bogeyman.

George LaBranche claimed in *The Dry Fly and Fast Water* that the knack of seeing fish under water can be learned by practice, but I incline to believe that either one is born with sharp eyes or one is not. On the other hand, there is a mysterious mental aspect of eyesight; sometimes it seems to be a quality separate from mere keenness of sight—visual acuity. Resolving power, the ability to see what we look at, seems to be a mental as well as a physical attribute. How else can we account for the almost incredible ability of the great British angler-writer G. E. M. Skues to discern whether trout were nymphing immediately *under*, or taking spent flies *in*, the surface film, when we know that he was virtually blind in one eye and had to aid the other with a monocle? Of course, knowledge plays a part. "The little brown wink under water," as Skues called it, means a feeding fish to the initiate but nothing at all to the tyro, just as that Pullman-plush patch in yonder bush, eighteen inches above the ground, means a deer in summer coat to the woodsman but is never noticed by the city yokel looking sixteen hands high for a hatrack spread of antlers.

The second method of finding fish, by learning to be "a judge of water," is to my way of thinking the highest attainment in this aspect of angling. Anyone who is willing to do the work can make himself a fair judge of water; like piano playing, a little of it is a simple thing to acquire. But mastery of the art is granted to but few, and a lifetime is not too long to achieve perfection.

It is remarkable what a good judge of water can do. Gene Russell, who learned the angler's trade on hard-plugged public streams around New York City, doesn't even set up a rod when he gets out of his car to fish a new piece of water. He just saunters along the bank for half a mile or so, smoking a pipe and looking; then he saunters back and either drives away or gets out his rod and goes to one, two, or maybe three places that he has mentally marked down during his stroll.

What did he see? Maybe it was a tiny patch of watercress on the opposite bank, or perhaps moisture on a rocky face above the stream; either would indicate a seepage of cold spring water below which a fish is apt to be lying in hot weather. Maybe it was a big stone in the current—not any stone but one so faced and undercut that it creates an eddy of quiet water in front of it in which a trout can rest at ease while the stream brings him his vittles. Maybe it was a smallish trout exposing himself where no trout ought to be, on a clean sand bottom in brilliant sunlight. If there is a good lie nearby, the chances are that a bigger fish has driven the little fellow out of it; he wants to go back but daren't.

Maybe Gene saw a long stretch of shallow, brawling water, the natural feeding grounds of the trout, without any cover for a sizable fish anywhere along it except one hollow about as big as a bathtub. Maybe such a fish is using it for an advanced base.

More likely, Gene didn't really *see* all this, for an experienced, capable angler's stream sense becomes a part of his subconscious. Probably all he *saw* were a few places that seemed to say: try me.

The third method of fish finding, that of learning a piece of water by experience, is, of course, a limited one, and yet it is remarkable how many miles of water an industrious and wide-ranging fisherman can learn by heart. I once heard the late John Alden Knight and a man named Crane, of Deposit, New York, testing each other's knowledge of some ten miles of excellent fly-rod bass water on the West Branch of the Delaware between Deposit and Hancock. They checked each other stone by stone on every pool and disagreed but once— as to whether there were four or five stones at the head of the Cat Pool. They finally agreed that there were five, but that there never was a bass behind the first one.

Still, the angler who depends on experience to know the stream is like the applicant for admission to the bar who had read nothing but the laws of the state. "Young man," thundered the judge, "some day the legislature may repeal everything you know." The stream is continually repealing much of what the local angler has learned; after every big storm, with its attendant filling of old holes and digging of new ones, he has to learn the water anew.

Thus far we have been able to follow a firm path. But it ends on the shores of an illimitable sea of controversy when we come to the second requirement of angling: to deceive the fish into taking an imitation of its food. Fortunately, it is not necessary for us to wet much more than the soles of our shoes in this sea.

First let us consider a few fundamentals. The trout is a very primitive creature with only two primary instincts. One is the spawning urge; it comes during the closed season so we need not consider it. The other is self-preservation. It cannot be emphasized too strongly that the trout spends all its time at the business of staying alive.

Unfortunately for the trout, its internal economy is such that it is never very far ahead of starvation; and the larder of the stream is not in the safest but in the most dangerous, i.e., exposed, places. The whole "food chain"— plankton, insects, minnows—lives in the fast, shallow places where there is lots of sunlight and quickly changing water. So when a fish gets hungry enough, it has to risk itself out where the food is. Aside from food, it has only two other requirements—oxygen (as you know, it is dissolved in the water) and cover—protection from its enemies and shelter from such elements as floods and ice. Obviously, the only instinct of the trout to which the fisherman can appeal is its appetite; the only lure which will interest it is an imitation of its food.

Trout eat about every living thing that they can catch and swallow, but in the main they feed on smaller fish and the various life forms of water insects. There is something in the composition of water insects that makes them preferred by the trout to any other form of food. But a big fish, which eats more, in proportion to its weight, than a man, just doesn't have the time or the energy to collect its nourishment one insect at a time, so it is forced to feed considerably on minnows, frogs, crawfish, and other sizable mouthfuls. But it is the glory of the brown trout that he never entirely ceases to feed on insects, no matter how big he grows, so that the fly-fisherman always has a chance—not a good one, but a chance—of setting his hook in the biggest fish in the stream. For the purpose of this article we shall assume that "food" means stream insects in their several life forms.

So to catch a trout the angler must deceive it into taking an imitation of some form of stream insect. There is a lot of dynamite in those two simple words "deceive" and "imitation," for they are the keys to the most uncompromising and violent disagreements in the whole world of sport.

Let us consider imitation first. The trout, being essentially a very simple creature, does not go through elevated mental processes in feeding but depends upon its reflexes; it has more automatic controls built into it than a guided missile. (They work a lot better, too.) It reacts to the approach in, or on, the current of an insect larva or winged fly according to the triggering of these automatic controls, varying with the circumstances. So imitation can only mean: whatever deceives the reflexes, the automatic controls, of the fish, *according to circumstances.*

That is an important qualification. An invitation to dinner doesn't look anything like a dinner, but, under different circumstances, each may bring a hungry man a-running. The angler may use a replica of the natural insect, complete even to its eyes, like Halford, or depend mostly on where he casts his fly and how it floats, like LaBranche, to deceive the fish. But if he does deceive the fish, that's all that counts; who will say he is wrong? For the purpose of our hypothetical perfect angler, it is sufficient to say, as regards imitation, that he knows how to imitate the natural food of the trout so well that the fish is deceived under every circumstance.

This involves a great knowledge of both aquatic biology and stream entomology and a great skill in expressing this knowledge in the concrete form of artificial flies. Our perfect angler must have the technical knowledge of such authorities as the late Dr. James G. Needham and his son Dr. Paul R. Needham (*Life of Inland Waters* and numerous other works, jointly or severally), and the late Dr. Ann Haven Morgan (*Field Book of Ponds and Streams* and others). And like Theodore Gordon, who was probably the first man to fish the dry fly in America, our perfect angler must have a large practical knowledge of stream insects and the ability to construct imitations of them.

Imitation of the fish's food, the stream insect, is only a part of deceiving it; the rest is presentation, which involves stalking—getting into casting position without alarming the fish—and casting, including also fishing out the cast.

Stalking is another of the fundamentals upon which one may judge the quality of an angler. The real expert is always willing to credit the fish with the inordinate wariness which it always manifests, and he is willing to take the trouble to stalk as he should, even if it is no more than taking pains to scare the little fish in the tail of the pool downstream, out of the way, rather than upstream where they will alarm the bigger ones.

The great Skues was well into his eighties, an enfeebled old man, when he wrote to a friend that he "found it increasingly difficult to adopt an attitude of becoming reverence to the fish." British chalk streams usually can't be waded, and, typically, their banks are bare except for a few bushes to which the angler creeps and behind which he kneels to cast. Skues was finding it "increasingly difficult" to do so; but he was kneeling, nevertheless.

Over on what used to be the "railroad" side of Cairns's Pool on the lower Beaverkill, there was a magnificently deep, boulder-lined run that was just right for big fish. Every day during the season, literally scores of fishermen flogged that run, carelessly and ineffectually, from the shallow, "road" side. It couldn't be fished properly from that side and they knew it; they just wouldn't bother to do it right.

But for an expert like Harry Darbee, it was not too much trouble to cross the stream above the pool, walk along the railroad track, slither down a dauntingly steep and loose embankment, and then work from one to another of the huge rough rocks that protected the railroad fill from floods. With the stream on his left, his casting arm had to contend with an abominable mess of high bushes, low-strung telegraph wires, poles, and the embankment itself, and most fishermen said it wasn't worth it. But I saw Harry perched like a chamois on one steep-faced boulder after another, holding his rod across his body and making niggling backhanded casts to every good spot within reach.

Seldom indeed will one see the average fisherman crawling to reach the right spot, or kneeling in the stream to reduce his visibility; but Ray Bergman used to wear out the knees of his waders before any other portion, and Otto v. Kienbusch not only fished but progressed upstream on his knees along a quarter mile of the flat, gravel-bottomed, fish-infested upper Nissequogue on Long Island. Otto was one of the few who could get into the big browns in that stretch.

Every dry-fly man knows that there are ways of casting a curve or loop in his line so as to allow his fly a natural float when he is fishing across varied currents. But Ray Bergman was speaking important truth when he told me, "Curves are too hard to throw and succeed too seldom for you to bother with them. For every fish there is one place from which you can cast to him with a straight line and still get a free float. Figure out where it is and go there even if it means walking back a hundred yards to cross the stream and come up the other side." My lady wife, who can fish like an otter, heeded well this advice. Although she learned her fishing from a whole galaxy of expert casters and anglers, she has never even tried to cast a curve. She wades around until she finds the right place and then makes the short straight cast which, too often for the comfort of my ego, takes a fish.

Having stalked the fish, the angler must now cast, and here all hell breaks loose, for there is more misconception, disagreement, and prevarication about casting than any other part of the sport. For one thing, practically no fisherman knows how far he really can cast, a fact which once nearly broke up one of the older Beaverkill clubs.

The clubhouse is right on the bank, and at noon the members come in for lunch and discuss the morning's fishing at the table. One low miscreant got tired of listening to these tales. Secretly he drove two stakes in the bank, a measured sixty feet apart. Next lunchtime, the first member to voice a standard fish story remark—"I made a medium cast, about sixty feet"—was challenged by the miscreant. Bets were made, and the whole party repaired to the riverside, where an appalling thing was quickly discovered. The storyteller couldn't cast sixty feet, and, what is worse, none of the others could either. Since it is obviously impossible to tell a fish story without mentioning a sixty-foot cast, the members lunched in gloomy silence until at last they rebelled, chucked the beggar out, and went back to making sixty-foot casts at the luncheon table.

As a matter of fact, long casting is not of much use in trout fishing, at least in the East. Few, indeed, are the times when an angler really has to make a cast longer than forty-five feet, and fewer still the times when such a cast raises *and hooks* a fish. But if distance is not necessary to the angler's cast, control—the ability to cast accurately and delicately—is. Accuracy is a prime necessity when obstacles make it difficult to reach the fish. When deep water, overhanging trees, or the lack of room for a backcast forbid the use of that best of all fish-getters, the short straight cast, the angler must resort to high art flavored with black magic—the skillful manipulation of rod and line which so defies analysis and classification that it is called, simply, tip work.

George LaBranche likely may have been the greatest of them all at this, his forte. His preference was for smallish water, and the limitations imposed by so restricted an environment required him to perform blackest magic with the tip. It is a revelation to watch the tip work of an artist like Guy Jenkins, whose almost imperceptible manipulations seem to endow the fly with independent ability to guide its own flight among bushes and brambles and still achieve a perfect float.

Delicacy is the other half of control. The average fisherman cherishes the delusion that his casts place the fly on the water as delicately as an alighting insect. But if he casts on still water so that he can walk down for a close look at his fly, he probably will be distressed, as I have been, to see that it is awash *in*, rather than riding high *on* the surface film. The reason, I think, is that most fishermen still believe in that ancient chestnut which one fishing writer has copied from another ever since the dry fly became popular. It is that the caster should check his line while his fly is three or four feet above the water and "allow the fly to flutter down onto the water like an alighting insect."

This is so much bilge, tosh, sheep-dip, and hogwash. Even without a line or leader attached to it, an artificial fly cannot be dropped onto the water "as delicately as a natural insect alighting" or anywhere near it, any more than you could do the same thing with a seaplane. Every winged creature uses its wings, and uses them a lot, in effecting a landing; a flying duck can make a beautiful three-pointer, but a shot duck can hit the water so hard he bounces.

The instant and universal popularity which fan-wing flies and long-hackled spiders achieved in the 1920s was due to the fact that their larger sail area permits them to parachute down slower and more gently than an ordinary fly when they are checked high in the air and allowed to drop.

George LaBranche had the most delicate presentation of any angler whom I have ever observed. In his books, George speaks repeatedly of checking the fly in the air to get a delicate delivery, but what he did was really more than that. He made each cast, short or long, with a deliberate powerful stroke; checked the line hard so that the fly whipped down until it was only an inch above the water, with its headway killed; and then seemed to lower it gently, through that remaining inch, onto the water. On short casts, he could put his fly on the surface before line or leader touched the water.

To sum up presentation: In this, as in imitation, our synthetic perfect angler must meet one test—the exacting standards of the trout. He must be able to stalk and cast so well that he always deceives the fish.

The final angling requirement—hooking, playing, and landing the fish—is universally slighted both in practice and in the literature, in spite of the axiom that a sale does the store no good until it is rung up on the cash register.

The average fisherman's record on big fish is brief and dismal. He loses practically all of them that rise to his fly, and on the average it takes him less than five seconds apiece to do it. He hits them too hard and holds them too tight; that's the whole story.

Striking and playing a fish correctly is a matter of iron self-discipline and rigid control of one's reflexes. One of the greatest examples of it that I know of is Tappen Fairchild's conquest of "Grandpa," a four-and-a-quarter-pound brown trout that each year in late summer was driven by the warming of the upper Neversink to take refuge in a little ten-foot feeder stream that is always 46° F.

There was just one pool, about fifty feet in diameter, in this little spring brook, and in it this veritable whale lived, nervous and wary because of its restricted, dangerous quarters.

Tappen studied that fish for most of two seasons. He was a very tall man, and he had arthritis, but whenever he found time, he *crawled* to the edge of the pool and *knelt* behind a bush in order to study, hour after hour, the feeding and harboring habits of this fish. He found that its lie was under a submerged, fallen tree on the other side, and that when feeding, it worked round the pool, vacuum cleaning occasional nymphs off the sandy bottom.

The trout was patrolling like that when Tappen finally went after it. Of course, laying a line anywhere near the fish, no matter how gently, would have sent it flying in panic. So Tappen cast a small nymph on 3x gut and let it sink to the bottom while the fish was at the other end of the pool. Imagine the mounting tension as he watched this enormous fish turn and start feeding back toward him. The faintest movement of rod, line, or lure would have sent it bolting off, but Tappen knelt like a bronze statue while the fish approached the nymph, inspected it, picked it up, started away with it, and by its own movement pulled it into the corner of its mouth and hooked itself!

The fish lashed the pool into foam when it felt the iron and darted irresistibly in among the sunken tree branches. Tappen backed off into the meadow so as to be out of sight, pointed his rod at the fish, and with his left hand gave a couple of very delicate, gentle pulls on the line. The fish quietly swam out the same way it had gone in.

To top it off, Tappen had lent someone his net. So he had to play his fish until it was broad on its side and completely exhausted, and then crowd it against his leg while he gilled it with his middle finger and thumb, thus completing a perfect demonstration of angling technique.

The tactics of playing a fish, like those of warfare, depend almost entirely on the "terrain," and it is difficult to establish doctrine on them, but there are a few principles on which knowledgeable anglers seem to be fairly well agreed.

Holding a fish hard when it is first hooked lets it break off.

"Let him go; tear line off the reel and throw it at him; don't put any pressure on him at all. He won't go far—maybe fifty yards," Ed Hewitt used to say. "Don't try to check that first run."

The time-honored adjurations to "keep the tip up" and "don't give any slack line" should not be observed strictly. They may be wrong or they may be right; it depends on the circumstances.

In order to breathe with any facility, a fish must face the current; even when migrating downstream it lets the current carry it tail first so it can breathe readily. So when a fish starts to take line downstream, it won't go far at any one time. Try to lead it into slacker water at the side of the stream. When a fish gets below the angler, it can hang in the current, breathing comfortably and doing no work to maintain its position. In this situation it is simply recuperating; unless the angler can get below it and put it to work, his chances of losing it are good.

A fish going straight away from the angler with the leader over its shoulder is like a horse in harness, in the best position for pulling. If it is held hard, it may easily break off. But a fish swims as a snake crawls through the grass, by moving its head from side to side and using its broad body surfaces against the current. A light sidewise pull will so hamper this serpentine movement that it will quickly abandon its effort and turn aside. Where there is room, it is possible to keep an active fish turning almost continuously in a figure-eight pattern and thus prevent it from dashing downstream or into a hole.

It takes long to tire a fish by swimming; the angler seeks to drown it by maintaining steady upward pressure so as to tire its jaw muscles and force its mouth open. A fish has to close its mouth to squeeze water through its gills; when it can no longer do so, it quickly drowns.

The harder a fish is held, the harder it fights; if pressure is released entirely it will stop fighting and swim around aimlessly or rest on the bottom, and sulk, jerking its head like a bulldog. This is hard on tackle and the hold of the hook; lightening the pressure will encourage the fish to come up and make an active, hence tiring, fight.

After the first five seconds of hooking and fighting his fish, the angler's greatest chance of losing it is through trying to net it before it is completely exhausted and broad on its side. Usually he unfurls his net immediately after hooking the fish. As soon as he can drag the still vigorous trout within range, he extends his rod hand far behind him, assumes a position like a fencer lunging, and extends the net at arm's length like a tennis player trying to stop a low shot. In this position the angler goes to work with his net like a man chopping down a tree, and unless his fish is well hooked and his leader sturdy, he's going to lose his prize.

Charlie Wetzel is the best netter I ever saw. He uses one of those big "snowshoe" nets, and he doesn't even get it out until the fish is on its side and completely tuckered. Standing erect, facing upstream with his elbows at his sides and his rod held just back of vertical, he sinks the net deep and draws the fish over it. Slowly, gently, he raises the rim of the net, tilting it from side to side to free the meshes from the fish's fins. Then he quietly, deliberately lifts the fish out of water, and it lies in the net as if hypnotized until Charlie grasps the upper meshes to hold it shut. It doesn't go into its final flurry until too late.

To sum up, we must require our hypothetical perfect angler always to hook his fish perfectly, in the corner of the mouth; to maintain utter, absolute control over his own reflexes, and to play and net the fish without committing an error.

Now we have constructed the perfect angler, but he's dead. To bring him to life we must infuse him with the spirit of a great angler. That is *not* the relaxed, gentle, lackadaisical spirit that delights in birds, flowers, wild animals, clouds, and the sweet clash of running waters. I have known great anglers who were thus benign, but it was not the spirit of their formative years, the thing that made them great, but a luxury they could afford after fishing had ceased to challenge them. Ed Hewitt pinpointed it when he said, "First a man tries to catch the most fish, then the largest fish, and finally the most difficult fish." After that, the birds and flowers.

The spirit that makes the great angler is compounded of terrifically intense concentration and a ferocious, predatory urge to conquer and capture. What less would drive Dick Jarmel, a well-known Beaverkill fisherman, to risk a bad battering and possible drowning by working his way for fifty yards along the retaining wall of the Acid Factory Pool, holding his rod crosswise in his mouth and clinging with fingertips and toes to rough projections of stones, simply to get to *the* spot from which the run can be fished effectively during high water?

Or impel Tom Collins (Ed Hewitt once called him the best fisherman ever) to climb down the face of a cliff, swing across a cleft on a rope affixed to a branch, and shinny down a convenient tree, all to get to a secret spot on a secret stream, down in a gorge? Tom had the heft of a grizzly as well as the strength and endurance of one, and he risked a broken neck and stove-in ribs time after time, as a matter of course. I laugh when I hear a doctor approving fishing as light recreation for a heart patient without finding out what sort of fishing it will be. He thinks of his man as soaking a worm while he dozes on the bank; he would be shocked to see, as I so often have, the hard-case angler coming in at eventide limp and sweat-soaked from prowling and galloping along the stream all day.

The furious urge of the great fisherman expresses itself in an intense competitive spirit. Some anglers conceal it very well, but it is there nevertheless, so strong that it can even bias their devotion to the truth. I still grin privately at what happened long ago when two really great anglers, who must remain nameless here, met by chance on a certain pool. They got into a discussion of wet fly versus dry fly and set up an informal competition, each fishing the pool in turn. I've heard the story from each of them, and you'd never guess that they were both talking about the same event. The only thing they agreed on was the name of the pool.

Ed Hewitt and George LaBranche were always tilting at each other. When both of them were aged men, Ed and I went up to George's office to surprise him one day. The two really dear old friends fell upon each other, and then George asked Ed what was new. Nothing, said Ed, except that he had another grandchild.

"How many grandchildren have you?" asked George. Ed fell for it.

"Eight."

"That's one thing I can beat you at," crowed George. "I have twelve."

Ed's eyes darted about as he sought furiously to redeem his defeat.

"How many great-grandchildren have you?" he demanded. This time George was under the guns.

"Five."

"Hah!" cried Ed triumphantly. "I have twenty-one!"

George's secretary looked shocked and beckoned me into the hall.

"Mr. LaBranche doesn't have twelve grandchildren!" she whispered.

"That's all right," I reassured her. "Ed doesn't have twenty-one great-grandchildren, either. They're just trying to beat each other."

Some twenty-five years ago I met on the stream a then well-known fishing writer, the late Albert C. Barrell, who, it developed, had fished a lot with LaBranche on the Konkapot in Massachusetts.

"George is a duelist," he explained. "The fish is his antagonist, his adversary. He'll return it to the water after he has conquered it, but he attacks it as furiously as if he were fighting for his life."

Here then, out of the zeal and the skills of many experts, we have synthesized the perfect angler. In the flesh this perfect dry-fly fisherman does not exist, and it is doubtless a good thing that he does not, for surely he would be intolerable to all us imperfect anglers.

Sport—and its inextricably associated rituals—is an often-tackled subject. This piece is something special—a journey of the spirit and a cleansing of the soul.

GEOFFREY NORMAN

Sea of Plenty

The boat was sixty feet long, broad in the beam, round at the bow, and painted white with green trim. It would have been charitable to describe it as "functional," or even "ungainly." Actually, it was ugly and something of a tub. Stacked on its roof were six smaller boats with outboard motors, and bunk beds were positioned all around the decks. It was named after a woman who had two names—*Sally Lou*, or something like that.

It was tied to a dock in Bayou La Batre, just a mile or two from a boatyard that was owned by the Reverend Moon and that produced dozens of big steel-hulled boats for shrimping. Those boats, built purely for function, looked more seaworthy and graceful than this craft, though it was built with just as much purpose.

Twelve of us were waiting to board. We carried our tackle and small duffel bags with clothes and shaving gear for three days. We also carried our beer and whiskey for the trip and some odds and ends such as cards and paperbacks.

It was late on a Sunday afternoon in September. The weather was so gentle that it was hard to believe that it was hurricane season on the Gulf Coast. There were a few harmless clouds blown a little ragged at the edges by warm south winds. A few solitary gulls rode the breezes, and an occasional mullet jumped into the bayou, catching the sun on a silver side, then disappearing in a green splash of water and a ring of ripples. We loaded up quickly, cast off, and headed for the mouth of the bayou under the power of a sturdy diesel. There was a television in the cabin, and somebody tuned in the Cowboys game.

In less than an hour, we were in the ship channel off the Mississippi coast, headed for the Chandeleur Islands. We had a four-hour to five-hour run before dark.

I had flown all night, from Africa, to make this trip. Which seemed curious, even to me, as I watched the boat traffic and the football game and thought about it. Travel for the sake of getting away from the routine is one thing. travel for the sake of more travel is something else. But I had wanted to make this trip badly, and I had turned down three previous invitations for what had seemed like good reasons at the time. You can't keep turning down invitations unless you want them to stop coming, and as I say, this was a trip that I wanted to make. Why, I wondered as I felt the relief that always comes when you leave the land behind, even if only for a few days and thirty or forty miles.

I knew most of the men on the boat. Three of them were blood kin and among my favorite people in the world. Yet over the years we had frequently passed within a few miles of one another with no more than a telephone call. I hadn't spent an extra night at the Johannesburg airport simply to spend time with them.

Nor was the fishing part of the trip a sufficient explanation. We stood to catch a lot of fish if the weather held, but there was no guarantee. And the fish themselves were not that exotic. I had caught hundreds just like them. I could catch them without going much farther than the back yard when conditions were right. You travel halfway around the world to catch trophy marlin or salmon, not speckled trout or redfish.

And it was not a matter of getting away. I had been away more than I cared to think about, and my back yard seemed like a fine alternative to airports and motel rooms for a while. Six months of food cooked in a real kitchen was a delightful prospect.

But there I was.

According to Robert Ardrey, who wrote *The Territorial Imperative*, and to others, men get together to hunt (and, I suppose, also to fish) because that is what their ancestors did. It has something to do with the racial memory of a time when we wore hides, chewed raw carrion, sat around fires, and ran animals to the ground and then killed them with spears and clubs. It was what men did and what, genetically, they still long to do. This is probably true.

The trouble with all deterministic explanations of human behavior is that they explain, in truth, so little. Of course, one wants to say to Marx, man is a creature determined by economic factors. Among other things. To say that men like to get together to hunt because that is the way we got started is not an explanation for the bewildering number of styles we adopt in doing it. Which may be all that free will comes down to; but that is enough.

About ten miles from where I live in Vermont, there is a little cabin that sits empty for eleven and a half months of the year. Then, for sixteen days it is deer season, and the cabin is packed with hunters, equipment, supplies, and big talk. The men who go up there all know one another and all live in the little towns that surround the camp. Most of them see the others all year long. They nod and speak at the post office, have a cup of coffee after church, get together now and then for dinner.

They could hunt easily enough without leaving home and going to the cabin. A few of them don't hunt very much when they get up there, and they could certainly stay home and *not* hunt. Judging from the smoke and the smells and the stories that come out of that cabin, they could stay home and eat a lot better, too.

They have all sorts of rituals that go back some twenty or thirty years and that are observed faithfully. You don't eat pickles until somebody in camp has killed a deer. First man to kill a deer does not have to wash dishes for the rest of the season. First man to miss tends the fire for the rest of the season. The poker game starts after the last dish is dried and put away and sometimes is still going when the first hunter slips out the door into the early, milky morning light. There are about a dozen men in the group and nobody ever drops out.

There was a group of men I knew of in Michigan who did the same thing to fish for trout. They were all senior executives in major corporations, and they could go more or less anywhere when they had the time. One of the places they chose to go was the cutover country around Grayling, to a little screened-in cabin on the Au Sable River. They fished early mornings and late afternoons, slept and played cards and talked during the day, watched the fleets of canoes pass and complained about what they were doing to the fishing. They posted a list of housekeeping chores, which rotated from day to day, and took turns in the kitchen. These men had more fun, I think, than a bunch of Boy Scouts on jamboree.

The common theme here is the men's familiarity with one another and with the place where they went to be together. The Au Sable River is a short hop by corporate airplane from Detroit and Grand Rapids. If you live in southern Vermont, you do not have to go up into the mountains and live in a shack to hunt deer. But it is different if you do.

Different, but not exotic, which is what the magazines sell and what, I assume, the people buy. Fly to Alaska to shoot sheep. Come to Texas to hunt

Sitka deer and red stag and thirty other species that are not native to the United States. Go to Panama for the really big billfish. You go if you can afford to, and you spend your time among a bunch of strangers, and sometimes you do not speak the language and are clearly despised by those who do (which might duplicate certain aspects of our ancestral experience). You cannot do anything on your own. A guide supervises, which is necessary because you don't know the land or the water. You are a tourist and are never allowed to forget it. You may or may not come home with a trophy, but the odds are you will be damned happy to get home with or without.

The other way, the way I had come across the Atlantic for, is less spectacular. But five years later I remember that trip better than the one to the trophy lake in Canada where I was a guest of the lodge.

We ate steaks that night when the boat was still under power. There was a young man who did all the cooking in a galley aft of the cabin and sunk about a half deck below the main deck, so that we sat around him at a horseshoe-shaped counter just like at an old-fashioned diner. He was good on the grill, fast and stylish. He could do ten different things with an ordinary spatula.

After the steaks we stood around and had some drinks and made some talk. We were, variously, lumberman, parole officer, newspaper editor, forester, dentist. We had in common, mainly, fishing.

So we made a lot of tall talk and some side bets on who would catch the most fish and the largest. Some of us went to bed later than we normally did. Drunker, too. We slept above deck and under the stars, with the boat rocking just enough so that when you rolled over and wondered where you were you'd feel it and remember.

In the morning the cook had eggs any way you wanted them. Toast, grits, bacon, coffee. We ate in the dark, and as the light gathered off our stern, the mate lowered the skiffs and checked the motor on each of them. We were told not to go too far from the mother ship and to be back at noon if we wanted lunch.

I fished with my brother. He had been on the trip the year before and was top boat, so I went where he took us. We were into fish in the first hour. They were big enough and they took eagerly and we caught plenty. Between fish we caught up on things. I told him what I could about Africa, and it seemed, already, like something lived in another life. We put on lotion as the sun climbed and stripped to the waist at ten or so when the heat seemed to close in on us like a tangible presence. By the time we quit for lunch, we were encrusted with two salts—the water's and that from our own bodies.

The water we fished was shallow, perhaps six feet at its deepest points. The bottom was covered with wide-bladed grass that you could see when the water was clear. It waved back and forth like a field of grain in a Midwestern breeze. There were low, sandy islands covered with saw grass all around us. They were protected, bird sanctuaries, and all sorts of species used them for nesting—pelicans, blue herons, terns. The shallow water was the native habitat of all kinds of small shrimp and crabs and fish. They drew, in the pattern of such shallows, larger fish. I hooked up with a tarpon but lost it after two jumps.

Lunch was gumbo and tea. And corn bread. A sea breeze came up and everyone fell asleep, except the mate, who spent the afternoon taking fillets from the fish and packing them in ice.

More fishing and more fish that afternoon. A weary return to the boat, followed by a cold freshwater shower, one of the most refreshing experiences in this world. Drinks on deck. More big talk. Supper. Bed. And so on for three days until we turned around and went back into the ship channel and up the bayou and back home.

My brother and I were top boat; I wish I could fish with him more often. Everybody paid up and made something of the pain it caused. There were suggestions that we had cheated. I had heard some wonderful jokes, too crude and too stupid for print. Caught up on some family business. Learned again that the end of sport is not to shoot an elephant or catch a black marlin. For two days I walked around swaying this way and that, as though I were still at sea. The bed pitched just slightly and I had a sunburn. It was good to be home, though in a way, I had never left.

Taxonomy has long held the unfortunate distinction of being the most tedious of the sciences, the most deserving of Latin as its principal language. It is only natural that steps have been taken to enliven the discipline by broadening its scope—to anglers, of course, and their myriad forms. Thaddeus Norris, legendary early American fisherman, dissects the species.

THADDEUS NORRIS

What and Who Is an Angler?

It is not my intention to offer any remarks on the antiquity of angling, or say much in its defense. Dame Juliana Berners, Izaak Walton, and more recent authors, have discoursed learnedly on its origin, and defended it wisely and valiantly from the aspersions and ridicule of those who cannot appreciate its quiet joys, and who know not the solace and peace it brings to the harassed mind, or how it begets and fosters contentment and a love of nature.

I ask any caviller to read Dr. Bethune's Bibliographical Preface to his edition of Walton; and then Father Izaak's address to the readers of his discourse, "but especially to THE HONEST ANGLER," and accompany him in spirit, as Bethune does, by the quiet Lea, or Cotton by the bright rippling Dove; and if he be not convinced of the blessed influences of the "gentle art," or if his heart is not warmed, or no recollections of his boyish days come back to him, I give him up without a harsh word, but with a feeling of regret, that a lifetime should be spent without attaining so much of quiet happiness that might have been so easily possessed, and quoting a few sad words from Whittier's Maud Muller, I only say "it might have been."

Many anglers, such as Sir Humphrey Davy and Sir Joshua Reynolds, besides some of my own acquaintance, have sought its cheering influences in advanced life. I know of one whose early manhood and maturer years were spent on the boisterous deep, and who, though now past eighty, is still an ardent, but quiet angler; and when no better spot can be found, he will even fish through the ice in winter for roach. No doubt his days have been lengthened out, and the burden of life lightened, by his love of angling.

But how sweetly memories of the past come to one who has appreciated and enjoyed it from his boyhood, whose almost first penny, after he wore jacket and trousers, bought his first fish hook; whose first fishing line was twisted by mother or sister; whose float was the cork of a physic vial, and whose sinkers were cut from the sheet lead of an old tea chest! Thus rigged, with what glad anticipations of sport, many a boy has started on some bright Saturday morning, his gourd, or old cow's horn of red worms in one pocket, and a jackknife in the other, to cut his alder pole with, and wandered "free and far" by still pool and swift waters, dinnerless—except perhaps a slight meal at a cherry tree, or a handful of berries that grew along his path—and come home at night weary and footsore, but exulting in his string of chubs, minnows, and sunnies, the largest as broad as his three fingers! He almost falls asleep under his Saturday night scrubbing, but in the morning, does ample justice to his "catch," which is turned out of the pan, crisp and brown, and matted together like a pancake.

In *my* school days, a boy might have been envied, but not loved for proficiency in his studies; but *he* was most courted, who knew the best fishing holes; who had plenty of powder and shot; the best squirrel dog, and the use of his father's long flintlock gun. And I confess, as I write these lines with my spectacles on, that I have still a strong drawing toward this type of a boy, whether I meet him in my lonely rambles, or whether he dwells only in my memory.

Sometimes the recollection of our boyish sports comes back to us after manhood, and one who has been "addicted" to fishing relapses into his old "ailment"; then angling becomes a pleasant kind of disease, and one's friends are apt to become inoculated with the virus, for it is contagious. Or men are informally introduced to each other on the stream, by a good-humored salutation, or an inquiry of *"What luck?"* or a display of the catch, or the offer of a cigar, or the flask, or a new fly; and with such introduction have become fast friends, from that affinity which draws all true anglers together.

But let me ask what is an angler, and who is a *true* angler? One who fishes with nets is not, neither is he who spears, snares, or dastardly uses the crazy bait to *get* fish, or who catches them on set lines; nor is he who is boisterous, noisy, or quarrelsome; nor are those who profess to practise the higher branches of the art, and affect contempt for their more humble brethren, who have not attained to *their* proficiency, imbued with the feeling that should possess the true angler.

Nor is he who brings his ice chest from town, and fishes all day with worm or fly, that he may return to the city and boastingly distribute his soaked and tasteless trout among his friends and brag of the numbers he has basketed, from fingerlings upwards.

Anglers may be divided into almost as many genera and species as the fish they catch, and engage in the sport from as many impulses. Let me give, "en passant," a sketch of a few of the many I have met with.

There is the Fussy Angler, a great bore; of course you will shun him. The Snob Angler, who speaks confidently and knowingly on a slight capital of skill or experience. The Greedy, Pushing Angler, who rushes ahead and half fishes the water, leaving those who follow in doubt as to whether he has fished a pool or rift carefully, or slurred it over in his haste to reach some well-known place down the stream before his companions. The company of these, the quiet, careful angler will avoid.

We also meet sometimes with the Spick-and-Span Angler, who has a highly varnished rod, and a superabundance of useless tackle; his outfit is of the most elaborate kind as regards its finish. He is a dapper "well got up" angler in all his appointments, and fishes much indoors over his claret and poteen, when he has a good listener. He frequently displays bad taste in his tackle, intended for fly-fishing, by having a thirty-dollar multiplying reel, filled with one of Conroy's very best relaid sea-grass lines, strong enough to hold a dolphin. If you meet him on the teeming waters of northern New York, the evening's display of his catch depends much on the rough skill of his guide.

The Rough-and-Ready Angler, the opposite of the aforenamed, disdains all "tomfoolery," and carries his tackle in an old shot bag, and his flies in a tangled mass.

We have also the Literary Angler, who reads Walton and admires him hugely; he has been inoculated with the *sentiment* only; the five-mile walk up the creek, where it has not been fished much, is very fatiguing to him; he "did not know he must wade the stream," and does not until he slips in, and then he has some trouble at night to get his boots off. He is provided with a stout bass rod, good strong leaders of salmon gut, and a stock of Conroy's "journal flies," and wonders if he had not better put on a *shot* just above his stretcher fly.

The Pretentious Angler, to use a favorite expression of the lamented Dickey Riker, once Recorder of the city of New York, is one "that prevails to a great extent in this community." This gentleman has many of the qualities attributed by Fisher, of the "Angler's Souvenir," to Sir Humphrey Davy. If he has attained the higher branches of the art, he affects to despise all sport which he considers less scientific; if a salmon fisher, he calls trout "vermin"; if he is a trout fly-fisher, he professes contempt for bait fishing. We have talked with true anglers who were even disposed to censure the eminent Divine, who has so ably, and with such labor of love, edited our American edition of Walton, for affectation, in saying of the red worm, "our hands have long since been washed of the dirty things." The servant should not be above his master, and certainly "Iz. Wa.," whose disciple the Doctor professed to be, considered it no indignity to use them, nor was he disgusted with his "horn of gentles." But the Doctor was certainly right in deprecating the use of ground bait in reference to trout, when the angler can with a little faith and less greed soon learn the use of the fly.

The *Shad-roe Fisherman.*—The habitat of this genus (and they are rarely found elsewhere) is Philadelphia. There are many persons of the aforesaid city, who fish only when this bait can be had, and an idea seems to possess them that fish will bite at no other. This fraternity could have been found some years back, singly or in pairs, or little coteries of three or four, on any sunshiny day from Easter to Whitsuntide, heaving their heavy dipsies and horsehair snoods from the ends of the piers, or from canal boats laid up in ordinary— the old floating bridge at Gray's Ferry was a favorite resort for them. Sometimes the party was convivial, and provided with a junk bottle of what they believed to be *old rye.*

Before the gas works had destroyed the fishing in the Schuylkill, I frequently observed a solitary individual of this species, wending his way to the river on Sunday mornings, with a long reed pole on his shoulder, and in his hand a tin kettle of shad roe; and his "prog," consisting of hard-boiled eggs and crackers and cheese, tied up in a cotton bandana handkerchief. Toward nightfall "he might have been seen" (as James the novelist says of the horseman), trudging homeward with a string of pan rock and white perch, or "catties" and eels, his trousers and coat sleeves well plastered with his unctuous bait, suggesting the idea of what, in vulgar parlance, might be called "a very nasty man."

But let us not turn up our scientific noses at this humble brother; nor let the home missionary or tract distributor rate him too severely, if he should meet with him in his Sunday walks; for who can tell what a quiet day of consolation it has been to him; he has found relief from the toils and cares of the week, and perhaps from the ceaseless tongue of his shrewish "old woman." If his sport has been good, he follows it up the next day, and keeps "blue Monday."

We have seen some very respectable gentlemen in our day engaged in fishing with shad roe at Fairmount Dam. The bar even had its representative, in one of our first criminal court lawyers. He did not "dress the character" with as much discrimination as when he lectured on Shakespeare, for he always wore his blue coat with gilt buttons: he did not appear to be a successful angler. "Per contra" to this was a wealthy retired merchant, who used to astonish us with his knack of keeping this difficult bait on his hooks, and his skill in hooking little white perch. Many a troller has seen him sitting bolt upright in the bow of his boat on a cool morning in May, with his overcoat buttoned up to his chin, his jolly spouse in the stern, and his servant amidship, baiting the hooks and taking off the lady's fish. The son also was an adept as well as the sire. Woe to the perch fisher, with his bait of little silvery eels, if these occupied the lower part of the swim, for the fish were all arrested by the stray ova that floated off from the "gobs" of shad roe.

As we love contrasts, let us here make a slight allusion to that sensible "old English gentleman," the Admiral, who surveyed the northwest coast of America, to see, if in the contingency of the Yankees adhering to their claim of "fifty-four forty," the country about Vancouver's Island was worth contending for. He was an ardent angler, and it is reported, that on leaving his ship he provided stores for a week, which comprised of course not a few drinkables, as well as salmon rods and other tackle, and started in his boats to explore the rivers and tributaries, which, so goes the story, were so crammed in many places with salmon, that they could be captured with a boat hook; and still with all the variety of salmon flies and the piscatory skill of the admiral and his officers, not a fish could be induced to rise at the fly. He returned to his ship disheartened and disgusted, averring that the country was not worth contending for; that the Yankees might have it and be——; but it would be indecorous to record the admiral's mild expletive.

The *True Angler* is thoroughly imbued with the spirit of gentle old Izaak. He has no affectation, and when a fly cast is not to be had, can find amusement in catching sunfish or roach, and does not despise the sport of any humbler brother of the angle. With him, fishing is a recreation, and a "calmer of unquiet thoughts." He never quarrels with his luck, knowing that satiety dulls one's appreciation of sport as much as want of success, but is ever content when he has done his best, and looks hopefully forward to a more propitious day. Whether from boat or rocky shore, or along the sedgy bank of the creek, or the stony margin of the mountain brook, he deems it an achievement to take fish when they are difficult to catch, and his satisfaction is in proportion. If he is lazy, or a superannuated angler, he can even endure a few days' trolling on an inland lake, and smokes his cigar, chats with the boatman, and takes an occasional "nip," as he is rowed along the wooded shore and amongst the beautiful islands.

A true angler is generally a modest man; unobtrusively communicative when he can impart a new idea; and is ever ready to let a pretentious tyro have his say, and good-naturedly (as if merely suggesting how it should be done) repairs his tackle, or gets him out of a scrape. He is moderately provided with all tackle and "fixins" necessary to the fishing he is in pursuit of. Is quietly self-reliant and equal to almost any emergency, from splicing his rod or tying his own flies, to trudging ten miles across a rough country with his luggage on his back. His enjoyment consists not only in the taking of fish: he draws much pleasure from the soothing influence and delightful accompaniments of the art.

With happy memories of the past summer, he joins together the three pieces of his fly rod at home, when the scenes of the last season's sport are wrapped in snow and ice, and renews the glad feelings of long summer days. With what interest he notes the swelling of the buds on the maples, or the advent of the bluebird and robin, and looks forward to the day when he is to try another cast! and, when it comes at last, with what pleasing anticipations he packs up his "traps," and leaves his business cares and the noisy city behind, and after a few hours' or few days' travel in the cars, and a few miles in a rough wagon, or a vigorous tramp over rugged hills or along the road that leads up the banks of the river, he arrives at his quarters! He is now in the region of fresh butter and mealy potatoes—there are always good potatoes in a mountainous trout country. How pleasingly rough everything looks after leaving the prim city! How pure and wholesome the air! How beautiful the clumps of sugar maples and the veteran hemlocks jutting out over the stream; the laurel; the ivy; the moss-covered rocks; the lengthening shadows of evening! How musical the old familiar tinkling of the cow-bell and the cry of the whippoorwill! How sweetly he is lulled to sleep as he hears

> The waters leap and gush
> O'er channelled rock and broken bush!

Next morning, after a hearty breakfast of mashed potatoes, ham and eggs, and butter from the cream of the cow that browses in the woods, he is off, three miles up the creek, a cigar or his pipe in his mouth, his creel at his side, and his rod over his shoulder, chatting with his chum as he goes; free, joyous, happy; at peace with his Maker, with himself, and all mankind; he should be grateful for this much, even if he catches no fish. How exhilarating the music of the stream! how invigorating its waters, causing a consciousness of manly vigor, as he wades sturdily with the strong current and casts his flies before him! When his zeal abates, and a few of the *speckled* lie in the bottom of his creel, he is not less interested in the wild flowers on the bank, or the scathed old hemlock on the cliff above, with its hawk's nest, the lady of the house likely inside, and the male proprietor perched high above on its dead top and he breaks forth lustily—the scene suggesting the song—

> The bee's on its wing, and the hawk on its nest,
> And the river runs merrily by.

When noon comes on, and the trout rise lazily or merely nip, he halts "sub tegmine fagi," or under the shadow of the dark sugar maple to build a fire and roast trout for his dinner, and wiles away three hours or so. He dines sumptuously, straightens and dries his leader and the gut of his dropper, and repairs all breakage. He smokes leisurely, or even takes a nap on the greensward or velvety moss, and resumes his sport when the sun has declined enough to shade at least one side of the stream, and pleasantly anticipates the late evening cast on the still waters far down the creek. God be with you, gentle angler, if actuated with the feeling of our old master! whether you are a top fisher or a bottom fisher; whether your bait be gentles, brandling, grub, or red worm; crab, shrimp, or minnow; caddis, grasshopper, or the feathery counterfeit of the ephemera. May your thoughts be always peaceful, and your heart filled with gratitude to Him who made the country and the rivers; and "may the east wind never blow when you go a-fishing!"

Retirement could be found pretty tame to a Raj colonel used to lighting barrels of gunpowder with his cheroot and blowing to hell bands of mutinous Sepoys in the Madras sun. Tame and colorless. Roland Pertwee's friend was such a colonel. A certain salmon in Wales brought them together for a moment, igniting much more than gunpowder and forever setting higher standards indeed for any colonel to follow.

ROLAND PERTWEE

The River God

When I was a little boy I had a friend who was a colonel. He was not the kind of colonel you meet nowadays, who manages a motor showroom in the West End of London and wears crocodile shoes and a small moustache and who calls you "old man" and slaps your back, independent of the fact that you may have been no more than a private in the war. My colonel was of the older order that takes a third of a century and a lot of Indian sun and Madras curry in the making. A veteran of the Mutiny he was, and wore side whiskers to prove it. Once he came upon a number of Sepoys conspiring mischief in a byre with a barrel of gunpowder. So he put the butt of his cheroot into the barrel and presently they all went to hell. That was the kind of man he was in the way of business.

In the way of pleasure he was very different. In the way of pleasure he wore an old Norfolk coat that smelled of heather and brine, and which had no elbows to speak of. And he wore a Sherlock Holmesy kind of cap with a swarm of salmon flies upon it, that to my boyish fancy was more splendid than a crown. I cannot remember his legs, because they were nearly always under water, hidden in great canvas waders. But once he sent me a photograph of himself riding on a tricycle, so I expect he had some knickerbockers, too, which would have been that tight kind, with a box cloth under the knees. Boys don't take much stock of clothes. His head occupied my imagination. A big, brave, white-haired head with cheery-red rugose cheeks and honest, laughing, puckered eyes, with gunpowder marks in their corners.

People at the little Welsh fishing inn where we met said he was a bore; but I knew him to be a god and shall prove it.

I was ten years old and his best friend.

He was seventy something and my hero.

Properly I should not have mentioned my hero so soon in this narrative. He belongs to a later epoch, but sometimes it is forgivable to start with a boast, and now that I have committed myself I lack the courage to call upon my colonel to fall back two paces to the rear, quick march, and wait until he is wanted.

The real beginning takes place, as I remember, somewhere in Hampshire on the Grayshott Road, among sandy banks, sentinel firs, and plum-colored wastes of heather. Summer-holiday time it was, and I was among folks whose names have since vanished like lizards under the stones of forgetfulness. Perhaps it was a picnic walk; perhaps I carried a basket and was told not to swing it for fear of bursting its cargo of ginger beer. In those days ginger beer had big bulgy corks held down with a string. In a hot sun or under stress of too much agitation the string would break and the corks fly. Then there would be a merry foaming fountain and someone would get reproached.

One of our company had a fishing rod. He was a young man who, one day, was to be an uncle of mine. But that didn't concern me. What concerned me was the fishing rod and presently—perhaps because he felt he must keep in with the family—he let me carry it. To the fisherman born there is nothing so provoking of curiosity as a fishing rod in a case.

Surreptitiously I opened the flap, which contained a small grass spear in a wee pocket, and, pulling down the case a little, I admired the beauties of the work butt, with its gun-metal ferrule and reel rings and the exquisite frail slenderness of the two top joints.

"It's got two top joints—two!" I exclaimed ecstatically.

"Of course," said he. "All good trout rods have two."

I marveled in silence at what seemed to me then a combination of extravagance and excellent precaution.

There must have been something inherently understanding and noble about that young man who would one day be my uncle, for, taking me by the arm, he sat me down on a tuft of heather and took the pieces of rod from the case and fitted them together. The rest of the company moved on and left me in Paradise.

It is thirty-five years ago since that moment and not one detail of it is forgotten. There sounds in my ears today as clearly as then, the faint, clear pop made by the little cork stoppers with their boxwood tops as they were withdrawn. I remember how, before fitting the pieces together, he rubbed the ferrules against the side of his nose to prevent them sticking. I remember looking up the length of it through a tunnel of sneck rings to the eyelet at the end. Not until he had fixed a reel and passed a line through the rings did he put the lovely thing into my hand. So light it was, so firm, so persuasive; such a thing alive—a scepter. I could do no more than say, "Oo!" and again, "Oo!"

"A thrill, ain't it?" said he.

I had no need to answer that. In my new-found rapture was only one sorrow, the knowledge that such happiness would not endure and that, all too soon, a blank and rodless future awaited me.

"They must be awfully—awfully 'spensive," I said.

"Couple of guineas," he replied offhandedly.

A couple of guineas! And we were poor folk and the future was more rodless than ever.

"Then I shall save and save and save," I said.

And my imagination started to add up twopence a week into guineas. Two hundred and forty pennies to the pound, multiplied by two—four hundred and eighty—and then another twenty-four pennies—five hundred and four. Why, it would take a lifetime, and no sweets, no elastic for catapults, no penny novelty boxes or airgun bullets or ices or anything. Tragedy must have been writ large upon my face, for he said suddenly, "When's your birthday?"

I was almost ashamed to tell him how soon it was. Perhaps he, too, was a little taken aback by its proximity, for that future uncle of mine was not so rich as uncles should be.

"We must see about it."

"But it wouldn't—it couldn't be one like that," I said.

I must have touched his pride, for he answered loftily, "Certainly it will."

In the fortnight that followed I walked on air and told everybody I had as good as got a couple-of-guineas rod.

No one can deceive a child, save the child himself, and when my birthday came and with it a long brown-paper parcel, I knew, even before I had removed the wrappers, that this two-guineas rod was not worth the money. There was a brown linen case, it is true, but it was not a case with a neat compartment for each joint, nor was there a spear in the flap. There was only one top instead of two, and there were no popping little stoppers to protect the ferrules from dust and injury. The lower joint boasted no elegant cork hand piece, but was a tapered affair coarsely made and rudely varnished. When I fitted the pieces together, what I balanced in my hand was tough and stodgy, rather than limber. The reel, which had come in a different parcel, was of wood. It had neither check nor brake, and the line overran and backwound itself with distressing frequency.

I had not read and reread Gamages' price list without knowing something of rods, and I did not need to look long at this rod before realizing that it was no match to the one I had handled on the Grayshott Road.

I believe at first a great sadness possessed me, but very presently imagination came to the rescue. For I told myself that I had only to think that this was the rod of all other rods that I desired most and it would be so. And it was so.

Furthermore, I told myself that, in this great wide ignorant world, but few people existed with such expert knowledge of rods as I possessed. That I had but to say, "Here is the final word in good rods," and they would accept it as such.

Very confidently I tried the experiment on my mother, with inevitable success. From the depths of her affection and her ignorance on all such matters, she produced:

"It's a magnificent rod."

I went my way, knowing full well that she knew not what she said, but that she was kind.

With rather less confidence I approached my father, saying, "Look, father! It cost two guineas. It's absolutely the best sort you can get."

And he, after waggling it a few moments in silence, quoted cryptically:

"There is nothing either good or bad but thinking makes it so."

Young as I was, I had some curiosity about words, and on any other occasion I would have called on him to explain. But this I did not do, but left hurriedly, for fear that he should explain.

In the two years that followed, I fished every day in the slip of a back garden of our tiny London house. And, having regard to the fact that this rod was never fashioned to throw a fly, I acquired a pretty knack in the fullness of time and performed some glib casting at the nasturtiums and marigolds that flourished by the back wall.

My parents' fortunes must have been in the ascendant, I suppose, for I call to mind an unforgettable breakfast when my mother told me that father had decided we should spend our summer holiday at a Welsh hotel on the river Lledr. The place was called Pont-y-pant, and she showed me a picture of the hotel with a great knock-me-down river creaming past the front of it.

Although in my dreams I had heard fast water often enough, I had never seen it, and the knowledge that in a month's time I should wake with the music of a cataract in my ears was almost more than patience could endure.

In that exquisite, intolerable period of suspense I suffered as only childish longing and enthusiasm can suffer. Even the hand of gut that I bought and bent into innumerable casts failed to alleviate that suffering. I would walk for miles for a moment's delight captured in gluing my nose to the windows of tackleists' shops in the West End. I learned from my grandmother—a wise and calm old lady—how to make nets and, having mastered the art, I made myself a landing net. This I set up on a frame fashioned from a penny schoolmaster's cane bound to an old walking stick. It would be pleasant to record that this was a good and serviceable net, but it was not. It flopped over in a very distressing fashion when called upon to lift the lightest weight. I had to confess to myself that I had more enthusiasm than skill in the manufacture of such articles.

At school there was a boy who had a fishing creel, which he swapped with me for a Swedish knife, a copy of *Rogues of the Fiery Cross*, and an Easter egg I had kept on account of its rare beauty. He had forced a hard bargain and was sure he had the best of it, but I knew otherwise.

At last the great day dawned, and after infinite travel by train we reached our destination as the glow of sunset was graying into dark. The river was in spate, and as we crossed a tall stone bridge on our way to the hotel I heard it below me, barking and grumbling among great rocks. I was pretty far gone in tiredness, for I remember little else that night but a rod rack in the hall—a dozen rods of different sorts and sizes, with gaudy salmon flies, some nets, a gaff, and an oak coffer upon which lay a freshly caught salmon on a blue ashet. Then supper by candlelight, bed, a glitter of stars through the open window, and the ceaseless drumming of water.

By six o'clock next morning I was on the river bank, fitting my rod together and watching in awe the great brown ribbon of water go fleetly by.

Among my most treasured possessions were half a dozen flies, and two of these I attached to the cast with exquisite care. While so engaged, a shadow fell on the grass beside me and looking up, I beheld a lank, shabby individual with a walrus moustache and an unhealthy face, who, the night before, had helped with our luggage at the station.

"Water's too heavy for flies," said he, with an uptilting inflection. "This evening, yes; now, no—none whateffer. Better try with a worrum in the burrun."

He pointed at a busy little brook that tumbled down the steep hillside and joined the main stream at the garden end.

"C-couldn't I fish with a fly in the—the burrun?" I asked, for although I wanted to catch a fish very badly, for honor's sake I would fain take it on a fly.

"Indeed, no," he replied, slanting the tone of his voice skyward. "You cootn't. Neffer. And that isn't a fly rod whateffer."

"It is," I replied hotly. "Yes, it is."

But he only shook his head and repeated, "No," and took the rod from my hand and illustrated its awkwardness and handed it back with a wretched laugh.

If he had pitched me into the river I should have been happier.

"It is a fly rod and it cost two guineas," I said, and my lower lip trembled.

"Neffer," he repeated. "Five shillings would be too much."

Even a small boy is entitled to some dignity.

Picking up my basket, I turned without another word and made for the hotel. Perhaps my eyes were blinded with tears, for I was about to plunge into the dark hall when a great, rough, kindly voice arrested me with:

"Easy does it."

At the thick end of an immense salmon rod there strode out into the sunlight the noblest figure I had ever seen.

There is no real need to describe my colonel again—I have done so already—but the temptation is too great. Standing in the doorway, the sixteen-foot rod in hand, the deerstalker hat, besprent with flies, crowning his shaggy head, the waders, like seven-league boots, braced up to his armpits, the creel across his shoulder, a gaff across his back, he looked what he was—a god. His eyes met mine with that kind of smile one good man keeps for another.

"An early start," he said. "Any luck, old feller?"

I told him I hadn't started—not yet.

"Wise chap," said he. "Water's a bit heavy for trouting. It'll soon run down, though. Let's vet those flies of yours."

He took my rod and whipped it expertly.

"A nice piece—new, eh?"

"N-not quite," I stammered; "but I haven't used it yet, sir, in water."

That god read men's minds.

"I know, garden practice; capital; nothing like it."

Releasing my cast, he frowned critically over the flies—a Blue Dun and a March Brown.

"Think so?" he queried. "You don't think it's a shade late in the season for these fancies?" I said I thought perhaps it was.

"Yes, I think you're right," said he. "I believe in this big water you'd do better with a livelier pattern. Teal and Red, Cock-y-bundy, Greenwell's Glory."

I said nothing, but nodded gravely at these brave names.

Once more he read my thoughts and saw through the wicker sides of my creel a great emptiness.

"I expect you've fished most in southern rivers. These Welsh trout have a fancy for a spot of color."

He rummaged in the pocket of his Norfolk jacket and produced a round tin which once had held saddle soap.

"Collar on to that," said he, "there's a proper pickle of flies and casts in that. As a keen fisherman, you don't mind sorting 'em out. They may come in useful."

"But, I say, you don't mean—" I began.

"Yes, go on; stick to it. All fishermen are members of the same club and I'm giving the trout a rest for a bit." His eyes ranged the hills and trees opposite. "I must be getting on with it before the sun's too high."

Waving his free hand, he strode away and presently was lost to view at a bend in the road.

I think my mother was a little piqued by my abstraction during breakfast. My eyes never, for an instant, deserted the round tin box that lay open beside my plate. Within it were a paradise and a hundred miracles all tangled together in the pleasantest disorder. My mother said something about a lovely walk over the hills, but I had other plans, which included a very glorious hour that should be spent untangling and wrapping up in neat squares of paper my new treasures.

"I suppose he knows best what he wants to do," she said.

So it came about that I was left alone and betook myself to a sheltered spot behind a rock where all the delicious disorder was remedied and I could take stock of what was mine.

I am sure there were at least six casts all set up with flies, and ever so many loose flies and one great stout, tapered cast, with a salmon fly upon it, that was so rich in splendor that I doubted if my benefactor could really have known that it was there.

I felt almost guilty at owning so much, and not until I had done full justice to everything did I fasten a new cast to my line and go a-fishing.

There is a lot said and written about beginner's luck, but none of it came my way. Indeed, I spent most of the morning extricating my line from the most fearsome tangles. I had no skill in throwing a cast with two droppers upon it and I found it was an art not to be learned in a minute. Then, from overeagerness, I was too snappy with my back cast, whereby, before many minutes had gone, I heard that warning crack behind me that betokens the loss of a tail fly. I must have spent half an hour searching the meadow for that lost fly and finding it not. Which is not strange, for I wonder has any fisherman ever found that lost fly. The reeds, the buttercups and the little people with many legs who run in the wet grass conspire together to keep the secret of its hiding place. I gave up at last, and with a feeling of shame that was only proper, I invested a new fly on the point of my cast and set to work again, but more warily.

In that hard racing water a good strain was put upon my rod, and before the morning was out it was creaking at the joints in a way that kept my heart continually in my mouth. It is the duty of a rod to work with a single smooth action and by no means to divide its performance into three sections of activity. It is a hard task for any angler to persuade his line austerely if his rod behaves thus.

When, at last, my father strolled up the river bank, walking, to his shame, much nearer the water than a good fisherman should, my nerves were jumpy from apprehension.

"Come along. Food's ready. Done any good?" said he.

Again it was to his discredit that he put food before sport, but I told him I had had a wonderful morning, and he was glad.

"What do you want to do this afternoon, old man?" he asked.

"Fish," I said.

"But you can't always fish," he said.

I told him I could and I was right and have proved it for thirty years and more.

"Well, well," he said, "please yourself, but isn't it dull not catching anything?"

And I said, as I've said a thousand times since, "As if it could be."

So that afternoon I went downstream instead of up, and found myself in difficult country where the river boiled between the narrows of two hills. Stunted oaks overhung the water and great boulders opposed its flow. Presently I came to a sort of natural flight of steps—a pool and a cascade three times repeated—and there, watching the maniac fury of the waters in awe and wonderment, I saw the most stirring sight in my young life. I saw a silver salmon leap superbly from the cauldron below into the pool above. And I saw another and another salmon do likewise. And I wonder the eyes of me did not fall out of my head.

I cannot say how long I stayed watching that gallant pageant of leaping fish—in ecstasy there is no measurement of time—but at last it came upon me that all the salmon in the sea were careering past me and that if I were to realize my soul's desire I must hasten to the pool below before the last of them had gone by.

It was a mad adventure, for until I had discovered that stout cast, with the gaudy fly attached in the tin box, I had given no thought to such noble quarry. My recent possessions had put ideas into my head above my station and beyond my powers. Failure, however, means little to the young, and walking fast, yet gingerly, for fear of breaking my rod top against a tree, I followed the path downstream until I came to a great basin of water into which, through a narrow throat, the river thundered like a storm.

At the head of the pool was a plate of rocks scored by the nails of fishermen's boots, and here I sat down to wait while the salmon cast, removed from its wrapper, was allowed to soak and soften in a puddle left by the rain.

And while I waited a salmon rolled not ten yards from where I sat. Head and tail, up and down he went, a great monster of a fish, sporting and deriding me.

With that performance so near at hand, I have often wondered how I was able to control my fingers well enough to tie a figure-eight knot between the line and the cast. But I did, and I'm proud to be able to record it. Your true-born angler does not go blindly to work until he has first satisfied his conscience. There is a pride in knots, of which the laity knows nothing, and if, through neglect to tie them rightly, failure and loss should result, pride may not be restored nor conscience salved by the plea of eagerness. With my trembling fingers I bent the knot and, with a pummeling heart, launched the line into the broken water at the throat of the pool.

At first the mere tug of the water against that large fly was so thrilling to me that it was hard to believe that I had not hooked a whale. The trembling line swung round in a wide arc into a calm eddy below where I stood. Before casting afresh I shot a glance over my shoulder to assure myself there was no limb of a tree behind me to foul the fly. And this was a gallant cast, true and straight, with a couple of yards more length than its predecessor, and a wider radius. Instinctively I knew, as if the surface had been marked with an X where the salmon had risen, that my fly must pass right over the spot. As it swung by, my nerves were strained like piano wires. I think I knew that something tremendous, impossible, terrifying, was going to happen. The sense, the certitude was so strong in me that I half opened my mouth to shout a warning to the monster, not to.

I must have felt very, very young in that moment. I, who that same day had been talked to as a man by a man among men. The years were stripped from me and I was what I was—ten years old and appalled. And then, with the suddenness of a rocket, it happened. The water was cut into a swathe. I remember a silver loop bearing downward—a bright, shining, vanishing thing like the bobbin of my mother's sewing machine—and a tug. I shall never forget the viciousness of that tug. I had my fingers tight upon the line, so I got the full force of it. To counteract a tendency to go headfirst into the spinning water below, I threw myself backward and sat down on the hard rock with a jar that shut my teeth on my tongue—like the jaws of a trap.

Luckily I had let the rod go out straight with the line, else it must have snapped in the first frenzy of the downstream rush. Little ass that I was, I tried to check the speeding line with my forefinger, with the result that it cut and burnt me to the bone. There wasn't above twenty yards of line in the reel, and the wretched contrivance was trying to be rid of the line even faster than the fish was wrenching it out. Heaven knows why it didn't snarl, for great loops and whorls were whirling like Catherine wheels, under my wrist. An instant's glance revealed the terrifying fact that there were not more than half a dozen yards left on the reel and the fish showed no signs of abating his rush. With the realization of impending and inevitable catastrophe upon me, I launched a yell for help, which, rising above the roar of the waters, went echoing down the gorge.

And then, to add to my terrors, the salmon leaped—a winging leap like a silver arch appearing and instantly disappearing upon the broken surface. So mighty, so all-powerful he seemed in that sublime moment that I lost all sense of reason and raised the rod, with a sudden jerk, above my head.

I have often wondered, had the rod actually been the two-guinea rod my imagination claimed for it, whether it could have withstood the strain thus violently and unreasonably imposed upon it. The wretched thing that I held so grimly never even put up a fight. It snapped at the ferrule of the lower joint and plunged like a toboggan down the slanting line, to vanish into the black depths of the water.

My horror at this calamity was so profound that I was lost even to the consciousness that the last of my line had run out. A couple of vicious tugs advised me of this awful truth. Then, snap! The line parted at the reel, flickered out through the rings and was gone. I was left with nothing but the butt of a broken rod in my hand and an agony of mind that even now I cannot recall without emotion.

I am not ashamed to confess that I cried. I lay down on the rock, with my cheek in the puddle where I had soaked the cast, and plenished it with my tears. For what had the future left for me but a cut and burning finger, a badly bumped behind, the single joint of a broken rod and no faith in uncles? How long I lay there weeping I do not know. Ages, perhaps, or minutes, or seconds.

I was roused by a rough hand on my shoulder and a kindly voice demanding, "Hurt yourself, Ike Walton?"

Blinking away my tears, I pointed at my broken rod with a bleeding forefinger.

"Come! This is bad luck," said my colonel, his face grave as a stone. "How did it happen?"

"I c-caught a s-salmon."

"You what?" said he.

"I d-did," I said.

He looked at me long and earnestly; then, taking my injured hand, he looked at that and nodded.

"The poor groundlings who can find no better use for a river than something to put a bridge over think all fishermen are liars," said he. "But we know better, eh? By the bumps and breaks and cuts I'd say you made a plucky fight against heavy odds. Let's hear all about it."

So, with his arm round my shoulders and his great shaggy head near to mine, I told him all about it.

At the end he gave me a mighty and comforting squeeze, and he said, "The loss of one's first big fish is the heaviest loss I know. One feels, whatever happens, one'll never —" He stopped and pointed dramatically. "There it goes— see! Down there at the tail of the pool!"

In the broken water where the pool emptied itself into the shallows beyond, I saw the top joints of my rod dancing on the surface.

"Come on!" he shouted, and gripping my hand, jerked me to my feet. "Scatter your legs! There's just a chance!"

Dragging me after him, we raced along by the river path to the end of the pool, where, on a narrow promontory of grass, his enormous salmon rod was lying.

"Now," he said, picking it up and making the line whistle to and fro in the air with sublime authority, "keep your eyes skinned on those shallows for another glimpse of it."

A second later I was shouting, "There! There!"

He must have seen the rod point at the same moment, for his line flowed out and the big fly hit the water with a plop not a couple of feet from the spot.

He let it ride on the current, playing it with a sensitive touch like the brushwork of an artist.

"Half a jiffy!" he exclaimed at last. "Wait! Yes, I think so. Cut down to that rock and see if I haven't fished up the line."

I needed no second invitation, and presently was yelling, "Yes—yes, you have!"

"Stretch yourself out then and collar hold of it."

With the most exquisite care he navigated the line to where I lay stretched upon the rock. Then:

"Right you are! Good lad! I'm coming down."

Considering his age, he leaped the rocks like a chamois.

"Now," he said, and took the wet line delicately between his forefinger and thumb. One end trailed limply downstream, but the other end seemed anchored in the big pool where I had had my unequal and disastrous contest.

Looking into his face, I saw a sudden light of excitement dancing in his eyes.

"Odd," he muttered, "but not impossible."

"What isn't?" I asked breathlessly.

"Well, it looks to me as if the top joints of that rod of yours have gone downstream."

Gingerly he pulled up the line, and presently an end with a broken knot appeared.

"The reel knot, eh?" I nodded gloomily. "Then we lose the rod," said he. That wasn't very heartening news. "On the other hand, it's just possible the fish is still on—sulking."

"Oh!" I exclaimed.

"Now, steady does it," he warmed, "and give me my rod."

Taking a pair of clippers from his pocket, he cut his own line just above the cast.

"Can you tie a knot?" he asked.

"Yes," I nodded.

"Come on, then; bend your line on to mine. Quick as lightning."

Under his critical eye, I joined the two lines with a blood knot. "I guessed you were a fisherman," he said, nodded approvingly and clipped off the ends. "And now to know the best or the worst."

I shall never forget the music of that check reel or the suspense with which I watched as, with the butt of the rod bearing against the hollow of his thigh, he steadily wound up the wet slack line. Every instant I expected it to come drifting downstream, but it didn't. Presently it rose in a tight slant from the pool above.

"Snagged, I'm afraid," he said, and worked the rod with an easy straining motion to and fro. "Yes, I'm afraid—no, by Lord Bobs, he's on!"

I think it was only right and proper that I should have launched a yell of triumph as, with the spoken word, the point at which the line cut the water shifted magically from the left side of the pool to the right.

"And a fish too," said he.

In the fifteen minutes that followed, I must have experienced every known form of terror and delight.

"Youngster," said he, "you should be doing this, by rights, but I'm afraid the rod's a bit above your weight."

"Oh, go on and catch him," I pleaded.

"And so I will," he promised; "unship the gaff, young 'un, and stand by to use it, and if you break the cast we'll never speak to each other again, and that's a bet."

But I didn't break the cast. The noble, courageous, indomitable example of my river god had lent me skill and precision beyond my years. When at long last a weary, beaten, silver monster rolled within reach of my arm into a shallow eddy, the steel gaff shot out fair and true, and sank home.

And then I was lying on the grass, with my arms round a salmon that weighed twenty-two pounds on the scale and contained every sort of happiness known to a boy.

And best of all, my river god shook hands with me and called me "partner."

That evening the salmon was placed upon the blue ashet in the hall, bearing a little card with its weight and my name upon it.

And I am afraid I sat on a chair facing it, for ever so long, so that I could hear what the other anglers had to say as they passed by. I was sitting there when my colonel put his head out of his private sitting room and beckoned me to come in.

"A true fisherman lives in the future, not the past, old man," said he; "though, for this once, it 'ud be a shame to reproach you."

I suppose I colored guiltily—at any rate I hope so.

"We got the fish," said he, "but we lost the rod, and the future without a rod doesn't bear thinking of. Now"—and he pointed at a long wooden box on the floor, that overflowed with rods of different sorts and sizes—"rummage among those. Take your time and see if you can find anything to suit you."

"But do you mean—can I—?"

"We're partners, aren't we? And p'r'aps as such you'd rather we went through our stock together."

"Oo, sir," I said.

"Here, quit that," he ordered gruffly. "By Lord Bobs, if a show like this afternoon's don't deserve a medal, what does? Now, here's a handy piece by Hardy—a light and useful tool—or if you fancy greenheart in preference to split bamboo—"

I have the rod to this day, and I count it among my dearest treasures. And to this day I have a flick of the wrist that was his legacy. I have, too, some small skill in dressing flies, the elements of which were learned in his company by candlelight after the day's work was over. And I have countless memories of that month-long, month-short friendship—the closest and most perfect friendship, perhaps, of all my life.

He came to the station and saw me off. How I vividly remember his shaggy head at the window, with the whiskered cheeks and the gunpowder marks at the corners of his eyes! I didn't cry, although I wanted to awfully. We were partners and shook hands. I never saw him again, although on my birthdays I would have colored cards from him, with Irish, Scotch, Norwegian postmarks. Very brief they were: "Water very low." "Took a good fish last Thursday." "Been prawning but don't like it."

Sometimes at Christmas I had gifts—a reel, a tapered line, a fly book. But I never saw him again.

Came at last no more postcards or gifts, but in the *Fishing Gazette*, of which I was a religious reader, was an obituary telling how one of the last of the Mutiny veterans had joined the great majority. It seems he had been fishing half an hour before he died. He had taken his rod down and passed out. They had buried him at Totnes, overlooking the River Dart.

So he was no more—my river god—and what was left of him they had put into a box and buried it in the earth.

But that isn't true; nor is it true that I never saw him again. For I seldom go a-fishing but that I meet him on the river banks.

The banks of a river are frequented by a strange company and are full of mysterious and murmurous sounds—the cluck and laughter of water, the piping of birds, the hum of insects and the whispering of wind in the willows. What should prevent a man in such a place having a word and speech with another who is not there? So much of fishing lies in imagination, and mine needs little stretching to give my river god a living form.

"With this ripple," says he, "you should do well."

"And what's it to be," say I—"Blue Upright, Red Spinner? What's your fancy, sir?"

Spirits never grow old. He has begun to take an interest in dry-fly methods—that river god of mine, with his seven-league boots, his shaggy head and the gaff across his back.

If conversation lags at your next dinner party, try canvassing the table: "Did the ancient Egyptians or did not the ancient Egyptians fish with the hair of the dead?" Smart money will collect on one answer. Which one?

WILLIAM RADCLIFFE

Fishing with the Hair of the Dead

This chapter owes its birth to a passage of intrinsic interest but gruesome nature.

Before quoting or dealing with it, I may be allowed a few words as to my running it to ground and the curiosity it excited among angling scholars.

Some years ago I read in an article that "fishing with the hair of a dead person, ἔδησεν νεκρᾷ τριχὶ δέλεαρ, was practiced by the Egyptians, as is shown by discoveries during the last thirty years." No authority, no reference was given. "Thirty years" opened up a search too extensive to waste on an anonymous statement.

Even so this fishing with an unknown gut, dead men's hair, kept worrying me. Aristotle and others had written of the use of horsehair, but none of my friends or I had ever come across this Egyptian tackle. A great authority suggested that it was possibly taken from a body of which the hair continued to grow after death, and thus possessed much value because of length and strength.

Instantly floated before us visions of obtaining by a new *Rape of the Lock* this most desirable gut. Two nefarious courses were discussed. First, to rifle the coffin of Edward I., which when last opened in Dean Stanley's time revealed (*teste* the Verger) long hair still growing. Second, to raid the tomb of the

Countess of Abergavenny (*née* Isabella Despencer) in Tewkesbury Abbey, in which (to use Canon Ernest Smith's words) "at the restoration of the Abbey in 1875 was disclosed bright auburn hair, apparently as fresh and as plentiful, as when the body was buried four and a half centuries ago."[1]

Do the Sagas or other ancient Scandinavian literature, in which descriptions of fishing frequently figure, allude to such use of dead men's hair? Two of the foremost Scandinavian scholars could recall none. *The Kalevala*—the great Finnish epic—yielded no help.

Nearest comes the account of "Gunnar's Slaying" in *Story of the Burnt Njal*.[2] After his bowstring has been cut by his foe, Gunnar said unto his wife, Hallgerda, "Give me two locks of thy hair, and ye two, my mother and thou, twist them together into a bowstring for me." "Does aught lie on it?" she says. "My life lies on it," he said; "for they will never come to close quarters with me, if I can keep them off with my bow." "Well," she says. "Now will I call to thy mind that slap in the face thou gavest me," and refused him her hair.

Gunnar, just ere he falls, sings:

> Now my helpmeet, wimple hooded,
> Hurries all my fame to earth.
> Woman, fond of Frodi's flour
> Wends her hand, as she is wont.[3]

The passage containing the Greek words quoted in the article was eventually discovered on page 82 of *Fayum Towns and their Papyri*, by Grenfell, Hunt, and Hogarth.

> καὶ δὴ χθόνα δυσπράπελον φθάσας
> ἀσχήμονας ἦλθε παρ' ἠόνας
> ἔνθεν δὲ πέτραν καθίσας ὅτε
> κάλαμον μὲν ἔδησεν νεκρᾷ τριχὶ
> δέλεαρ δὲ λαβὼν καὶ ψωμίσας
> ἄγκιστρον ἀγηγε βύθει βυθῷ

[1] Aristotle (*H. A.*, III. II) states that the hair does grow in dead bodies. Since his time many descriptions of remarkable growth after death have been published, and many people believe that such growth does take place. Erasmus Wilson pronounces that "the lengthening of the hairs observed in a dead person is merely the result of the contraction of the skin towards their bulb."

[2] Blakey, *op. cit.*, 207, states an engraving was found at Herculaneum "representing a little Cupid fishing with the ringlets of her (*sic*) hair for lovers." So far I have failed to track this hermaphroditic representation, nor is Sir C. Waldstein aware of its existence.

[3] Translated by Dasent. *Frodi's flour* = gold.

$$\overset{.}{\omega}\varsigma\ \overset{.}{\delta}'\ o\overset{.}{\vec{v}}\delta\grave{\varepsilon}v\ \overset{.}{\ddot{o}}\lambda\omega\varsigma\ \overset{.}{\tau\acute{o}\tau}'\ \overset{.}{\grave{\varepsilon}\lambda}\alpha\mu\mu\acute{\varepsilon}vov.^4$$

I subjoin a translation:

"And so hastening over the rugged ground he came unto the unsightly shores, and there seated on a rock tied the rod with dead hair, and taking bait and feeding with little morsels, drew the hook along (or up and down) in the deep pool. But as naught was caught," and as $\alpha\mathring{v}\tau\eta\ \mu\grave{\varepsilon}v\ \mathring{\eta}\ \mu\eta\rho\iota\nu\theta\acute{o}\varsigma\ o\mathring{v}\delta\varepsilon\nu\ \mathring{\varepsilon}\sigma\pi\alpha\sigma\varepsilon\nu,^5$ both in its literal and proverbial sense held true, he returned to the place whence he came, the place of corpses.

The Editors' introduction to the Papyrus runs: "The matter of the poem is hardly less remarkable than the manner in which it was written down. The subject is the adventures of a man whose name is not given. After some talk, the hero proceeds to a place which is full of corpses being devoured by dogs. He then makes his way to the seacoast and proceeds to sit down on a rock, and fish with rod and line. He did not, however, succeed in catching anything: we then revert to the corpses, the gruesome picture of which is further elaborated. The language and style of the composition, the literary qualities of which are poor enough, clearly show its late date, not posterior to the second century."

I am indebted to Professor Grenfell for further information. "The Papyrus," he writes me, "is certainly a poem describing the descent of some one to the underworld. An Austrian, A. Swoboda,[6] wrote an article to show that it belonged to a Naassene[7] psalm describing the descent of Christ to Hades. The beginning of a poem on this subject, in the same meter as the Papyrus, is known from Hippolytus, *Refutatio Hereticorum*. The second column of the Papyrus seems to be an address to a Deity, and would fit in with Swoboda's theory.

"The composition being, in any case of a mystical and imaginative character, I do not think the description of the fishing incident is to be regarded as in any way real, and, from the fisher's point of view, it is not to be taken literally. *No parallel for the use of dead men's hair in fishing has ever been suggested.* In none of the Papyri are there any details about the modes of Angling. $\mathring{\Varepsilon}\delta\eta\sigma\varepsilon\nu$, which I should translate *tied*, has been generally supposed to refer to the

---

[4] Professor Grenfell tells me that $\ddot{o}\tau\varepsilon$ here has no connection, unless the main verb came in line 16, where there is a lacuna, but the traces do not suggest any verb. He also approves my rendering of $\psi\omega\mu\acute{\iota}\sigma\alpha\varsigma$ having the sense of "baiting the swim" with bits of flesh from the corpses.

[5] Aristophanes, *Thesm.*, 928. Cf. also *Wasps*, 174–76.

[6] *Wiener Studien*, XXVII (1905), pp. 299 ff.

[7] Or early Gnostic, also called Ophite, who honored serpents.

angler's line, and considering the composition is poetical, this seems the natural interpretation."

This coupled with the Introduction to the Papyrus appears to shatter the statement that fishing with the hair of a dead person was practiced in ancient Egypt. But although in such a mystic adventure as a Descent to Hades all is possible and all is pardonable, the passage can hardly from its extremely abrupt and casual mention of hair be regarded as heralding in the use of this substance as a quite new adjunct to fishing. It partakes of the nature of a simile.

If it be true that an ancient simile was intended to throw light from the more familiar on the less familiar, but never to illustrate the moderately familiar by the wholly strange, one might, despite the absence of all reference to such tackle in the representations or in classical writers, possibly argue that lines made of the hair of the dead were known and were used by the Egyptians. The substitution of the hair of a dead person for the hair of a horse may be but a bold and not ineffective attempt to heighten the mysticism of the picture.

Apart from the pleasant gain which the quest and the running down of this hare in "a mare's nest" (to mix metaphors boldly) entailed, one's only real satisfaction is that the Egyptian angler, notwithstanding his gruesome gut and loathsome bait, caught NOTHING!

There is a pier somewhere in southern California whose denizens had their exploits chronicled with a touch as lovingly maudlin as Steinbeck's. James Safley fished that pier and caught some of the finest yarns this side of Cannery Row.

JAMES CLIFFORD SAFLEY

Mutiny on the Annie B

"Barge boat! Barge boat!"

The man who was shouting wore a nautical cap, a double-breasted blue coat with brass buttons, and white trousers. He was master of the launch that plied between Fisherman's Pier and the barge, *Annie B*, anchored a mile offshore. Also, he was captain of the barge.

"Barge boat! Barge boat!" he cried. "Get your tickets now for the fishing barge, *Annie B*! Out where the big fish are! No disappointments! Fish all day for a dollar with pole, line, and live bait furnished."

A half-dozen men, two women, and two boys paid a dollar each at the ticket office.

"Right this way," the skipper directed. "Right this way, please."

He unlocked the wire-covered gate of the cagelike structure on the wharf and herded the passengers, each of whom carried a burlap gunny sack, down the ramp that led toward the water. Carefully they watched their step as they picked their way down the wet and slippery boards, thence across the gangplank to the throbbing, rocking launch that strained at its ropes in eagerness to get away.

"All aboard! Last call!" barked the operator of the barge boat in a final plea for fares. "They're catching plenty of big fish off the barge, folks. Who else wants to go on the barge? Barge boat! Room for a few more. Last call for the barge boat!"

The happy, laughing passengers planted themselves on seats in the stern of the open craft. Abandoning further quest for customers, the master locked the wire gate behind himself and descended the passageway to the boat. The mate raised the gangplank and cast off the ropes that had held the launch fast. The captain gave the starting signal, and the engine, which had been idling, chugged viciously, the propeller churning the water into a mass of white foam. The ten adventurers waved a gay farewell to those who hung over the rail at the side of the pier, and the party was off for the barge "out where the big fish are."

The *Annie B* in her days of glory had served her owners well, carrying freight and passengers across the sea. But the passing of the years had told on her. She had grown old, as all things do, and her period of usefulness was rapidly drawing to a close. No longer fit for service on the high seas, she had been dismantled and was now a mere hulk of wood sold for a pittance at San Pedro and towed by a tug to her new anchorage off Fisherman's Pier. Here she would spend her remaining days as a fishing barge, yielding a meager living to her new owner until, some day, under the lashing of a severe storm, her anchor cable would give way and she would be hurled to pieces on the sandy beach.

But this day was calm, and the *Annie B* rode lazily at anchor. The launch drew to her side, the ropes were made fast, and up the steps from the water's surface to the deck of the barge climbed the ten who were the passengers of the barge boat.

Excited at the opportunity of angling in deep water, they baited their hooks and dropped the lines over the gunwale. Down went a line with a sudden jerk, then away, and the fisherman thrilled in bringing his catch to the deck of the barge. Soon all ten anglers were dragging out fish almost as fast as they could drop their baited hooks into the sea. A great school of fish had been encountered and they were ravenous. The burlap sacks the anglers had brought were filling rapidly with a green-backed catch whose sides were as silvery as though made of metal. Many were a foot and a half long.

Barge fishing was great sport. But there was keen disappointment among those who had paid for the privilege of fishing from the barge, for all they caught was mackerel. And who wants mackerel? Seeking to avoid the mackerel, which are a surface fish, the anglers tried at a lower level, a hundred feet or more down, but there no fish would bite. It was mackerel or nothing.

The disappointed anglers held consultation. Ten dollars the mackerel had cost them and they were not worth ten cents. Better fish could be caught from Fisherman's Pier, and there the expense would be nothing. Besides, it would be extremely embarrassing to return to the wharf with a boatload of mackerel and face the good-natured ridicule of those who had not made the trip to the barge. It would be better, some thought, to return with no fish at all. But that would be embarrassing too. Finally it was agreed to protest to the captain who had induced them to make the trip.

"Captain," spoke up a man with a brown mustache, "I can't understand why we catch nothing but mackerel."

"It's just one of those days," the ship's master informed his paying guest, "when the mackerel are running and no other fish will bite. Try again tomorrow. Perhaps your luck will be better."

"You told us 'no disappointments,' " put in one of the women, "and I surely am disappointed. Why, mackerel are fit only for cats to eat."

"Sorry, madam, if you are disappointed," answered the captain. "Why don't you try it another day?"

"I thought we would get halibut and yellowtail," remarked a man who was evidently an office worker and had acquired a bad sunburn while fishing.

"Plenty of yellowtail yesterday and halibut the day before," said the captain. "They will be running again. Come some other day."

"I want my money back," pleaded one of the boys. "I worked all day yesterday for that dollar I gave you, and all I got was a no-account mackerel."

"Sorry, lad, I can't regulate the fish in the sea."

"You told us they were catching plenty of fish from the barge," said the second woman angrily.

"Lady," answered the captain, "I did not misinform you. Don't you have plenty of fish? If not, perhaps some of the gentlemen will give you a portion of what they have caught."

"If you would give us another try, say tomorrow—a free trip, I mean—we'd all be better satisfied," suggested a man in blue jeans and a farmer's straw hat.

The suggestion struck a popular chord.

"Sure!" one agreed.

"You bet!" yelled another.

"Now you're talking!"

"Just what I was about to say."

"Okay with me."

But the suggestion was not agreeable to the captain.

"I haven't misrepresented anything," he informed the crowd. "You have had plenty of fun even if you caught only mackerel. The only time a rain check is issued is when a storm arises which stops the fishing. There has been no sign of a storm today. My price is a dollar a day for each fisherman. But to show you I am willing to do the right thing I will compromise with you. You came aboard at eleven o'clock this morning. A day, in reality, means twenty-four hours. It is now four o'clock in the afternoon. You may remain on the barge until eleven o'clock tomorrow morning, if you like, for the dollar you paid. Maybe better fish will be biting tonight or tomorrow. But there are no sleeping accommodations on the barge and there is very little food. Also, remember, it gets mighty cold out here at night.

"The barge boat will shove off for the pier at five o'clock this evening, or sooner if you agree to an earlier time. Those who want to stay all night may do so. How many are going ashore? Let me see your hands."

Everyone raised his hand.

"When shall we shove off?" asked the captain.

"Now."

"Now."

"Now."

"Any want to stay?"

There was not a murmur. The barge boat was quickly loaded with six men, two women, two boys, and ten gunnysacks filled with mackerel, and was off for Fisherman's Pier and the jibes and jests of a welcoming committee.

The mutiny on the *Annie B* was at an end and no one was put in irons.

Schwiebert knows his bugs, where they've been, where they hide, where they go. Sure, he knows gnats, leeches, stoneflies, and hellgrammites—but does he know 'hoppers? You better believe it. Everything you always wanted to know, and more.

ERNEST SCHWIEBERT

Grasshopper Wind

Many trout-water summers ago, my fishing apprenticeship began with live grasshoppers in Michigan. Getting bait was sport in itself, and we gathered the grasshoppers in the mornings when they were cold and clambered stiff-legged in meadows still beaded with dew. The grass was wet against our boots, and we picked them like berries.

My first trout was caught below a timber-sluice culvert above the farmhouse. Its pool was sheltered under a huge elm, with the trout lying tight in the run along its roots. Our rods were stiff in three pieces of pale split-cane popular in those days. They were well-suited to dapping the live, wriggling grasshoppers over the trout. The first trout came on a windy afternoon in August. Our stalk was made on hands and knees through the alfalfa until we sprawled belly-flat under the elm, its roots pressing up into our ribcages. My father crawled close and outlined tactics with whispers and gestures.

The grasshopper dangled five feet below the agate tip of the rod and I lowered it slowly between the tree and the fence that crossed below the culvert. The action was eager and immediate. There was a splash and the stiff rod dipped down and I reacted. The trout was derricked violently up into the elm and it hung there, struggling feebly in the breeze. Somehow we extricated it from the branches and sat in the meadow admiring its beauty. Wild twelve-inch brook trout are still treasured in the world of adults, but to my boyhood eyes that fish seemed bigger and more beautiful than any other I have ever caught.

The next summer saw my introduction to the dry fly. June was a good month and the mayfly hatches were heavy, and I caught my first dry-fly trout with a spentwing Adams in the Little Manistee. But that first dry-fly trout was only nine inches long, and in August there was grasshopper feeding in the meadows. My father gave me several Michigan Hoppers and told me to try them when it got hot in the middle of the day. They worked and along a sweeping bend in the river where the coarse grasses trailed in the current I caught my first big trout.

My casts with the grasshopper imitations came down along the undercut bank or ticked into the grass until I coaxed them loose. One cast came free and dropped nicely along the bank and the fly floated past the trailing grass. After three feet of float the fly was suddenly intercepted by a shadowlike trout and the rise was vicious, and I was into a fat seventeen-inch brown.

This meadow water was open and undercut along the deep grassy side and I fought the fish down over a pale rippled-sand bottom. There were no visible snags or deadfalls and I was able to handle such a trout in spite of my tremble-fingered excitement and the errors of my inexperience. After this grasshopper triumph came a week of doldrums. The trout became sluggish and fed little. One could see them lying on the pale bottom against the sand and gill-panting weakly as they waited for cooler water.

We gathered in the local tackle store and talked of fishing. *You be nice to your boy,* they told my father, still twinkle-eyed about the big grasshopper trout. *You be nice to your boy,* they laughed, *and maybe he'll tell you how he did it.*

My father always smiled. *Maybe he will!* he was pleased and generous about the trout. *I've never caught one any larger,* he said, *even during the caddis hatch!*

Talk always returned to the late August doldrums. *No decent rise of fish for two weeks,* observed the town doctor and the others nodded in agreement.

What we need is a mackerel sky, said the ice-cream proprietor, *and then some good windstorms and rain to clear the weather.*

We sure do, agreed the old logger who fished at night in the marl swamps, *that and a grasshopper wind.*

The season ended in doldrums that lasted until after Labor Day and I did not see the grasshopper wind that summer. That winter was spent learning to tie flies. My father bought some Michigan Hoppers tied by the late Art Kade and I used them as models. The copies were less than elegant, but the originals were exquisite: scarlet hackle tail-fibers cocked down under a tufted yellow-floss body palmered with brown multicolor hackle. Brown turkey-feather wings lacquered with feather glazer held the body hackles flat along the sides. Stiff multicolor hackles completed the flies. The hooks were elegant long-shank English up-eyes. These patterns were so classic in proportions that they still influence the style of my flies.

Several summers later I saw my first grasshopper wind. The incident occurred on the upper meadows of the Arkansas in Colorado during the late-August haying. Rock Creek was low and clear and the trout had not been rising well for several days. Then the haying started and the irrigation ditches were closed off to dry the fields for the mowing. The irrigation water was diverted back into the stream, and it came up several inches and the water was measurably colder. The trout became active again and the men began working in the fields. Grasshoppers rose up in front of the mowing machines and the hay rakes, and the warm wind moved up the valley and carried them in shaky, precarious flight patterns over the water.

The lower reaches of the creek were once dammed by beavers, and their leavings consist of two long chest-deep flats divided by a shallow gravelly riffle. Both flats are deeply undercut along the banks and their bottoms are soft and pin-cushion thick with old beaver sticks. Approach from the hay-meadow side was easy and that bank was well worn with the boots of fishermen. Everyone fished from there. But this approach was in plain view of the trout, and I never saw any there except small fish.

On the morning of the grasshopper wind I came down through the willows and brush on the other side, keeping some distance below the stream. The evening before I had been reading my fishing bible of those years, Ray Bergman's now-mellow classic *Trout*, and had covered several passages about fishing difficult pools from their less-traveled sides. I was absorbed with this idea and the ranch was quiet when I put the book down and turned out the lights in the bunkhouse.

It worked on the beaver-dam flats. The brush was thick where the creek riffled out into the wide Lake Creek shallows, and I was sweating heavily when I finally stumbled out and sat down on the bank. I checked my clothes for cattle ticks and washed my face and wetted my hat while I watched the mowing machine pass in the meadow. Grasshoppers rose up ahead of the sickle bar and the warm wind carried them over the creek. Several faltered and came down like mallards in the lower flat. Wakes appeared in the smooth water, and the unfortunate grasshoppers were collected swiftly in a series of calm showy rises that spelled size.

I was spellbound. The trout were large, larger than any I had seen before except for hatchery breeders or mounted fish on tackle-shop walls, and I watched them cruise the flat like hungry alley cats. There were no more grasshoppers on the water and the big trout vanished. The mowing machine chattered back toward the creek and I hastily got ready. The fragile 4x gut tippet was clipped off and I searched frantically for a grasshopper in my fly boxes. One battered split-winged hopper crouched forlorn and neglected in a compartment full of Hendricksons. Hooking it out of the box with my index finger, I clinch-knotted it firmly to the tippet. I tested the leader and crawled up the riffle to wait for the mowing machine and the grasshopper wind.

Three grasshoppers settled into the quiet current and started kicking toward shore. There was a heavy boil and the fish were feeding again, and my artificial flicked over the pool to drop near the undercut bank. Two big browns came cruising down the flat and each took a grasshopper as he came. I held my breath. One came toward my floating grasshopper and then detoured swiftly to take a kicking natural. I twitched the slowly drifting artificial, and the trout turned like a shark and came ten feet with his dorsal fin showing.

The fish wallowed clumsily when I struck, and bulldogged deep into the beaver sticks under the bank. I felt the leader pluck and catch as it slipped over the sunken branches, but it did not foul and the trout turned out into the open water of the channel. Then the fish made its mistake. It bolted down over the shallows where I crouched, its spotted back showing as it came, and I followed the trout with much splashing into the open water below.

The rest was easy. The fish finally recognized its danger and tried to get back into the pool again, but I splashed and kicked and frightened it back. It was tired now when it circled close, but pumped out again when it saw me waiting with the net in the shallows. It measured an even twenty-six inches, heavy and hook-jawed with maturity, and I ran back up through the meadows to the house with its strong-muscled bulk threshing convulsively in the net.

That was my biggest dry-fly trout for several years, and he held the title until my second encounter with a grasshopper wind. It occurred in the Cooper meadows of the Gunnison in Colorado. There are high-water side channels of the big river in these meadows, and there are big trout under the brush piles, trapped in the side channels by the receding water of summer.

On this afternoon I hooked and lost two dry-fly fish, both brutes, and returned talking to myself. The first was grasshopper feeding under a high bank. I changed to a big wool-bodied hopper and clinch-knotted it hastily. The trout saw the fly land above it and came upstream and splashed water wildly as it felt the hook. It bored up the pool, rolled deep along the bottom and turned. It came back strong and I stripped line clumsily and it wallowed in the shallows, smashing the leader at my feet.

Five pounds, I whispered.

The second fish was slashing at grasshoppers above a log tangle that bridged the narrow channel. It took my imitation on the first float and spurted upstream

in a series of bucking rolls. Then it hung high in the current above the logs and reconsidered. It turned and bored brazenly through the log tangle. The fish was below me now, below the jumbled logs and brush, rolling feebly on the leader in the quiet water downstream. Several seconds passed. It was too big to force back through the brush.

Then I remembered the brush-pile trout Charlie Fox once hooked on Cedar Run in Pennsylvania and passed the rod carefully through the logs to continue the fight below. The trout shifted gears as I tightened up and he tore back through the brush. This time he broke off and hung in the current above the jam, shaking his head at the annoying fly and leader before he drifted back into the logs trailing five feet of nylon.

There had been only two grasshoppers in my jacket and both were lost in trout, and I went downstream toward the ranch and the fly vise. Just above the junction of the side channel with the main river was a deep log-lined pocket, and Frank Klune crouched beside the water. He was studying the water and not casting. I yelled and he waved me away and continued to watch the water. I circled through the meadow well away from the stream and I could not see the water, but Frank was casting again. Then he yelled and stood up to handle his flailing rod. The fish was running now, and I was running too and the reel was going. The trout was high and rolling in the deadfalls before Frank finally turned it. Then the fish writhed and turned and flashed silver deep at our feet, and bored back upstream. It seemed confused and I watched its big rose-colored gills working slowly.

What did he take? I asked.

Grasshopper, said Frank. *The one you tied yesterday.* He gained some line and had the big rainbow back on the reel.

Took right up there in the brush!

Can't see the fly, I said. *He must have taken it deep.*

Then the fish exploded. *He's got it deep all right*, yelled Frank and we were running again.

The trout porpoised down the side channel toward the big-water Gunnison. The reel was going again and we were running down the high meadow bank. Thirty yards downstream was a narrow gully. I was running ahead with the net and broad jumped the gully, but Frank was busy playing the fish and missed. The fish was still on and Frank was trying to scramble out of the gully and handle the rod. The rod was bucking dangerously and suddenly the fish was gone.

Good one! he said sadly. *You get a good look?*

Yes! I said. *At least six pounds!*

The artificial grasshoppers I was tying now were still similar to the Kade patterns I had used for prototypes as a boy. The yellow-silk floss had been abandoned. Floss turned dark when it was wet, and floss bodies were too delicate and slim for bulky grasshopper bodies. Dubbed yellow wool was the best we could do, and it achieved a fat hopperlike body silhouette and did not change color when wet. Between the wings was an underwing of fox squirrel to achieve more buoyancy and counteract the absorption of the wool.

This version seemed good for several years, particularly on the less-selective trout of the big western rivers. But the hyper-selective brown trout of the small Pennsylvania limestone streams were another matter. The old patterns worked much of the time, but there were also many refusals, particularly from the larger wild trout. Anglers on limestone water had long experimented with hopper patterns: many used the traditional Michigan and Joe's Hopper flies, and some even tried the more radical fore-and-aft-dressings. Charlie Fox had used fore-and-aft grasshoppers for years on the difficult fish of his Letort Spring Run, and these flies had been tied for him by the late Ray Bergman. But the selective Letort trout seem to become more difficult every year, and they were refusing these old-time imitations with nose-thumbing frequency. New variations seemed necessary.

The first attempt was created in the Turnaround meadow on Charlie Fox's Letort water. Western experiments with deer hair had worked well on the big Jackson Hole cutthroats, and many anglers had reported good luck with the Muddler Minnow fished dry during sessions of grasshopper feeding. Using this information as a beginning, we concocted some lightly dressed wingless hoppers with deer hair and yellow nylon wool. They seemed to work better than the earlier patterns, but it was July and the grasshoppers were still small and not many fish were looking for them yet.

Subsequent refusals and successes caused us to restore the old-time turkey wings to the new hoppers and alter the deer-hair dressing. The silhouette of the wings and the trailing deer hair proved important. The absence of hackle permitted the bulk of the fly and its yellow-dubbed body to float flush in the surface film. The light pattern created by the dressing in the surface film looked hopperlike and promising.

Looks good, observed Ross Trimmer. *Maybe we'll name it the Letort Hopper.*

The trout liked it fine. We used it with good success on the Letort and pulled up trout that were not feeding on many occasions. But there were some refusal rises too, and that was disconcerting. We experimented some more and the final improvement came near the end of the season when the grasshoppers were at full growth. Tying bigger imitations resulted in the change: when the deer hair was looped and pulled tight it flared out like thick stubby hackles tightly bunched, and these butts were scissor trimmed in the blocky configuration of the grasshopper head and thorax. The earlier versions had these deer-hair butts trimmed close and covered with the head silk. The bulky version was better. We tried the following pattern that next morning on the Letort and it worked wonders on demanding fish:

> Tails—none
> Body—yellow nylon wool dubbed on yellow silk
> Wings—brown-mottled turkey glazed with lacquer
> Legs—brown deer-body hair
> Head—trimmed deer body-hair butts
> Silk—oo yellow
> Hook—sizes 6 through 16 2x long down-eye.

We found our final proving ground on a small privately owned limestone stream in central Pennsylvania. The browns were big and stream-spawned, and they were trout that had been caught and released many times during the season. Charlie Fox and our host walked down through the meadows with me to the stream in the early afternoon. Five hundred yards below the deep sapphire-colored spring, where the stream comes up full-size from limestone caverns, is a long marl-bottomed flat. The flat is smooth and clear and colder than sixty degrees through the heat of August. One side is bordered by limestone ledges and sheltered with trees. The shallow side is bordered by a marl shelf and a sizable hay meadow. Charlie Fox decided to try the water above the flat where he had spotted a big brown that morning. Our host walked with me where the meadow was alive with grasshoppers.

We reached the flat and moved cautiously down the path toward the water. The sun was high and the hot wind moved down across the valley and its hay meadows. We stopped short when we saw the water: big wild browns were cruising the flat in twos and threes.

We crouched low along the flat and studied the rise-forms to see what they were taking. The rises were quiet and we decided the Jassid was the probable answer, since it had produced several fine trout that morning. The little Jassid was already on my leader when we felt the hot wind and saw the grasshoppers. They rose up as the hot wind crossed the meadow and were parachuted out over the flat. The water was quiet, too wide for them to cross once they were committed to the wind, and they came down hard. Their shallow, faltering trajectory was futile and the big trout stalked them when they fell. The trout had learned that the grasshoppers were helpless, and their rises quiet and calm, completely lacking the splashy eagerness characteristic of most grasshoppers. *It's the wind*, I said, *it's grasshopper wind!*

Five of the new 'hoppers were in my fly box, tied the night before at my inn on the Letort. I changed to a grasshopper pattern but neglected to change the fragile Jassid-sized tippet to something heavier. It was a mistake. Two big fish came up above us over the marl shelf and I placed the imitation between them. One turned and took the 'hopper without hesitation and bolted thirty yards into a brush pile. The delicate leader sheared like wet tissue paper.

I replaced the grasshopper after cutting the leader back to a heavier calibration. Under the trees a big muskie-sized trout took another natural. The roll cast dropped the fly in the sun, but the trout had disappeared somewhere in the shadows along the bank. The float was good and it flirted with the bank shadows and I was already picking up the cast when he slashed at the fly. The big mouth closed and I tried to set the hook, but the fly came back in a loose leader tangle at my feet. The heavy trout rolled in panic and bolted up the length of the flat, brush-pile black and leaving a frightened wake.

My shout of disappointment died. *My fault*, I said.

Five pounds, consoled our host.

The other fish were still feeding, and the first cast with the fresh grasshopper produced a fat reddish-bronze two-pounder. The fish was released after a strong fight. The fish were so intent on their grasshopper prey that they ignored the heavier nylon tippet. The new grasshopper patterns worked beautifully, and none of these big selective browns refused to rise after a brief inspection.

Three casts later I was into another. *Should have brought my rod!* said our host.

The fish went eighteen inches and had the reddish tail and adipose coloring of wild limestone-stream browns. It was released and I promptly hooked and lost another.

You have an extra 'hopper? asked my host.

Sure. I laughed and he disappeared to get his rod.

The fishing was fast and Charlie Fox appeared at the head of the flat fifteen minutes later. The best fish of the afternoon was recovering its strength on the marl shelf at my feet, hook-jawed and heavy at twenty-three inches.

Grasshoppers! I yelled.

He was already casting over a good brown. His rod doubled over and there was a heavy splash under the trees at the head of the flat. We took twelve browns between us from fifteen to twenty-three inches, releasing them all.

Our host arrived late in the rise and promptly left my last grasshopper in a heavy fish. Light rain misted down the valley and the wind turned cool and the grasshopper activity was over. There were no rises when the rain finally stopped, and five big suckers were the only fish in sight.

Good score for the new 'hopper, said Charlie. *These big wild browns were a really perfect test.*

No refusals mean something, I agreed.

Our host was amazed at the grasshopper feeding. *They haven't come that fast all year,* he said.

We stopped to feed a fat brook trout from the suspension bridge over the big spring. *Had some refusals on the fore-and-aft 'hoppers,* said Charlie, *so it was a good comparison.*

How do you tie the legs and head? Our host was examining the tie.

Like a bass bug, I said. *Bunched and clipped.*

Charlie and I drove back down to the Letort that night, and we had a final day with the grasshoppers before the end of the season. Ross Trimmer met us in the Turnabout Meadow early that afternoon and went upstream with me above the Barnyard. We were in high spirits and Ross periodically stained the stream with tobacco. We were paying an end-of-season visit to the logjam.

We ought to try the Bolter, Ross had suggested at the Buttonwood corner.

The Bolter was a heavy brown trout several of us had hooked and lost when he bolted and broke off. The fish was an estimated twenty-two inches. It was feeding quietly along a cressbed cover when we approached under the trees. The rises were methodical and gentle, but several ugly white ducks squatted on the logs just below the trout. The ducks were notorious on the Letort for swimming ahead of an angler and spooking his fish.

Ross crouched and moved above the ducks. *I'll drive 'em downstream away from the fish,* he said.

The ducks waddled along the logs and dropped clumsily into the current. The trout continued to feed. The ducks drifted downstream, protesting noisily. When they were twenty yards below the fish I slipped into the stream and edged slowly into casting position. Ross sat on the logs and we waited. Five minutes later the trout came up again.

There he is! said Ross. *How's that for gillying?*

You make a good gillie. I grinned.

Well, my part's done and I'm waiting. The heavy trout came up noisily again and its rise was impressive.

Okay, I said.

The cast was difficult and the first two attempts failed, and finally the grasshopper fell right. I could not see its line of drift down the face of the watercress, but I heard the soft rise and saw the rings push gently into the current as I set the hook. There was a heavy splash instead of the usual rapier-quick bolt and the trout wallowed under the cress. It probed deep up the channel and I turned it short of the tree. The fish was under the cressbed again and I forced it out into the open water with my rod tip deep in the current. It was getting tired now and I kept the fish high in the water and out of the elodea. The light was wrong and we could not see the fish. Then it rolled head down and the broad tail fanned weakly at the surface. I turned the light rod over for the strain of the infighting and it turned slowly headfirst into the net.

Looks better than twenty, said Ross.

I pushed the hook free carefully. *Henfish,* I said. *She's really perfectly shaped and colored.*

Well, Ross said, *let her go.*

We crossed the current and walked back along the railroad. That evening we gathered at the Buttonwoods and celebrated the end of the season. The old stories were recounted again about Hewitt and LaBranche going fishless on the Letort, and the heavy sulfur hatches on Cedar Run in the old days, and the record fifteen-pound brown taken on a fly from the Upper Mill Pond on Big Spring.

For big trout I'll take the shad flies anytime, somebody was talking about Penns Creek.

They only last a week, said Charlie Fox, *but the grasshopper season lasts over a month.*

Right, said Ross. *I'll take the 'hoppers.*

I'll take the 'hoppers too, I agreed happily. *'Hoppers and meadow water and a grasshopper wind.*

The others murmured agreement. We fell silent and the little Letort whispered past the bench in the moonlight. The year was over again. Somewhere above the buttonwoods a trout came up in the darkness and we turned to listen.

Friend and neighbor to Sir Walter Scott, in his day Scrope was just as well known as a painter and deerstalker as a fisherman. Arnold Gingrich, who should know, once said that leaving out Scrope in a book about fishing would be as sinful as "passing up the roast beef when you're at Simpson's in the Strand."

WILLIAM SCROPE

The River Sneak

If I were to write an account of half the poaching stories that are common to all Salmon rivers, I should produce a book, the dimensions of which would terrify the public, even in this pen-compelling age.

In times when water bailiffs in Tweed had very small salaries, they themselves were by no means scrupulous about the observance of close time, but partook of the good things of the river in all seasons, lawful or unlawful. There is a man now, I believe, living at Selkirk, who in times of yore used certain little freedoms with the Tweed Act, which did not become the virtue of his office. As a water bailiff he was sworn to tell of all he saw; and indeed, as he said, it could not be expected that he should tell of what he did not see.

When his dinner was served up during close time, his wife usually brought to the table in the first place a platter of potatoes and a napkin; she then bound the latter over his eyes that nothing might offend his sight. This being done, the illegal salmon was brought in smoking hot, and he fell to, blindfolded as he was, like a conscientious water bailiff,—if you know what that is; nor was the napkin taken from his eyes till the fins and bones were removed from the room, and every visible evidence of a salmon having been there had completely vanished: thus he saw no illegal act committed, and went to give in his annual report at Cornhill with his idea of a clear conscience. This was going too near the wind, or rather the water; but what would you have?—the man was literal, and a great eater of salmon from his youth.

People who are not water bailiffs have not always so delicate a conscience. Let us examine the style and bearing of such marauders as have fallen under our notice.

In the first place, there is your man with a pout net, which resembles a landing net, only that it is very considerably larger, and is in shape only half of a circle; with this he scoops out foul salmon during floods, when, from weakness, they are unable to stem the current, and get close under the banks. This he transacts very snugly, under pretence of taking trouts; so indeed he does, and welcome too, if he would stop there; but this he is perfectly averse from.

Next in consequence comes your Triton, who walks the waters with a long implement in his hands, namely a leister, alias a waster; with this weapon, "quocunque nomine gaudet," the said deity, quick of eye and ready of hand, forks out the poor fish that are spawning on the streams; and this in close time. Vile, vile Triton!

Then comes your lawless band of black fishers, so called from their masks of black crape with which they disguise themselves: these men come forth in the darkness of the night to burn for salmon. When the winds are hushed, you may sometimes hear the dipping of oars and the clanking of a boat chain, and see at a distance a small light, like a glow-worm. In a little while the light blazes forth, and up rise a set of Othellos who are about to take a private benefit. These minions of the night are generally men of a desperate character, and it is not easy to collect water bailiffs sufficient in number or willing to encounter them; but if water bailiffs would fight, how very picturesque the attack would be! The rapids,—the blazing,—the leisters,—the combatants driven headlong into the river. Why, the battle of Constantine and Maxentius, and the affair of the bridge, as seen in the famous fresco, would be nothing to it. The only thing I should apprehend would be, that the bailiffs would eventually sport Marc Antony and run.

In contradistinction to these illuminati comes your plausible poacher, a sort of river sneak. This man sallies forth with apparent innocence of purpose; he switches the water with a trout-rod, and ambulates the shore with a small basket at his back, indicative of humble pretensions; but has a pocket in his jacket that extends the whole breadth of the skirts. He is trouting, forsooth; but ever and anon, as he comes to a salmon-cast, he changes his fly, and has a go at the nobler animal. If he hooks a salmon, he looks on each side with the tail of his eye to guard against a surprise; and if he sees any danger of discovery from the advance of the foeman, he breaks his line, leaves the fly in the fish's mouth, and substitutes a trout one;—said fish swims away, and does not appear in evidence.

I once came upon one of these innocents, who had hold of a salmon with his trout-rod in a cast a little above Melrose bridge, called *"The Quarry Stream."* He did not see me, for I was in the copsewood on the summit of the bank immediately behind him. I could have pounced upon him at once, I and my fisherman. Did I do so? I tell you, no. He would have broken his line as above, and have lost the fish; and I wanted a salmon, for it is a delicate animal, and was particularly scarce at that time.

So I desired Charlie to lie down amongst the bushes, and not to stir till the fish was fairly landed, and was in the capacious pocket, which has already been described. Then I counselled him to give chase, and harry the possessor. Judging, however, that if the man crossed the river at the ford a little below, which he was very likely to do, that he would have so much law of Charlie before he could descend the steep brae, that he might escape: I drew back cautiously, got into the road out of sight, and passed over Melrose bridge, taking care to bend my body so as to keep it out of sight behind the parapet; I then lay concealed amongst the firs in the opposite bank. Thus we had Master Sneak between us. I was at some distance from the scene of action to be sure, and somewhat in the rear, as I could advance no further under cover; but I had the upper ground, and was tolerably swift of foot in those days, which gave me confidence. I took out my pocket glass, and eyed my man. He was no novice: but worked his fish with great skill. At length he drew him on the shore, and gave him a settler with a rap of a stone on the back of his head; he then, honest man, pryed around him with great circumspection, and seeing no one, he took the salmon by the tail, and, full of internal contentment, deposited it in his well-contrived pocket: he then waded across to the south side of the river, with an intention, as it seemed, of revisiting his household gods and having a broil.

Charlie now arose from his lair, and scrambled down the steep. The alarm was given, but he of the salmon had a good start, with the river between him and his pursuer. So he stopped for a moment on the haugh to make out what was going forward on all sides, much after the fashion of an old hare, who runs a certain distance when she apprehends any thing personal, then rests for a moment or two, and shifts her ears in order to collect the news from all quarters of the compass. Even so did our friend, and having satisfied himself that he was a favoured object of attraction, he was coy, and took to flight incontinently; I now sprang up from the firs, the game being fairly afoot, and kept the upper ground. The pursuit became close and hot, but as the fugitive, like Johnny Gilpin, carried weight, I soon closed with him.

"You seem in a hurry, my good friend; your business must be pressing. What makes you run so?"

"Did ye no see that bogle there by the quarry stream, that garred me rin this gait, haud on for yer lives, sirs, for if he overtakes us, we are deid men."

"Why, the truth is, Sandy, that I do not choose to haud on at present, because I came forth in quest of a bonny salmon, and cannot go home without one; could you not help me to such a thing?"

At this Sandy took a pinch of snuff from his mull, and seeing my eyes fixed upon the length and protuberance of his pocket, answered quaintly enough,—

"Aye, that can I, and right glad am I to do ye a favour, ye shall no want for a salmon whilst I have one."

So saying, he pulled forth a ten pounder, which occupied all the lower regions of his jacket. "How the beast got here," said he, as he extracted him gradually, "I dinna ken, but I am thinking that he must have louped intill my pocket, as I war wading the river."

"Nothing more likely, and I will admit him to have done so for once, but, mark me, I will not admit of any salmon doing so in future without my permission in writing. You have been trouting, it seems, pray what sort of a fly do you use?"

"Whiles I use a wee ane, and while a muckle flee, ane for rough and deep water, and the ither for shallow streams. That is the way to trout, both in loch and river."

"True! I see you have some bonny little flies in your hat; take it off carefully, Purdie—you understand me,—and let me admire them."

Charlie advances, and taking off the man's hat with great care so as to keep the crown undermost, he pulls out from the inside six well tied salmon flies of the most approved colours, which he transferred to his own pocket. I actually saw *"Meg with the muckle mouth"* amongst them.

"Aye, ye are as welcome to the flees as ye are to the sawmont, and I am proud to do ye a good turn at ony gait."

"Well now, bear in mind, that I will never permit you to throw a fly wee or muckle in the Pavilion-water again; and if you darken the shores with your presence a second time, I will have you up at Melrose."

"I'm thinking I shall tak' your advice, for ye seem a sensible chiel. Will ye accept a pinch of snuff?"

"Good morning, good morning, get home to Selkirk as quick as ye can; we know ye well for a souter of that town. Run, run, the bogle is after you!"

"Run, aye that will I, and the deil tak' the hindmost," said he, and off he went at his best pace; leaving this blessing and the salmon to solace us.

If Dobie Gillis ever went fishing, it would surely be in the company of Max Shulman. The man can't help chumming a seemingly effortless slick, trolling one-liners and dispatching his prey with gaffes.

MAX SHULMAN

Stalking the Red-Nosed Captain

Until a year ago I knew absolutely nothing about salt-water game fishing. Today I am an expert, loaded with lore. I have learned how to tempt a tuna, master a marlin, seduce a sailfish, beguile a barracuda, and tell big lies.

I've been attracted by deep-sea fishing for many years, but somehow I never got around to it. It seems like every time I planned to go, something annoying would come up to prevent it, like root canal or a job. But early in November of 1968—it was shortly before Election Day—I looked over the list of presidential candidates and it was clear to me that if ever there was a time for a man to go fishing, this was it.

Asking advice from knowledgeable friends, I was directed to a recently opened resort in the Bahamas—Great Harbour Cay, a sun-blessed, breeze-kissed isle that has been turned into a paradise for fishermen, yachtsmen, golfers, and other unemployables. I arrived at Great Harbour Cay late one afternoon, unpacked my deep-sea gear (a kapok T-shirt, inflatable drawers, and six bottles of Dramamine) and turned in early for a good night's sleep.

The next morning I boarded my chartered fishing boat, the *Uninsurable*, a trim craft with merrily gurgling bilges and a captain named Rummy Rafferty, an attractive red-nosed man with palsy. The mate, a lovable native named

Black Power, cast off the lines, the captain threw the throttles open, and we leaped away from the dock with a roar.

Some hours later, after a passing dory pulled us off the sandbar, we reached open water. What excitement flooded my breast as I gazed for the first time at the incredible blues and greens of the Bahamian sea! How my pulses pounded and my eyeballs shone as the mate baited the hooks with mullet and balao and dropped them over the stern!

"Captain," I said eagerly to the Captain, "what kind of fish will we catch?"

"Bless you, sir," said the Captain, "what kind would you like?"

"Are there any marlin around?" I said.

"Lordy, yes!" said the Captain. "Why, I declare we must have raised thirty or forty yesterday."

"Where?" I said.

"Bless you, sir," said the Captain. "Right here where we are."

Marlin! I fairly trembled with anticipation. Could it be that I—a tyro, a novice—would catch the mightiest fish in the sea on my very first trip? No, it was too much to hope for.

But suddenly my reel was whirling and shrieking and my line was running out at blinding speed!

"Oh, joy!" I cried. "A strike! A strike! Oh, joy!"

"Shut up and reel," said the Captain.

Now began the titanic struggle: man, the wily hunter (me) against raw, savage, and elemental nature (the fish). Back and forth the battle seesawed, the outcome always in doubt. I reeled in; he ran out. I reeled in again; he ran out again. Sometimes I thought my strength would give out, but somehow, I know not whence, at the last second I summoned up just a little more. And under the waves my adversary too was finding hidden reserves. A hundred times it seemed he could fight no more, but a hundred times he turned and plunged and fought again. How long the battle lasted I truthfully cannot say, for I was unaware of time or space. In all the world there were only two things— I at one end of the line, he at the other.

At last it was over. One final plunge and then—his noble heart broken—he came to the side of the boat and the mate's sharp gaff slashed downward.

My every sinew aching, my voice a dry croak, I said to the mate, "What is it?"

"Kelp," said the mate.

"However, sir," said the Captain, "that's no reason not to have a drink."

We drank. We trolled. We waited. Then we drank and trolled and waited some more.

"Can't understand it," said the Captain. "They were sure here yesterday."

"Where do you think they've gone?" said I.

"Aha!" said the Captain. "I know exactly where they've gone, the foxy devils." He pointed off to his left. "See that rip?"

"Yes," said I.

"That's where they are," said the Captain and whipped the wheel hard aport.

Some hours later, after the mate had replaced the broken rudder with a toilet seat, we reached the rip. And—you're not going to believe this—no sooner did we get there when—wham! zap! zowie!—I had another strike!

I will not attempt to recount the landing of this one; even Herman Melville's powers would be strained to describe the action and passion, the drama and strife, the cosmic contest of atavistic guile against brute protein. Suffice it to say that when it was over, the monster lay gaffed in the boat.

"Marlin?" I said to the mate.

"Barracuda," said the mate to me.

"Oh," I said, crestfallen. But my spirits quickly rallied. "Well," I said, "it must be the biggest barracuda ever taken in these parts."

"I doubt it," said the Captain. "Looks to be about four pounds."

"But a fighting fool!" said I.

"Officially the record for barracuda is 103 pounds," said the Captain. "*Officially*, that is. Actually I got one last year that went well over 120."

"Do tell," said I.

"Happened on my way back to port one evening," said the Captain. "Getting around sundown when she hit. Lordy, how she hit! Three and a half hours I fought that 'cuda. Pitch dark it was when I finally pulled her in. Got back to the dock and the weighing shed was closed for the night. Had to leave her on the dock till morning—which is how come I don't have the record."

"Goodness," I said. "What happened?"

"Tinker Bell," said the Captain. "That's my cat. Tinker Bell. She came out during the night and must have ate fifty pounds off that fish."

"Heavens to Betsy," I said.

"If you think *you're* surprised, imagine how I felt when I saw Tinker Bell next morning," said the Captain. "Bigger than a St. Bernard, she was."

"Where is she?" I said. "I'd certainly like a look at her."

"Dead," said the Captain. "Choked to death on her flea collar, poor thing."

"Have a drink," said I, "and see if you can remember some other world records you got tragically diddled out of."

"Much obliged," said the Captain. "Well, sir, I guess the most tragic happened back on April 17, 1961, when I caught the record blue marlin."

"How big?" said I.

"Can't say for sure," said the Captain. "All I can say is I've seen the *official* record marlin—814 pounds—and mine went anyhow twice as big, maybe three times."

I wiped away a tear.

"Hooked her off the Isle of Pines about eight in the morning," said the Captain. "Fought her all that day and half the night. Dragged me all over the sea, she did, but I hung tough. Finally I brought her in and lashed her to the boat and headed for the nearest land. If only it hadn't been that particular night!"

"What particular night?" said I.

"April 17, 1961," said the Captain. "Bay of Pigs."

Later that day I learned some more of the Captain's heartrending history. Not only had this gallant, luckless man been bilked out of the records for marlin and barracuda, but also for dolphin, sailfish, and tuna. His dolphin, at least 180 pounds, was hijacked by a Japanese trawler. His sailfish, 200 pounds by the most conservative estimate, was carried away by Hurricane Esther. His tuna, 1,200 pounds if it was an ounce, was lost when the Apollo 7 spacecraft landed on his leader.

I could well sympathize with the Captain's misfortune, for I had a little of my own that day. Three times I got tremendous strikes, and three times the fish got off.

"What a crying shame!" said the Captain after each loss. "You had a marlin."

"Did you see him?" I asked each time.

"Plain as day," said the Captain.

"Oh, mice and rats!" I cried, stamping my foot testily, but the Captain passed the bottle till I was calm again.

And so with good talk and good fishing the day raced by. Before we knew it, the setting sun was turning the sea to gold, and the Captain set his course for home. (Actually, as it turned out, we landed in Haiti because he neglected to compensate for drift in the toilet seat. How we chuckled over that in the days ahead, the Captain and Papa Doc and I!)

But I digress. I was speaking of the end of my first day's deep-sea fishing. Tired but content, I sat and looked out at the burnished sea and reviewed what I had learned. Even to one as new at the game as I was, certain profound truths were already clear. To wit:

1. Fishing boats leak.
2. Fishing boat captains drink.
3. Any fish you lose is a marlin.
4. Fishing was always better the day before you got there.
5. Though deep-sea fishing is a very difficult sport, it can be mastered by any man or woman with average strength and inherited money.

Believing a solicitor should practice what he preaches, Skues could never be found on his beloved chalk streams without his trusty marrow spoon—to thoroughly cross-examine the stomachs of his first caught fish for feeding evidence. One willingly defers to Skues, ever the tactician, in his wisdom on filing the Great Appeal.

G. E. M. SKUES

Well, I'm ——!

Mr. Theodore Castwell, having devoted a long, strenuous, and not unenjoyable life to hunting to their doom innumerable salmon, trout, and grayling in many quarters of the globe, and having gained much credit among his fellows for his many ingenious improvements in rods, flies, and tackle employed for that end, in the fullness of time died and was taken to his own place.

St. Peter looked up from a draft balance sheet at the entry of the attendant angel.

"A gentleman giving the name of Castwell. Says he is a fisherman, your Holiness, and has 'Fly-fishers' Club, London,' on his card."

"Hm-hm," says St. Peter. "Fetch me the ledger with his account."

St. Peter perused it.

"Hm-hm," said St. Peter. "Show him in."

Mr. Castwell entered cheerfully and offered a cordial right hand to St. Peter.

"As a brother of the angle—" he began.

"Hm-hm," said St. Peter.

"I am sure I shall not appeal to you in vain for special consideration in connection with the quarters to be assigned to me here."

"Hm-hm," said St. Peter. "I have been looking at your account from below."

"Nothing wrong with it, I hope," said Mr. Castwell.

"Hm-hm," said St. Peter. "I have seen worse. What sort of quarters would you like?"

"Well," said Mr. Castwell. "Do you think you could manage something in the way of a country cottage of the Test Valley type, with modern conveniences and, say, three-quarters of a mile of one of those pleasant chalk streams, clear as crystal, which proceed from out the throne, attached?"

"Why, yes," said St. Peter. "I think we can manage that for you. Then what about your gear? You must have left your fly rods and tackle down below. I see you prefer a light split cane of nine foot or so, with appropriate fittings. I will indent upon the Works Department for what you require, including a supply of flies. I think you will approve of our dressers' productions. Then you will want a keeper to attend you."

"Thanks awfully, your Holiness," said Mr. Castwell. "That will be first-rate. To tell you the truth, from the Revelations I read, I was inclined to fear that I might be just a teeny-weeny bit bored in heaven."

"In H—hm-hm," said St. Peter, checking himself.

It was not long before Mr. Castwell found himself alongside an enchantingly beautiful clear chalk stream, some fifteen yards wide, swarming with fine trout feeding greedily; and presently the attendant angel assigned to him had handed him the daintiest, most exquisite, light split cane rod conceivable—perfectly balanced with reel and line—with a beautifully damped tapered cast of incredible fineness and strength—and a box of flies of such marvelous trying as to be almost mistakable for the natural insects they were to simulate.

Mr. Castwell scooped up a natural fly from the water, matched it perfectly from the fly box, and knelt down to cast to a riser putting up just under a tussock ten yards or so above him. The fly lit like gossamer, six inches above the last ring; and next moment the rod was making the curve of beauty. Presently, after an exciting battle, the keeper netted out a beauty of about two and a half pounds.

"Heavens!" cried Mr. Castwell. "This is something like."

"I am sure his Holiness will be pleased to hear it," said the keeper.

Mr. Castwell prepared to move upstream to the next riser when he became aware that another trout had taken up the position of that which he had just landed, and was rising. "Just look at that," he said, dropping instantaneously to his knee and drawing off some line. A moment later an accurate fly fell just above the neb of the fish, and instantly Mr. Castwell engaged in battle with another lusty fish. All went well, and presently the landing net received its two and a half pounds.

"A very pretty brace," said Mr. Castwell, preparing to move on to the next of the string of busy nebs which he had observed putting up round the bend.

As he approached the tussock, however, he became aware that the place from which he had just extracted so satisfactory a brace was already occupied by another busy feeder.

"Well, I'm damned!" cried Mr. Castwell. "Do you see that?"

"Yes, sir," said the keeper.

The chance of extracting three successive trout from the same spot was too attractive to be forgone, and once more Mr. Castwell knelt down and delivered a perfect cast to the spot. Instantly it was accepted and battle was joined. All held, and presently a third gleaming trout joined his brethren in the creel.

Mr. Castwell turned joyfully to approach the next riser round the bend. Judge, however, his surprise to find that once more the pit beneath the tussock was occupied by a rising trout, apparently of much the same size as the others.

"Heavens!" exclaimed Mr. Castwell. "Was there ever anything like it?"

"No, sir," said the keeper.

"Look here," said he to the keeper, "I think I really must give this chap a miss and pass on to the next."

"Sorry! It can't be done, sir. His Holiness would not like it."

"Well, if that's really so," said Mr. Castwell, and knelt reluctantly to his task.

Several hours later he was still casting to the same tussock.

"How long is this confounded rise going to last?" inquired Mr. Castwell. "I suppose it will stop soon?"

"No, sir," said the keeper.

"What, isn't there a slack hour in the afternoon?"

"No afternoon, sir."

"What? Then what about the evening rise?"

"No evening, sir," said the keeper.

"Well, I shall knock off now. I must have had about thirty brace from that corner."

"Beg pardon, sir, but his Holiness would not like that."

"What?" said Mr. Castwell. "Mayn't I even stop at night?"

"No night here, sir," said the keeper.

"Then do you mean that I have got to go on catching these damned two and a half pounders at this corner for ever and ever?"

The keeper nodded.

"Hell!" said Mr. Castwell.

"Yes," said his keeper.

Suppose you're Red Smith—ace scribe on the old New York *Herald Tribune*. You come across a rumor so alarming it requires several medicinal martinis just to stop your ears from ringing. The first thing you'd want to do is shake things up, get to the bottom of the pitcher. Then, if there's time, you'd want to check this story out.

RED SMITH

Anglers' Club

It was in the Anglers' Club of New York a few years ago that a petrifying potion called martini-on-the-rocks ("O true apothecary! Thy drugs are quick") was encountered for the first time. It was an experience never to be buried deep in memory, and recently there were stories in the papers which brought it back to the surface.

The stories told how scholars at Princeton had discovered "startling similarities" between Izaak Walton's *The Compleat Angler* and a work called *The Art of Angling* published seventy-six years earlier than Izaak's master opus. The boys at Princeton didn't like to say so bluntly, but the facts seemed to be that the revered Mr. Walton was a skulking plagiarist.

Inevitably a question presented itself: What manner of depth charge were they consuming in the Anglers' Club, now that the truth was out?

"Just the usual thing," a member reported in a tone that was like a shrug. "Did I say the usual?" he asked. "That may be stretching it a bit. Back in prohibition days we not only mixed our own recipes but made up our own ingredients. Once somebody making up the gin forgot to add the distilled water. There was a dinner featuring straight grain alcohol flavored with essence of juniper."

320

"The speeches," the member recalled happily, "never were so witty before, and haven't been since."

But how about those horrifying revelations regarding The Master, whose "delightful innocence" charmed Charles Lamb, whose "fascinating veins of honest simplicity" bewitched Washington Irving? To discover now that Father Izaak was a contemptible literary thief—

"Pooh," the member said. "You're talking about that book of Kienbusch's. We knew it all the time."

Recently Carl Otto v. Kienbusch, of New York, came upon the only copy of *The Art of Angling* which is known to exist.

"Kienbusch," said the Brother of the Angle, "is a member of the club. He showed the book around to all of us. It may be big news at Princeton, but we've known for a good while that Walton swiped from everybody whose stuff he read, same as all those writing johnnies do. How did Kipling put it—

"When 'Omer smote 'is bloomin' lyre,
He'd 'eard men sing by land an' sea;
An' what 'e thought 'e might require,
'E went an' took—the same as me!"

All the same, it comes hard to think of the gentle old ironmonger as a calculating hack lifting paragraphs and passages from authors who had gone before him, and never giving credit to his sources. It wasn't as though he were a young guy struggling to get into some slick-paper paradise like *Sports Illustrated*.

Izaak was a churchly man and no rookie in the writing dodge when he produced the first edition of *The Compleat Angler, or The Contemplative Man's Recreation* in the sixtieth year of his life. He had already done two biographies—of the poet John Donne, and his old fishing companion, Sir Henry Wotton—and if there wasn't an aura of sanctity about his graying skull he managed to create one.

"Anglers," he wrote, meaning himself, "they be such honest, civil, quiet men." Honest? Why, the old rummy! A fellow pictures him now in that little stone hut of his which had three sides facing the River Dove so he might see if a trout was dimpling the water. He's dipping into barley wine, "the good liquor that our honest forefathers did use to drink—the drink which preserved their health and made them live so long and to do so many good deeds," and poring through the works of his betters for passages that he could steal.

It is not easy to believe this of Walton. A guy would as lief believe that Dame Juliana, who wrote the very first treatise on fly-fishing—

"Dame Juliana!" said the member of the Angler's Club. "Good heavens, don't you know about her? Fact is, she probably wasn't a her. The language used in her *Treatyse of Fysshinge wyth an Angle* went out of style seventy years before the time she is supposed to have been born, and the chances are that whoever faked her stuff was a man, not a woman."

From beginning to end, these had been shaking discoveries. One would have thought that the mere unmasking of Walton as a plagiarist would have shaken the Angler's Club until the stuffed trout fell from its walls.

"You mean those big fish hanging over the doors?" the member said. "Don't worry about them. One was caught on a worm, one was netted and the other was killed with a pitchfork."

Nothing is sacred.

Father takes son fishing. It happens every day. Nothing special. Unless your father is the poet William Jay Smith and you are fishing for albacore.

WILLIAM JAY SMITH

Fishing for Albacore

I

Past oil derricks, gray docks, intricate layout of oil pipes, search-
lights wheeling overhead, oil rigs working in darkness with
the motion of praying mantises,

Through gray streets, at 10:00 p.m., down to Pierpont Landing,
Long Beach, where, in the window of a shop offering every
type of fishing gear,

Are displayed fish carved from driftwood by the natives of Bali,
each representing in true colors and exact dimensions a fish
found on their reefs,

Colors derived from bark and root (each fish, when completed,
is bartered for rice; no money is involved);

Then to the Pier, where sixty anglers wait, a bobbing bamboo
wood, to board the Liberty, eighty-five feet long, twenty-
three foot beam, twin diesels, twin stacks painted red, white,
and blue;

And the bamboo surges forward, rustling as in a slow wind, up
    the gangplank.

We sail at eleven; stand the poles against the bulkheads, and line
    up for rotation tags, my ten-year-old son and I—

Far from those mountains, where, in clear, shallow streams, slim,
    speckled trout flicker through massive shadows—

Sail out into San Pedro Bay—Long Beach, San Pedro, Wilming-
    ton, and below, Huntington Beach and Newport Beach,

Spreading behind us their red, green, and yellow fan of light,
    while one pale blue searchlight, directed from the city's center,
    draws customers to a used-car lot;

On until we pull alongside a boat to pick up our live bait, thou-
    sands of anchovies, handed from a wide brown net, in small
    dipnets on long aluminum poles,

Anchovy-colored, manipulated deftly like giant darning needles,
    anchovies threaded through the nets, dropping into the tanks;

On past the lighthouse, out through the breakwater, where, be-
    hind us, lit-up oil rigs perched in oily water are grotesque
    festive birds.

Passengers secure their gear; we seek out our bunks below while
    the boat plows ahead into black San Pedro Channel.

We toss for an hour, rough blankets up to our chins; then my
    son wakes me, needing air,

And we climb back on deck, proceed to the bow, where water is
    played out like the scalloped inside of a shell;

Phosphorescence breaks, has broken, into glowing bits of foam
    and then the foam bursts into sprays of flying fish drawn to the
    light;

Our wake swerves into a thousand foaming wings; and then,
    where the waves rise and fall, two waves break, and then two
    more, greener than green,

Not waves but porpoises, darting in and out; the high prow rides
    as if harnessed by dolphins, and my son's head on my shoulder,
    we fly through the night.

II

Below again. 5:00 a.m.; the engines pause, and groggy, back up:
far off to starboard, an island rides in the water, a carrier;

We sit in the galley and wait, or weave along the decks, following
the flying fish, until dawn, and gray water breaks against gray
sky.

8:00 a.m. We stop; rag lures sweep astern; the crew stands aft,
chumming, tossing dipnets of anchovies into the sea to lure
the albacore—if there are albacore—alongside.

And I picture that fish, dark blue above, shading into smoky silver
below, built for great speed, all its fins fitted and grooved, so
that stream-lined, steel-blue,

It makes its way in less than a year between Mexico and Japan;
and its spawning grounds are unknown, although one was
found once with ripening ovaries in the late summer off
Hawaii,—

The long-winged tuna, *Thunnus alalunga*, esteemed for its white
flesh, weighing up to forty pounds and a real fighter, taking a
trolled lure at eight to ten miles an hour,

That fish the Arabs named *al bukr*, "young camel" of the sea,
watching it weave, blue-humped, with long pectoral fins,
through warm water.

A strike astern; one of the crewmen reels in, and it *is* an albacore;
all sixty poles go over the side, and the deck palpitates with
poles, lines bobbing, weaving, thread tangling;

The waves boil with albacore: fat white bellies, long fins sweeping up and down in green water and through the school race
the sharks, bloodhounds, blue-green, and the next albacore
comes in, a great chunk chewed from its gut.

The captain fires a shot through the poles to kill the scavenger
while the bloody fish flops his bloated half-belly on the deck
with a hollow gourdlike drumming, and blood runs between
our feet;

Still the poles bend and the fish come in; albacore swoop down,
away, lines play out;

The cry, "Color!" from every side; deckhands rush up with gaffs,
  white gasping bodies are hoisted on deck, lines tangle;

Blood on deck, blood in the scuppers, blood and color—
  "Color!"—and a fat Japanese boy slips in blood, a fat-bellied fish
  throbbing at his feet;

And through the bamboo forest the sun beats, the sea boils,
  tempers break with breaking lines; gulls sweep over the bloody
  blue-green, churning cauldron of the sea.

III

After an hour we rotate positions, moving up toward the bow
  along the boat's striped divisions.

My son gets a strike; I follow him forward, the pole seeming to
  grow from his body, and past the other poles I follow his
  tense face

As he dips with the weight of the fish, bobbing, a bright-painted
  Russian doll, and I bend to help him steady the pole

And slowly he winds in his prize, boat throbbing, wild water
  thrashing,

Boat heaves, pole heaves, blood on water, blood on deck, on
    clothes, and steady, slowly, in . . .

And there he is—"Color!"—right at the prow where the porpoises
    had guided us through the night

And the deckhand with his gaff hoists an albacore more than half
    the size of my son, thrashing and throbbing, its dark eye gazing
    up and out like a button unthreaded and cut.

Hours pass: fish piling up, sun beating down, blood flowing; the
    school of albacore somewhere behind us,

The anglers, winded now, sprawling, the Liberty skims along,
    giving form to a formless ocean.

Off to port, sudden activity—not albacore, but waterspouts, a
    pod of whales . . .

I think of those young Leviathan amours, that harem and its lord
    in their indolent rambling, and there somewhere among them,
    tail to head, all ready for the fine spring, the unborn whale
    lying bent like a Tartar's bow. . . .

Silence . . . diesel-smell, fish-smell, salt-smell, slip-slap of waves,
    the afternoon sun drawing into its wrinkled round all the
    blood of the waves.

We speed back to harbor: the boat become a factory, crewmen
    aft cleaning fish, blood blowing, hoses running . . .

Throbbing of engines, gulls following, sun riding, winking low,
    ribbons of light trailing the horizon,

Waves changing, gray, blue-green, orange, gray, and then the
    whole surface weighted, leaden,

Until night comes down, and a semicircle of light dances before
    us, and we whip through the channel, past the lighthouse, a
    squat owl in black water,

Back to the Pier, the blue searchlight spanning the sky, oil rigs
    pumping in the dark, cold light sweeping the Liberty as she
    eases in;

And then, plumped down on the pier, in sacks, one hundred
   twenty albacore, whose steel-blue bodies will no longer flash
   on that mysterious migration,

Through that boiling ocean, past whales coupling in foaming
   water, resting mid-earth in the green wavering circle of their
   families,

And we come down to the dock, in hot light, past skeletal poles,
   raw laughter, lights flashing—

Come there to my mother who waits proudly to greet us; and
   then one bright, final flash against the gray (her camera), and
   there, in a circle of light,

As on some permanent atoll, I see my son, smiling, holding his
   fish, reflected, blue and silver, in my mother's eyes.

Some anglers become wedded to a certain aspect of technique, favoring one way of doing things over all others. Traver called this plain stubbornness, as he roll-casted across Michigan's Upper Peninsula. Since this announcement comes from the author of *Anatomy of a Murder*, one hesitates to disagree.

ROBERT TRAVER

Big Secret Trout

No misanthropist, I must nevertheless confess that I like and frequently prefer to fish alone. Of course in a sense all dedicated fishermen must fish alone; the pursuit is essentially a solitary one; but sometimes I not only like to fish out of actual sight and sound of my fellow addicts, but alone too in the relaxing sense that I need not consider the convenience or foibles or state of hangover of my companions, nor subconsciously compete with them (smarting just a little over their success or gloating just a little over mine), nor, more selfishly, feel any guilty compulsion to smile falsely and yield them a favorite piece of water.

There is a certain remote stretch of river on the Middle Escanaba that I love to fish by myself; the place seems made of wonder and solitude. This enchanted stretch lies near an old deer-hunting camp of my father's. A cold feeder stream—"The Spawnshop," my father called it—runs through the ancient beaver meadows below the camp. After much gravelly winding and circling and gurgling over tiny beaver dams the creek gaily joins the big river a mile or so east of the camp. Not unnaturally, in warm weather this junction is a favorite convention spot for brook trout.

One may drive to the camp in an old car or a jeep but, after that, elementary democracy sets in; all fishermen alike must walk down to the big river—*even* the arrogant new jeepocracy. Since my father died the old ridge trail has become overgrown and faint and wonderfully clogged with windfalls. I leave it that way. Between us the deer and I manage to keep it from disappearing altogether. Since this trail is by far the easiest and closest approach to my secret spot, needless to say few, secretive, and great of heart are the fishermen I ever take over it.

I like to park my old fish car by the camp perhaps an hour or so before sundown. Generally I enter the neglected old camp to look around and, over a devotional beer, sit and brood a little over the dear dead days of yesteryear, or perhaps morosely review the progressive decay of calendar art collected there during forty-odd years. And always I am amazed that the scampering field mice haven't carried the musty old place away, calendars and all. . . . Traveling light, I pack my waders and fishing gear—with perhaps a can or two of beer to stave off pellagra—and set off. I craftily avoid using the old trail at first (thus leaving no clue), charging instead into the thickest woods, using my rod case as a wand to part the nodding ferns for hidden windfalls. Then veering right and picking up the trail, I am at last on the way to the fabulous spot where my father and I used to derrick out so many trout when I was a boy.

Padding swiftly along the old trail—over windfalls, under others—I sometimes recapture the fantasies of my boyhood: once again, perhaps, I am a lithe young Indian brave—the seventh son of Chief Booze-in-the-Face, a modest lad who can wheel and shoot the eye out of a woodchuck at seventy paces—not bound riverward to capture a great copper-hued trout for a demure copper-hued maiden; or again, and more sensibly, I am returning from the river simply to capture the copper-hued maiden herself. But copper fish or Indian maid, there is fantasy in the air; the earth is young again; all remains unchanged: there is still the occasional porcupine waddling away, bristling and ridiculous; still the startling whir of a partridge; still the sudden blowing and thumping retreat of a surprised deer. I pause and listen stealthily. The distant blowing grows fainter and fainter, "*whew*" and again "*whew*," like wind grieving in the pines.

By and by the middle-aged fisherman, still gripped by his fantasies, reaches the outlet of the creek into the main river. Hm . . . no fish are rising. He stoops to stash a spare can of beer in the icy gravel, scattering the little troutlings. Then, red-faced and panting, he lurches up river through the brambles to the old deer crossing at the gravel ford. Another unseen deer blows and stamps— this time across the river. "*Whew*," the fisherman answers, mopping his forehead on his sleeve, easing off the packsack, squatting there batting mosquitoes and sipping his beer and watching the endless marvel of the unwinding river. The sun is low, most of the water is wrapped in shadow, a pregnant stillness prevails. Lo, the smaller fish are beginning to rise. Ah, there's a good one working! Still watching, he gropes in the bunch grass for his rod case. All fantasies are now forgotten.

Just above his shallow gravel ford there is a wide, slick, still-running and hopelessly unwadable expanse of deep water—a small lake within the river. I have never seen a spot quite like it. On my side of this pool there is a steep-sloping sandy bank surmounted by a jungle of tag alders. On the far opposite bank there is an abrupt, rocky, root-lined ledge lined with clumps of out-curving birches, rising so tall, their quivering small leaves glittering in the dying sun like a million tinkling tambourines. But another good fish rises, so to hell with the tambourines. . . . For in this mysterious pool dwell some of the biggest brown trout I know. This is my secret spot. Fiendishly evasive, these trout are not only hard to catch but, because of their habitat, equally hard to fish. The fisherman's trouble is double.

A boat or canoe invariably invokes mutiny and puts them down—at least any vessel captained by me. My most extravagant power casts from the ford below usually do the same or else fall short, though not always. The tall fly-catching tag alders on my side discourage any normal bank approach consistent with retaining one's sanity. (Hacking down the tag alders would not only be a chore, but would at once spoil the natural beauty of the place and erect a billboard proclaiming: BIG TROUT RESIDE HERE!) Across the way the steep rocky bank and the clusters of birches and tangled small stuff make it impossible properly to present a fly or to handle a decent trout if one could. The place is a fisherman's challenge and a fisherman's dream: lovely, enchanted, and endlessly tantalizing. I love it.

Across from me, closer to the other side and nicely out of range, there is a slow whirl-around of silky black water, endlessly revolving. Nearly everything floating into the pool—including most natural flies—takes at least one free ride around this lazy merry-go-round. For many insects it is frequently the last ride, for it is here that the fat tribal chieftains among the brown trout foregather at dusk to roll and cavort. Many a happy hour have I spent fruitlessly stalking these wise old trout. The elements willing, occasionally I even outwit one. Once last summer I outwitted two—all in the same ecstatic evening. Only now can I venture coherently to speak of it.

I had stashed my beer in the creek mouth as usual and had puffed my way through the tangle up to the deep pool. There they were feeding in the merry-go-round, *both* of them, working as only big trout can work—swiftly, silently, accurately—making genteel little pneumatic sounds, like a pair of rival dowagers sipping their cups of tea. I commanded myself to sit down and open my shaking can of beer. Above and below the pool as far as I could see the smaller brook trout were flashily feeding, but tonight the entire pool belonged to these two quietly ravenous pirates. "Slp, slp" continued the pair as I sat there ruefully wondering what a Hewitt or LaBranche or Bergman would do.

"They'd probably rig up and go fishin'," at length I sensibly told myself in an awed stage whisper. So I arose and with furious nonchalance rigged up, slowly, carefully, ignoring the trout as though time were a dime and there were no fish rising in the whole river, dressing the line just so, scrubbing out the fine twelve-foot leader with my bar of mechanic's soap. I even managed to whistle a tuneless obbligato to the steady "Slp, slp, slp. . . ."

And now the fly. I hadn't the faintest idea what fly to use as it was too shadowy and far away to even guess what they were taking. Suddenly I had *the* idea: I had just visited the parlor of Peterson, one of my favorite fly tiers, and had persuaded him to tie up a dozen exquisitely small palmer-tied creations on stiff gray hackle. I had got them for buoyancy to roll-cast on a certain difficult wooded pond. Why not try one here? Yet how on earth would I present it?

Most fishermen, including this one, cling to their pet stupidities as they would to a battered briar or an old jacket; and their dogged persistence in wrong methods and general wrongheadedness finally wins them a sort of grudging admiration, if not many trout. Ordinarily I would have put these fish down, using my usual approach, in about two casts of a squirrel's tail. Perhaps the sheer hopelessness of the situation gave me the wit to solve it. Next time I'll doubtless try to cast an anvil out to stun them. "The *only* controlled cast I can possibly make here," I muttered, hoarse with inspiration, "is a *roll* cast . . . yes—it's that or nothing, Johnny me bye." If it is in such hours that greatness is born, then this was my finest hour.

Anyone who has ever tried successfully to roll-cast a dry fly under any circumstances, let alone cross-stream in a wide river with conflicting currents and before two big dining trout, knows that baby sitting for colicky triplets is much easier. For those who know not the roll cast, I shall simply say that it is a heaven-born cast made as though throwing an overhand half-hitch with a rope tied to a stick, no backcast being involved. But a roll cast would pull my fly under; a decent back cast was impossible; yet I had to present a floating fly. *That* was my little problem.

"Slp, slp, slp," went the trout, oblivious to the turmoil within me.

Standing on the dry bank in my moccasins I calmly stripped out line and kept rolling it upstream and inshore—so as not to disturb my quarry—until I figured my fly was out perhaps ten feet more than the distance between me and the steadily feeding trout. And that was plenty far. On each test cast the noble little gray hackle quickly appeared and rode beautifully. "God bless Peterson," I murmured. Then I began boldly to arc the cast out into the main river, gauging for distance, and then—suddenly—I drew in my breath and drew up my slack and rolled out the fatal business cast. *This was it.* The fly lit not fifteen feet upstream from the top fish—right in the down whirl of the merry-go-round. The little gray hackle bobbed up, circled a trifle uncertainly and then began slowly to float downstream like a little major. The fish gods had smiled. Exultant, I mentally reordered three dozen precious little gray hackles. Twelve feet, ten feet, eight . . . holding my breath, I also offered up a tiny prayer to the roll cast. "Slp, slp . . ." The count-down continued—five feet, two feet, one foot, "slp"—and he was on.

Like many big browns, this one made one gorgeous dripping leap and bore down in a power dive, way deep, dogging this way and that like a bulldog shaking a terrier. Keeping light pressure, I coaxed rather than forced him out of the merry-go-round. Once out I let him conduct the little gray hackle on a subterranean tour and then—and then—I saw and heard his companion resume his greedy rise, "Slp, slp." *That* nearly unstrung me; as though one's fishing companion had yawned and casually opened and drunk a bottle of beer while one was sinking for the third time.

Like a harried dime-store manager with the place full of reaching juvenile delinquents, I kept trying to tend to business and avoid trouble and watch the sawing leader and the other feeding trout all at the same time. Then my trout began to sulk and bore, way deep, and the taut leader began to vibrate and whine like the plucked string of a harp. What if he snags a deadhead? I fretted. Just then a whirring half-dozen local ducks rushed upstream in oiled flight, banking away when they saw this strange tableau, a queer man standing there holding a straining hoop. Finally worried, I tried a little more pressure, gently pumping, and he came up in a sudden rush and rolled on his side at my feet like a length of cordwood. Then he saw his tormentor and was down and away again.

The nighthawks had descended to join the bats before I had him folded and dripping in the net, stone dead. "Holy old Mackinaw!" I said, numb-wristed and weak with conquest. A noisy whippoorwill announced dusk. I blew on my matted gray hackle and, without changing flies, on the next business cast I was on to his partner—the senior partner, it developed—which I played far into the night, the nighthawks and bats wheeling all about me. Two days later all three of us appeared in the local paper; on the front page, mind you. I was the one in the middle, the short one with the fatuous grin.

Next season I rather think I'll visit my secret place once or twice.

The surest way to grasp the essence of angling is to explore the alternatives. There is a risk, however, of becoming seduced. Trawick, it is sadly reported, succumbed to the temptation. Alas.

LEONARD TRAWICK

Feeling for Fish

Even in daylight, in murky waters,
As the ooze slides between your toes,
You can sense them around you, cautious,
Curious, nosing up close,

And often, swimming at night, you feel
Small ones nip at your flesh,
Then flick away with a little swirl.
But to make your catch,

Lie in the dark on a weedy ledge
Where the bank drops off sharply,
And troll your arm over the edge
Into the blind water.

You'll feel them nudging, cruising about;
Then one will strike your hand—quick,
Cock your thumb in the gills, hook
Your fingers through the mouth

And wrestle the slippery, thrashing thing
Out of its element into your own.
Later you'll find raw streaks the teeth have torn
And aching little holes from fins,

But you'll never use hook or net again;
You'll keep feeling back into black water,
And one night sooner or later
You'll wade out deep for the big one.

You'd never catch Van Dyke tubing the Yellowstone, float-planing Alaska, or wahooing wahoo. It just wasn't his style. But even though he lived in gentler times we can still nod our heads and profit from the good Reverend's comportment lessons.

HENRY VAN DYKE

Fisherman's Luck

Has it ever fallen in your way to notice the quality of the greetings that belong to certain occupations?

There is something about these salutations in kind which is singularly taking and grateful to the ear. They are as much better than an ordinary "good day" or a flat "how are you?" as a folksong of Scotland or the Tyrol is better than the futile love ditty of the drawing room. They have a spicy and rememberable flavor. They speak to the imagination and point the way to treasure trove.

There is a touch of dignity in them, too, for all they are so free and easy—the dignity of independence, the native spirit of one who takes for granted that his mode of living has a right to make its own forms of speech. I admire a man who does not hesitate to salute the world in the dialect of his calling.

How salty and stimulating, for example, is the sailorman's hail of "Ship ahoy!" It is like a breeze laden with briny odors and a pleasant dash of spray. The miners in some parts of Germany have a good greeting for their dusky trade. They cry to one who is going down the shaft, *"Glück auf!"* All the perils of an underground adventure and all the joys of seeing the sun again are compressed into a word. Even the trivial salutation which the telephone has lately created and claimed for its peculiar use—"Hello, hello!"—seems to me to have a kind of fitness and fascination. It is like a thoroughbred bulldog, ugly enough to be attractive. There is a lively, concentrated, electric air about it. It makes courtesy wait upon dispatch, and reminds us that we live in an age when it is necessary to be wide awake.

I have often wished that every human employment might evolve its own appropriate greeting. Some of them would be queer, no doubt; but at least they would be an improvement on the wearisome iteration of "Good evening" and "Good morning," and the monotonous inquiry, "How do you do?"—a question so meaningless that it seldom tarries for an answer. Under the new and more natural system of etiquette, when you passed the time of day with a man you would know his business, and the salutations of the marketplace would be full of interest.

As for my chosen pursuit of angling (which I follow with diligence when not interrupted by less important concerns), I rejoice with every true fisherman that it has a greeting all its own and of a most honorable antiquity. There is no written record of its origin. But it is quite certain that since the days after the Flood, when Deucalion

> Did first this art invent
> Of angling, and his people taught the same,

two honest and good-natured anglers have never met each other by the way without crying out, "What luck?"

Here, indeed, is an epitome of the gentle art. Here is the spirit of it embodied in a word and paying its respects to you with its native accent. Here you see its secret charms unconsciously disclosed. The attraction of angling for all the ages of man, from the cradle to the grave, lies in its uncertainty. 'Tis an affair of luck.

No amount of preparation in the matter of rods and lines and hooks and lures and nets and creels can change its essential character. No excellence of skill in casting the delusive fly or adjusting the tempting bait upon the hook can make the result secure. You may reduce the chances, but you cannot eliminate them. There are a thousand points at which fortune may intervene. The state of the weather, the height of the water, the appetite of the fish, the presence or absence of other anglers—all these indeterminable elements enter into the reckoning of your success. There is no combination of stars in the firmament by which you can forecast the piscatorial future. When you go a-fishing, you just take your chances; you offer yourself as a candidate for anything that may be going; you try your luck.

There are certain days that are favorites among anglers, who regard them as propitious for the sport. I know a man who believes that the fish always rise better on Sunday than on any other day in the week. He complains bitterly of this supposed fact, because his religious scruples will not allow him to take advantage of it. He confesses that he has sometimes thought seriously of joining the Seventh-Day Baptists.

Among the Pennsylvania Dutch, in the Alleghany Mountains, I have found a curious tradition that Ascension Day is the luckiest in the year for fishing. On that morning the district school is apt to be thinly attended, and you must be on the stream very early if you do not wish to find wet footprints on the stones ahead of you.

But in fact, all these superstitions about fortunate days are idle and presumptuous. If there were such days in the calendar, a kind and firm Providence would never permit the race of man to discover them. It would rob life of one of its principal attractions, and make fishing altogether too easy to be interesting.

Fisherman's luck is so notorious that it has passed into a proverb. But the fault with that familiar saying is that it is too short and too narrow to cover half the variations of the angler's possible experience. For if his luck should be bad, there is no portion of his anatomy, from the crown of his head to the soles of his feet, that may not be thoroughly wet. But if it should be good, he may receive an unearned blessing of abundance not only in his basket, but also in his head and his heart, his memory and his fancy. He may come home from some obscure, ill-named, lovely stream—some Dry Brook, or Southwest Branch of Smith's Run—with a creel full of trout, and a mind full of grateful recollections of flowers that seemed to bloom for his sake, and birds that sang a new, sweet, friendly message to his tired soul. He may climb down to "Tommy's Rock" below the cliffs at Newport (as I have done many a day with my lady Greygown), and, all unnoticed by the idle, weary promenaders in the path of fashion, haul in a basketful of blackfish, and at the same time look out across the shining sapphire waters and inherit a wondrous good fortune of dreams—

> Have glimpses that will make him less forlorn;
> Have sight of Proteus rising from the sea,
> Or hear old Triton blow his wreathèd horn.

But all this, you must remember, depends upon something secret and incalculable, something that we can neither command nor predict. It is an affair of gift, not of wages. Fish (and the other good things which are like sauce to the catching of them) cast no shadow before. Water is the emblem of instability. No one can tell what he shall draw out of it until he has taken in his line.

Herein are found the true charm and profit of angling for all persons of a pure and childlike mind.

Look at those two venerable gentlemen floating in a skiff upon the clear waters of Lake George. One of them is a successful statesman, an ex-president of the United States, a lawyer versed in all the curious eccentricities of the "lawless science of the law." The other is a learned doctor of medicine, able to give a name to all diseases from which men have imagined that they suffered, and to invent new ones for those who are tired of vulgar maladies. But all their learning is forgotten, their cares and controversies are laid aside, in "innocuous desuetude." The Summer School of Sociology is assembled. The Medical Congress is in session. But they care not—no, not so much as the value of a single live bait. The sun shines upon them with a fervent heat, but it irks them not. The rain descends, and the winds blow and beat upon them, but they are unmoved. They are securely anchored here in the lee of Sabbath Day Point.

What enchantment binds them to that inconsiderable spot? What magic fixes their eyes upon the point of a fishing rod, as if it were the finger of destiny? It is the enchantment of uncertainty: the same natural magic that draws the little suburban boys in the spring of the year, with their strings and pin hooks, around the shallow ponds where dace and redfins hide; the same irresistible charm that fixes a row of city gamins, like ragged and disreputable fish crows, on the end of a pier where blear-eyed flounders sometimes lurk in the muddy water. Let the philosopher explain it as he will. Let the moralist reprehend it as he chooses. There is nothing that attracts human nature more powerfully than the sport of tempting the unknown with a fishing line.

Those ancient anglers have set out upon an exodus from the tedious realm of the definite, the fixed, the must-certainly-come-to-pass. They are on a holiday in the free country of peradventure. They do not know at this moment whether the next turn of Fortune's reel will bring up a perch or a pickerel, a sunfish or a black bass. It may be a hideous catfish or a squirming eel, or it may be a lake trout, the grand prize in the Lake George lottery. There they sit, those gray-haired lads, full of hope, yet equally prepared for resignation; taking no thought for the morrow, and ready to make the best of today; harmless and happy players at the best of all games of chance.

"In other words," I hear some severe and sour-complexioned reader say, "in plain language, they are a pair of old gamblers."

Yes, if it pleases you to call honest men by a bad name. But they risk nothing that is not their own; and if they lose, they are not impoverished. They desire nothing that belongs to other men; and if they win, no one is robbed. If all gambling were like that, it would be difficult to see the harm in it. Indeed, a daring moralist might even assert, and prove by argument, that so innocent a delight in the taking of chances is an aid to virtue.

Do you remember Martin Luther's reasoning on the subject of "excellent large pike"? He maintains that God would never have created them so good to the taste, if He had not meant them to be eaten. And for the same reason I conclude that this world would never have been left so full of uncertainties, nor human nature framed so as to find a peculiar joy and exhilaration in meeting them bravely and cheerfully, if it had not been divinely intended that most of our amusement and much of our education should come from this source.

"Chance" is a disreputable word, I know. It is supposed by many pious persons to be improper and almost blasphemous to use it. But I am not one of those who share this verbal prejudice. I am inclined rather to believe that it is a good word to which a bad reputation has been given. I feel grateful to that admirable "psychologist who writes like a novelist," Mr. William James, for his brilliant defense of it. For what does it mean, after all, but that some things happen in a certain way which might have happened in another way? Where is the immorality, the irreverence, the atheism in such a supposition? Certainly God must be competent to govern a world in which there are possibilities of various kinds, just as well as one in which every event is inevitably determined beforehand. St. Peter and the other fishermen-disciples on the Lake of Galilee were perfectly free to cast their net on either side of the ship. So far as they could see, so far as any one could see, it was a matter of chance where they chose to cast it. But it was not until they let it down, at the Master's word, on the right side that they had good luck. And not the least element of their joy in the draft of fishes was that it brought a change of fortune.

Never believe a fisherman when he tells you that he does not care about the fish he catches. He may say that he angles only for the pleasure of being out-of-doors, and that he is just as well contented when he takes nothing as when he makes a good catch. He may think so, but it is not true. He is not telling a deliberate falsehood. He is only assuming an unconscious pose, and indulging in a delicate bit of self-flattery. Even if it were true, it would not be at all to his credit.

Watch him on that lucky day when he comes home with a full basket of trout on his shoulder, or a quartet of silver salmon covered with green branches in the bottom of the canoe. His face is broader than it was when he went out, and there is a sparkle of triumph in his eye. "It is naught, it is naught," he says, in modest depreciation of his triumph. But you shall see that he lingers fondly about the place where the fish are displayed upon the grass, and does not fail to look carefully at the scales when they are weighed, and has an attentive ear for the comments of admiring spectators. You shall find, moreover, that he is not unwilling to narrate the story of the capture—how the big fish rose short, four times, to four different flies, and finally took a small Black

Dose, and played all over the pool, and ran down a terribly stiff rapid to the next pool below, and sulked for twenty minutes, and had to be stirred up with stones, and made such a long fight that, when he came in at last, the hold of the hook was almost worn through, and it fell out of his mouth as he touched the shore. Listen to this tale as it is told, with endless variations, by every man who has brought home a fine fish, and you will perceive that the fisherman does care for his luck, after all.

And why not? I am no friend to the people who receive the bounties of Providence without visible gratitude. When the sixpence falls into your hat, you may laugh. When the messenger of an unexpected blessing takes you by the hand and lifts you up and bids you walk, you may leap and run and sing for joy, even as the lame man, whom St. Peter healed, skipped piously and rejoiced aloud as he passed through the Beautiful Gate of the Temple. There is no virtue in solemn indifference. Joy is just as much a duty as beneficence is. Thankfulness is the other side of mercy.

When you have good luck in anything, you ought to be glad. Indeed, if you are not glad, you are not really lucky.

But boasting and self-glorification I would have excluded, and most of all from the behavior of the angler. He, more than other men, is dependent for his success upon the favor of an unseen benefactor. Let his skill and industry be never so great, he can do nothing unless *la bonne chance* comes to him.

I was once fishing on a fair little river, the P'tit Saguenay, with two excellent anglers and pleasant companions, H. E. G——and C. S. D——. They had done all that was humanly possible to secure good sport. The stream had been well preserved. They had boxes full of beautiful flies, and casting lines imported from England, and a rod for every fish in the river. But the weather was "dour," and the water "drumly," and every day the lumbermen sent a "drive" of ten thousand spruce logs rushing down the flooded stream. For three days we had not seen a salmon, and on the fourth, despairing, we went down to angle for sea trout in the tide of the greater Saguenay. There, in the salt water, where men say the salmon never take the fly, H. E. G——, fishing with a small trout rod, a poor, short line, and an ancient red ibis of the common kind, rose and hooked a lordly salmon of at least five-and-thirty pounds. Was not this pure luck?

Pride is surely the most unbecoming of all vices in a fisherman. For though intelligence and practice and patience and genius, and many other noble things which modesty forbids him to mention, enter into his pastime, so that it is, as Izaak Walton has firmly maintained, an art; yet, because fortune still plays a controlling hand in the game, its net results should never be spoken of with a haughty and vain spirit. Let not the angler imitate Timoleon, who boasted of his luck and lost it. It is tempting Providence to print the record of your wonderful catches in the sporting newspapers; or at least, if it must be done, there should stand at the head of the column some humble, thankful motto, like *"Non nobis, Domine."* Even Father Izaak, when he has a fish on his line, says, with a due sense of limitations, "There is a trout now, and a good one too, *if I can but hold him!"*

This reminds me that we left H. E. G——, a few sentences back, playing his unexpected salmon, on a trout rod, in the Saguenay. Four times that great fish leaped into the air; twice he suffered the pliant reed to guide him toward the shore, and twice ran out again to deeper water. Then his spirit awoke within him: he bent the rod like a willow wand, dashed toward the middle of the river, broke the line as if it had been pack thread, and sailed triumphantly away to join the white porpoises that were tumbling in the tide. *"Whe-e-ew,"* they said, *"whe-e-ew! psha-a-aw!"* blowing out their breath in long, soft sighs as they rolled about like huge snowballs in the black water. But what did H. E. G——say? He sat him quietly down upon a rock and reeled in the remnant of his line, uttering these remarkable and Christian words: "Those porpoises," said he, "describe the situation rather mildly. But it was good fun while it lasted."

Again I remembered a saying of Walton: "Well, Scholar, you must endure worse luck sometimes, or you will never make a good angler."

Or a good man, either, I am sure. For he who knows only how to enjoy, and not to endure, is ill fitted to go down the stream of life through such a world as this.

I would not have you to suppose, gentle reader, that in discoursing of fisherman's luck I have in mind only those things which may be taken with a hook. It is a parable of human experience. I have been thinking, for instance, of Walton's life as well as of his angling: of the losses and sufferings that he, the firm Royalist, endured when the Commonwealth men came marching into London town; of the consoling days that were granted to him, in troublous times, on the banks of the Lea and the Dove and the New River, and the good friends that he made there, with whom he took sweet counsel in adversity; of the little children who played in his house for a few years, and then were called away into the silent land where he could hear their voices no longer. I was thinking how quietly and peaceably he lived through it all, not complaining nor desponding, but trying to do his work well, whether he was keeping a shop or writing books, and seeking to prove himself an honest man and a cheerful companion, and never scorning to take with a thankful heart such small comforts and recreations as came to him.

It is a plain, homely, old-fashioned meditation, reader, but not unprofitable. When I talk to you of fisherman's luck, I do not forget that there are deeper things behind it. I remember that what we call our fortunes, good or ill, are but the wise dealings and distributions of a Wisdom higher, and a Kindness greater, than our own. And I suppose that their meaning is that we should learn, by all the uncertainties of our life, even the smallest, how to be brave and steady and temperate and hopeful, whatever comes, because we believe that behind it all there lies a purpose of good, and over it all there watches a providence of blessing.

In the school of life many branches of knowledge are taught. But the only philosophy that amounts to anything, after all, is just the secret of making friends with our luck.

The Compleat Angler holds some sort of record for having more editions extant (400 and still counting) than any other work except the Bible. Some would argue that it inspired nearly as many disciples. The source, the wellspring, and fountainhead. The Master.

IZAAK WALTON

The Third Day

PISCATOR. The Trout is a fish highly valued both in this and foreign nations. He may be justly said, as the old poet said of wine, and we English say of venison, to be a generous fish: a fish that is so like the buck that he also has his seasons; for it is observed, that he comes in and goes out of season with the stag and buck. Gesner says his name is of a German offspring, and says he is a fish that feeds clean and purely, in the swiftest streams, and on the hardest gravel; and that he may justly contend with all fresh-water fish, as the Mullet may with all sea-fish, for precedency and daintiness of taste, and that, being in right season, the most dainty palates have allowed precedency to him.

And before I go further in my discourse, let me tell you that you are to observe, that, as there be some barren does, that are good in summer, so there be some barren Trouts that are good in winter; but there are not many that are so, for usually they be in their perfection in the month of May, and decline with the buck. Now you are to take notice, that in several countries, as in Germany and in other parts, compared to ours, fish do differ much in their bigness, and shape, and other ways, and so do Trouts. It is well known that in the Lake Leman, the Lake of Geneva, there are

345

Trouts taken of three cubits long, as is affirmed by Gesner, a writer of good credit; and Mercator says, the Trouts that are taken in the Lake of Geneva are a great part of the merchandise of that famous city. And you are further to know, that there be certain waters that breed Trouts remarkable both for their number and smallness. I know a little brook in Kent that breeds them to a number incredible, and you may take them twenty or forty in an hour, but none greater than about the size of a gudgeon. There are also in divers rivers, especially that relate to, or be near to the sea, as Winchester, or the Thames about Windsor, a little Trout called a Samlet or Skegger-Trout,—in both which places I have caught twenty or forty at a standing,—that will bite as fast and as freely as minnows; these be by some taken to be young Salmons, but in those waters they never grow to be bigger than a herring.

There is also in Kent near to Canterbury a Trout called there a Fordidge Trout, a Trout that bears the name of the town where it is usually caught, that is accounted the rarest of fish; many of them near the bigness of a Salmon, but known by their different color, and in their best season they cut very white, and none of these have been known to be caught with an angle, unless it were one that was caught by Sir George Hastings, an excellent Angler, and now with God; and he hath told me, he thought that Trout bit not for hunger but wantonness; and is the rather to be believed, because both he then, and many others before him, have been curious to search into their bellies, what the food was by which they lived: and have found out nothing by which they might satisfy their curiosity.

Concerning which you are to take notice, that it is reported by good authors, that grasshoppers, and some fish, have no mouths, but are nourished and take breath by the porousness of their gills, man knows not how; and this may be believed, if we consider that, when the Raven hath hatched her eggs, she takes no further care, but leaves her young ones to the care of the God of nature, who is said in the Psalms, (Psalm clxvii. 9,) "to feed the young ravens that call upon him." And they be kept alive, and fed by a dew, or worms that breed in their nests, or some other ways that we mortals know not; and this may be believed of the Fordidge Trout, which, as it is said of the Stork, Jerem. viii. 7, that "he knows his season," so he knows his times, I think almost his day of coming into that river out of the sea; where he lives, and, it is like, feeds, nine months of the year, and fasts three in the river of Fordidge. And you are to note that those townsmen are very punctual in observing the time of beginning to fish for them; and boast much that their river affords a Trout that exceeds all others. And just so does Sussex boast of several fish; as namely, a Shelsey

Cockle, a Chichester Lobster, an Arundel Mullet, and an Amerly Trout.

And now for some confirmation of the Fordidge Trout: you are to know that this Trout is thought to eat nothing in the fresh water; and it may be the better believed, because it is well known that swallows and bats and wagtails, which are called half-year birds, and not seen to fly in England for six months in the year, but about Michaelmas leave us for a hotter climate; yet some of them that have been left behind their fellows have been found, many thousands at a time, in hollow trees, or clay caves, where they have been observed to live and sleep out the whole winter without meat. And so Albertus observes, that there is one kind of frog that hath her mouth naturally shut up about the end of August, and that she lives so all the winter: and though it be strange to some, yet it is known to too many among us to be doubted.

And so much for these Fordidge Trouts, which never afford an Angler sport, but either live their time of being in the fresh water by their meat formerly gotten in the sea, not unlike the swallow or frog, or by the virtue of the fresh water only; or as the Bird of Paradise and the Chameleon are said to live, by the sun and the air.

There is also in Northumberland a Trout called a Bull-Trout, of a much greater length and bigness than any in these southern parts: and there are in many rivers that relate to the sea Salmon-Trouts, as much different from others, both in shape and in their spots, as we see sheep in some countries differ one from another in their shape and bigness, and in the fineness of their wool; and certainly, as some pastures breed larger sheep, so do some rivers, by reason of the ground over which they run, breed larger Trouts.

Now the next thing that I will commend to your consideration is, that the Trout is of a more sudden growth than other fish: concerning which you are also to take notice, that he lives not so long as the Perch and divers other fishes do, as Sir Francis Bacon hath observed in his "History of Life and Death."

And next you are to take notice, that he is not like the Crocodile, which, if he lives never so long, yet always thrives till his death: but 't is not so with the Trout; for after he has come to his full growth, he declines in his body, and keeps his bigness or thrives only in his head, till his death. And you are to know, that he will about, especially before, the time of his spawning, get almost miraculously through weirs and flood-gates against the streams: even through such high and swift places as is almost incredible. Next, that the Trout usually spawns about October or November, but in some rivers a little sooner or later: which is the more observable, because most other fish spawn in the spring or summer, when the sun hath warmed both the earth and water, and made it fit for generation. And you are to note, that he continues many months out of season: for it may be observed of the Trout, that he is like the Buck or the Ox, that will not be fat in many months, though he go in the very same pasture that horses do, which will be fat in one month; and so you may observe, that most other fishes recover strength, and grow sooner fat and in season, than the Trout doth.

And next you are to note, that till the sun gets to such a height as to warm the earth and the water, the Trout is sick, and lean, and lousy, and unwholesome: for you shall in winter find him to have a big head, and then to be lank, and thin, and lean: at which time many of them have sticking on them Sugs, or Trout-lice, which is a kind of a worm, in shape like a clove or pin, with a big head, and sticks close to him and sucks his moisture; those, I think, the Trout breeds himself, and never thrives till he free himself from them, which is when warm weather comes; and then as he grows stronger, he gets from the dead still water into the sharp streams and the gravel, and there rubs off these worms or lice; and then, as he grows stronger, so he gets him into swifter and swifter streams, and there lies at the watch for any fly or minnow that comes near to him: and he especially loves the May-fly, which is bred of the Cod-worm, or Cadis; and these make the Trout bold and lusty, and he is usually fatter and better meat at the end of that month than at any time of the year.

Now you are to know, that it is observed that usually the best Trouts are either red or yellow; though some, as the Fordidge Trout, be white and yet good; but that is not usual: and it is a note observable, that the female Trout hath usually a less head and a deeper body than the male Trout, and is usually the better meat. And note, that a hog-back and a little head, to either Trout, Salmon, or any other fish, is a sign that that fish is in season.

But yet you are to note, that as you see some willows, or palm-trees, bud and blossom sooner than others do, so some Trouts be in rivers sooner in season: and as some hollies or oaks are longer before they cast their leaves, so are some Trouts in rivers longer before they go out of season.

And you are to note, that there are several kinds of Trouts; but these several kinds are not considered but by very few men, for they go under the general name of Trouts: just as Pigeons do in most places; though it is certain there are tame and wild Pigeons: and of the tame, there be Helmits and Runts, and Carriers and Cropers, and indeed too many to name. Nay, the Royal Society have found and published lately, that there be thirty and three kinds of Spiders: and yet all, for aught I know, go under that one general name of Spider. And 't is so with many kinds of fish, and of Trouts especially, which differ in their bigness, and shape, and spots, and color. The great Kentish Hens may be an instance compared to other hens; and doubtless there is a kind of small Trout, which will never thrive to be big, that breeds very many more than others do that be of a larger size: which you may rather believe, if you consider that the little Wren or Titmouse will have twenty young ones at a time, when usually the noble Hawk, or the musical Thrassel or Blackbird, exceed not four or five.

And now you shall see me try my skill to catch a Trout, and at my next walking, either this evening or to-morrow morning, I will give you direction how you yourself shall fish for him.

VENATOR. Trust me, Master, I see now it is a harder matter to catch a Trout than a Chub: for I have put on patience, and followed you these two hours, and not seen a fish stir, neither at your minnow nor your worm.

PISCATOR. Well, Scholar, you must endure worse luck some time, or you will never make a good Angler. But what say you now? there is a Trout now, and a good one too, if I can but hold him, and two or three turns more will tire him. Now you see he lies still, and the sleight is to land him: reach me that landing-net. So, Sir, now he is mine own, what say you now? is not this worth all my labor and your patience?

VENATOR. On my word, Master, this is a gallant Trout; what shall we do with him?

PISCATOR. Marry, e'en eat him to supper: we'll go to my Hostess, from whence we came: she told me, as I was going out of door, that my brother Peter, a good Angler and a cheerful companion, had sent word he would lodge there to-night, and bring a friend with him. My Hostess has two beds, and I know you and I may have the best: we'll rejoice with my brother Peter and his friend, tell tales, or sing ballads, or make a catch, or find some harmless sport to content us, and pass away a little time without offence to God or man.

VENATOR. A match, good Master: let's go to that house, for the linen looks white, and smells of lavender, and I long to lie in a pair of sheets that smell so. Let's be going, good Master, for I am hungry again with fishing.

PISCATOR. Nay, stay a little, good Scholar: I caught my last Trout with a worm; now I will put on a minnow and try a quarter of an hour about yonder trees for another, and so walk towards our lodging. Look you, Scholar, thereabout we shall have a bite presently, or not at all. Have with you, Sir! o' my word, I have hold of him. Oh! it is a great logger-headed Chub; come, hang him upon that willow-twig, and let's be going. But turn out of the way a little, good Scholar, towards yonder high honeysuckle hedge; there we'll sit and sing whilst this shower falls so gently upon the teeming earth, and gives yet a sweeter smell to the lovely flowers that adorn these verdant meadows.

Look, under that broad beech-tree I sat down, when I was last this way a-fishing, and the birds in the adjoining grove seemed to have a friendly contention with an echo, whose dead voice seemed to live in a hollow tree, near to the brow of that primrose hill; there I sat viewing the silver streams glide silently towards their centre, the tempestuous sea; yet sometimes opposed by rugged roots, and pebble-stones, which broke their waves, and turned them into foam: and sometimes I beguiled time by viewing the harmless lambs, some leaping securely in the cool shade, whilst others sported themselves in the cheerful sun; and saw others craving comfort from the swollen udders of their bleating dams. As I thus sat, these and other sights had so fully possessed my soul with content, that I thought, as the poet has happily expressed it,

> I was for that time lifted above earth,
> And possessed joys not promised in my birth.

As I left this place, and entered into the next field, a second pleasure entertained me; 't was a handsome Milkmaid that had not yet attained so much age and wisdom as to load her mind with any fears of many things that will never be, as too many men too often do; but she cast away all care, and sung like a nightingale. Her voice was good, and the ditty fitted for it; 't was that smooth song, which was made by Kit Marlowe, now at least fifty years ago: and the Milkmaid's mother sung an answer to it, which was made by Sir Walter Raleigh in his younger days.

They were old-fashioned poetry, but choicely good, I think much better than the strong lines that are now in fashion in this critical age. Look yonder! on my word, yonder they both be a-milking again. I will give her the Chub, and persuade them to sing those two songs to us.

God speed you, good woman! I have been a-fishing, and am going to Bleak Hall to my bed; and having caught more fish than will sup myself and my friend, I will bestow this upon you and your daughter, for I use to sell none.

MILK-WOMAN. Marry, God requite you! Sir, and we'll eat it cheerfully; and if you come this way a-fishing two months hence, a-grace of God I'll give you a syllabub of new verjuice in a new-made hay-cock for it, and my Maudlin shall sing you one of her best ballads; for she and I both love all Anglers, they be such honest, civil, quiet men. In the mean time will you drink a draught of red cow's milk? you shall have it freely.

PISCATOR. No, I thank you; but I pray do us a courtesy that shall stand you and your daughter in nothing, and yet we will think ourselves still something in your debt: it is but to sing us a song that was sung by your daughter when I last passed over this meadow, about eight or nine days since.

MILK-WOMAN. What song was it, I pray? Was it "Come, Shepherds, deck your heads"? or, "As at noon Dulcina rested"? or "Philida flouts me"? or Chevy Chace? or Johnny Armstrong? or Troy Town?

PISCATOR. No, it is none of those: it is a song that your daughter sung the first part, and you sung the answer to it.

MILK-WOMAN. O, I know it now; I learned the first part in my golden age, when I was about the age of my poor daughter; and the latter part, which indeed fits me best now, but two or three years ago, when the cares of the world began to take hold of me: but you shall, God willing, hear them both, and sung as well as we can, for we both love Anglers. Come, Maudlin, sing the first part to the gentlemen with a merry heart, and I'll sing the second, when you have done.

THE MILK-MAID'S SONG

Come, live with me, and be my love,
And we will all the pleasure prove
That valleys, groves, or hills, or field,
Or woods and steepy mountains yield,—

Where we will sit upon the rocks,
And see the shepherds feed our flocks,
By shallow rivers, to whose falls
Melodious birds sing madrigals.

And I will make thee beds of roses,
And then a thousand fragrant posies;
A cap of flowers, and a kirtle
Embroidered all with leaves of myrtle,

A gown made of the finest wool,
Which from our pretty lambs we pull;
Slippers lined choicely for the cold,
With buckles of the purest gold;

A belt of straw, and ivy-buds,
With coral clasps and amber studs;—
And if these pleasures may thee move,
Come, live with me, and be my love.

Thy silver dishes for thy meat,
As precious as the Gods do eat,

Shall on an ivory table be
Prepared each day for thee and me.

The shepherd swains shall dance and sing
For they delight each May morning:
If these delights thy mind may move,
Then live with me, and be my love.

VENATOR. Trust me, Master, it is a choice song, and sweetly sung by honest
Maudlin. I now see it was not without cause that our good Queen Elizabeth
did so often wish herself a Milkmaid all the month of May, because they
are not troubled with fears and cares, but sing sweetly all the day, and
sleep securely all the night: and, without doubt, honest, innocent, pretty
Maudlin does so. I'll bestow Sir Thomas Overbury's Milkmaid's wish upon
her,—"that she may die in the Spring; and, being dead, may have good
store of flowers stuck round about her winding-sheet."

THE MILK-MAID'S MOTHER'S ANSWER

If all the world and love were young,
And truth in every shepherd's tongue,
These pretty pleasures might me move
To live with thee, and be thy love.

But time drives flocks from field to fold:
When rivers rage, and rocks grow cold,
Then Philomel becometh dumb,
And age complains of cares to come.

The flowers do fade, and wanton fields
To wayward Winter reckoning yields:
A honey tongue, a heart of gall,
Is fancy's spring, but sorrow's fall.

Thy gowns, thy shoes, thy beds of roses,
Thy cap, thy kirtle, and thy posies,
Soon break, soon wither, soon forgotten;
In folly ripe, in reason rotten.

Thy belt of straw, and ivy-buds,
Thy coral clasps and amber studs,
All these in me no means can move
To come to thee, and be thy Love.

What should we talk of dainties then,
Of better meat than's fit for men?
These are but vain: that's only good
Which God hath blest, and sent for food.

But could youth last, and love still breed,
Had joys no date, nor age no need,—
Then those delights my mind might move,
To live with thee, and be thy love.

MOTHER. Well, I have done my song. But stay, honest Anglers, for I will make
Maudlin to sing you one short song more. Maudlin, sing that song that
you sung last night, when young Coridon the Shepherd played so purely
on his oaten pipe to you and your Cousin Retty.

MAUD. I will, Mother.

I married a wife of late,
The more's my unhappy fate:
I married her for love,
As my fancy did me move,
And not for a worldly estate:

But oh! the green-sickness
Soon changed her likeness,
And all her beauty did fail.
But 't is not so
With those that go,
Through frost and snow,
As all men know,
And carry the milking-pail.

PISCATOR. Well sung! Good woman, I thank you. I'll give you another dish of
fish one of these days; and then beg another song of you. Come, Scholar,
let Maudlin alone: do not you offer to spoil her voice. Look! yonder comes
mine Hostess, to call us to supper. How now! is my brother Peter come?

HOSTESS. Yes, and a friend with him; they are both glad to hear that you are
in these parts, and long to see you, and long to be at supper, for they be
very hungry.

Fishing now and then, fishing then and now. Waterman completes a cycle he began fifty years ago in the Ozarks. And if his reel's backing line is wound with the strings of his heart, it's because he's prepared for a long tug.

CHARLES WATERMAN

Ozarks and Time Passing

The two men didn't talk very much and every day they built another johnboat and painted it dark red like an Ozark barn. When the paint had dried they put a chain on the bow of each and slid it into the James River at Galena, Missouri. The planks soon swelled tight and the boat was ready to run the river and come back on a flatcar.

There were green johnboats, too, but the first ones I saw were barn red, and I assumed that was the true johnboat color. It was more than fifty years ago, and the origin of the boat's name was already forgotten. I asked an Ozark kid of my own age why they called them johnboats, and he said he wasn't sure but he had an uncle named John and maybe that was the reason. I doubt it.

Those flatboats were pretty simple. There was no raised transom for an outboard motor in those days, nor any oarlocks; just a board seat in the stern for a paddler and another in the bow, more to hold the boat together than to sit on, I suppose. They nested together pretty well, piled on flatcars and then on trucks in later years.

They still make johnboats in the hills, but nowadays they're mostly aluminum and fiber glass, and factories smelling of resin and paint turn out glossy bass boats that run fifty miles an hour. They would have been apparitions on the old James River. The new bass boats flash across the big impoundments and study the bottoms with clicking, whirring things—they show the old and silent riverbeds where the johnboats slipped along half a century ago. The big lakes are lined with resorts and homes today; but then, except for the occasional town, there were only a few houses along the old rivers, most of them presiding over little rocky hill farms.

The first of the White River dams I saw was the Taneycomo at Forsyth, downstream from Branson, and even fifty years ago there were resorts there. Tour boats would show you the lake, with everything named after characters from Harold Bell Wright's *Shepherd of the Hills*, which had its setting there. Now there's a Dogpatch, U.S.A., a little farther south in Arkansas, with characters from much later literature.

The big johnboats were sluggish under homemade paddles of the mountain men who guided them down the smallmouth rivers for a day, a week or even more at a time, but they rode the rapids softly, taking the steep waves below the "shoals" in measured thumps. There were two casters to a boat, seated on folding canvas chairs, and the guide on his burlap cushion of spare clothing, with room even for a modest sideswipe with a short rod.

A few of the guides fished themselves, and their choice of stubby tubular-steel bait-casting rods—sometimes less than three feet long—evidently began with the convenience of laying the weapon aside quickly when the paddle needed attention. Sportsmen in khaki might use split bamboo, but a hill-country guide in bib overalls and felt hat used short tubular steel, and so did kids who mimicked him. "Takapart" found its way into the names of some of the reels to emphasize their simplicity, and well into the thirties many did not have level wind. I recall admiring the Meisselbach Takapart, but my own reel was a Shakespeare Precision. Braided silk was the plugging line of vacationing float clients—smooth-casting but needing to be dried after use. The guides and I used crochet thread, which seemed to work about as well and cost much less.

There was no doubt about the favorite bait-casting lure along the James and White rivers. For years it was the Peck's feather minnow, referred to simply as Black Peck or Yellow Peck. It had a spinner in front of a weighted head and a long feather body, often with a pork rind attached to the single big hook, or the occasional trailer hook.

I still have an old Tom Thumb casting plug, a fast-wiggling little diver with metal "lips" both front and rear, and when I first began fishing on James River, it was second to the Peck's in popularity. The fly-fishermen used the Callmac bass bug, the Tuttle's devil bug, Tuttle's mouse and feather minnows like the Wilder-Dilg.

News traveled fast among river fishermen, even if its interpretation was questionable. One evening, two float boats came downstream to Galena, both with heavy strings of smallmouths, one of them a four-pounder, and all but that one fish were caught on the Yellow Peck. The big one was caught on a Black Peck and the general store at Galena sold out of Black Pecks the next morning. Those river smallmouths run bigger in memory than in fact, and I am surprised that the yellowed snapshots show them so small.

I was not an Ozark boy. I was raised on a flatland farm in southeastern Kansas almost 100 miles away, but an unreasoning passion for the river began during a family vacation there, with the Model T Ford and white canvas tent, sightseeing in the "mountains."

I was less than ten years old, but I had a craze for fishing, not just a healthy love for the outdoors but an obsession that has lasted until after I should have grown up and accepted more productive pursuits. My father did not fish, but tolerated my weakness regretfully, and was ashamed that I would somehow get back to the James River during much of school vacation when I should have been helping with the farm work. I was ashamed, too, but I must use the word "obsession" again. I slept on the riverbank and cooked poorly balanced meals over an old stump soaked in kerosene.

I have taken very few real river floats with guides, but I soaked up the river scene and fished mostly alone, wading in overalls and casting the Peck and the Tom Thumb, or struggling for half a day upstream with a johnboat to enjoy an hour of bliss floating downstream like the vacationing businessmen. I would cast frantically as I drifted, reeling too fast most of the time so that no inch of water would be wasted. That was in the late twenties, and it wasn't until the thirties that I used a fly rod much.

All of the smallmouth rivers were fickle. In spring, when most of the heavy rains had finished and the water, still cool, began to clear, there would be times of excellent fishing. Low, warm water could turn the fishing poor in midsummer, and guides would paddle continually in the slow stretches, and would often have to drag and shove the loaded johnboats over the gravel bars. With fall came the reddened oaks, flocks of ducks that flared over a float boat as they came upon it suddenly in a river bend, and energetic bronzebacks with enmity for Pecks and Tom Thumbs.

The smallmouths were black bass, and the largemouths caught in sloughs off James River and in the slower, wider parts of White River below, where the James emptied in, were called linesides. The occasional walleyes were jack salmon and the rock bass were goggle-eye. Many years later when I returned to the rivers I found the smallmouths called brownies.

* * *

Once, as a reward for some now forgotten high school triumph, my father paid for a full day's float with a guide, downstream from Galena, and went along to watch, not knowing that I had become a better caster than most guides. I'd worked at it harder and longer.

I had not slept the night before and was suffering nerve-racking anticipation. When the boat actually began to slide downstream and plopped over the steep "shoal" with the big boulder just below Galena, I somehow managed to produce a mammoth backlash, a supertangle I can still see, and prodded it helplessly with quivering fingers while the guide threw his lure over shadowy chunk rock and against willowed banks. I had no spare reel and I heard the guide land two fish and remark condescendingly that I could use his outfit, while my father asked if he could help me. It was a long time before I untangled the mess, my parent's worried sympathy hanging over me like a rain cloud, and it now seems incredible that such a little mishap could be so important. All that expensive fishing time lost was catastrophic, and when I finally straightened in my canvas chair the sweat of humiliation ran down my neck— but it was then I saw the muddy creek pouring in from the right. It had rained the night before somewhere back in those hills, and the creek water boiled into the James River, leaving a sharp line where it met the clear river current and turned downstream.

For some reason I had neither a Peck nor a Tom Thumb on my line— but whatever the forgotten reason, the choice of a jointed Pikie minnow had been made with deliberation. I threw it at the juncture of bright river and muddy creek, and the big smallmouth came storming up and took it crosswise in his jaws, lunged in a half jump and went down in clear water where I could see his gyrations, a blur of twisting fish and flashing plug, distorted by curling currents. When he was in the boat my confidence came back.

And then I could do no wrong, the plug breaking the little eddies above the shoreline rocks and against the drowned willows, the gentle bulges over the upthrust boulders and the foamy vees of undecided water at the edge of the rapids. The burnished fish came out from underwater shadows in quick streaks, sometimes in twos and threes. They sometimes turned about the plugs before they struck. I remember them much larger than they must have been.

"He casts just as good as I do," the guide said, and then admitted he had been keeping score.

Then, "He puts it up there against the bank better than I do," he conceded, and although the guide was a mediocre caster, I can recall no greater angling triumph. It is true that he used the paddle a bit, but the day's score was so one-sided, I'm sure I would have caught more fish, even if he had cast full-time. And my father, who had suffered through my fishing addiction, could see I had at least become reasonably proficient at a game the niceties of which had never before occurred to him.

But when the day of glory had ended and I was back splashing the side channels and tugging on waterlogged johnboats, priding myself in my casting of three-eighths-ounce lures, I met a wading hill-country boy with a great string of smallmouth bass he had caught on a gigantic Dowagiac torpedo plug with five big trebles and two spinners and twenty-five-pound line on his Montgomery Ward reel. I doubt if I ever equaled that catch.

It was the long float trips that made the Ozark rivers famous, the parties made up of several fishermen. There might be a commissary boat as well, to carry the camping gear and cook, going mushily with little freeboard. The man with the commissary rig would paddle on through and set up camp on a high bar, ready for the guests' comfort when they arrived in late afternoon—a procedure that was still followed much later when most of the fish to be caught might be rainbow trout. For the charm of floating remains in the hill country, changed though it may be by engulfing progress, the rivers shortened by great impoundments painted like blue dragons on Missouri and Arkansas maps.

But in those days of fifty years ago there was instant wilderness when the boat rounded the first bend. The home landing was probably a little town, mostly unpainted, but with a false-fronted store or two and a neat church, the streets of gravel and generally tilted. And if the float began in early morning, there would probably be mist on the river, so that a cat-fisherman running his trotline or limb lines might seem suspended in dark silhouette as the boats went by. Some said the fishing wasn't good until the mist cleared, but it wasn't always true.

Later generations of float fishermen would frequently see whitetail deer at the water's edge, but when I first went to the rivers there were few deer in the hills, and I never saw one on James or White River then. There were nesting ducks in spring, gray squirrels in the oaks, and barred owls to startle a kid under a tarpaulin at night. Always there was the wood smoke as there is today, sometimes in faint blue wraiths through the valleys.

Although their presence was not obvious to a man engrossed in casting a plug or fly-rod streamer, the hill folk lived near the rivers, if not on their banks, and the rocky roads strayed from cabin to cabin. Here and there would be a steep trail coming down to the river and probably some kind of boat, often a sort of caricature of a johnboat. At evening there might be the sound of an axe in some unseen clearing and, inevitably, the call of a hound. Later, the tired fisherman in his blankets might hear the rising and falling tones of a distant coon pack, crossing ridge and hollow, and the next thing he sensed would be wood smoke, coffee and bacon, with the mist on the river not yet burned through by the sun.

Float fishing became big business and some of the companies were famous. Perhaps the best known of all was the Jim Owen outfit at Branson, and I sent Jim Owen the first angling telegram I ever wrote—carefully counted words to learn how the fishing was—and I can quote his answer:

> RIVER HIGH BUT CATCHING SOME FISH.
> —JIM OWEN.

Almost everyone tries to go back and no one will admit that things are better, for always something has been lost. I fished Lake of the Ozarks when it was new, and after I had caught some largemouth bass, a smallmouth took the popping bug against the shoreline and went deep, then to be netted by a St. Louis surgeon named Tremaine who could cast and paddle a canoe with hardly a pause at either.

A world war later I went back to Galena after many of the dams were built, and I could not find the place where I camped below town, near Mighty Barnes's service station. I was not sure of the spot where Charley Barnes, the famous guide, let me help him with a trotline.

Then, when most of the familiar rivers down in Arkansas had been backed up, I floated the Ouachita and the Buffalo for bass. I caught trout below a dam or two, but I always felt hill rivers should have smallmouths instead. Then, the last time I returned, I tried to get back the whole thing.

It was one of only a few uncrowded smallmouth stretches left, and I would do it in the grand manner, I decided. There was no big boat company there, but I found a man with a johnboat, even if it was made of plywood and smaller than the old ones, and I found a guide who had been very drunk for several days. I wondered if he could paddle all day, but he did, while I waved a fly rod from dawn until dark. I caught some bass and a great many sunfish, and I don't know if the fish were as big as those of my youth or not. That night the man who owned the johnboat picked us up in a shiny truck, but somehow I guess I had expected a snorting old Model T, or even a mule with a flatcar. I was very tired, and it struck me like a blow that I was fifty years old—and even that was quite a few years ago.

Of course, there are float trips today and perhaps they are better, for the equipment is, and those who float on their own are partial to canoes. And since most of the bass rivers have been swollen into reservoirs, I am sure there are more bass than there ever were when I cooked over the old stump. Many of the old cabins with rough stone fireplaces are long drowned, along with the rocky roads that led to them, and the people who build homes along the lake shores wouldn't have room for their bass boats on a mumbling little river.

And of course there were not enough bass for the thousands of later vacationers. Perhaps it was best to leave only some token stretches for the folks with canoes. I don't know if I'll go back or not.

Burke's Steerage. The title of this guide to British social order is enough of a clue to the author's point of view. In this excerpt, Arthurian scholar and master falconer T. H. White demonstrates his ability to cast barbs with wicked accuracy.

T. H. WHITE

Fishing

There are four main types of salmon river in these islands: *The Financier's*, or water of which half a dozen inferior pools were withdrawn at £50,000 at the last sale but two—the sales are pretty frequent because the financiers keep getting put in prison; *The Laird's of That Ilk*, or water of unknown value because it has never passed out of the possession of The Ilk, and probably never been fished by them; *The Hotel*, or water of known inferiority, which is fruitlessly flogged by such members of the rising bourgeoisie who cannot get their noses in anywhere else; and *Worm Water*, which is patronized by a solitary solicitor of great age who caught a salmon there in 1881 while fishing for trout and has since been back every year (the fishing is free) with a bouquet of worms threaded on enormous hooks. All these waters can be defined within a single *pensée*, which occurred to us while fishing a heavy spate, in a snowstorm, in February, before the fish had run up: "If you are a millionaire, you can afford to own a catch which is full of salmon, in which case, why trouble to catch them? If you are not a millionaire, you cannot afford to own a catch which has any salmon in it at all, in which case why trouble to catch them?"

The Financier's water is situated in El Dorado, and any one financier may during a good season kill five hundred fish of which those below twenty pounds

361

are called small and those above thirty, large. As his rental will be in the neighbourhood of £2,500 per annum, these fish will have cost him £5 apiece, a figure that is considerably above their market value, but not so much so as is the case with the pheasant, which will be dealt with in a later section. Uneconomic as is the prospect, exclusive of rates, it is found that financiers are not deterred by it. They have been so economic all their lives that now, sitting back to enjoy the fruits of their various bankruptcies after fifty years, they are only too glad of a little change. They are rowed about the water in brightly painted boats by indignant Scotsmen (to whom they are very rude, as is fitting with servants), and as they dabble their gaily-feathered hooks in the murmuring waters, so do the flotillas of enormous fish fight it out among themselves which shall have the first bite.

The Laird of the Ilk owns water on one of the smaller though excellent Scottish streams, say the Deveron or the Awe. But he is ninety-seven years of age and lives at Monte Carlo, having since the early years of last century been quite sick of the Ilk and interested in practically nothing but steam trams. His water is fished (a) by a friend of a nephew of his great-grandson, to whom he occasionally gives a grudging permission for the snow water in February; (b) by a ghillie who goes down once a week with a hand line and kills three fish in ten minutes for the Laird's table; (c) by a certain Major Green, who, since 1903, has been under the misapprehension that this water belongs to him, owing to a conversation he then had with the McInvert of McInvert's keeper. The McInvert, who also lives in Monte Carlo and collects seashells, has let a totally different stretch of water to the Major. This water is situated upon the other coast of Scotland, and is fished by the editor of *Rivers in Britain*, who discovered it accidentally during one of his tours in 1908, and has since had the sense to keep it dark. Major Green, the ghillie, and the friend of the nephew of the great-grandson often clash over their fishing rights, but as they all feel that there is something wrong somewhere, they prefer to leave it at that.

Hotel Water is perfectly uneconomic for all concerned, except the landlord who lets it. The stretches on either side of it hold some good pools that either command a high rental or are reserved because of their goodness for the land-lord's own recreation. The Hotel Water, which lies between these stretches, has been cursed with some sort of blight and recognized for the last fifty years as hopeless. It is therefore let to a hotelkeeper, at a rental exaggerated by the high prices on either side, on the grounds that it can be of no use to any one else. The hotelkeeper, in his turn, vainly attempts to win back his outlay by charging half a dozen retired business men 5 guineas a week each, plus 8/6 a day ghillie, plus 15/- a day salmon fishing, plus £1 a fish. The latter fee is rarely earned, but the hotelier just manages to keep his head above water by catering for the summer tourists who are making in their thousands for the Pass of Glencoe, and they do not care a fig about fishing, anyway.

Worm Water is a subject we would commend to the attention of the Amateur Gentleman. It is a matter for melancholy reflection that less than a hundred years ago all salmon fishing was virtually free, while in earlier times the self-respecting retainers of noble northern families would stipulate in their contracts of service that they were not to be given salmon for dinner more than twice a week. But that self-satisfied and cruel old humbug Izaak Walton, with his crucifixion of frogs and his eternal condescension from Piscator to Venator, somehow succeeded in fixing the attention of the upper classes upon fish—presumably as a means of humiliating each other far more brutally and improbably than Holmes ever humiliated Watson, if the *Compleat Angler* is anything to go by—and free water gradually began to go out of circulation. A few moments' conversation with any ghillie past middle age will show us that even within his own memory the rent of a given piece of water has risen by thousands per centum. This rise has taken place in all waters where the salmon has been found to be susceptible of temptation with the sunken fly—the method of temptation still the most common and, until 1903, the one invariably pursued. Since 1903, however, a new means of duping the Salmonidæ has been discovered: the method of greased-line fishing with a lightly-dressed fly, which, although valuable at all seasons of the year provided that the air is warmer than the water, is particularly suitable for low summer water. It was the low summer water that had been regarded, until 1903, as totally unsuitable for the accepted practice of the sunken fly and that, under the scornful reputation of being possible only with the worm, has therefore remained at a low rental and sometimes even at none at all. Here the solicitor of 1881 caught a salmon when trout fishing with the dry fly (i.e., when using the greased line method by mistake, before Mr. Hills had time to invent it), and here he has since frequented with his worming tackle, catching two or three free salmon every year because the stretch has possessed the reputation of being impossible among orthodox anglers. His main terror during all these years has, of course, been that some interfering young gentleman should come along and kill a salmon on the fly; thus giving the place a correct fishing reputation, causing the impoverished little hotel that owns it to make a charge for the fishing, and quite spoiling his happy preserve by throwing it into the thousand-per-centum market of orthodox rivers. The hotel is on the upper reaches of the river, holds no fish in the spring, and possesses at present only the solicitor's summer season.

We make these revelations only because we are particularly fond of the reader, but we do suggest that an observant Amateur Gentleman who can master the greased line can still with luck congratulate himself upon not having been born too late to get his hook into a salmon at reasonable cost. He has been born too late to catch the sunk fly bus, but still not quite too late for the greased line in Worm Water. We have ourselves ousted the solicitor (who committed suicide), but we do not feel that we know the reader quite well enough to tell him the exact locality of this particular grave.

If the Amateur Gentleman possesses a great deal of money he can immediately purchase a good salmon river, and two or three ghillies with their wives and dependents will naturally be included in the deal. In this case he will automatically become a Professional Gentleman (since the local master of hounds will need his subscription) and, the ghillies being perfectly able to hook, gaff, or indeed play his fish for him, he will no longer stand in need of the services offered by this invaluable little book. So our public must be assumed not to be in possession of a great deal of money.

The average day for such a public, which is probably too poor to belong to a good syndicate, even, must consist, if we leave out the deep and beautiful mystery of Worm Water, of one out of two alternatives: either the Amateur Gentleman must borrow a first-class river in February from some rich acquaintance who knows there are no fish in it during that month, or he must discover a good salmon fishing hotel. He should, if a reasonably heavy drinker, be prepared to pay about fifteen guineas a week at one of these resorts, inclusive of fishing, ghillie, bed, board, and drink. The hotel will list its prices somewhat lower than his, but that is what they are likely to average out at when the bill comes round. It is at such an hotel that we shall be most helpful in spending our average day. A description of the alternative average, on the rich February river with no fish in it, would become monotonous. It snows all the time in the latter case, and all you have to do is to provide yourself with eleven empty bottles of whiskey and one full, together with a good supply of celluloid chicken rings. The empty bottles are attached one by one to the spinning line, by means of the chicken rings, and floated off in the vain effort to salvage snagged minnows. By the time you have lost eleven traces and a few score yards of line, you will have finished the contents of the twelfth bottle, and it is then advisable to go home.

The average day on hotel water at its best time (say May) begins at half-past eight, when the Amateur Gentleman springs out of bed, full of optimism, determination, and constipation. He hurries downstairs, almost unshaven, and hastily gobbles (but does not digest) a few mouthfuls of the excellent breakfast served by this hotel. The hotel serves this breakfast as a conscience offering, for it knows that no luncheon except sandwiches is included in its five guineas a week. In the course of the fevered meal the Amateur Gentleman calls confusedly between mouthfuls for tepid water in a saucer (to soak his casts in), for his waders, his line drier, and various other oddments, which occur to his maddened brain as being of cosmic importance. He winds his line from the drier to the reel with one hand and feeds himself with alternate mouthfuls of porridge and gut cast with the other. All things having reached a kind of conclusion, and none having reached a complete one, he throws down his spoon and rushes out into the passage, under the stuffed salmon of thirty-eight pounds, to pull on his waders. This done, he infuriates the lady of the house by bursting into the kitchen to claim his luncheon basket, not yet ready, and assembles all his gear in a pile on the front doorstep, so as to be ready for the car and the ghillies the moment they arrive. At this instant an elderly angler who is to share the car with him and to exchange beats in the afternoon comes slowly down the stairs to begin his breakfast.

The Amateur Gentleman may now sit down under the stuffed salmon for forty minutes or so, and he may pass his time in reflecting upon the following problems:

1. Do salmon take at any particular time of day?
2. If so, is this time (a) merely any time when you are not there, or (b) a particular time when you are not there?
3. For instance, do they perhaps take before breakfast and after dinner?
4. Would it be wise to warn the proprietor of this possibility and to arrange to fish from 6 A.M. to 11 P.M., or to sleep out on the bank?

The answer to all these questions is "No." The proprietor knows, and the aged angler now enjoying his breakfast knows, that not only do salmon not take before breakfast, but that they rarely if ever take at all. This is why the car and ghillies are not ready, for the proprietor supposes and the aged angler recognizes as a fact that the famished fisherman will suffer more than the fed one in the almost certain event that neither of them sees a fish.

These matters having been satisfactorily pondered, the car and ghillies will arrive, and your doddering partner will come out of the breakfast room wiping his moustache. Harrying everybody about in all directions, you will bundle the party into the motor, choose the nearer of the two beats, and arrange to be dropped at the nearest pool of this beat while the car goes on to drop your companion at the farthest pool of the farthest beat. By this means you hope to start fishing about twenty minutes before he does. You jump out of the car as it comes to a standstill, dig out your rod and tackle with trembling fingers, and practically run down to the river, urging a reluctant Highlander before you. It is at this moment, just as the car is disappearing up the glen, that you will remember your reel, which was left on the breakfast table. Sit down then, for the car will not be back for half an hour, and get the ghillie to tell you a few Highland legends. He probably knows none either.

If we were a truthful sporting writer we could end this description here, merely adding that from now onward (as soon as the car has been back for the reel) you will continue to splash your line in the water and to disentangle your hook from trees, until it is time to go home. But we intend to give full value for money, and, since such things have been known to occur, you shall have a fish.

It is important to keep on good terms with the ghillie, and to remember that he has probably fished this water since before you were born. A good way of winning the affection and cooperation of a ghillie is to ask him to bring his rod and to fish down the water after you. Such a course of action will at the same time deliver you from the great vice of ghillies—supposed by many gentlemen to be a virtue—which is, the habit of tying on your flies. By all means learn knots from ghillies, and get them to show you how to tie them, but do the actual job yourself. Then, if anything does go wrong, you will know who is to blame, and be spared much useless regret and indignation. The truest word ever spoken about this clumsy world was: if you want to do anything well, do it yourself. But in order to be allowed to do it yourself, you will probably have to interest the ghillie in his own fishing.

The ghillie leads you to the top of the pool, looks dubiously at a rock, a rabbit hole and a tree stump, and demands your fly box. He opens this with exaggerated precaution (who knows but what the latest gadget perfected for these expensive southron gentry may not contain a jack-in-the-box?) and peers inside it with still greater dubiety. Finally he shuts the box, which contains two dozen assorted lures at three shillings each, and withdraws one of the two rusty hooks, each adorned with half a moth-eaten feather, which ornament his own hat. Do not attempt to prevent him from making this first attachment, but go down with it to the riverbank at the point he indicates, and begin to throw it sheepishly in. If you are not an expert caster, do not pretend to be one, nor produce any excuses, such as a new rod, out of practice, veering wind, et cetera. Remember that you are being watched by a past master in this lovely art, and ask for advice if necessary.

You have fished half the pool now, paying particular attention, as the ghillie directed you, to that smooth wet rock one-third of the way down. The wind has been blowing diagonally upstream and only one cast in three has truly reached its approximate destination, but apart from this, and apart from the feeling that you can't cast as far as you would like, and apart from the knot that has somehow tied itself in your gut cast and the bother that was caused when you got caught up in the ash tree, you feel that you have covered the water reasonably well, particularly that bit above the smooth rock. The gentle splash and subdued commotion you now hear is the ghillie, who has hooked a fish behind you, just at that rock.

He is calling you now to come and run the fish. If your self-respect is of Homeric proportions, you will tell him that since he has hooked it he had better run it himself. If you are a humble man, you will accept his offer (which he will make easier for you by looking very cross at your preliminary hesitation) because even running a fish will give you a chance to learn something. He hands you the rod with only a gentle bend in it, holding it with one hand by the butt and putting no check on the reel except the mechanical one that is already there. You seize the rod, take hold of the handle of the reel, wind in a few turns and bend the rod double. "Too hard," says the ghillie. The fish shows for a moment near the surface, his great silver side looking rusty in the water, wallows another moment, and the fly, coming away, whistles past your ear to land on the bank behind you.

Amateur Gentleman, do not cry or curse. Reflect upon this misadventure with a mind that desires to better itself. The ghillie, who is an angler of the old school, said that you were too hard on the fish. But it was he who hooked it, and upon him rests the responsibility of the hold. For you can be too hard on a fish at the moment of hooking him, but you cannot be too hard afterward— short of breaking your tackle. It stands to reason. A hold that is going to give will give. Ten minutes of fierce strain will not be any more likely to lose it than half an hour of light pressure: indeed, it will be less likely to lose it, just as you will be less likely to pull a nail out of a wall with one strong pull than with very many little wriggles. The fact that spring salmon have light mouths, a fact that will be advanced by the ghillie, has nothing to do with it. Once the hold is established, hard treatment is no more dangerous than light: it was the ghillie who established this hold, and you have no cause to reproach yourself.

But you will reproach yourself.

You will feel that you are a fool and a rogue to have missed the fish in the first place, letting the ghillie hook it behind you—more than 50 percent of this was pure chance—that you are a scoundrel and an imbecile to have lost the glorious creature which he obtained. Barratry, simony, arson, matricide, and every other tort, these you will consider to be your bedfellows, shame and remorse your only portion for the few remaining years of a disgraced and decrepit existence.

The next pool is Black Murdoch, a long broad elbow of water with the main current on the other side. There it has cut a small precipice out of the bank, while on your side the shingle slopes into the stream with a more gentle graduation down which it is necessary to wade. Black Murdoch means deep wading, and you look piteously at the ghillie because it seems quite impossible to fish it. The ghillie points sternly forward, indicating a position that will place a hawthorn tree exactly behind you, just within reach of your back cast, while the elbow of Black Murdoch is exactly in front of you, just out of reach of your forward cast. There is nothing for it but to wade in as far as possible without total immersion, pay out line, and do your best to reach the main current on the opposite side. If you ever had any ability to cast in the first place, it will vanish when you discover that a continuation of your previous action now means dipping your elbows and forearms into the water twice at each cast, while the force of the water against the submerged part of your body is such that any movement whatever is fraught with extreme peril. Go on, however, and splash about as best you may.

While you are sporting in the whirlpool, frozen between fury and tears in your ability to make more than one true cast out of six, the ghillie will sit down on the bank and go to sleep. He does this because after the briefest inspection he has realized that it will be politer not to watch you. If he did watch you, you would be paralyzed by the suspicion that he was finding you amusing; but now that he does not watch you, you are infuriated by the suspicion that he finds you boring. You are just casting a malevolent glance at him over your shoulder, a glance in which indignation at being made to fish an apparently impossible distance, shame at being unable to fish that distance, and reproach for his seemingly callous indifference are striving for mastery, when you hear a splashing noise at the other side of Black Murdoch. Your last cast went astray and you are quite out of touch with your fly, which is, as far as you know, lying tangled in the slack at the edge of the current about fifty yards away. This is the reason why you have, as a matter of fact, hooked a beautiful fish, which is making the splashing noise you noticed, and, since you are a beginner, it is almost certain to be a forty-pounder. You may now tighten up on our fish and retreat backward out of the water, in the perfect certainty that the hold is good. You were not in contact with your fly and had no opportunity of striking. The current did all this for you, drawing the hook backward into the corner of his jaw as he turned away, before you noticed anything, and he is firmly held. Come out as quickly as possible, hoping that the ghillie really was not looking after all.

It turns out that the fish is of at least thirty pounds, and you, after your experience of losing the last fish apparently through violent methods, will submit to every suggestion made by the ghillie. He for his part takes your hand right off the handle of the reel while the fish makes his first rush. He reiterates that if "He" wants to go you must let "Him" go, and that this will tire "Him" out. It does nothing of the sort, however, for this fresh and powerful fish merely takes advantage of the current, leaning against it on the other side just sufficiently to balance the timorous pull, which has been dictated to you by your mentor. Two hours later, with arms feeling like those of that gentleman in the Bible who had to hold them up in the air while a battle was going on, you will be compelled, and the ghillie will inconsistently exhort you, to resort to the violent methods that you might as well have adopted in the first instance; and you will drag the fish into shallow water by main force. There the ghillie will pierce it with his meat hook, heave it ashore, and bash it on the head. By that time you will have visited about three pools, walked several miles, seen your line five times down to the dangerous end of the backing, quarrelled twice with the ghillie, and experienced all the limits of human passion. You may well stand trembling beside that glorious junket-white belly, from which the golden oil of health is oozing, and quaff a hero's dram.

Elated with this success—it is evidently a taking day—you hurry off to Gowrie's Pot, as soon as proper respect has been paid to the dead monster, in the certainty that you are going to find a fish there too. Nor is your certainty ill-founded. Gowrie's Pot has the current on your side of the river and thus seems much easier to fish. You need cast only about fifteen yards, obliquely downstream, and the current immediately straightens out even the most amateur throw. Pleased with this, you cast about twenty-five yards, and this means that you are fishing almost directly downstream. The fish is there, just as you thought, and comes at you from below. You are in contact with your fly and haul back at him (or "strike") just as he begins his haul at you. "Got you, you beggar!" But the ghillie, who was standing high up on the bank, is running down to you exclaiming, "Too hard! Too hard!" just as he did before. The words are scarcely out of his mouth before the hook is out of the fish's, and here you are again with the fly lying on the bank at your feet.

This time the ghillie was right. The fish, coming from below you, took your hook in the hardest part of his mouth, the front of it, and you have simply pulled the hook away from him. It slipped out between hard palate and hard dentary. If you had possessed the self-control to *pay out* line when you felt him below you, you *might* have hooked him in the corner of the mouth, just as you hooked the fish you never had a chance to strike at in Black Murdoch.

There. We fancy that we have given you a run for your money, and now it is time to go back to your hotel. Here comes the aged angler in the motor car that is to take you home, and if we know anything about it he has got a bigger fish than you have or more of them. So don't hold up your trophy in triumph, the moment he comes into sight, or you will give him the opportunity of displaying his own superiority by means of affected humility. Go home quietly instead, and send off the fish by the earliest train, to the most influential person that you know.

To analyze competitions, you don't have to dissect a single fishing tournament. The shrewd critic lets them compare themselves. Conservation writer Edward (Ted) Williams remains disturbed by what he observed.

TED WILLIAMS

Fishing to Win

I object to fishing tournaments less for what they do to fish than what they do to fishermen. They have invaded one of the last refuges of civilized man, transmuted a noble art into something it isn't and shouldn't be, and fouled our perception of wild, lovely life forms. I would not argue that fish tourneys should be banned, even if there were a possibility of this, just that they be recognized for what they are—distractions from what's truly important.

In all my research for *Audubon* nothing that I read, heard, or saw taught me more about fishing tournaments than competing in the Bass Masters Classic as a "press angler." The stakes were $500 a day (which is a lot for most freelance writers who specialize in subjects other than sex). If the pro you shared the boat with had any reservations about an amateur's tagging along, they were eased by the organizer's promise to "dig right back into [his] pocket" and haul out another $500 for the pro who accompanied the winner.

In a sheltered, rock-strewn cove of the St. Lawrence River beside a wooded island full of blue herons, I hung a good bass. Immediately, she vaulted into the air, thereby revealing herself to be a smallmouth. A big smallmouth, as big as any I had taken that season. Whenever I hook a big fish my throat gets dry—not because I give a damn if I lose it but because I need desperately to see it before I *might* lose it. For me the worst blow in fishing is losing unseen big fish. I am haunted by hundreds of them.

My throat was dry now, but when I saw this fish I didn't relax. It was not a smallmouth on the end of my line; it was $1,000, and the worst part was that $500 of it belonged to someone else. Instead of trying to make the fish jump by giving her the wood, I found myself, for the first time since puberty, holding the rod low and backpedaling the reel—not fighting but nagging. I wasn't enjoying it at all. In fact, I was happy when it was over. My pro slipped a hand under the hard, handsome, ruby-eyed fish, and lifted her into the boat. "I think you did it," he said.

But I didn't. Some other writer caught a bigger one.

MULLETS IN THEIR GULLETS

As an official observer at the Marathon Tarpon Tournament, I had watched perhaps half a dozen hundred-pound-plus tarpon caught and killed. In this kind of fishing the boat drifts or is anchored in deep water, usually at night; and a live mullet, impaled through the mouth, is floated in the current. When a tarpon takes, you let it swallow the mullet so it will get the hook in the soft gut or gullet rather than the hard mouth.

The Marathon tournament got going just about the time angling for recognition and prize money started becoming very big business in America. During its nineteen-year history, fish tourneys have grown from oddities and casual, yacht-club-style socializing to a multimillion-dollar industry. "Gone soft in the head?" inquires an ad for Softhead trolling lures. "One angler did, and won $220,000." He won the first $200,000 with just one fish—a 144-pound blue marlin, small for the species, taken in the Poco Bueno tournament at Port O'Connor, Texas. That's the kind of money being thrown around in fishing tournaments these days.

As tournaments go, the Marathon affair isn't very big or especially well known. Nor is there much prize money; but with side betting—technically illegal but tolerated—the captain of a winning boat can expect a haul of about $5,000.

Libby Baumeister, a pretty brunette with a quick smile, has a reputation around Marathon as a hard worker. This is why local businessmen, who sponsor the tournament, asked her to direct it. Most everyone attending the kickoff party at the Buccaneer Lodge seems happy with the choice. Libby, they say, adds a touch of class that the tournament hasn't always had.

Perhaps the most challenging part of this kind of tarpon fishing is netting and keeping live mullet. There is constant talk of who has mullet and who does not. When captains and anglers compete, wives and girl friends buy mullet and throw mullet nets. "Every day," says Libby, "you pull the dead ones out of the mullet cars." Mullet cars are wooden or wire cages that are tethered to docks or boats and through which seawater can flow. "It's survival of the fittest. Sometimes you get what's called a 'hard mullet.' You stick a hook through a hard mullet and he won't die on you."

"What's a hard mullet?" I ask.

"Hey, Thad," says Libby, "tell what's a hard mullet."

Thad pauses reflectively. "A hard mullet," he begins, "is a mullet who has acclimated his system to taking stuff out of the water rather than out of the bottom, kinda like osmosis. I've seen 'em live nine or ten months. They get all skinny and slimy."

"A hard mullet can win a tournament," says Libby.

A little before midnight at the Bahia Honda Marina Captain Don Braswell flips open the bait well aboard the *Finest Kind* and furthers my education on mullet. "Your mullet," instructs Captain Don, "is a very nervous fish. You spook 'em and blood comes right through their scales and turns 'em red. These here are all red or dead. Ain't any of 'em worth fishing with."

"You got any hard mullet?" I ask. Captain Don looks at me intently and says, "Nope." Fortunately, however, he's been able to catch some fresh mullet. I help him transfer them from the mullet car.

Our angler this evening is Annette Kennedy, Captain Don's girl friend and a newcomer to tarpon fishing. My duties will be to report any cheating and to record time fishing begins, time fishing ends, and the number of fish hooked, released (if under seventy-five pounds), and boated. We'll be fishing at Bahia Honda Bridge.

The night is warm and black with a haze over the stars. We drift in front of the twinkling bridge. The only sounds are the occasional clatter of a truck or car, the revving of an engine as one of the captains changes position, and the long, sleepy "whoooosh" of exhaling sea turtles. I lie across the seat in the bow of the long, low, slightly dilapidated tarpon boat. Annette sits in the fighting chair, holding the heavy boat rod, and waits. Captain Don sits on the inboard engine and waits. Every fifteen minutes or so he says, "Let's see your mullet." Annette cranks the reel, Captain Don hoists the mullet over the side, scrutinizes it, strips out slack, casts out, and passes the rod back to Annette. Then they start waiting again.

"Hey," hisses Captain Don, "you got a nervous mullet!" The mullet is on the surface, splashing. "C'mon baby," says Captain Don. The mullet sounds. We wait. Then the mullet rises and splashes more frantically. Another small swirl and the mullet disappears. "Easy," whispers Captain Don. "Easy . . . easy . . . easy . . . Okay. Give it to him, A! Give it to him!"

Annette flips the reel out of free-spool and rears back on the rod. "Again!" shouts Captain Don. The rod bends sharply, then snaps straight. Annette looks at Captain Don with big, questioning eyes. "Reel in! Reel in!" he shouts. He snatches the mullet, looks at it, then grunts. " 'Cuda."

Captain Don rips the mangled mullet from the hook and hurls it into the night. He gropes in the bait well for a fresh one and, holding it under the running light, carefully splits its lower lip with the point of Annette's hook: "So's he'll breathe better." Then he pushes the hook up into the roof of the mullet's mouth and out through the top of the head. He strips out slack, casts, and passes the rod to Annette.

I prove to be a malfeasant observer. I am jarred from sound sleep by Captain Don's "Okay, give it to him, A! Again! Again!" I sit up quickly. God knows what cheating might have gone on while I lay snoring in the bow. I scan the black water for swirls. I see none. What I do see, however, is six feet of iridescent silver fish suspended in the air about ten feet in front of me and maybe five feet over my head. I never heard it leave the water. It hangs across a tropic sky, now lit with stars. It hangs there for an impossibly long time. Then it starts to fall toward the sea, twisting and shimmering, finally obliterating the reflected stars in an explosion of white foam. There is an obscene pop, and Annette's thick, hookless, monofilament line snaps back and coils around her shoulders like a corn snake on a rat. "Ooooh," she moans.

Captain Don smacks his left palm with his right fist. "Someday," he says, "I'm gonna teach this little gal to fish." He clips off ten feet of line with his fishing pliers, ties on another hook, and impales a fresh mullet. "Well, that's fishin'," he announces. He explains that he and Annette had quarreled the day before—a rare occurrence. "Since then," says Captain Don, "ain't nothing gone right."

Annette, rerigged, grips her rod with both hands. Now there are big tarpon breaking all around us. Most are just rolling, but a few are feeding. Occasionally, one will launch high and crash loud. It isn't long before we have another nervous mullet.

The mullet itself leaps into the air. There is an enormous, violent upwelling of water, and the mullet leaps again. Another upwelling, and the mullet disappears. "Let him swaller it," says Captain Don. "Easy . . . Eeeasy. Not yet. Okay, now! Again! Again!"

The fish is hooked well and deeply. It leaps six times in quick succession, a very big tarpon. Then it streaks off on a long, dazzling run slowed not at all by the murderous drag. Annette is pulled almost to her knees. Her thick rod points directly at the fish. She cranks furiously.

The tarpon doesn't last long against the heavy tackle. After perhaps ten minutes it is alongside the boat, finning in feeble circles. Captain Don loops the hand gaff around his wrist and, gently gripping the line with his left hand, reaches down and drives the point through the soft spot in the lower jaw. With both hands on the gaff now he straightens bent knees, hoisting the fish out of its element. The wide mouth appears, the big luminous eye, the flaring gill plates. Captain Don pauses and draws a breath. The head and two feet of hard, wide body hang over the gunwale. One last heave and the fish slides up and over, and plops onto the fiber glass floor. It gasps, showing blood-red gills, and drums weakly with its broad tail. Its scales are the size of canning lids.

The big tarpon takes twenty minutes to die. The whole port side of the *Finest Kind* is smeared with blood, mucus, and feces the color and consistency of mustard. Finally, Captain Don wraps the carcass in a green plastic tarp.

Annette says: "I don't like him wrapped up in that green tarp. It gives me the heebie-jeebies."

Captain Don says: "That's just what they done with the bodies in Vietnam—wrapped 'em up in green tarps."

Clouds of laughing gulls swirl up from the scrubby shorelines of Bahia Honda Channel where full-rigged pirate ships used to lie in ambush, heeled over with their masts tied to palm trees. I announce that legal fishing has officially ended.

Back at the Buccaneer, the blackboard proclaims that Captain Don and Annette will coast easily into first place. The fishing has been slow. Libby says she fished all night and never had a nervous mullet. The seven or eight tarpon that had baked and bloated in the sun until midafternoon have now been disposed of by the Tarpon Disposal Committee, which Thad directs. To avoid "waste," the tarpon are given to local taxidermists who, before dumping them in the ocean, make plaster casts of the carcasses. From these casts fiber glass "mounts" are made in advance for the coming tourist season. Whenever a tourist kills a tarpon in the Keys he is always impressed with the quick service he gets from taxidermists. If they don't have your size, they'll sell you a bigger one. There are few complaints.

Presently the director of the Tarpon Disposal Committee rises to brief the participants on the committee's activities. "Today," he declares, "we was run off the road by this Cuban in a big Chevy. 'Señor,' he says, 'I must buy one of your beeg feesh for to feed my beeg family of seexteen.' He had all this luggage in his trunk, but he said for us just to put the fish underneath it, right on the carpet. By this time, a course, they was all thick as watermelons with all kinds a yellow stuff coming out. So we hauled out his luggage an' stuffed in a fish. But here's the best part: The wife says, 'How ees ze meat?' [Laughter.] I say, 'Well, uh . . . uh . . .' [More laughter.] 'How do I clean eet? Do I scale eet? Do I fillet eet?' and I say, 'No, you take a chain saw and steak it.' 'What price, Señor?' he says. 'Ten dollars,' I say. Well, they thought and thought and thought. And finally the wife says, 'Okay.' "

With the ten dollars the Tarpon Disposal Committee purchased a fifth of Canadian Club, which is now passed around the room.

GOOD TOURNAMENTS

In Florida I had encountered Romanesque games and pit humor. But if I was going to deliver a reasonably comprehensive report on fishing tournaments in America, I needed the antithesis as well—a high society, putting-on-the-Ritz affair where cheating would be simply unthinkable, and where money prizes would be in just plain bad taste and superfluous anyway. I needed a "good" tournament, too, where all fish caught are released or at least eaten by the contestants.

After a morning on the phone and a salvo of letters, I found precisely what I was looking for: the Cat Cay Tuna Tournament. It's said by those who know to be the "best, oldest, and most respected" fishing tournament in North America. Unless bitten by sharks, all fish are released. There is no prize money.

The tuna are globe-tripping giant bluefins that funnel through Hemingway's deepwater "Alley" off Bimini, riding the waves north whenever the spring wind blows up from the south. When they reach the Gulf of Maine they mill about, glutting themselves on squid, herring, and mackerel. They grow fat and lazy, follow chum lines to anchored boats, allow themselves to be hauled in on handlines, further enriching the "Moonies," and travel to Japan—by jet.

In the Bahamas they are different fish. They are hard and lean, capable of hitting sixty miles an hour. They travel in small pods, moving very fast, not feeding. But if a boat can get ahead of them, adjust precisely to their speed, and waggle a realistic bait in their faces, sometimes they will take. Before the fishing can begin, the bluefins must be spotted and stalked like African big game, a good deal of which they exceed in weight.

Like Fantasy Island, Cat Cay has no landing strip. One arrives by amphibian, orbiting over turquoise flats dotted with eagle rays, hitting the sea in a burst of water that obliterates the view, taxiing up onto the palm-fringed beach in front of the lavish clubhouse, and almost expecting a grimacing dwarf to shout, "Ze plane, Boss!"

After I have been ushered quickly through customs I am presented with keys to my cottage and golf cart (one does not walk on Cat Cay). The boats tied to the dock are custom-made Ryboviches, Andy Mortensens, and the like. The biggest Rybovich, a sixty-five-footer, is owned by contestant Bob Fisher, who has recently acquired the company that made it. Its cabin roof has been specially reinforced so that he may land his helicopter on it.

With map in hand I steer my golf cart along narrow asphalt paths, through dazzling gardens, lush, tropical vegetation, and palm groves where wild turkeys scratch and strut. A hundred yards or so beyond the golf course I locate my cottage. It backs up to an inviting flat where a big barracuda fins in the late sun and watches me with baleful eyes. Alas, there is no time for fishing now. I transfer camera, duffel bag, and bonefish rod to the cottage, then proceed to the house of the club commodore, from whose boat I shall be observing the competition.

The commodore's wife, Marion—aptly referenced in the daily *Poop Sheet* as "the commadorable"—greets me at the door. I am half through my drink when the commodore himself, Jim Hunt, who is said to have built half of Fort Lauderdale, appears in his bathrobe. He is stocky, silver-haired, with a sun-washed, wind-etched face—a perfect commodore. I have rousted him from a nap, but he seems genuinely glad to see me.

Hunt says he doesn't expect the tournament to be that productive in terms of fish caught. Sportfishing for giant bluefins has been all but ruined by the Japanese. Because of a loophole in the two-hundred-mile limit exempting tuna, Japan's longlining fleet has moved to within fifty miles of the U.S. mainland, festooning migration routes with mile after mile of super trotline that trails thousands upon thousands of baited hooks. "And they use nets, too," says Hunt. "They'll hang a net around a whole school—eight hundred fish—and they'll get every damn one. Then they stab them, winch them on board, chain-saw their heads off, stack them like cordwood, and two hours later they're on a plane to Japan." Hunt says he hasn't seen a bluefin yet this spring. "It used to be you'd see the big ones leading all the little ones up north. Now there're just a few big ones, and they're getting fewer and bigger each year." And on that sour note our chat ends. It is time for us to dress for the evening meetings.

The first meeting, says the schedule stapled to my map, will be at the Haigh House for the captains and mates. Having failed to impress the barracuda with a four-inch marabou streamer, I propel myself toward the Haigh House through the balmy, flower-scented twilight. The sign on the door says "Save the Bluefin Tuna." Inside, Hunt is advising the crews of the twenty competing boats of old rules, new rules, and rule changes. At last he discloses that this year they are invited to one of the ceremonial dinners. "I'm upsetting the apple cart on this," he declares. "So please, no shorts. And please don't get drunk again."

At the anglers' meeting there is much talk of the release rule. Merely snipping the wire is said not to be an adequate test of crew competence. One of the displeased anglers is sitting beside me—Carl Doverspike of Hawthorn, Pennsylvania. He says that the natives are getting restless because the natives aren't getting enough tuna. "You lay a tuna on the Bimini dock," he argues, "and twenty minutes later there's nothing but bones."

An angler with a thick Cuban accent rises to announce that he would prefer that the tuna be boated, killed, and fed to the sharks—a common practice at tournaments before the price per pound of tuna went from ten cents to four dollars—but that this, unfortunately, is no longer possible because of the paucity of sharks. Doverspike chuckles at that one. "He's going to have his eyes opened tomorrow," he tells me. I ask Doverspike if it is really necessary to kill a tuna just to test the crew. "Look," he says, "thirty percent of those tuna are going to be shark-bit anyway. I guarantee it. And to bring the others back to life you've got to tow them. You tell me one captain who will spend tournament time doing that."

The commodore rises: "I'd like to go back to four years ago when we brought them all on board. [Murmured amens.] Boating them is fifty percent of it. And I can't see saving them for the Japanese. But God forbid that this tournament should turn into a *fishery* for the Japanese." Hunt calls the issue to a vote. Releasing wins.

On the dock at eight o'clock in the morning of the third day of competition dark glasses are already necessary. The wind, at last, is obligingly out of the south. Today, it is said, the tuna will be up and moving.

Jim Hunt's three-man crew is making much ado about setting the drag on the big, two-speed Fin-Nor reel. Second Mate Eric Bingham of Australia stands on the dock and hooks a scale to the line, then hauls back on it with a melodramatic grunt, backing toward the water. Captain Tom Morrison of Miami Beach fusses with the reel. Bingham loudly announces that at sixty-five pounds the drag is now "just right."

The drag is nowhere near sixty-five pounds. It is all a charade for the newcomer in the next slip whose green crew really does set the drag at sixty-five pounds. Jim Hunt smiles indulgently. "When a fish hits," he tells me, "*pow.* That guy's never going to know what happened."

According to contestant Bobby Erra, who taught Hunt tuna fishing, no other fish strikes as savagely as a bluefin. "The strike," he says, "is incredibly intense." Erra used to race motorboats, and after one flip he came up minus four-fifths of his left hand. Only his little finger remained. So Erra had a metal ring welded to the butt of his tuna rod, and by inserting his left little finger—now as thick as his right thumb—he is still able to pump in giant bluefins faster than most of his competition.

Hunt's boat—the *Huntress*—is a fifty-five-foot Andy Mortensen with all the new devices for navigating and communicating, two heads, two showers, air conditioning, microwave oven, bar, TV with videotape and camera, built-in stereo, wall-to-wall carpeting, burglar alarm—a little long and beamy for tuna fishing, not quite agile enough for the quick maneuvering required in getting into position.

As we idle in the channel, waiting for the shotgun blast that signals the traditional Bimini start, a photographer snaps photos from Bob Fisher's helicopter. Pop. We're off. A quarter-mile to starboard and a little ahead of us Dinny Phipps's *Fighting Lady* cuts across the clean line from turquoise to azure sea, kicking up a steady shower of flying fish that arc from her bow like welding sparks. Now in the Alley, engines quiet and boats settle back into their own wash. The fleet spreads out, and each captain climbs the flying bridge to squint all day for brown cigar silhouettes.

First Mate Ray Waggener of Lake Worth, Florida, rigs a thawed "split-tail mullet." Mullet are made with one-piece tails, but a few years ago some genius thought to split one longitudinally with a filleting knife. "Watch this," declares Waggener, and flips the finished bait over the side. The wire leader tightens around his wrist, and the mullet swims two feet below the surface, wagging its double tail seductively. It looks as if it could fool even another mullet.

Being a first mate on a tuna boat can be a bit dangerous. A man can hang from the tip of a tuna rod and barely bend it, so if it slips out of the angler's sweaty hand during the fight it can snap down and crush a mate's skull. Or if the waxed Dacron line breaks, it can slice deep into his flesh. Unless he grabs the wire exactly right, he is likely to lose fingers, and even the best mates get pulled overboard. When a wired fish shakes its head and pops its gills Waggener says he can feel it through his whole body. But he loves it all. One of the things he loves best is the way bluefins light up when they get excited. "Their backs get all blue," he says, "and every little finlet glows bright yellow."

As we work along the coral shelf Ray explains strategy: sometimes you hook up in the shallow water, and they'll go out over the lip and down. Then they've got you. This is the reason for the whistle that hangs around Hunt's neck. When he feels the fish, he blows it. Then the *Huntress* will turn and race the tuna to deep water. Occasionally, however, you'll hang them in the Alley and they'll turn and go up over the lip. Then you've got *them*.

"Sometimes," says Ray, "you're fighting a fish in thirty feet of water and you can see everything. They bleed sometimes and look like bombers going down, trailing fire."

Suddenly the engines roar, and Hunt scrambles to the fighting chair, Ray helping him into the harness. I can see brown cigar silhouettes all around us. A black fin rise from the sea, then another and another. The engines fall silent again. The silhouettes are pilot whales.

The day wears on. At last Hunt and I retreat from the relentless sun to the dizzying cool of the cabin, where we sip cold beer at the bar. After three days, I have finally figured Jim Hunt out. Basically, he's a nice guy who likes to go fishing. His money, perhaps because he has worked for it, seems not to have affected his grasp on reality. No sooner have we adjusted to the new environment than the engines roar again.

This time it really is tuna—a pod of six, moving very fast in shallow water. When we are in position Ray hurls the mullet and Jim free-spools. The seconds pound by. Then the blast of the whistle and we are racing for the edge even as Jim is slamming in the hook.

Ray pours water on the reel as line hisses out of it. After the first run Eric Bingham squirts laundry soap on Jim's seat so that his rear end can slide back and forth as he pumps with his legs.

Over by the controls Ray tells me to keep an eye on Jim because in a few minutes no one else will be able to. Already Hunt is bleeding from the elbow. "Don't say anything," says Ray. He explains that a few years ago Jim had been bothered by chest pains. A doctor friend and Marion had conspired to provide him with nitro pills and secretly instruct the crew to cut the line if a tuna started to get the best of him. Somehow Jim had found out about it. "Boy are you guys lucky," he said. "God help anyone who cuts me off while I'm into a fish. I don't care if I'm on the deck."

After half an hour I climb the flying bridge to take pictures. The tuna is coming in now—straight up through 150 feet of clear water. He grows from herring size to shad size to striped bass size to seal size. It seems impossible that any fish can be this big. Still he comes and still he grows. Jim says to Ray and Eric: "Don't be posing for pictures now. Remember what you're doing."

The big tuna spirals in our wake, wallows and flashes in the sun. Ray strains for the wire. He will not tag this fish because the information from U.S. tagging studies—all the whens and wheres of migration—is said by club members to provide a how-to manual for Japanese tuna killers. Ray gets a wrap on the wire, holds the fish briefly, then cuts it free. The tournament clock is running. No time for towing and reviving.

"Don't go belly up," Jim Hunt says. But the fish does.

NUTS AND GUTS

No one can say for sure what happens to played-out bluefin tuna after they are cut loose, but I have spoken at length with lots of people who know bluefins, and the feeling seems to be that many if not most of these remarkable gamefish fight to the death. Even if a bluefin survives the stress of being wrestled to boatside with rod and reel, there is an excellent chance that it will be mauled by sharks.

If the "best, oldest, and most respected" fishing tournament was killing a species that is endangered in fact, if not by official decree, and for no reason other than to see who could do it best, then maybe I wasn't going to find a "good" fishing tournament. Still, I knew that a great deal of good accrues from even "bad" ones. For one thing, they provide biologists with valuable data.

Shark research and management, for example, would be paralyzed without tournaments. Biologists rarely see dead sharks elsewhere because the carcasses of sharks caught elsewhere are usually dumped at sea. And since sharks tend to be highly migratory, many species are available for only a short time. John G. Casey, who heads the National Marine Fisheries Service's shark program, says that the kind of information he collects at organized shark-fishing meets is simply not available anywhere else.

Casey piqued my interest even more when he told me that there was a "good" sharking affair: the Bay Shore Mako Tournament, a Long Island tourney in which many different kinds of sharks are caught. Casey's right-hand man, Wes Pratt, goes so far as to call it the best shark tournament in the East. Its value to man's understanding of sharks cannot, without great creativity, be overstated.

Forty miles straight out from Bay Shore, Joe Winn cuts the engines of the *Vento*, and we drift with the tide in clean, green water. Joe's crew—Leo Piscopo and Walt Boren—is unpaid. Walt peels newspaper from around the mossbunker chum, still frozen after two and a half hours in the late-June sun. "Newspaper is a good insulator," he says. "That's what the bums in the Bowery wrap up in at night." The blocks of chum are inserted in two ventilated plastic buckets, which are capped, hitched to ropes, and lowered over the side. The seawater will melt the chum, and the wave action will disperse it. Joe and Leo rig three boat rods with a one-pound Boston mackerel and two slightly smaller mossbunkers.

A high, black fin appears, flapping back and forth in the waves. There is a moment's excitement, but the fish turns out to be only an ocean sunfish—a strange, unworldly beast, a detached pewter head with silver-dollar eyes, propelled less by fins than wind and tide. Ocean sunfish are grazers of walnut-sized comb jellyfish and so have no interest in dead fish, whole or ground. Ours—a small one of maybe two hundred pounds—flops its way over to the stern of the *Vento*, actually touches it, and stares at us as if in disbelief.

Another fin appears. This time it belongs to a big blue shark. The shark circles one of the mossbunkers, sucks it in, and floats off, not knowing that it is hooked. Walt holds the rod, turns, and talks to Joe. Presently the shark is no longer hooked. It swings slowly back to the bait and sucks it in again. Again it is hooked. Again it swims off. Again the hook pulls out. Again it returns. Again it sucks in the bait. This time, however, it does not get hooked. A smaller blue shark appears, eats all three baits, and is caught on all three lines. The rod Joe picks up breaks near the butt, not because of the strain (there is barely any) but because it is twenty-five years old. He picks up another. "Makos," he explains, "are different."

The large blue returns and mounts the hooked shark. (The significance of the event is lost on us at the moment; but, later, Wes Pratt reveals that the handful of human beings who have witnessed shark copulation is now larger by four.) The coupled sharks thrash together on the surface. Leo gaffs the large one, then gaffs the hooked one. He points to the prominent claspers that extend from the male's pelvic fins and through which sperm is transferred to the female. "They got two penises," he says. "One for port and one for starboard."

Back at tournament field headquarters, on the wide cement pier, the big blue registers 171 pounds/points on the official scale. The female doesn't count because she is under 100 pounds.

The scene here is right out of the French Revolution. Whole and eviscerated carcasses of close to two hundred large sharks are strewn about the pier. There are makos, blues, sandbars, a dusky, a sexually immature male great white of 405 pounds (sometimes the females are immature at 1,500 pounds), and a "brand X"—the kind biologists have to identify later from fin measurements. I wade into it all—literally, because the cement is awash with blood, bile, and stomach contents. I can feel it seeping through my canvas sneakers. Its sickly sweet smell hangs in the air like tear gas. Occasionally the crowd, of several hundred, bulges into the fenced-off area, breaks off shark teeth, and is herded back by guards. An Oriental, who shields his face when I point my camera at him, darts from the shadow of a cement building, straddles a small blue, slashes off the basics of shark-fin soup, is yelled at by the owner, and darts back. Here and there someone hacks a steak from a mako. In the middle of it all Jack Casey and Wes Pratt are squatting over sharks and portions of sharks, reaching past their elbows into body cavities, dropping red, dripping things into plastic bags—doing, as they call it, "nuts and guts."

The crowd is getting increasingly unruly. The announcer, booming at it over the loudspeaker, is getting increasingly ugly. He seems drunk with power: "Get back. Get back," he screams. "Are you deaf?" He is also getting increasingly pompous: "Makos," he declares, "are the name of the game. And makos we're getting."

A garbage truck backs onto the pier to take the day's catch to the landfill. Each shark sags heavily as the driver and his helper pick it up by the head and tail and swing it up into the back of the truck. A little black girl, whose daddy has just gotten her a piece of a real shark says: "It's better that we catch them than they catch us."

THE TEST OF THE BEST

Not only do fishing tournaments provide a lot of useful scientific information, they pep up the economy. Certainly the fish whose pursuit by American tournament anglers has had the greatest economic impact is the freshwater black bass. And the man most responsible for this—the Henry Ford–P. T. Barnum of the "pro bassin' circuit," as it is called in hook-and-bullet literature—is Ray Scott: fifty-two, tall, green-eyed, ruggedly handsome, and almost always wearing a big Stetson. In 1967 Scott was an insurance underwriter in Montgomery, Alabama. He saw an unmet demand from what he calls "the biggest special-interest group in America." "Bass fishermen," says Scott, "had no group like the NRA." As some of his press material explains: "The idea of an invitational bass tournament, similar to golf's play-for-pay events, came to him with such startling impact that 'I sat straight up in bed and hollered.' "

Today, the Bass Anglers Sportsman Society, or BASS, with close to 400,000 members, is the largest fishing organization in the world. Essentially, it is one big tournament. Local chapters and affiliated clubs hold thousands of tournaments of varying size and difficulty from which, through a kind of bass-fishing Darwinism, the most proficient "bassin' men" are selected and sent on to the ultimate, grandest bassin' match of them all—the Bass Masters Classic, "the test of the best." This arduous process of natural selection has, BASS explains, "done more than anything else to create an entirely new breed of fisherman, a wondrously equipped, aggressive, and scientifically calibrated angler, labeled the bass fishing pro."

Many terrible things are said and written about Ray Scott—mostly by people who object to the way he puts personal profit before the greater good of pro bassin'. For my part, I liked Scott—for his fine sense of humor, for his lack of pretense, and, especially, for his honesty. He told me he is indeed in it for the money. He has never pretended otherwise. "Every time I see one of those [BASS] patches," he said, "I get a lump, right in my wallet."

I saw no reason why someone with drive and brains—the person, in fact, who invented pro bassin'—ought not to get rich from it. Scott hasn't done anything very awful and, in fact, has done some things that are pretty good. For instance, he insists that all fish caught in BASS tournaments be released, an example that is being imitated by bass fishermen everywhere. It is not, after all, as if he were selling cigarettes or hard pesticides. All he is selling is pro bassin', and selling it as if it were Dr. Kickapoo's Elixir for Rheum, Ague, Blindness, and Insanity.

Competition among journalists to observe BASS tournaments is keen, but once you're in, Ray Scott treats you right. The day after I'd been notified of my selection to the 102-member press entourage for the Bass Master Classic (the location of which changes but which would be held this year at New York's Thousand Islands area on the St. Lawrence River) the postman didn't even try to fit my mail into the box. First to arrive was BASS literature, in a blizzard that hasn't let up since. Then came a Plano tackle box. Then lures to put inside it. Then all manner of stickers and arm patches and metal buttons, then round-trip plane tickets between Boston and Syracuse. (A chartered bus would meet us in Syracuse.)

At tournament headquarters in Alexandria Bay the stuff piled up even faster: a Mercury Outboards/Classic duffel bag; a jacket with "Ranger Boats" written all over it; a metal BASS belt buckle; a New York fishing license; I-love-New-York maps and pamphlets; three or four adjustable hats bearing various commercial messages; the keys to a prepaid hotel room overlooking the river; a BASS life vest; all the fishing line I could, without embarrassment, carry away; considerably more printed product hype than I could, without a wheelbarrow, carry away; more patches, stickers, buttons . . .

In the press room were typewriters, free paper, free prewritten stories called "news releases," free liquor, free telephones, free machines for transmitting copy and photographs. When not tied down by work, journalists could select such prepaid diversions as grouse and woodcock hunting, skeet and trap shooting, muskie fishing, trout and salmon fishing, smallmouth bass fishing . . . Press conferences, with free beer for all, were held on a tour boat. We dined on gourmet food in the plush Pine Tree Point Resort and were entertained like sultans by singers, dancers, and world-famous bands that could cause three-quarters of the people in the room to leap to their feet just by playing "Dixie." There was even a singer who crooned about bassin': "Chunking and winding, dreaming of finding a bigmouth . . . There ain't no feeling like fighting and reeling . . ." I was beginning to piece together an hypothesis about why the hook-and-bullet press seems always to be so enthused about BASS tournaments.

Salesmen, offering private consultations and public seminars, descended on us like a hatch of flying ants. There were tackle salesmen, bassin' boat salesmen, electronic-fish-finder salesmen, outboard-motor salesmen . . .

The shrewdest salesmen seemed to be those peddling Stren line—a top-quality nylon monofilament put out by Du Pont, which developed both nylon and monofilament. Du Pont paid $500 each to twenty contestants for using Stren in the Classic, a tactic the firm says it resorted to only because its competition had employed it first. On top of this, Du Pont kicked in $13,000 to the overall jackpot—$10,000 for the winner, $2,000 for the runner-up, and $1,000 for the third-place finisher. The only catch was that they had to be using Stren. They were.

The winner of the Classic, Bo Dowden of Natchitoches, Louisiana, is described in my press material as "living proof 'weekend anglers' can compete successfully in professional bass tournaments." He is also living proof that, given the right commercial climate, weekend anglers can be quickly stripped of their innocence. At the press conference the evening before his victory Bo is already learning the game.

Bo—six feet one inch and 220 pounds—looks as if he is a long way from Natchitoches. He shuffles up to the front of the floating auditorium and explains that only Basil Bacon can catch him now and that right after the press conference he is going to go back to his room and, even though he really doesn't need to, just as one last extra precaution, he is going to strip all the old Stren off his reels and load them back up with new Stren.

The next night Bo's dream has come true. Ray Scott, with Bo's shoulder in one hand and a wad of checks in the other, says, "This is like waking from a big drunk and wondering what all you've done." Bo's check from BASS is for $31,000—$30,000 for catching the most pounds of bass and $1,000 for catching the biggest bass. Then there is the $10,000 from Du Pont. The big money, though, hasn't been collected yet. It is estimated that Bo can knock down $60,000 in product endorsements.

For the benefit of the press Bo explains everything he did that day. *Everything.* Beginning with swinging his feet out of bed. When at last he gets to the part of the day when he hung the big fish, Bo says: "I knew I had a big one on by that retaining wall, and I said, 'Lord, let this not be a pike.' I drug her up alongside the boat, and my line got caught in the trolling motor . . . Then I see it was a bass, and you coulda heard the war whoop across the bay." Bo observes that the other forty contenders "are good fishermen all" and that "they derned sure didn't get here by jackleggin' around." Of Alexandria Bay, Bo says: "I never knew a Yankee town could be so friendly."

I had wanted Bo to win even before he was in the running. Being a good ol' boy who, for instance, competes in shirtless hulas organized by Ray Scott to determine which BASS angler has the biggest belly, he is easily misread. The fact is that Bo Dowden, like every Classic contender I met, is a sportsman and a gentleman. In a way I'm happy for Bo, but I also know that something very special will never be the same for him again.

A REFINED TASTE IN NATURAL OBJECTS

The fish I love more than any other is the brook trout, a dweller of springwater, a little land-locked char with chestnut flanks flecked with scarlet—each fleck with a sapphire halo—ivory-trimmed fins, and a belly the color of a New England sunset. I love the brook trout not because he is the biggest and strongest of all gamefish (he is nowhere near it). Not even because I perceive him to be the most beautiful of all gamefish (although I do). But because he belongs to the Yankee forest that I live near and often in, because he is the part of stillness, loon song, and balsam-scented air that I can touch.

Without being too pious about it, I think that Americans are forgetting what fish are, and that this lapse of memory, more than anything, has been responsible for the boom in fishing tournaments. As wild, beautiful creatures reflecting the wildness and beauty of the places in which they abide, fish no longer count for much. What we have lost is what Teddy Roosevelt's friend George Bird Grinnell, in his old sporting weekly *Forest and Stream*, used to call "a refined taste in natural objects." This is why the Bass Research Foundation can underwrite a project to develop an artificial bass called the "meanmouth" by crossbreeding smallmouths and largemouths. This is why in my own state of Massachusetts—where almost all trout fishing is "put-and-take"—it becomes increasingly difficult even to pretend that the hatchery-reared western rainbows are wild. The Division of Fisheries and Wildlife now feels constrained to fit some of them with tags that say things like "Make it in Mass."—the shibboleth conceived by panicked commerce officials in hope of slowing the headlong flight of industry from "Taxachusetts."

The gadgets used in fishing tournaments are considered more important than the natural setting, and they breed discontent in all the fishermen who used to think they were happy soaking sun on the bank and doughballs in the creek. My favorite outdoor scribe has this to say about gadgets: "I have the impression that the American sportsman is puzzled; he doesn't understand what is happening to him. Bigger and better gadgets are good for industry, so why not for outdoor recreation? It has not dawned on him that outdoor recreations are essentially primitive, atavistic; that their value is contrast-value; that excessive mechanization destroys contrasts by moving the factory to the woods or to the marsh.

"The sportsman has no leaders to tell him what is wrong. The sporting press no longer represents sport; it has turned billboard for the gadgeteer."

The scribe is Aldo Leopold, and he wrote all this in the 1940s. I scarcely dare imagine what he would write today.

For twenty years, readers of the *Saturday Evening Post* chartered the cruiser *Poseidon*, left Miami on full throttle for the Gulf Stream, and fished with Crunch and Des. Philip Wylie guaranteed a good time every trip. Maybe he figured he should hoard goodwill in anticipation of his cage-rattling, bearbaiting *Generation of Vipers*.

Wylie drew upon his own war record to fashion this thinly disguised tale. It's not often that someone gets the chance to defend a day's fishing as a patriotic duty.

PHILIP WYLIE

The Shipwreck of Crunch and Des

The argument began in New York City—if so mild a term as "argument" may be used to describe an altercation which came fairly near costing three people their lives. It happened on a March afternoon in 1942, when the local weather was threatening everybody with pneumonia by an assortment of changes from rainy warmth to frigoric drizzle and back again to tepid. The subject was the relative efficiency, as a fish-catching device, of those small artificial lures known as plugs, and that other category of single-hooked bait which includes feathers and squids.

Eight persons pored over this matter in the board room of the brokerage firm of Smith, Gladwyl, Chevvy, and Kitteridge. The room had windows on four sides because it occupied one floor of a tower. A decorator had used thick gray carpeting, pink velvet drapery, and chrome furniture to turn it into a chamber that was not an office at all, but resembled the boudoir of a merchant princess. Even the upper strata of Wall Street regarded it as ultra.

Chauncey C. S. Smith, senior partner of the firm, had called the meeting at the behest of various government officials and military personages, to study, modernize, and improve the fishing tackle used on lifeboats and life rafts. The men summoned by Smith, who was a world-renowned big-game angler, were experts all—an ichthyologist, two tackle manufacturers, a writer of books on fish and fishing, and three guides, hand-picked by Florida's association of charter boatmen. These three had flown from Florida to New York—Crunch Adams, Desperate Smith, and Captain Bill.

They sat in session around a huge table in the center of the office. Ranged on the table were samples of the tackle that had been aboard lifeboats and life rafts at the commencement of the war; some of it so primitive and inadequate that, as Captain Bill said, "it hadn't been improved or changed since the old Moby Dick days." Also on the table was a glittering collection of the baits, hooks, lures, nets, lines, sinkers, leaders, and other impedimenta used by the most up-to-date commercial anglers and sportsmen.

"Our task," Mr. Smith had said as he opened the meeting, "will be to discard outmoded gear, to winnow the new material, and to devise from it a simple kit, light, strong, durable, which will give a fighting chance—maybe I should say a fishing chance—to every man adrift in a lifeboat or an airplane's rubber boat or on a raft." Mr. Smith had spoken with a broad *a*, while elegantly fingering his gaudy foulard tie and removing two or three flecks of lint from his hand-stitched gray woolen suit.

Mr. Smith was a shock to Crunch and Des. They had known about him—his New Zealand marlin, his Chilean broadbill, his Nova Scotia tuna—but they had never seen him. Indeed, save for old Bill, they were acquainted with none of the gentlemen at the conference. Their eyes, meeting humorously at the outset of the discussion, had at once classified Mr. Smith—the fisherman elegant, the deep-water dandy, the rich sportsman whose angling consists of taking the fighting chair when the gamester strikes, whipping it with heavy, expensive tackle, dusting genteel hands lightly afterward, and turning the fifty-thousand-dollar cruiser toward shore for cocktails and the applause of thrilled dowagers.

Now Crunch and Des were locked in argument with Smith. "I think," Crunch said, his sunburned face dark among the pale countenances of the broker, the writer, the scientist and the manufacturers, "that we ought to have a couple of plugs in every one of these emergency kits. A man on a raft can fasten a sinker above a plug, twirl it, throw, and yank back the plug so that it gets a lot of action. That'll attract fish—and fish mean staying alive, to him."

"Plugs," Mr. Smith answered, rising, pouring water from a silver vacuum bottle and sipping it like vintage wine, "are a bit too chi-chi for our need, Crunch. The squid"—he picked one up as if it were a jewel—"is the thing. A mere lead thickening of the shaft of a hook. Scrape the lead with a knife, and it glitters. It is simple. Rugged." The word seemed inappropriate on his lips. "Yes, Crunch, old boy, the squid and the feather are our meat. The feather is

a simple bait. But the plug! Too complicated, old man. Breaks easily. Tangles. Picks up weed everywhere. Rather a gadget, you know."

Des was embarrassed, but he spoke. "Why can't we have all three in every fishing set? Plugs, feathers and squids too?"

Mr. Smith sipped again. "My dear Des! For many reasons. Space must be saved; it's vital. Weight and bulk, old boy. This gear must consist of the absolute minimum. Essentials only. Besides, the men adrift won't be anglers, mostly. Few plug casters among 'em. Can't employ anything that's tricky or needs practice. Your plug—"

The plug was not Desperate's invention and he resented the word "your." He flushed. "Any fool can learn to use a plug on a hand line in ten minutes. These guys are adrift for months sometimes. And we're going to have instructions in every kit, aren't we?" He looked at the writer.

Mr. George Calden, author of *Game Fish the World Over*, was pained that anybody should disagree with Mr. Smith. "I am afraid," he said, "that I, too, hold against the plug."

"We," Crunch said, "are talking as practical men. Not theorists."

Mr. Smith smiled. That is, his thin mouth curved up. He shrugged his thick but obviously padded shoulders. "I think, gentlemen, that I may be considered as a 'practical' fisherman also."

"Hear, hear," said one of the tackle-makers pompously, and with a needling look at Crunch and Des.

Crunch came back into the argument. "All I mean is, if I were adrift in the Pacific, north or south, or the Atlantic, either one, I'd want a couple of small plugs—white with red heads and a good wiggle—in my kit. They're light and they don't take much room. Feathers and squids are good—I don't deny that—but—"

"We'll go on," Mr. Smith interrupted. "After all, gentlemen, there's a war. We're in a hurry about this business."

"Not too much of a hurry to get it right," Crunch said vigorously.

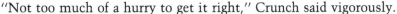

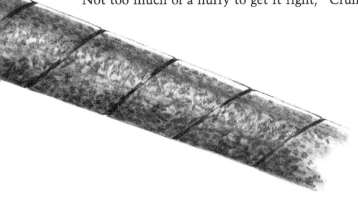

Smith—Chauncey C. S. Smith III—turned his narrow, indolent-looking face. "You Florida boatmen are stubborn lads, I must say! Look here. I'll let you in on a confidential matter. We're going to give whatever we select a field test under Navy and Coast Guard auspices. I'll have you demonstrate the plug at that time."

Crunch was mollified. So was Des. A field test was more to their taste than bickering in a plush Manhattan office.

"The C. S. in the middle of Smith's name," Crunch said later to Des at their hotel, "stands for Café Society. Why the government picked that vanilla custard to head this committee is one of those things not even a New Dealer can explain with graphs! Spends his nights in hot spots and his days in Turkish baths."

"Hot spot to hot spot," Des agreed. "But we'll prove what a plug can do, if we ever get a chance."

The chance eventually came. On a warm spring morning, partly overcast and lightly breezy, a Coast Guard patrol boat with no name and a number put out toward the Gulf Stream after passing through a drawbridge on the Highway that Goes to Sea between Miami and Key West. The boat was painted blue-gray. She carried a heavy machine gun forward and depth charges aft. Aboard her, besides certain special officers and her crew, were Smith and the members of his committee, flown south on a special plane.

She proceeded some miles into the ocean. Her engines were then cut and she swung about, rocking in the moderate chop. No ship and no other small boat was to be seen anywhere in the vast sweep of purple water. Such traffic as passed the Keys moved at night, and in convoy whenever possible, for here, at this time, Hitler's submarines were trying to make good the Führer's boast.

"We want," said Mr. Smith, gathering the officers and his committee in a clear space amidships, "to dispose, first of all, of Crunch and Des's claims for the plug. I therefore suggest that we put them over in the rubber boat. We will keep them in view and allow them, say, eight hours of fishing with the plugs they have brought along. Meanwhile, we on this craft will experiment with the various trolling devices chosen for testing. . . . Is that satisfactory, Commander?"

Commander Evans nodded. "You're the boss, Mr. Smith."

"Crunch?"

The skipper eyed the New Yorker. No hand-sewn gray woolens adorned him now, but a costume just as ostentatious—pearl-gray corduroy shorts, a light doeskin shirt, also gray, sandals, and a pith helmet.

Crunch grinned. "Suits Des and me."

"Later," said Mr. Smith, "we'll try squids and plugs under the same conditions."

Neither Crunch nor Des bothered to argue that the "same conditions" might not arise for weeks at this season. They did not protest that eight hours was too short a period for a fair test. They had become accustomed, by then, to the arbitrary manner of Mr. Smith. They merely hoped that they would be lucky enough to nail some fish from the rubber boat before sundown.

The boat was inflated by turning a valve in a cylinder attached to its peak, or forward end. It filled with a hiss, like a child's balloon. It had a cushiony, air-packed seat in its middle, a rubberized canvas seat forward, oarlocks, a pair of aluminum oars that came in sections, zipper pockets for holding equipment, and a life line around the edge. It was bright yellow, so that it could be spotted on the blank sea. The crew dropped it overboard. The ship's cook brought some sandwiches and a canteen of water. Crunch and Des put their tackle aboard and stepped into the craft with care.

"Just like standing on a hot-water bottle," Des said. He took the oars. Crunch lounged astern. A few strokes separated them from the Coast Guard boat. Crunch waved.

"I doubt," Mr. Smith called, "if you get a single strike. We'll be around."

"Lovely guy," Crunch murmured, trailing his fingers in the warm Gulf Stream. "I betcha when he caught his big mako he had himself locked in his cabin below until somebody killed the fish."

Des chuckled and rowed. With every stroke, the life craft moved a length forward. It was very easy. Des kicked off his shoes. His bare feet on the fabric could feel the run of water beneath. "Thin," he murmured. "You'd hardly expect these things to stand up for months, but they seem to. Just the same, what an annoyed marlin or a shark could do to one in about ten seconds isn't anything you like to think about."

Crunch was already unpacking the gear. He looked back toward the Coast Guard boat. She was under way again; a trolling line was visible astern.

"Smitty," said the captain irreverently, "is sitting among those ash cans, dragging a spoon. Likes to take things easy. Probably he'll have one of the sailors hold an umbrella over him and somebody else fan him before long. It's hot out here."

"You said it."

By and by, Des stopped rowing. The lifeboat drifted, bobbing on little waves. The shore was a smoky pencil line to the west. A lighthouse stood above the horizon like a matchstick. The patrol boat dwindled. Waves splashed. The sun burned through more clouds. Gulls squeaked like rusty hinges. A man-of-war bird towered in the blue altitude.

Crunch sniffed and smiled. "Nice day."

"Nice day." Des reached for a rig. He inspected it. "Jumping Josephine," he said with approval. It was one of his favorite plugs. He coiled his line carefully on the round yellow bulge that formed the craft's side. He spun the plug in a widening circle and flung it, downwind, some twenty yards. Crunch, at the other end of the boat, followed suit with a Manitoba Bobber. Each man retrieved his bait with a series of quick yanks, recoiling line carefully as it was brought in. A half hour passed and nothing happened.

"You'd get a sore arm," Des finally said, "if you had to do this forever."

"You're gonna get a sore arm. We gotta have fish. Otherwise a few thousand guys are going fishing without plugs, and fishing for real, too, not for fun."

The sun rose higher and hung in the sky like a burning glass. They passed the canteen back and forth and patiently tossed their plugs out on the water.

"According to Pinchot," Crunch said, after a deep draft of the warming water, "we don't need this. All we need is fish. Cube the meat, squeeze it, and presto, drinking water. I wonder how thirsty you have to be to hanker after fish juice?"

"First catch your fish," Des answered.

But they didn't get a strike. Toward noon, the Coast Guard boat cruised close to them. Its motors slowed and Commander Evans hailed them, "You guys O.K.?"

"Oke!" Crunch yelled back.

"Any luck?"

"We're catching nothing but a sunburn!"

It was after four when they had a hit. Crunch had not been precisely kidding when he had spoken of sunburn. It penetrated their basic, year-round tan, heated their cheeks, dried their lips and scalded their bare shoulders. They were wearied by incessant casting. They were limp with the heat and stiff from the confinement of the boat. The continual splash of the small waves had repeatedly dampened them and the dampness had dried in fine crystals. Crunch threw for the five hundredth time. The instant his plug touched water there was a bluish swirl under it. The Manitoba Bobber vanished in such a splash as would be made by a thrown brick. Crunch yelled jubilantly. The line slid through his fingers and cut them; he had long since taken off his fishing gloves. Now, he wrapped the line in a handkerchief.

Des asked excitedly, "What is it?" and was answered by the emergence of a big dolphin—a bull—that came out shaking his head like a slugged boxer, twisted once completely, and hit the sea with a smack. It was a thirty-pounder at least.

Desperate's eyes narrowed and the corners of his mouth sank. He saw the fish shoot around in a circle some forty feet from the boat and a foot below the surface. It took off on a straightaway after that and Crunch's line snapped.

"Too big for us," Crunch said ruefully.

Des nodded. "I wonder how many guys have had that happen? Too big to hold with the tackle that can be carried in a small craft. If we'd tied the canteen or something for a float on the end of the line, we could have tossed it overboard. We'd have had a buoy on the fish then, and I could have chased it till it wore itself out."

"A point," Crunch nodded. He was already rigging a new line, unmindful of the cuts on his fingers. "Still, if we weren't just playing shipwreck, we wouldn't dare risk losing the canteen. A big dolphin like that might tow it miles—probably would steal it—and, anyway, if you were bushed from floating around the ocean, you couldn't row that much."

Des said, "Yeah," and they went on fishing.

Toward six, Crunch coiled his line on the yellow-rubber side of the boat, blinked his eyes tiredly, set the plug in the center of the coil and rose on his knees. He shaded his hand toward the lowering sun and saw nothing. He looked north and saw nothing. He looked south.

"Our ship's a doggone long way off down there," he reported. He kept on kneeling, his eyes squinted to azure slots. "She ought to be coming up here or it'll be so near dark we'll be hard to spot, but darned if it doesn't look as though she were heading straight out to sea!"

Des, in turn, coiled his line and stared. The distant speck seemed to gather speed as they viewed it, and it was presently evident that she was, indeed, making off toward the east at full throttle. Presently, she could be spotted only at intervals, and before long she disappeared.

"Now that," Des said, "looks like Smith's work."

"He wouldn't dare risk it," Crunch answered. "Not as a test or as a joke. Too much water out here. Weather too uncertain this time of year. After all, she can do twenty-five knots and she isn't too far away—"

They sat down then. They resumed fishing in a desultory manner. The sun slid behind the level bars of low stratus cloud, which glowed scarlet and gold. The hues faded and the high clouds overhead took on the cosmetics of afterglow. Gulls banked, turned, and winged west. The coastline dissolved into the seascape. Overhead, the vault grayed and twilight descended. The day-long variable breeze died and picked up again, coming more steadily from the northwest.

A faint false light, like a stage effect, gave them one more chance for a circular sweep of the sea. Then it was gone and night hurried over them, full of stars.

"Fine thing," Crunch said.

"We're a cinch," Des replied. "After all, they know about where we are. They know how fast the Stream is running north today. At least, if they're any good, they've estimated. They can calculate our drift. They can cruise around where they think we are, and we can hear the motors. There ought to be some kind of signaling gear in one of the pockets."

They looked. There wasn't.

"Anyway," Des said, "they'll cut their engines every so often, and we can holler when they get near where we are." He didn't believe it.

"Sure." Crunch picked up the canteen and shook it. "About a cupful. Smart guys, we are. Not a sandwich left. Going to be a long sit, pal."

"You said it." Without saying so, they were agreed that rescue would have to wait for morning.

"Think you could sleep? Now, I mean? We'll have to guess the watches. I'll take it for a few hours and wake you."

"Okay." Des stretched out, his knees bent up over the center seat. "Comfortable, with only two of us. Hate to have about six here. Better save the water for tomorrow, hunh?"

"Yo."

Crunch watched his mate relax and presently heard his regular breathing. The skipper's muscles were painful from throwing the light plug all day long, but he began again. If they were leaving the boat out on purpose—as a test— he might as well do his best.

Des slept. The stars rode up the sky. Crunch fished.

It was much later when Des sat up suddenly and shook himself. He looked up at the Dipper. "Say. It's past my turn, hunh? Must be one or two o'clock. You sleep now." He saw the white spot of the plug in the sea. "Still at it?"

"I was. After all, there's guys doing it tonight all over the world by the hundreds, and nobody coming for them in the morning. We might as well carry on with the experiment. But if I find out Smith ordered this little routine on purpose, he'd better talk fast or I'll hang a lamp he can show to café society for the next fortnight—and I do mean fortnight!"

Des took over. Crunch lay down.

When he woke, the rubber boat was tossing uncomfortably. The east exhaled a pallor that was not yet light, but it silhouetted the determined jaw of Desperate as he threw, once again, line, leader, and lure. The wind carried it out of sight. A crisp wind now, and cool. Nor'west. Crunch yawned and his lips felt as though they were cracking. He licked them. Salt. He leaned over the side and washed his face. The water was warm. He rinsed out his mouth and wanted to swallow, but spat instead. Thirsty already. It grew light. Des was watching him. He looked haggard and his beard had pricked through his skin during the night.

"Can you sleep some more?" Crunch asked.

The mate shook his head. "Naw. Blowing up. Going to get rough. I've been sitting here the last couple of hours thinking what I'd say to Mr. Smith. They better find us soon. Want some water?"

"I'll take a sip." Crunch took one. Then Des.

They judged the passing of time by the sun. The day was clear and the wind chilly. It brought aboard spray enough to dampen them every time they began to dry out. Crunch could feel the gritty powder of salt on his face when it was dry and the bite of the wind when it was wet. The sun burned them without providing warmth enough to relieve the shiver of their wet bodies.

"Wouldn't care much about this as a steady thing," Des said. "Wanna fish?"

Crunch started again. His arms hurt, but the exercise was restorative. He kept rising up and looking, but there wasn't anything to see—no land, no boats, no planes—zero.

"If the Gulf Stream happens to be really running," Des said toward noon, "we may be heading north from where we were at about six knots."

Crunch grunted. "And we've been at it a long time. Say twenty hours from when they last had a bead on us. That's maybe a hundred and twenty miles. Whither, so to speak, are we drifting? Of course, though, the Stream probably isn't running that fast and the wind's holding us back."

"But just the same, there's a lot of water to hunt in by now, and this isn't much of a thing to spot."

"No."

They kept talking. They ran out of cigarettes. After a while, they realized that their growing thirst made conversation a luxury. So they stopped talking and fished.

In the middle of the afternoon, Crunch got another hit. He yanked in his line, hand over hand, with great energy. A three-pound dolphin came aboard. Crunch picked up the flopping fish and looked at it. "I could kiss you," he said. "At least, we don't have to starve."

A second dolphin hit Desperate's line a moment later, and he boated his fish. Quickly, he produced the knife which was to accompany the fishing kit they were helping to design. He cut off the tail and fins of the dolphin and tossed them overboard. He handed the knife to Crunch. "There must be a school of these babies. Chum for them." They chummed, throwing in the entrails and the heads, cut in pieces. They saw the flash, several times, of other dolphin feeding on the gobbets, but they were able to hook no more. The school swam out of range.

When they were sure of that, they looked at the two fish they had on board. Des said, "Well?"

Crunch nodded. He stripped off his jersey—neither of them had worn a shirt when they had embarked the day before. He washed out as much of the dried salt as he could, and wrung it. He and Des carefully fileted the fish. They cut the slabs of meat into small cubes. They put a double handful of the cubes into the jersey. They next shared the balance of the water. After that, Crunch held the canteen between his knees and took one end of the jersey. Des took the other. They twisted, wringing out a trickle of clear liquid from the meat—perhaps a cupful and a half in all.

Crunch took a sip. He lifted an eyebrow. "By golly, it isn't salty, at that! Tastes like something familiar—like clam juice. Like unsalted clam juice!" He sipped again and passed to Des his share.

Afterward, they looked at the white fish meat that remained. Des tasted it. "Okay," he said.

But Crunch shook his head. "Me, I'm not that hungry yet."

They went back to fishing, relieved by the liquid. If they could keep getting fish, they could stave off severe thirst indefinitely. And they were beginning to think about the length of their sojourn as indefinite. They resumed casting.

In the late afternoon a plane crossed their area of vision, but it was many miles away. They didn't even bother to wave, as sailors, they knew the futility of that. They watched it and went on fishing. The sea piled up five or six feet high. The rubber boat rode with a combination of motions—a buoyant wallow. Dusk ultimately descended.

"If it weren't for the dim-out," Crunch said, "we might get some idea of where we are. We can't be so doggoned far off the coast yet. If it were peacetime, we'd catch the glow of Miami. And if there weren't so much west in the wind, I'd try rowing. Kind of useless, the way it is. With any kind of a wish we could go the other way and hit into the Bahamas someplace."

"Yeah. Someplace. Before the Stream takes us north of there, and the next points are in Europe."

They thought that over. Crunch laughed. "A fine bunch of sailors we are! Pile into this bath-mat dinghy without water enough or provision, a sea anchor, a sail, a compass! We deserve to spend a week out here!"

"Yeah. Get a free ride as far as maybe Charleston."

"Scared?" Crunch asked.

Des thought. "Yeah. You?"

Crunch shrugged. "Sure, I'm scared. If you hadn't been, I'd have given you a devil of an argument. Figured they'd find us today."

"Me too. If the wind hauls, of course, we'll be okay. We can lash the shirts and our pants on the oars and paddle with our shoe soles and start making in toward the Florida coast. If it doesn't, we better start thinking hard."

"But we better just drift tonight. Best way. They'll try to figure our position on the basis of drift. Tomorrow—"

Tomorrow was a long time coming. The wind blew harder. It pushed and whistled on the jagged sea, scouring salty crests into their faces. They bailed with their hands and with their jerseys, sopping up the water and wringing it out. In the blackest part of the night an extra steep wave turned them over.

Crunch had been resting groggily, sitting on the boat's elastic bottom. He was thrown out into the warm sea. As he went, he grabbed the light Manila line that encircled the craft. When he came up, he was still holding on.

He bellowed, "Des!"

"O.K., pal! I'm right behind you! Let's flip her back!"

It was easier to say than to do. Every time they turned the craft up on edge, the wind shoved it back. They tried a half dozen times before they got the boat righted. They climbed in and kept low, with the water gushing around their chins. They bailed furiously, but they were exhausted by the time they had the boat empty.

When morning came, they sorted out their gear. They'd kept the canteen, the tackle and the knife tied to the boat. These articles floated around them now. They brought them back aboard and untangled the lines with stiff, shaky fingers. They coiled them and recommenced to fish.

"I don't know when I've enjoyed fishing less," Des said.

"And I can't remember wanting a fish more. I'm hungry enough for it now. Two days! Golly! You sure change your appetite fast!"

"Your lips are cracking pretty bad," Des said.

"Yours too. And my tongue feels big. Funny. I don't suppose we're thirsty, as thirsty really goes. But—"

"We may be yet."

"Yeah. We may be yet. Let's fish." The forenoon wore on. The wind grew fresher. A real sea began to build. Crunch's eyes, glazed, bloodshot, uncertain, kept watch. Within himself he struggled to decide whether to go on drifting, to try to row toward Florida or to attempt to sail southeast before the wind. It seemed to him that he had never been faced by a problem so difficult. But at last he made up his mind. "A northwester'll blow out in a day or two, Des, as a rule. She'll haul northeast or east, and shove us back across the Stream slantwise, so I say we save our strength and drift."

"Just about the answer I was getting myself. . . . Hey!" Des shouted the last word and pointed. They rose on another wave. Not far away was the Coast Guard boat—or another like it. They staggered to their knees on the unsteady bottom and waved and yelled. The boat saw them and plunged forward, with a sailor fanning his hat on the forward deck, and bow waves flying out like wings. Somebody threw a rope.

Commander Evans himself helped them on board. He was ghost white and the muscles in his cheeks showed. "Thank the Lord!" He pumped their hands. "You all right?"

"We could use a drink."

"Cook!" the commander bellowed. "Break into my private stock of bourbon—"

"Water," Crunch said somewhat thickly.

They gurgled it down and followed it with hot coffee and cigarettes.

Commander Evans was abjectly apologetic. "You see, on that first afternoon we got word from a plane south of us—out of sight of you, I guess—that a sub was running on the surface not more than a couple of miles from our position. Naturally, we ran for it. She must have dived—we never saw a thing. And right in the middle of the uproar both our engines cut out. We've been looking for all you guys ever since. We thought you'd lie doggo. Only thing to do. We figured the Gulf Stream drift as closely as we could. Of course, everybody available is out—planes, blimps—but there's a lot of water here, and it seems that the Stream ran backward for about ten hours. It does, occasionally."

"Yeah. It does." Crunch looked at the red-rimmed eyes of the Coast Guard crew. He thought over the words he had just heard. "What do you mean—'all' you guys?"

"Smith," said the Commander. "We put him over too. In a Navy raft. An hour after we planted you. He's still unsighted."

Crunch murmured his opinion in whispered, knotty words. He had more coffee, eggs, and some bacon. So did Des. Commander Evans went out on deck. A plane zoomed noisily. The radio operator kept talking near by. It seemed to Crunch that he said, "Roger," thousands of times.

Crunch was falling asleep when the man yelled through a window, "Commander! The blimp's sighted a raft! One man on it! Sounds like ours!"

The patrol boat put on her last ounce of speed and headed for the position of the raft. Crunch and Des roused themselves and went out on deck. The blimp could be seen hanging low in the sky some five miles off.

"Imagine." Des muttered it in Crunch's ear. "Navy raft! One with a slat deck that lets down, hunh? He has to stand waist deep in the water. And he was out as long as we were! Doggone, I'll take bets he's dead, the screwball!"

Mr. Smith was not dead. When they came alongside, he waved placidly. He was, it is true, standing waist deep in the water and he had been wet continuously during his sojourn. However, he seemed to be in good shape. A shark—a little one weighing perhaps a hundred pounds—was moored to the raft by its life rope. The shark was still alive, roped by the tail, and swimming feebly. Lashed to the top of the canvas-covered balsa ring that made the oval raft were slabs of fish meat—a dozen or more. On Mr. Smith's head was a broad, stiff contraption of fishskin and fishbones, tied under his chin with fishline. It was not a hat of any known pattern, but it shaded his face from the burning sun. As the patrol boat drew near, Mr. Smith took a small waterproof sack from the breast pocket of his doeskin shirt. He opened it and fumbled a moment. He closed it and returned it to his pocket. When he looked up, he was smoking a cigarette. And he came aboard unassisted.

His first words were, "What about the other chaps?" Then he saw them.

The cook hurried forward with water. Mr. Smith drank a little. Then he waved the pitcher aside.

"No real thirst. Used to it, anyway. Africa, you know. . . . Well, how'd you do, boys?"

They told him.

"Two dolphin, eh?" He yawned delicately. "Bit sleepy. Good. Maybe we'll include a plug, at that, if you nailed a couple of dolphin. I got eight. Two kingfish. Snagged three turbot yesterday. A tripletail—stole that. Got one mackerel and two bonitos, so I had plenty to eat and drink. And a meat bank, besides—that shark alive, in case it began to get tough. He attracted fish too. Chilly, though, wasn't it?"

Crunch understood Mr. Smith then. He grinned, although it hurt his mouth to do it. "I think I'll change my vote. Squids and feathers will do."

Mr. Smith tapped the ash from his cigarette and threw his fishskin hat overboard. "Suppose we get a little shut-eye and then try the trolling gear—what say?"

Crunch felt his insides rebel. He denied them. "Suits me."

Commander Evans spoke then. "I think, Mr. Smith, we'd better put in. That writer has been seasick for forty-eight solid hours. One of those other men—Mr. Stevens—is in the same shape. And provisions are low."

"Very well, Commander." Mr. Smith walked with Crunch and Des toward the staterooms below. Toward sleep.

"I owe you one terrific apology," Crunch said. "I thought—"

Mr. Smith lighted a fresh cigarette and stood on the companionway looking down at Crunch. "Yeah. It was written all over you in New York. You thought I was a phony. Fair-weather sailor and pretty-boy angler. Well, you know, I am something of a meadow lark, at that, in my lighter moments. But I'll tell you one. I thought, from the way you and Des argued with me, that your reputations had gone to your heads. Wise guys. Just now, when you were willing to keep on going if I was, I changed my mind. Matter of fact, I'm falling apart from the knees down and the shins up. We've got a swell practical kit for the fellows at sea in this way. Afterward, when it's all over, I want to charter you two guys and take you clear to New Zealand."

"It's a go," Crunch said—and all three shook on it, widening the salted cracks in one another's hands and widening their grins to match.

Zern falls somewhere between zebras and zwieback, one hell of a sandwich. What he doesn't know about fishing couldn't fill a brook. There's a reason he gets stuck in the back of books; it's called saving the best for last.

ED ZERN

A Trio

HOW TO DISPOSE OF DEAD FISH

A recent survey showed that roughly two-thirds of all fishermen never eat fish. This should surprise nobody. Fish is brain food. People who eat fish have large, well-developed brains. People with large, well-developed brains don't fish. It's that simple.

The question a fisherman faces, then, is how to get rid of the fish he has caught. There are several schools of thought on this problem.

The Pilgrim Fathers buried a dead fish in each hill of corn to make it grow. Unfortunately, few fishermen have access to cornfields. Most farmers would sooner have a cyclone.

Some fishermen try to palm off their catch on kindhearted friends and neighbors. Naturally, it doesn't take *those* folks long to learn that when a trout has been lugged around all day in a hot creel, it is poor competition for a pork chop.

Other methods of fish disposal are (1) stuffing them in a corner mailbox when nobody is looking, (2) hiding them under potted palms, (3) checking them at the Union Depot and throwing away the check, (4) hurling them from fast-moving cars on lonely roads late at night, (5) mailing them to the Curator of

400

the Museum of Natural History, requesting an identification of the species and giving a phony name and return address, and (6) baiting walrus traps with them.

None of these methods is satisfactory. (1) is probably illegal, (2), (3), (4), and (5) are in lousy taste, and (6) brings up the problem of walrus disposal. Walrus disposal makes fish disposal seem like child's play.

My friend Walt Dette throws back all the trout he catches in the Beaverkill, and keeps only chubs to feed to his seven Siamese cats. This is dandy for people who have (a) sense enough to put back trout for future sport and who also have (b) seven Siamese cats. Few fishermen have both.

Both, hell, *Either.*

HOW TO CATCH FISH WITH FLIES

Some wiseguy once defined a fishing line as a piece of string with a worm on one end and a damn fool on the other.

This is a silly definition, of course—for many fishermen use flies instead of worms. They think it is more hoity-toity. If worms cost two bits apiece, and you could dig Royal Coachmen and Parmacheene Belles out of the manure pile, they would think differently. This is called human nature.

Fly-fishermen spend hours tying little clumps of fur and feathers on hooks, trying to make a trout fly that looks like a real fly. But nobody has ever seen a natural insect trying to mate with a Fanwing Ginger Quill.

Of course, every once in a while a fly-fisherman catches a trout on a trout fly, and he thinks this proves something. It doesn't. Trout eat mayflies, burned matches, small pieces of inner tube, each other, caddis worms, Dewey buttons, crickets, lima beans, Colorado spinners, and almost anything else they can get in their fool mouths. It is probable they think the trout fly is some feathers tied to a hook. Hell, they're not blind. They just want to see how it tastes.

Trout flies are either wet flies or dry flies, depending on whether they are supposed to sink or float. If you ask a wet-fly fisherman why a natural insect would be swimming around like crazy under water, he gets huffy and walks away.

Many fishermen think trout are color-blind, but that is nothing to what trout think of fishermen.

WHY DUMB PEOPLE CATCH MORE TROUT THAN SMART PEOPLE

If you hang around Charley's Hotel Rapids on the Brodheads Creek, or Frank Keener's Antrim Lodge on the Beaverkill, and pay close attention to the inmates, you will notice that the lamer the brain, the heavier the creel.

The reason for this is very simple. When a fisherman gets to the stream he looks it over and decides where he would go if he were a fish. Then he takes out his worm can or his fly box and decides which worm or which fly he would prefer if he were a fish.

Then he drifts his worm or casts his fly into the spot he has decided on. If he catches a fish, he is very proud, because he knows he thinks like a fish. And naturally, fishermen who think like fish catch more trout than fishermen who think like armadillos or duck-billed platypuses or mongooses.

Of course, the reason a fish thinks the way he does is that his brain is very tiny in relation to his body. So the tinier the fisherman's brain the easier it is for him to think like a fish, and catch trout right and left.

The same principle explains why fishermen with big mouths catch the most large-mouth bass, and fishermen with banjo eyes catch the most wall-eyed pike, and fishermen with jaundice catch the most yellow perch, and so forth.

The virgin sturgeon has never been caught on rod and reel.

The editors wish to acknowledge the following for permission to include the selections listed:

Ares Publishers, "Fishing with the Hair of the Dead," from *Fishing from the Earliest Times* by William Radcliffe, copyright 1921 by William Radcliffe, reprinted by permission of Ares Publishers. "No Wind in the Willows," from *The Angler's Coast* by Russell Chatham, copyright © 1976 by Russell Chatham, previously published by Doubleday and Company, 1976, reprinted by permission of the author. The University of Chicago Press, "A River Runs Through It," from *A River Runs Through It* by Norman Maclean, copyright © 1976 by Norman Maclean, reprinted by permission of the University of Chicago Press. Country Life, "The Fisherman," from *An Angler's Anthology* by Robert Bell, copyright 1930 by Robert Bell, reprinted by permission of Newnes Books, a division of The Hamlyn Publishing Group Ltd, originally published by Country Life, Ltd. "Fishing Walton's Favorite Rivers," from *The Incompleat Angler* by Robert Deindorfer, copyright © 1977 by Robert Deindorfer, originally published by E. P. Dutton and Company, reprinted by permission of the author's representative. Delacorte Press, "The Hunchback Trout," from *Trout Fishing in America* by Richard Brautigan, copyright © 1967 by Richard Brautigan, reprinted by permission of Delacorte Press/Seymour Lawrence; "Great Point," from *Open Season* by William Humphrey, to be published in 1987 by Delacorte Press/Seymour Lawrence, copyright © 1977 by William Humphrey, originally published in *Sports Illustrated* under a different title, reprinted by permission of Delacorte Press/Seymour Lawrence. Doubleday and Company, Inc., "Anglers' Club," from *Red Smith on Fishing* by Red Smith, copyright © 1959 by the *New*

404